A SEASON IN GRANADA

Federico García Lorca

A SEASON IN GRANADA

Uncollected Poems & Prose

Edited and translated by
Christopher Maurer

ANVIL PRESS POETRY

First published in 1998
by Anvil Press Poetry Ltd
Neptune House, 70 Royal Hill, London SE10 8RF

This book is published with financial assistance from
The Arts Council of England

Designed and set in Monotype Fournier by Anvil
Printed in Great Britain at Redwood Books, Trowbridge

ISBN 0 85646 300 0 hardback
ISBN 0 85646 299 3 paperback

A catalogue record for this book
is available from the British Library

This translation is for
Patricia Findiesen (D/P)

ACKNOWLEDGMENTS

Some of the pieces in this book have previously appeared in Christopher Maurer's translations (since revised) in other editions of works by Federico García Lorca: "Holy Week in Granada" in *Deep Song and Other Prose* (New York: New Directions, 1980, and London: Marion Boyars, 1980); "How a City Sings from November to November" and the music for the two songs "El Café de Chinitas" and "Las tres hojas" (calligraphy by Carolyn Cassady) in *How a City Sings from November to November*, limited edition (San Francisco: Cadmus Editions, 1982). The publishers are grateful for permission to reprint them here.

A NOTE ON THE TEXT

All translations are by Christopher Maurer. All quotations from the letters of Federico García Lorca are from *Epistolario completo*, edited by Andrew A. Anderson and Christopher Maurer (Madrid: Cátedra, 1997). Sources for the Spanish texts of the individual poems, prose poems and essays are given in the notes.

CONTENTS

Preface

In these pages the Spanish poet Federico García Lorca (1898–1936) celebrates the city in which he grew up and where he wrote some of his best work.

What we glimpse here is the ideal Granada – the "murmur of perfect beauty" – which quickened his poetic imagination and gave him insight into his own work.

García Lorca is an elegiac poet, who looks at what *is* and always thinks of what is *not*. His work sings not of love but of desire, and in desire there is more absence than presence. And thus the Granada presented here has little to do with the city around him, which he described, months before his death, as a "poor cowardly city, a miser's paradise, with the worst bourgeoisie in all of Spain." Looking beyond the here and now, shunning the "facile, abominable phenomenon known as the sketch of manners," begging "not for local, but for *spiritual* color," Lorca sought, and helped create, a Granada both eternal and universal. "From the local to the universal" was a phrase he often heard applied to the art of his friend and mentor Manuel de Falla. And his path to the universal was lyricism.

He thinks of his city, at serious moments, as a "murky palimpsest" where Christians commingle with Jews, Moors, Romans, Gypsies; where East blends with West in a drama that has made Andalusia into a true "island of culture." At more whimsical moments he imagines Granada as "a great legendary city: the perfectly realized poem that every true poet secretly hates." He evokes a time when "fresh garlands of roses and mulberries girded the city walls, and the cathedral, with its round rump, came forward like a centaur over rooftops of green glass; and at midnight, from eaves and balconies, oil lamps and cats in flight hissed at the perfection of the reflecting pools."

Custom did not blind him to the beauty before his eyes: the Sierra Nevada he could see from his window; the Alhambra ("jasmine of pain" in the moonlight); the verdant farmland of the Vega, with its clear, winding streams and cool poplar groves. Even the air seemed to possess a greater "spiritual density" than elsewhere. All this is caught here both in verse and in prose: in passages from his letters, in talks and lectures, in the early poetic sequences he called *Suites*, and in poems from three of his best lyrical works: *Songs*, *The Gypsy Ballads*, and *The Divan of the Tamarit*.

These writings, some of which are presented to English and American readers for the first time, give us a special insight both into Lorca's art and into the popular art which nourished it. Granada, he once remarked, "has given me her light and her themes and has opened for me the vein of her lyrical secrets... If God continues to help me, and if, some day, I win glory, half of that glory will belong to Granada, which shaped and molded the creature I am: a poet from birth, an incurable one."

It is an ironic truth that in 1936, in the first days of Spanish Civil War, Lorca was brutally executed near the city evoked so lovingly in these pages. "The crime was in Granada, *in his Granada!*" Antonio Machado exclaimed bitterly in a famous elegy. And yet Lorca's Granada lies outside history, beyond the reach of envy: a "perfectly realized poem," bright figure of desire.

CHRISTOPHER MAURER

A SEASON IN GRANADA

Every day I am more convinced of how marvelous this country is. If you were here with me, you'd be spinning like a top to see all four points of the compass at once. A few days ago, a green-purple moon appeared in the bluish mist of the Sierra Nevada, and just across the street a woman was singing a cradle song that tangled itself into the landscape like a golden streamer. Above all at sunset one lives in the totally fantastic, in a half-effaced dream. There are times when everything evaporates and we are left in a desert of pearly grey, rose, and dead silver. I cannot tell you how enormous this Vega is, and this little white village in its dark poplar groves. At night our flesh aches from so many stars, and we grow drunk on breeze and water. I doubt that in India there are nights so charged with fragrance and so delirious.

FROM A LETTER TO ADOLFO SALAZAR,
AUGUST 2, 1921

POEM OF THE FAIR

Under the sun of the tuba
the fair goes by,
sighing for old
captive Pegasuses.

The fair
is a wheel:
wheel of lights
against the sky.

The concentric circles
of the merry-go-round
ripple the air
up to the moon.

And there is a child
lost by all poets
and a music box
on the breeze.

Merry-Go-Round

Sad little horses
pierced
by lances of evil knights.

Down to earth you flee,
from a tale told backward,
from a field of old dragons
who have vanquished the saints.

Sad little horses
pierced
by lances of evil knights!

Fair in the Stars

The night open wide.

Spinning on the moon's axis,
God's carousel.

Far from the crowd
Sirius the poet
is sobbing.

Among the girl-stars
Ursa Major is dancing.

The cylinder of the breeze
spins over the treetops.

Dawn on the way,
and a little old star
sells snowy nougat.

The night open wide.

Fair in the Evening

When you go to the fair
in the evening
you enter a house of fireflies.

Rat-a-tat-tat
tat-tat.

You'll never see a ladybug,
they've flown away home.

Rat-a-tat-tat
tat-tat.

Madness of love,
what pain:
my heart feels delight,
exposed,
awaiting the arrow.

Rat-a-tat-tat
tat-tat.

Scream

Mosquito
moth,
bird,
and star.

What?

Star,
bird,
moth,
and mosquito.

On the ground,
my pierced heart
flies over the girls
of the fair.

Drum

Heart
of the fair.

Withered heart
beating
like a boy's.

No musician
has seen it.

It's the true
Pierrot, singing lyrically
to the moon,
which fits into
its ring
with a melody
of unknown love.

The drum glows
like parchment
(musical will o' the wisp)
and on summer nights
a thousand old moths
pursue its throbbing.
The drum is the nostalgia
of the road.
It sounds like the cloudy sky,
like infinite distance.

On the beached boat
of the circus,
on the country breeze,
listen to it throbbing!
Oh coffin
of the full moon!

Paper Roses

That man,
huge constellation,
Atlantis,
multicolor star
lost in the wounds
of flares.

That man,
with his cloud of laughter,
offers roses
to the winds
of childhood.

And that man,
the ghost of autumn,
saves roses
for dead children
and sends them
on a kite.

Moon at the Fair

At the fair
you don't see the moon.
There are too many moons
on the grass!

Everything plays at being a moon.
The fair itself,
a wounded moon
that fell upon the city.

Microscopic moons
dance in the glass,
and some of them pause
in the stormclouds
of the band.

At the fair
you don't see the moon
up in the blue.
You wait for it, sighing.
"My eyes are hurting!"

Dark Song

I'd love to lose myself
in your dark country,
María del Carmen.

Lose myself
in your deserted eyes
and play the keyboard
of your ineffable mouth.

In your endless embrace
the air would be dark,
the breeze would be downy
as your skin.

I would lose myself
in your trembling breasts,
in the black depths
of your soft body.

I would lose myself
in your dark country,
María del Carmen.

Swing Ride

The girl on the swing
heads north to south
and south to north.
In the parabola
a red star trembles,
beneath all the stars.

Confusion

Over the sleepless houses,
sonorous streamers.

Red   Yellow   Green!

The little square is flooded
with pipes and whistles.

Red   Yellow   Green!

The people go astray
in labyrinths of music.

Red   Yellow   Green!

The clock tells no hour,
the eyes have no looks.

Black   Black   Black!

Sunset of the Fair

Balconies close,
making cages for kisses.

So many stars,
so many of them!

A hurdy-gurdy
dies on the breeze.

More stars
and more of them!

But the poor Pegasuses
cannot close their eyes.

Just one star,
just one of them!

Variation

(Final trill)

Before the deserted fair
the poet is sighing

(wind beats on canvas).

His bird flies away,
over the frond.

Fairytale bird,
bird with no home,
singing its *pío pío*,
singing its *pío pa*.

27 July 1921
ASQUEROSA

Just now a great storm is beginning. The thunderbolts, like great black iron bars rolling down a slope of smooth stone, rattle the windowpanes in my house. Oh Lord, remember the flocks in the mountain and the wheat abandoned in the stubble! In the ashen light my mother, brother, and sisters say "Holy, holy holy!" Like a snail, I pull in my horns of poetry.

FROM A LETTER TO JOSÉ MARÍA CHACÓN Y CALVO,
JULY 1923

SUMMER HOURS

Knife grinder.
(Three o'clock.)
The soul of Pan
on the lips
of the knife-grinder.

What dusty
sadness!

He evokes
a green pool,
and something
in the branches.

He carries
St. Catherine's
wheel.

What sadness!

Five o'Clock

(Colt)

Down the deserted street
goes a black horse,
the wandering horse
of bad dreams.

The breeze of sunset
comes from far away.
A window is weeping
with the wind.

Six o'Clock

Birds push
on the evening,
their beaks carry off
the blue tail of day.

The sunset,
tattooed with weather vanes
holds up the boat
of the half moon.

In the cool fountain,
a serpent is singing.

Seven o'Clock

First star.
Everything looks toward Venus.
Like a girl
who has fallen down the well,
she shivers and trembles
as if to ask,
"Will I come back tomorrow?"

Eight o'Clock

Sky pulled off
its blindfold
and the thousand-eyed dragon
licks us with tongues
of wind.

Venus goes astray
in the crowd
and I remember a sweetheart
I never really had.

Nine o'Clock

Bloodless blue.
Velvet breeze.

Oh, my girl,
we can
go down to the well
of the heart,
down the river of words
to the island
of the kiss.
We can
sink into the thirsty
olive grove.

Thistledown at Night

In pulsing water
under the briars,
the stars are growing longer.

The light presses against my temples like a golden kerchief.
The trees dream of their fruit, the little leaves of their wind.
The cathedral bells are ringing and the airplanes are dancing
the rigadoon they do every evening. The Guardia Civil kills a
gypsy each day and writes down his name on a long undulating
list like a Chinese dragon.

FROM A LETTER TO BENJAMÍN PALENCIA,
JULY 1925

PALIMPSESTS

FOR JOSÉ MORENO VILLA

City

The ancient forest
pushes into the city,
but the forest
is in the sea.

There are arrows in the air,
and warriors lost
in the branches
of coral.

Over the new houses
a grove of holm oaks is stirring
and the sky
has enormous crystal curves.

Corridor

Down the high corridors
go two gentlemen.

>   (New
>   sky
>   Blue
>   sky!)

…two gentlemen
who once were two white monks.

>   (Half
>   sky.
>   Mauve
>   sky!)

…two gentlemen
who once were hunters.

>   (Old
>   sky.
>   Gold
>   sky!)

…two gentlemen
who once were…

>   (Night.)

Air

Full of scars
it sleeps,
full of signs
and spirals.
Trail of the bird,
trail of a scream.

From the dust
of words and rhythms
two tones emerge:
black and yellow.

Madrigal

Oh, Lucy of Granada!
Dark little girl
who live at the foot of the Red
Towers... If your hands...
your hands...

(Full moon.)

Oh girl of April!
Oh Melisendra!
You of the high towers
and spindle.
If your breasts... your breasts...

(Half moon.)

Oh woman of my white
adolescence.
Fierce and fecund
Eve,
twisting in my arms
like the dry branches
of a holm oak
in the dance of the bonfire.

And my heart?
Was it wax?
Where is it?
And my hands?
And…

(Blind moon.)

First Page

TO ISABEL CLARA, MY GODCHILD

Clear fountain.
Clear sky.

Ah, how the birds
get bigger!

Clear sky.
Clear fountain.

And how the oranges
shine!

Fountain.
Sky.

Ah, how the wheat
is tender!

Sky.
Fountain.

Ah, how the wheat
is green!

In the rain Granada has that divine light from a pensive brow... light that reminds us of childhood. Light of six-thirty in the evening when we could come out of school and turn the corner.

FROM A LETTER TO MELCHOR FERNÁNDEZ ALMAGRO, 1927

LITTLE TALES
OF THE WIND

The wind was red
over the hill in flames,
and it has turned deep green
by the river.

Later it will be violet,
yellow and...
Over the sown fields
it will stretch out like a rainbow.

Pent-up wind.
The sun above.
Below,
the trembling algae
of the poplars.
My heart
is trembling too.

Pent-up wind
at five in the afternoon,
without birds.

The breeze
is wavy
like the hair
of certain girls,
like the little oceans
painted long ago
on wooden tablets.
The breeze
wells up like water
and spills
 — tenuous white balsam —
on the sheep trails,
and faints
when it gets to the hardness
of the mountain.

School

TEACHER
Which maiden marries
the wind?

PUPIL
The maiden of all
desires.

TEACHER
What does the wind
give her?

PUPIL
Whirlwinds of gold
and maps superimposed.

TEACHER
Does he offer anything to him?

PUPIL
Her open heart.

TEACHER
Tell me what her name is.

PUPIL

Her name is a secret.

> (The window
> of the schoolroom
> has a curtain
> of stars.)

Granada looks splendid. Autumn has begun, with all the elegance and light sent by the Sierra. The first snow has already fallen. The yellows begin, deep and infinite, playing with twenty shades of blue. It is an astounding richness, which, no matter how stylized, cannot be captured. Granada isn't pictorial, even for an Impressionist. It isn't pictorial, just as a river is not architectonic. Everything runs, plays, and slips away. Poetry and Music. A city of fugues without a skeleton. Melancholy with vertebrae.

FROM A LETTER TO MELCHOR FERNÁNDEZ ALMAGRO,
OCTOBER 27, 1926

WATER JETS

Interior

From my room
I hear the water jet.
A finger of grapevine
and a ray of sun
point to the place
in my heart.
Clouds are moving
through the August air.
I dream I am not dreaming
inside the water jet.

Country

Water jets from dreams,
with no water
and no fountains!

You see them from the corner
of the eye,
never face to face.

Like all ideal things,
they are moving
on the very edge
of Death.

Aside

The blood of night
goes through the arteries
of the water jets.

Ah, what a marvelous
trembling!
I think
of open windows,
without pianos
and without maidens.

Garden

In the dark, four knights
with their water swords.
Four swords are wounding
the world of the roses,
and they will wound your heart.
Do not go down to the garden!

I am in Granada, and it's infernally hot... I've been working hard, and have "composed" some poems to the cuckoo (admirable, symbolic little bird) and the daydreams of a river, *pathetical poems which I feel deep within me, in the deepest part of my unhappy heart. You have no idea how I suffer to see myself portrayed in the poems. I imagine myself to be an immense violet-colored dragonfly over the backwaters of emotion ...*

*These days I feel pregnant, for I have "seen" an admirable book that has to be written, one which I would like to write: "Meditations and Allegories of the Water." What profound, living miracles one can tell about the water! The water-poem of my book has blossomed in my soul. I see a great poem about the water, part Oriental and part Christian-European: a poem that sings, in ample verses or (*molto rubato*) in prose, the passionate life and martyrdom of the water. A great Life of the Water with meticulous analysis of the concentric circle, the reflection, the drunken music (unblent with silence) of the currents. The river and the irrigation ditches have come deep inside me. Now one can truly say that the Guadalquivir or the Miño is born in Fuente Miña and empties out into Federico García Lorca, small-time dreamer and son of the water. I ask God to grant me strength and joy (yes joy!) so that I can write this book ... of devotion for those who travel through the desert ... I can already see the chapters and stanzas (there would be prose and verse), for example: The Looms of the Water, Map of the Water, The Ford of Sounds, Meditations on the Spring, Backwaters. And later, when I study (yes, study!) (pray to the saints to give me joy!) the dead water, I will write an incredibly moving poem about* the Alhambra, seen as the water's pantheon. I believe that if I were really to tackle this I could do something fine, and if I were a great poet, really a great poet, perhaps this would be my masterpiece . . .

From a little poem (Daydreams of the River), a stone in the portico of what I'm thinking about:

Slow Current

My eyes go down the river,
down the river.

My love goes down the river,
down the river.

(My heart is counting
the hours it is asleep.)

The river brings dry leaves,
the river.

It is clear and deep,
the river.

(My heart is asking
if it can change place.)

FROM A LETTER TO MELCHOR FERNÁNDEZ ALMAGRO,
JULY / AUGUST 1922

Meditations and Allegories of the Water

For many years now, as a happy boy and modest dreamer, I have spent the summer on the cool bank of a river. In the afternoon, when the admirable bee-eaters feel the wind coming and break into song, and the cicada is in a frenzy rubbing together its two little plates of gold, I sit down near the living depths of the pool and allow my poor frightened eyes to settle on the water or on the round tops of the poplars.

Under the weeping willows, near the tongue of the water, I feel the open afternoon gently settle its weight on the green surface of the pool, and gusts of silence cool the astonished crystal of my eyes.

At first I was moved by the splendid sight of the reflections, the fallen groves of poplar, which twist like Baroque columns at the least little sigh of the water, the briars and reeds which curl like the habit of a nun.

I saw that my soul was turning into a prism; that it was filling with immense perspectives and trembling phantoms. One afternoon, as I stared at the moving green, I noticed a strange curved bird of gold riding the ripples of a reflected poplar. I looked at the real poplar, which was flooded with setting sun, but saw that only the invisible little birds of the wind were playing in its leaves. The bird of gold was gone.

A marvelous coolness came over my whole body, tangled in the last little strands of sunset, and a broad avenue of light traversed my heart. Can this be possible?

Does my soul really journey to these waves and ripples rather than visit the stars?

The tinkling of sheep-bells placed a dark echo on my throat, and clear, tiny droplets spattered the marvelous skin of my soul. Ah soul, have you forgotten shivering Venus and the violin of the winds? Why do you hold to the resonant algae of the cascades, the huge bloom of the concentric circle? And I saw all of my memories reflected in the water!

Border

I was returning from the dry lands. Down below was the Vega, swathed in shimmering blue. The pulsing ribbons of the crickets were floating in the night summer air, which lay flat as a corpse.

The music of the dry lands has a markedly yellow taste.

I now understand that the cicadas are made of real gold, and that a song can turn to ash in the olive groves.

The dead who live in these cemeteries, so far from others, must turn yellow like the trees in November.

Near the Vega we seem to enter a green fishbowl, and the air becomes a sea of blue waves, a sea made for the moon, where countless frogs play their flutes of dry cane.

Coming down from the dry lands to the Vega, one must cross a mysterious ford which few people can feel, the Ford of Sounds. This is a natural border where a strange silence tries to deaden two contrary musics. If we had a well-constituted spiritual retina we would see how a man tinged gold by the dry lands turns green on entering the Vega, after disappearing into the murky musical current of the border.

For a moment I have tried to follow that wonderful dividing line (frogs on one side and crickets on the other), and where those two sounds collide almost imperceptibly, I have drunk fresh, cold little trickles of silence.

Who can go down this long road without his soul being covered with a confusing arabesque? Who would dare to say, "I have walked a road in my head; a road belonging not to fish or fowl or man but only to the ears?"

Is this the road that goes to No Man's Land, the land of those who have died waiting? From the tail of the olive grove to the first poplars, what admirable algae, what invisible little lights must be floating by!

I have drawn up before the current and the long antennae of my hearing have explored its depths. Here it is wide and full of whirlpools, but in the mountains it will be buried under blue sands of silence. Here it has the sublime confusion of a dream we cannot remember.

The waning moon, like a golden clove of garlic, gives the fuzz of an adolescent to the curve of the sky.

Daydreams of the River

The poplar groves are gone,
but they leave their reflection.

    (Ah, what a lovely
    moment!)

The poplar groves are gone,
but they leave us the wind.

The long sky has placed
a shroud on the wind.

    (Ah, what a sad
    moment!)

But the wind has left its echo
floating on the rivers.

The world of fireflies
has invaded my memory.

    (Ah, what a pretty
    moment!)

And a tiny heart
blossoms on my fingers.

*

On the pool, the lotuses
of concentric circles.
On my temples I bear
the majesty of silence.

Marvelous bevels
make the poplars shiver.
White snails are moving
along the grassy bank.

How lovely and how sad the Carrera del Darro must be, and what clouds there must be over Valparaíso! I remember Granada the way one remembers a dead fiancée or a day of sunshine from childhood. Have all of the leaves fallen?

FROM A LETTER TO EMILIA LLANOS MEDINA,
NOVEMBER 28, 1920

Granada: Paradise Closed to Many

Granada loves tiny things, and so does the rest of Andalusia. Popular speech places even verbs in the diminutive, making it easier to trust and love. But the diminutives one hears in Malaga and Seville are but charm and rhythm. Seville and Malaga are cities on the crossroads of the water, cities that thirst for adventure and slip away to sea. Granada, tranquil and refined, girded by her sierras, riding eternally at anchor, sets her own horizons, takes pleasure in her small jewels, and offers her bland diminutive: a diminutive without rhythm, almost without grace and charm when one compares it with the phonetic dance of Malaga and Seville, but cordial, domestic, affectionate. A diminutive frightened as a bird, one which opens secret chambers of feeling and reveals the subtlest, best-defined nuances of the city.

The diminutive's only mission is to limit, enclose, bring indoors and place in our hands objects and ideas which seem too large: time and space, the sea, the moon, distances, and even action.

We don't want the world to be so big, the sea so deep. We need to limit and domesticate anything huge.

Granada cannot leave her house. She isn't like other cities, which are on the edge of the ocean or of great rivers: cities that travel and return enriched by what they have seen. Lonely and pure, Granada grows smaller and binds up her extraordinary soul. Her only escape is her high natural port of stars. And thus, with no thirst for adventure, she doubles back upon herself, using the diminutive to rein in her imagination, just as she reins in her body to avoid excessive flight, and soberly harmonizes her interiors with the living architecture that lies around her.

In a word, the true aesthetic of Granada is the aesthetic of the diminutive, of tiny things, and her true creations are the little chamber, the mirador of lovely, small proportions, the small garden or statue.

The so-called artistic "schools" of Granada are groups of artists who work lovingly on small-scale works. They do other things, of course, but it is this type of work that best reveals their personality.

One might say that the schools of Granada, her most perfect representatives, are given to preciosity. The tradition of the arabesque of the Alhambra, complicated and small in scope, weighs on every great artist in the city. The palace of the Alhambra – a palace which Andalusian fantasy looked at through the wrong end of the telescope – has always been the aesthetic axis of the city. Granada seems never to have realized that the palace of Carlos V and the well-drawn cathedral rise in her midst. There is no Caesarean tradition, no tradition of the massive column or clustered pier. She is still frightened by the great, cold cathedral tower, and withdraws into her ancient little rooms, with a pot of myrtle and a stream of cold water, to carve little ivory flowers, inlaying them in hard wood.

When the Renaissance tradition comes to the city, Granada simply flees, or, mocking its grand dimensions, constructs the unlikely little tower of Santa Ana: tiny tower more fit for doves than for bells, made with all the elegance and ancient charm of Granada.

In years when the triumphal arch is reborn, Alonso Cano is carving his little virgins, precious examples of virtue and intimacy. When the Castilian tongue is mature enough to describe the elements of nature and supple enough for the most poignant mystical constructs, Fray Luis de Granada gives us his delectable descriptions of small objects and things.

It is Fray Luis who, in his *Introduction to the Symbol of the Faith*, tells how God's wisdom and providence shine more brightly in small things than in large ones. Humble, reserved, a "preciosista," he is a master of the loving look, like all good people of Granada.

When Gongora issues his proclamation on behalf of pure, abstract poetry – a proclamation taken up avidly by all the most lyrical spirits of his day – Granada reappears on the literary map of Spain. Soto de Rojas takes the difficult, exacting orders of Góngora. But while the subtle Cordovan poet toys with oceans, forests, and the elements, Soto de Rojas encloses himself in his garden and discovers water jets, dahlias, finches and gentle breezes. Moorish, half-Italian breezes rustle the boughs and fruits and thickets of his poetry.

In a word: what characterizes him is his preciosity. He orders his nature instinctively, as though decorating a room. He flees from the great elements of Nature and prefers the garlands and fruit baskets he can make with his own hands. That is what has always happened in Granada. Beneath the impression made by the Renaissance, native blood was pulsing, producing its virginal fruit.

The aesthetic of small things is our most distinctive trait, the very most delicate play of our artists. It is not a matter of patience but of time; not of work but a labor of virtue and love. This could happen in no other city.

*

Granada is a city of leisure, a city for contemplation and fantasy, a city where, better than in any other, the lover can write on the ground the name of his beloved. The hours are longer, more delectable in Granada than in any other city in Spain. There are complicated sunsets with unheard-of colors that seem to go on forever.

We carry on long conversations with friends in the middle of the street.

Granada lives on fantasy. It is full of initiatives, but short on action.

Only in a city of leisure and tranquility could there be such exquisite tasters of waters, of temperatures, of sunsets.

Her people are surrounded by the most splendid nature imaginable, but they do not go to it.

The landscapes are extraordinary, but the person from Granada prefers to look at them from his window. He is frightened of the elements, and feels scorn for the noisy rabble. Because he is a man of fantasy, he has little courage. He prefers his own gentle snow-cooled breeze to the terrible, harsh wind heard in Ronda, for example, and he is ready to place his entire soul in the diminutive and bring the world into his room. Wisely, he realizes that he can understand it better that way. He renounces adventure, travel, the curiosities of other lands. Most of the time he rejects luxury, fine clothes, the city.

He scorns all this and makes his garden more beautiful. He retires into himself, a man of few friends (isn't the reserve of Granada proverbial in the rest of Andalusia?)

He stares lovingly at the objects around him. He is in no hurry. Perhaps this is why the artists of Granada have taken such pleasure in carving small things or describing worlds of reduced dimensions. Someone will say that these traits lead to philosophizing, but philosophy demands a certain constancy, a mathematical equilibrium that is rather difficult in Granada. Granada is fit for dream and daydream, and it borders everywhere on the ineffable. Besides, there is a great difference between dreaming and thinking, although they begin with similar attitudes. Granada will always be more plastic than philosophical, more lyrical than dramatical. Her tender personality is hidden away inside her houses and her landscape. Her voice comes down from a little mirador, or rises from a dark window. Impersonal, poignant voice, full of ineffable aristocratic melancholy. Who is singing? Where does it come from, that slender voice, night and day at the same time?

To hear that voice, one must enter the tiny chambers and corners of the city, live the city's unpeopled interior and well-girded solitude. And, what is even more admirable, explore one's own intimacy, one's own secret, taking a definitively lyrical perspective on things.

One must make oneself a little poorer, forget one's name, renounce what people call "personality."

Just the opposite of Seville. Seville is man in the full complexity of his sensuality and emotion. It is political intrigue and the triumphal arch. Don Pedro and Don Juan. It is full of the human element, and its voice brings tears, because anyone can understand it. Granada is like the narration of what already happened in Seville.

There is the emptiness of something that is gone forever.

When one understands the intimate, cautious soul of the city – soul of the interior, of the small garden – one can also explain the aesthetics and techniques of many of our most representative artists.

Everything has a sweet domestic air. And yet, who can understand, who can penetrate this intimacy? The poet Pedro Soto de Rojas defined it in the seventeenth century. Returning from Madrid, full of sorrow and disenchantment, he wrote on the cover of one of his books these words, giving the most exact definition possible of Granada: "Paradise Closed to Many."

Paquito is going to Oxford in October... I imagine him as an Englishman — very serious, very elegant, with that air of a wild duck that all those strange, insular people have. You and I will remain in Spain: billy goat, rooster, bull, fiery auroras, the white light of courtyards, where the humidity spots the heartless old walls with incredible shades of green. If only you could see Andalusia! When you walk you have to open galleries in the golden light, like the moles in their dark world. The brilliant silks Michaelangelize the fannies of well-to-do women, the roosters nail their banderillas into the shoulders of the dawn, and I turn brown from the sun and from the full moon.

FROM A LETTER TO PEPÍN BELLO,
JULY 1925

August.
Against the sunset
peaches and sugar,
and the sun inside the afternoon
like the stone in a fruit.

The ear of corn is holding
its hard, yellow laughter.

August.
Children eat
dark bread and tasty moon.

Evening

(Was my Lucy dangling
her feet in the stream?)

Three huge poplars
and a star.

The silence bitten
by frogs resembles
a gauze painted
with green polka dots.

In the river
a dry tree
flowers
into concentric circles.

On the waters I have dreamed
the dark little girl of Granada.

Ballad of the Three Rivers

The river Guadalquivir
passes through olive and orange trees.
The two rivers of Granada
descend from the snow to the wheat.

Ah, love
that went away forever!

The river Guadalquivir
has garnet-colored beards.
The two rivers of Granada,
one blood, the other tears.

Ah, love
that fled on the breeze!

For sailing ships
Seville has a path.
In the water of Granada
only sighs can row.

Ah, love
that went away forever!

Guadalquivir, high tower
and wind in the orange groves.
Dauro and Genil, little towers
dead in the pools below.

Ah, love
that fled on the breeze!

Who doubts that the water carries
a will-o'-the-wisp of screams?

Ah, love
that went away forever!

It carries olives and orange blossoms,
Andalusia, to your seas.

Ah, love
that fled on the breeze!

Tree, tree,
dry and green.

The girl with the pretty face
is picking olives.
The wind, suitor of towers,
takes her by the waist.

Four riders went by
on Andalusian ponies,
with suits of blue and green,
and long, dark capes.

"Come to Córdoba, girl."
The girl does not listen.

Three little bullfighters pass,
with slender waists
in bright orange suits
and swords of old silver.

"Come to Seville, girl."
The girl does not listen.

When the evening turned
mauve with scattered light
a boy came by carrying
roses and moonlit myrtle.

"Come to Granada, girl."
And the girl does not listen.

The girl with the pretty face
goes on picking olives,
the gray arm of the wind
wrapped around her waist.

Tree, tree,
dry and green.

St. Michael

(Granada)

TO DIEGO BUIGAS DE DALMÁU

You can see them from the railings
on the mount, the mount, the mount,
mules and shadows of mules
carrying sunflower seed.

Their eyes, in the shady places,
cloud over with huge night.
The salty dawn is rustling
in river-bends of breeze.

A sky of white mules
closes its quicksilver eyes,
making the calm penumbra
a resting place for hearts.
And the water turns cold
so no one will touch it.
Crazy, uncovered water
on the mount, the mount, the mount.

*

St. Michael, full of lace
in the alcove of his tower
shows his lovely thighs
ringed in lantern light.

Domesticated archangel
pointing to twelve o'clock
feigns a sweet anger
of feathers and nightingales.
St. Michael sings in the glass,
ephebe of three thousand nights,
fragrant with cologne
and far away from flowers.

*

On the beach the sea is dancing
a poem of balconies.
The shores of the moon
gain voices and lose reeds.
Women in bright costume
are eating sunflower seeds,
their huge bottoms hidden
like copper planets.
Tall gentlemen come by
and ladies of sad mien,
dusky with nostalgia
for a yesterday of nightingales.
And the Bishop of Manila,
saffron-blind and poor,
says a double-bladed mass
for the men and women.

*

St. Michael was resting calmly
in the alcove of his tower,
his petticoats frozen
in spangles and lace.

St. Michael, king of balloons
and of uneven numbers,
in the berberesque grace
of shouts and miradors.

Sleepwalking Ballad

FOR GLORIA GINER AND FERNANDO DE LOS RÍOS

Green I want you green.
Green wind, green boughs.
The ship on the sea
and the horse on the mountain.
With shadow at her waist
she dreams at her railing,
green flesh, green hair,
and eyes of cold silver.
Green I want you green.
Under the gypsy moon
things are looking at her,
and she cannot return their gaze.

*

Green I want you green.
Great stars of frost
come with the shadow-fish
that opens the way for dawn.
The fig tree rubs its wind
with the sandpaper of its branches,
and the hill, a wildcat,
bristles with bitter cactus.
But who will come? From where?
She remains at her railing,
green flesh, green hair,
dreaming of the bitter sea.

"Compadre, I want to trade
my horse for your house,
my saddle for your mirror,
my knife for your blanket.
Compadre, I've come here bleeding
from the passes of Cabra."
"If I could, young man,
that deal would be done.
But I am no longer I,
and my house is no longer mine."
"Compadre, I want to die
decently in bed.
A steel one, if I can,
with the best linen sheets.
Don't you see this wound
from my chest to my throat?"
"Three hundred brown roses
cover your white shirt.
Your blood oozes and smells
around your sash.
But I am no longer I,
and my house is no longer mine."
"Let me climb, at least,
up to the high railings.
Let me climb! Let me,
up to the high rails!
Big railings of the moon
where the water roars."

*

The two compadres climb
up to the high railing.
Leaving a trail of blood.
Leaving a trail of tears.
Little tin-leaf lanterns
tremble on the rooftops.
A thousand crystal tambourines
were wounding the dawn.

*

Green I want you green,
green wind, green boughs.
The two compadres climbed.
The long wind was leaving
a strange taste in their mouth
of basil, gall and mint.
"Compadre, where is she?
Where is your bitter girl?"
"How often she awaited you,
how often did she wait,
fresh face, black hair
upon this rail of green!"

*

Over the face of the rain-well
the gypsy girl was rocking.
Green flesh, green hair
and eyes of cold silver.
An icicle of the moon
holds her over the water.

The night became as intimate
as a little village square.
Drunken Civil Guards
were knocking at the door.
Green I want you green.
Green wind. Green boughs.
The ship on the sea.
And the horse on the mountain.

I wish I could be with you to enjoy the spring air of Granada, the pagan odor of the temples, the green gusts of wind sent by the Vega, dressed as a bride by the bean vines in blossom.

FROM A LETTER TO EDUARDO RODRÍGUEZ VALDIVIESO,
APRIL 8, 1933

Holy Week in Granada

The untroubled traveler, full of smiles and the screams of locomotives, goes to the carnival of Valencia. The bacchant goes to the Holy Week of Seville. The man burning for nudes goes to Malaga. But the melancholy, contemplative man goes to Granada, in order to be alone with a breeze of sweet basil, dark moss, and trilling nightingales. To be alone with the breeze that comes from the old hills of the Alhambra – from the bonfire of saffron, deep gray, and blotting-paper pink of its walls. To be alone. To ponder an atmosphere full of difficult voices, in an air so beautiful it is almost thought, at a nerve center of Spain where the "meseta" poetry of St. John of the Cross fills with cedars, cinnamons, and fountains, and Spanish mysticism can receive that Oriental air, that "wounded stag" (wounded by love) who "comes to the hill."

To be alone: to have the solitude one would want in Florence. To understand not the water's play, as at Versailles, but the water's passion, the water's agony.

Or to be with one's beloved and feel the springtime pulsing in the trees and in the skin of the delicate marble columns and see how the yellow orbs of the lemons climb through the glades and push back the frightened snow.

Whoever wants to feel the sweet ticktock of blood in his lips, and feel the stamina of the bull, should be off to the baroque tumult of universal Seville. But whoever would like to sit down at a café table among phantasms and perhaps find a wonderful old ring somewhere along the corridors of his heart should go to the inner, hidden

Granada. He will soon be surprised to learn that there is no Holy Week in Granada. Holy Week does not suit the Christian, antispectacular spirit of her people. When I was a child I sometimes went to the Holy Burial. But only a few times, for the rich people of Granada did not always want to spend money on that parade.

These past few years, out of commercialism, they have put on processions wholly devoid of the seriousness and poetry of the Holy Week I knew as a child. Back then it was a Holy Week of lace, of canaries flying amid the tapers, of an air that was lukewarm and sad, as if the whole day had fallen asleep on the opulent throats of the old maids who promenaded on Holy Thursday pining for some soldier, judge, or foreign professor to carry them far, far away.

In those days the entire city was like a slow merry-go-round moving in and out of fantastically beautiful churches that were both fun-houses and the apotheosis of the theater. Some of the altars were sown with wheat, others had little cascades, and some had the tenderness and poverty of a shooting gallery at the village fair. This one was nothing but reeds, like a celestial henhouse of firecrackers, and that one was immense, with the cruel purple, the sumptuous ermine of the poetry of Calderón.

In a house on the Calle de la Colcha, the street where wreaths and coffins were sold to poor people, those dressed as Roman soldiers would gather for practice. These "soldiers" were not a formal confraternity like the saucy *armaos* of the marvelous Sevillian neighborhood of the Macarena. They were hired hands – moving men, bootblacks, sick people just out of the hospital in need of a few pesetas. They put on the red beards of

Schopenhauer or of flaming cats or ferocious professors. The captain was a military technician, and he taught them to mark the rhythm, which went like this — *porón... chas!* — and they would strike the ground with their lances in a deliciously comical way. As an example of Granada's natural genius, I will tell you that one year the Roman soldiers did very poorly at rehearsal and spent more than fifteen days furiously striking their lances on the ground before they could do so in unison. And then the captain shouted desperately, "Enough! Enough! If you go on like this we'll end up carrying the lances in candleholders!" A saying very characteristic of Granada, and already commented on by several generations.

I would like to ask Granada to restore that old-fashioned Holy Week and have the good taste to hide that hideous procession of the Last Supper and not profane the Alhambra — which is not and never will be Christian — with the jangle of processions where false elegance mocks good taste and the crowd breaks laurels, tramples on violets, and urinates by the hundred on the illustrious walls of poetry.

Granada must save for herself and for the traveler her inner Holy Week, one so intimate and so silent that, as I remember, a startled breeze from the Vega would enter the city by the Calle de la Gracia and would reach the fountain in the Plaza Nueva without hearing a single noise or song.

That way Granada's snowy spring will be perfect, and through this festival the intelligent traveler will be able to converse with her classic types: the human ocean of Ganivet, whose eyes are on the secret lilies of the Darro; the watcher of sunsets who climbs anxiously to the rooftop; the fellow who loves the Sierra as a form, without ever having gone near it; the dark beauty who yearns for love and sits by her mother in the garden; a whole admirable town of contemplatives who are surrounded by unique natural beauty, want nothing, and only know how to smile.

Amid an incredible variety of forms, landscapes, light and aromas, the uninformed traveler will get the feeling that Granada is the capital of a kingdom with its own art and literature, and will find a curious mixture of Jewish and Moorish Granada which will seem to have been blended by Christianity but are really alive and incorruptible in their ignorance.

Neither the prodigious mound of the cathedral nor the great imperial and Roman stamp of Carlos V have effaced the little shop of the Jew who prays before an image recast from a menorah, just as the sepulchers of the Catholic Kings have not kept the crescent from showing at times on the chest of Granada's finest sons. The dark struggle continues, without being expressed. Well, not without expression, because on the Colina Roja are two dead palaces, the Alhambra and the palace of Carlos V, which continue to fight the fatal duel that throbs in the heart of each of Granada's citizens.

All this the traveler should look at when he gets to Granada,which at this very moment is putting on her long dress of springtime. As for the caravans of noisy tourists who like cabarets and luxury hotels – those frivolous groups that the people on the Albaicín call "Tío Turista" – to them the city's soul is closed.

In Madrid the autumn has been delightful. With true melancholy I remember the great yellow treetops in the Plaza de Campillo, and that solitary Plaza de los Lobos, full of acacia leaves, and the divine, first cold wind which sends a shiver through the fountain in the Plaza Nueva. All of this is the Granada of my dreams and my loneliness, when I was an adolescent and no one had yet loved me.

FROM A LETTER TO EDUARDO RODRÍGUEZ VALDIVIESO,
OCTOBER OR NOVEMBER, 1932

Casida of One Wounded by Water

I want to go down to the well,
I want to climb the walls of Granada,
to look at the heart pierced
by the dark awl of the waters.

The wounded boy was moaning
with a crown of frost.
Pools, cisterns and fountains
lifted their swords in the air.
Oh, what a fury of love, what a wounding edge,
what nocturnal murmur, what white death!
What deserts of light were sinking
the sandbacks of early morning!
The boy was all alone.
The city drowsed in his throat.
A water jet that comes from dreams
defends him from the hungry algae.
The boy and his agony, face to face,
were two green rains entwined.
The boy lay flat on the earth,
and his agony made a curve.

I want to go down to the well,
I want to die my death by the mouthful.
I want to fill my heart with moss,
to see the boy wounded by the water.

Casida of the Boughs

Through the groves of Tamarit
the dogs of lead have come
to wait for the boughs to fall,
to wait for them to break by themselves.

The Tamarit has an apple tree
with an apple of sobs.
A nightingale snuffs out sighs
and a pheasant chases them through the dust.

But the boughs are happy,
the branches are like us.
They do not think of the rain and like trees
they have suddenly fallen asleep.

Seated with the water on their knees
two valleys were waiting for autumn.
The dusk, with the tread of an elephant,
was pushing the treetrunks and branches.

In the groves of the Tamarit
there are many boys with veiled faces,
waiting for my boughs to fall,
waiting for them to break by themselves.

Ghazal of the Love Which Hides from Sight

Just to hear
the bell of the Vela,
I gave you a crown of verbena.

Granada was a moon
drowned in the ivy.

Just to hear
the bell of the Vela,
I tore up my garden of Cartagena.

Granada was a doe,
pink among the weathervanes.

Just to hear
the bell of the Vela
I burned in your body
without knowing whose it was.

Ghazal of the Dead Child

Every afternoon in Granada,
every afternoon a child dies.
Every afternoon the water sits down
to converse with its friends.

The dead wear wings of moss.
The clouded wind and clean wind
are two pheasants that fly around the towers
and the day is a wounded boy.

No blade of lark remained in the air
when I found you in the wine caverns.
No crumb of cloud remained on the earth
when you were drowning in the river.

A giant of water fell upon the hills
and the valley went tumbling, with dogs and iris.
Your body, in the violet shadow of my hands,
dead on the bank, was an archangel of cold.

Ghazal of the Morning Market Place

Through the gate of Elvira
I want to see you pass,
to learn your name
and break into tears.

What grey moon at nine o'clock
drained your cheek of blood?
Who collects your seed,
aflame in the snow?
What little cactus needle
murders your crystal...?

Through the gateway of Elvira
I want to see you pass,
to drink your eyes
and break into tears.

What a voice, to punish me,
you raise in the market place!
What an estranged carnation
in the mounds of wheat!
How far I am when with you,
how close when you depart!

Through the gateway of Elvira
I want to see you pass,
to feel your thighs
and break into tears.

Autumn turns the Vega into a submerged bay. In the ramparts of the Alhambra... haven't you ever felt the desire to embark? Haven't you seen the spectral little boats that nod sleepily at the foot of its towers? Today I realize, in the midst of this gray, mother-of-pearl sunset, that I live in a marvellous Atlantis.

I am eager to leave [for Madrid], and yet, I don't want to depart until everything has turned completely golden. Now, in autumn, the valleys of the Darro and the Genil are the only paths in the world that lead directly to the land of Noplace, *lost somewhere in those murmuring mists.*

I am neither happy nor sad, I am inside the autumn; I am...

> *Ay, heart, heart*
> *Cupid's St. Sebastian!*

FROM A LETTER TO MELCHOR FERNÁNDEZ ALMAGRO,
NOVEMBER 1921

How a City Sings from November to November

Like a boy gazing in wonder at his mother dressed in bright colors for a party, I want to show you the city where I was born, the city of Granada. To do so, I want to give you examples of her music, and I will have to sing them. That will be difficult, for I do not sing like a professional but like a poet, or rather as the farm boy sings while goading along his oxen. My voice is weak, my throat delicate; so please do not be surprised if you hear me let out one of those false notes known in our language as "roosters." If one escapes, at least it won't be the corrosive "rooster" of professional singers, terrible bird that pecks at their eyes and ruins their glory. I will turn it into a little silver rooster, and lovingly place it upon the sweet neck of the most melancholy girl in this room, here in Montevideo.

A man from Granada blind from birth and absent from his city for many years would know the season by what he heard sung in the streets. We are not going to take our eyes on this little visit. We shall leave them on a plate of snow, so that St. Lucy won't feel quite so proud.

Why must we always use only our sight, and never our smell or taste to study a city? The special pastries, the *alfajor*, the *torta alajú*, the *mantecado* of Laujar, tell us quite as much about Granada as do its glazed tiles or Moorish arches. And the marzipan of Toledo with its monstrous vestment of plums and anise pearls, invented by a cook of Carlos V, speaks more poignantly of the Emperor's Germanic origins than does his ruddy chin. While a

97

cathedral remains fastened to its own epoch, its profile slowly crumbling away, eternally unable to step into the next day, a song leaps suddenly from its epoch into ours, live and nervous as a frog, with its fresh melancholy or fresh happiness, as miraculous as the seed that flowers when taken from the Pharaoh's tomb. So then, let us *hear* the city of Granada.

The year has four seasons, namely winter, spring, summer and autumn.

Granada has two rivers, eighty bell towers, four thousand irrigation ditches, fifty fountains, a thousand and one jets of water, and one hundred thousand inhabitants. It has a factory where they make guitars and bandurrias, a store where they sell pianos and accordions and harmonicas and especially drums. It has two promenades for singing – the Paseo del Salón and the Paseo del Alhambra – and one for crying, the Alameda de los Tristes, true acme of all European Romanticism, and it has a legion of pyrotechnicians who build towers of noise, with an art equal to that of the Court of the Lions, to irritate the square water of the reflecting ponds.

The Sierra Nevada lends a background of boulders or of snow or of green dream to the songs that cannot fly: songs that fall upon the rooftops or burn their little hands in the hot earth, or drown in the dry spikes of July wheat.

Those songs are the physiognomy of the city, and in them we shall feel its rhythm and temperature.

Using our hearing and our sense of smell, we draw closer, and our first sensation is the smell of sedge, of mint, of a vegetable world gently crushed under the hoofs of the mules and horses and oxen that criss-cross the Vega. And then, the rhythm of the water. But not mad water that goes wherever it wants. Water with tempo, rather than murmur, water that is well-measured and precise as it follows its geometrical, rhythmic course through the irrigation ditches. Water that irrigates and sings here below, and water that suffers and weeps, full of tiny white violins, on the hill of the Generalife.

There is no play of water in Granada: that is left for Versailles where the water is a spectacle and where it is as abundant as the sea: proud mechanical architecture with no sense of song. The water of Granada slakes our thirst. It is living water that becomes part of whoever drinks it or hears it or wants to die in it. It suffers a passion of *jets d'eau* and lies down to die in the reflecting pool. Juan Ramón Jiménez has said it like this:

> What pain and what despair
> at being led about!
> And what somnambulistic
> repetition as
> she reaches the last corner!
> What banging of her head
> against the final walls!
> The water falls asleep and dreams
> of being stripped of tears!

There are also two valleys. Two rivers. In them the water no longer sings; it is a deaf murmur, a mist that mingles with the windspouts sent down by the Sierra. The Genil, crowned with poplars, and the Dauro, crowned with lilies.

But everything is exactly right, everything has human proportion. Air and water in just the right tiny doses. This is the distinction, the special charm of Granada: things for inside the room. Small courtyard, small music, small water, air to dance on our fingertips.

The Cantabrian Sea or the high wind that hurls itself over the cliffs at Ronda frighten the Granadan who peers out the window that frames and defines him. The air grows tame and so does the water, for when the elements come to a boil they smash the tonic of the human scale and annihilate, exhaust the personality of man, who cannot master them and who has to let go of his landscape and his dream. The Granadan sees things through the wrong end of the binoculars. That is why Granada never produced any heroes. That is why Boabdil, the most famous Granadan ever, surrendered her to the Castilians. And that is why, in every age, the Granadan has withdrawn into his tiny chambers, with only the moon for decoration.

Granada is made for music, for it is a city enclosed by mountain ranges, where the melody is returned and polished and blocked by walls and boulders. Music is for cities away from the coast. Seville and Malaga and Cadiz escape through their ports, but Granada's only way out is its high natural port of stars. Granada is withdrawn, enclosed, apt for rhythm and the echo, the marrow of music.

Her highest expression is not poetical but musical, with a wide avenue that leads to mysticism. And so she does not have, as does Seville (city of Don Juan, city of love), a dramatical expression, but a lyrical one. And while Seville reaches its heights in Lope and Tirso and in Beaumarchais and Zorrilla and in the prose of Bécquer, Granada reaches hers in an orchestra of water jets charged with Andalusian pain, and in Narvaez's music for the *vihuela*, and in Falla and in Debussy. And while in Seville the human element dominates the landscape, and Don Pedro and Don Alonso and Duke Octavio of Naples and Figaro and Mañara stroll through closed spaces, in Granada phantasms stroll through the two empty palaces, and the spur turns into a slow ant racing across an endless marble pavement, and the love letter turns into a fistful of grass, and the sword turns into a delicate mandolin that only spiders and nightingales are unafraid to play.

We have arrived in Granada toward the end of November. It smells like burnt straw, and the piles of leaves are beginning to rot. It is raining and people are indoors. But in the middle of the Puerta Real there are already a few stalls selling noisemakers (*zambombas*). The Sierra is covered with clouds, and there is room enough here for all the music of northern Spain. A girl from Armilla or Santa Fe or Atarfe, a servant, buys a *zambomba* and sings this song:

> Of the four muleteers
> who go to the water,
> the one with the grey mule
> steals my heart.

> Of the four muleteers
> who go to the river,
> the one with the grey mule
> is my husband.

> Why do you look for warmth
> farther up the street
> if your face
> is glowing with heat?

This is the folk rhythm that is heard all over the Vega, and which the Moors carried from Granada to Africa. Today in Tunis they play it like this. [*He plays*].

The song of the four muleteers is sung beside the glowing embers of beanstalks burnt for heat in the numerous villages outside Granada, the crown of villages that climbs into the Sierra.

But December advances, the sky is clear, flocks of turkeys arrive, and the sound of tambourines and chicharras takes over the city. At night, from inside the closed houses, one goes on hearing the same rhythm. It comes out the windows and the chimneys, as though born directly from the earth. The voices climb a little higher, the streets fill with brightly-lit booths, with huge mounds of apples, the bells of midnight join the little bells that the nuns ring at daybreak, the Alhambra grows darker and more remote than ever, the hens abandon their eggs on the frosty straw. By now the nuns of the Convent of Santo Tomás de Villanueva are putting a flat, yellow hat on St. Joseph and a mantilla, with its curved comb, on the Virgin Mary. By now the clay sheep, the little woollen dogs are climbing the stairs toward the artificial moss.

The sound of *carrañacas* begins to be heard and amid castanets and potcovers, graters and copper mortars, they sing the joyous Christmas ballad of the two pilgrims:

> Two pilgrims
> are going to Rome
> so the Pope can marry them,
> for they are cousins.

The young man is wearing
a hat of oilcloth,
the pilgrim girl
a velvet one.

While they were crossing
Victoria Bridge
the bridesmaid stumbled,
the bride fell down.

They have come to the palace
and go upstairs.
In the Pope's chambers
they discourage them.

The Pope has asked
what are their names.
He says Pedro,
and Ana, she.

The Pope has asked
how old they are.
She says fifteen,
seventeen, he.

The Pope has asked
where they are from.
She says from Cabra,
Antequera, he.

The Pope has asked
if they have sinned.

Yes, he answers,
he has given her a kiss.

The pilgrim girl
is rather shy.
Her face has turned
red as a rose!

The Pope has replied
from inside his room:
"Wish *I* were a pilgrim
and could do the same!"

The bells of Rome
are pealing now,
for at last the pilgrims
are married.

People sing this song on the streets in bacchic throngs,
little children sing it with their nannies, and so do drunken
prostitutes behind the closed curtains of their carriages,
and soldiers remembering their home towns as they have
their pictures taken by the balustrade along the Genil. It is
the gaiety of the streets, the humor of Andalusia, the subtle
refinement and wit of a people steeped in culture.

But we leave the streets and head for the Jewish neigh-
borhood, and find it deserted. We hear this song full of
hidden melancholy, the opposite of "The Little Pilgrims."

Just who is singing this song? It is Granada's very
purest voice, her elegiac voice, the clash of East and West
in the two broken palaces that are full of ghosts, the Palace
of Charles V and the Alhambra:

Down the street
goes the man I love.
I can't see his face
under his hat.

A curse on the hat
that covers all that!
I'll buy him a new one
for Christmas.

The last Christmas carol scurries away, and the city falls asleep in the ices of January.

In February, with the sun shining and giving us fresh air, people go on picnics and hang swings from the olive trees, and one hears the same cry – the same *uyuí* – as in the mountains of northern Spain.

People are singing on the outskirts of Granada, where the water is still hidden under a thin layer of ice. The grown boys stretch out on the ground to see the legs of the girls on the swings, the older ones peeping at them from the corners of their eyes. The air is still cold.

The streets in the poor, outlying neighborhoods are calm now. A dog or two, a breeze from the olive groves, and suddenly, *plop!* Somebody tosses a pail of dirty water out the door. But the olive groves are full of life:

The girl is swinging,
her lover is watching,
and he says, "My darling,
this rope won't hold."

This rope won't hold.
Where will she land?
In the last little alleys
of San Nicolás.

Some of these songs have all the purity of the folk-
songs of the fifteenth century:

I go to the olive groves,
I go in the evenings,
to see how the air
is moving the leaf.
To see how the air
is moving the leaf.

This is the same as that marvelous song of 1560, with a
melody by Juan Vázquez, that says:

I come from the poplars, mother,
to see them moving in the breeze.

From the poplars of Seville,
from seeing my sweet friend.

From the poplars of Granada,
from seeing my beloved.

To see them moving in the breeze,
I come from the poplars, mother.

The purest classical reminiscences enliven these songs
of the olive groves. And this is not at all rare in Spain

where songs by Juan del Encina, Salinas, Fuenllana, and Pisador turn up suddenly in Galicia or Avila, sung in all their purity.

At nightfall people come home from the olive groves and often the gatherings go on indoors.

But when spring arrives and leaves are beginning to bud and balconies begin to open, the landscape is strangely transformed. We have come down from the snow, down to the laurel tree and all the sharp profiles of the south.

Children have already begun to play in the streets, and in my childhood a popular old poet whom they used to call "Look-at-the-Sky" would come outside and sit on a bench in the park. Casks of new wine are arriving from the coast, and at twilight the city sings this song heralding the bullfights, a song with a form as pure as the air of the last day of March:

> In the Café de Chinitas
> Paquiro said to his brother:
> I'm so much braver than you,
> more *torero*, more of a Gypsy.
>
> Paquiro took out his watch
> and this is what he said:
> "This bull must die
> by four-thirty this afternoon."
>
> When it struck four in the tower
> they left the café,
> and Paquiro went strutting about
> like a big-name bullfighter.

But what's this, what's going on? Two women friends from one of the villages meet at the Humilladero gate, through which the Catholic Monarchs entered Granada:

> Comadre, where are you coming from?
> Comadre, from Granada.
> Comadre, what's happening there?
> Comadre, nothing at all:
> they're making the same old baskets
> and ringing the same old bells.

In May and June the bells of Granada ring incessantly. The students cannot study. In the Plaza de Bibarrambla, the cathedral bells – bells that seem to ring underwater, with seaweed and clouds – make it impossible for the farmers to hear one another. The church bells of San Juan de Dios hurl through the air their Baroque reredos of lamentation and banging bronze. The Alhambra is lonelier and more forlorn than ever, dead and flayed, alien to the city, more and more remote. But there are ice cream vendors in the streets, and stalls with raisin bread with sesame seeds, and men selling honey bars with garbanzo beans.

Along come the dragon and dwarfs of Corpus Christi, and in the streets Granada's women, with their lovely naked arms and wombs like dark magnolias, suddenly open their green, orange, blue parasols, in the frenzy of lights and violins and carriages, in a carousel of love, gallantry and nostalgia, in the Castle-of-No-Return of the fireworks.

From the Vega comes a swarm of whistles (sold at the village fairs), and on the Calle de Elvira, most ancient

Elvira Street
where the *manolas* live,
the ones that go up to the Alhambra
by twos and threes, alone…

we hear this song, so expressive of Granada:

Under the leaf
of the vervain
my lover is sick,
Jesus, how sad!

Under the leaf
of the lettuce
my lover is sick
with a fever.

Under the leaf
of the parsley
my lover is sick,
I'll stay by his side.

The last firecracker, the so-called "thunderbolt," is shot off, and in a single day all Granada leaves for the country. The city is abandoned to summer, which comes in an hour. The ladies cover their armchairs with white dropcloths and close the doors of the balcony. Those who stay behind are living in the courtyards and in the downstairs rooms sitting in their rockers and drinking cool water from the wet red clay of the water jugs. One begins to think and to live by night. And this is the time when the city sings, to the accompaniment of guitars, those *fandangos* and *granadinas* that are so peculiar and have such a depth of landscape.

The whole of traditional balladry comes to the lips of the children. The most beautiful ballads, unmatched by any Romantic poet, the bloodiest legends, the most unexpected plays on words. Among countless examples I have chosen this one, sung by the children in some of the villages and by the boys who live around the Plaza Larga in the Albaicín. In the August night, no one can resist this tender melody. It is the ballad of the Duke of Alba:

> "It is rumored, it is rumored,
> it is rumored in Seville
> that the Duke is getting married
> to another, and forgetting you."
>
> "Let him marry if he wants.
> Why should I care?"
> "You ought to care, sister,
> for your honor is lost."
> She went upstairs to a room
> where she used to embroider and sew.
> Now she goes to a window
> that overlooks the square.
> She sees the Duke coming
> with another woman.
> She makes him a secret sign,
> to see if he will catch it.
> "What does Ana, Ana want?
> What can she want, this Ana María?"
> "Duke of Alba, Duke of Alba,
> Duke of Alba of my life,

they tell me you are marrying
a lady of great worth."
"Who told you that? Who told you
the truth and not a lie?
The wedding is tomorrow,
I was coming to invite you."
When she heard those words,
she fell dead to the ground.
Doctors and surgeons
hurried to her side.
They tried to open her breast
to see why she was dying.
To one side of her heart
she had two slips of gold.
One of them said "Duke,"
the other, "of my life."
"If only I had known
that you loved me so,
I would not have forgotten you,
dove of my soul."

But it is time now for us to tiptoe down a certain road
of red clay, bordered by prickly pears, to a gathering in a
remote corner of the hills. They are singing and dancing.
We hear guitars, castanets and rustic instruments,
tambourines and triangles. These are the people who sing
the *roas* and *alboreás*, the *cachuchas* and the *zorongo*, which
has greatly influenced the music of Manuel de Falla. [*He
plays*]

In the hills the yellow light of dawn brings us the songs
of reapers and threshers. But those rural songs never enter
the city.

September. The air is nippy. The wheel is coming full circle.

> Round and round we go,
> and autumn appears in the poplar groves.

And so do the village fairs. The fairs, with walnuts, jujubes, red haws, crowds of quinces, towers of sugar bread and tarts from the Corzo pastry shop.

St. Michael on his hill brandishes his sword, surrounded by sunflowers. Remember my ballad?

> St. Michael full of lace
> in the alcove of his tower
> shows his lovely thighs
> ringed in lantern light…

> St. Michael, king of balloons
> and of uneven numbers
> in the Berberesque grace
> of screams and miradors.

Berberesque grace of screams and miradors. That is Granada, seen from the Cerro del Aceituno. The song one hears is chaotic. It is all Granada singing at once: rivers, voices, ropes, foliage, processions, an ocean of fruits, the music of the swing rides at the fairs.

But when the happiness of Michaelmas is gone, autumn with its noise of water comes knocking at every door.

Knock, knock.
Who's there?
Autumn again.
What do you want?
The coolness of your temple.
You can't have it.
Then I'll take it.
Knock, knock.
Who's there?
Autumn again.

With the first rain, the threshing floors fill with grass.
The air is a bit chilly now, and no one goes to the park.
Look-at-the-Sky is sitting at his table, his legs tucked
cozily under the green felt tablecloth, his feet warmed
by a charcoal brazier. But the sunsets fill the entire
sky. Enormous clouds annul the landscape and strange
lights go skittering over the rooftops or fall asleep in
the cathedral tower. And here again is the voice of true
melancholy.

Through that window
over the river
toss me your kerchief,
for I am hurt.

Through that window
over the garden
toss me your kerchief,
for I am dying.

Through that window
over the water
toss me your kerchief,
I'm nearly dead.

It happens that the boys do not want to go to school:
they are playing with their tops.

It happens that in drawing rooms they are lighting
candles for the deceased.

It happens that we are in November.

It smells like burnt straw, and the piles of leaves (do
you remember?) are beginning to rot. It is raining, and
people are indoors.

But in the middle of the Puerta Real there are already a
few stalls selling noisemakers.

A girl from Armilla or Santa Fe or Atarfe, a year older,
dressed perhaps in mourning, is singing for her master's
children:

Of the four muleteers
who go to the water,
the one with the grey mule
steals my heart.

Of the four muleteers
who go to the river,
the one with the grey mule
is my husband.

We have gone round the year. It will always be like this.
Before and now. We must leave, but Granada remains.
Eternal in time but fleeting in these poor hands – these
hands of mine, the smallest of her children.

Notes

OC refers to volume and page number of Federico García Lorca, *Obras Completas*, ed. Miguel García-Posada (Barcelona: Círculo de Lectores, 1997).

Poem of the Fair (p. 13)
In July 1921, shortly after his twenty-third birthday, Lorca returned to his family's house in the village of Asquerosa, away from the heat and fumes of Madrid, where he had been studying at the Residencia de Estudiantes. A few days after his arrival he wrote to a friend: "I think my place is here, in the midst of these musical poplars and the continuous backwaters of these lyrical rivers. For here my heart is definitively at rest and I can poke fun at my passions, which are always waiting for me, in the tower of the city, like a band of panthers."

In July and August, during his stay in Asquerosa, a few country miles by train and carriage from Granada, he settled down to work on his *Suites*: loosely structured sequences of short poems. The title, *Suites*, is drawn from the world of music, and the structural ideas and whimsical tone seem reminiscent of one of Lorca's favorite composers, Claude Debussy. The idea was to capture some phenomenon – the moon, the hours of evening, the ocean, wheatfields, flamenco – in a series of stylized *estampas* (prints) or "moments." Lorca's first book of verse, *Libro de poemas*, arrived that July from Madrid, but by the time the first copy reached his hands he had grown tired of its sometimes ponderous rhetoric – "path of the essay, path of declamation" – and was struck by the possibilities of the short poem. At the Residencia he had become interested both in haiku and in the lyrics of Andalusian folksong: a fine example of lyrical concentration "for those of us who must prune and care for the over-luxuriant lyrical tree left to us by Romanticism."

Gracefully, with a touch of irony, the *Suites* capture a range of lyrical events and metaphysical conundrums (the longing for childhood, the mystery of language, or the anguish of unrealized possibilities). One of them, dated July 27, 1921, pays homage to the fairs that come to Spanish villages on saints' days in summer and autumn.

This little sheaf of poems, *Poema de la feria*, was tucked away with other *Suites* awaiting revision, and, except for two poems, remained unknown for more than 60 years. In 1931, Lorca had given the MS. to the French Hispanist Mathilde Pomès. Sold at auction after her death, it was bought by the Barcelona bookseller and bibliophile Ramón Soley who published it in facsimile in spring 1997. It is presented here in English for the first time. I have translated from Soley's edition, but have also consulted an unpublished critical edition of the *Suites* by Melissa Dinverno of the University of Michigan.

p. 22 In "Dark Song," Lorca drew a box around lines 12–15, as though considering them for omission.

p. 26 In the final lines of "Variation," Lorca is remembering the traditional Spanish ballad, often sung by children, "Mambrú se fue a la guerra…". Spanish text, *Ferias* (Barcelona: Edicions Delstre, 1997).

Summer Hours (p. 29)
Written August 11, 1921. Complete manuscript published for the first time by C. de Paepe in *Boletín de la Fundación Federico García Lorca*, and given here in English for the first time. Spanish text: *Boletín de la Fundación Federico García Lorca*, no. 16 (December 1994), 16–19.

Palimpsests (p. 37)
Probably written in spring 1922, and published in 1936 in *Primeras canciones*, without "Air" and "Madrigal." The "Vermilion Towers" (*Torres Bermejas*) form part of a wall near the Alhambra. The libidinous Melisendra is the protagonist of a well-known traditional ballad. Spanish text: *OC*, I: 184–186.

Little Tales of the Wind (p. 45)
Written in Asquerosa in July 1922. Spanish text: *OC*, I: 211–213.

Water Jets (p. 51)
Composed 1921–1922. One page of the manuscript is missing.
Lorca published the first poem in *Songs* (1927), entitling it "Granada y 1850." Spanish text: *OC*, I: 266–267.

Meditations and Allegories of the Water (p. 57)
Written, like the preceding letter, in spring 1922, according to Dinverno, but never finished. The Vega is the green, fertile plain at the foot of the Sierra Nevada, where Lorca's father, Federico García Rodríguez, a rich landowner, cultivated sugar beets and other crops. The "border" or "dividing line" mentioned by Lorca lies to the west of the Cubillas, the river mentioned in the opening paragraph. See Ian Gibson, *Lorca's Granada. A Practical Guide* (London: Faber and Faber, 1992), p. 146. Spanish text: *OC*, I: 294–296.

Daydreams of a River (p. 60)
"Ensueños del río" is from the same period as "Meditations...". Both were published in *Collected Poems*, ed. C. Maurer (New York: Farrar, Straus and Giroux, 1990), pp. 324–327 and 318–321.

Granada: Paradise Closed to Many (p. 63)
Published in the catalogue of the Seville Exposition of 1929, and given here for the first time in English, following the text in C. Maurer, ed., *Conferencias*, vol. I (Madrid: Alianza Editorial, 1984), pp. 133–136. Lorca read these lines for the first time in 1926 as part of a lecture on the poet Pedro Soto de Rojas (1584–1658), a friend of Lope de Vega and Góngora. His masterpiece, *Paraíso cerrado para muchos, jardines abiertos para pocos*, describes his house and walled garden in Granada. Spanish text: *OC*, III: 79–83.

August (p. 71)
Written *ca.* 1924 and published in *Songs* (1927). Spanish text: *OC*, I: p. 354.

Evening (p. 72)
From *Songs* (1927). Spanish text: *OC*, I: 368.

Ballad of the Three Rivers (p. 73)
From *Poem of the Deep Song*, written 1921 and published 1931. Spanish text: *OC*, I: 305–306.

Tree, tree / dry and green (p. 75)
Written in 1923 and published in *Songs* (1927). Spanish text: *OC*, I: 370–371.

St. Michael (Granada) (p. 77)

From *The Gypsy Ballads* (1928). Written in August 1926. The poem describes the break of dawn on the feast of St. Michael (Sept. 29), an occasion celebrated in Granada with a pilgrimage to the shrine of San Miguel el Alto on the hill over the gypsy quarter of the Albaicín. Lorca is referring to a peculiar Baroque statue portraying a somewhat effeminate archangel. Ramsden explains: "Behind the altar a glass screen [*glass*] separates the nave from the 'camarín' [*alcove of his tower*] where the statue of St. Michael stands surrounded by four lights [*lantern light*]. The boyish figure of the saint [*ephebe of three thousand nights*] [...] sumptuously attired in female dress [...] and with a fine plume of feathers on his head [*feathers*] is treading, somewhat delicately, on the prostrate figure of a demonic, tailed Satan, his right arm upraised with three arrows in his hand [*pointing to twelve o'clock*], threatening the demon beneath his feet." H. Ramsden, *Lorca's Romancero gitano. Eighteen Commentaries* (Manchester: Manchester University Press, 1988), p. 148. Words in italics, mine. Spanish text: *OC*, I: 427–429.

Sleepwalking Ballad (p. 80)

Lorca said of this ballad (written 1924; published in *The Gypsy Ballads*, 1928) that it was "thought by many to express Granada's longing for the sea and the anguish of a city that cannot hear the waves and seeks them in the play of her underground waters and in the undulous clouds with which she covers her mountains. That is true, but this poem is also something else. It is a pure poetic event, of Andalusian essence, and will always have changing lights, even for me, the man who communicated it. If you ask me why I wrote, 'A thousand crystal tambourines / were wounding the dawn,' I will tell you that I saw them in the hands of angels and trees, but I will not be able to say more; certainly I cannot explain their meaning. And that is the way it should be. By means of poetry a man more rapidly approaches the cutting edge that the philospher and the mathematician turn away from in silence." *Deep Song and Other Prose* (New York: New Directions, 1980), pp. 111–112. The mention of the "passes of Cabra," a mountain pass in Córdoba province, suggests that one of the men is a smuggler, wounded in an encounter with the Civil Guard. Spanish text: *OC*, I: 420–422.

Holy Week in Granada (p. 85)
Broadcast on the radio in Madrid in April 1936, a few months before
Lorca was murdered in Granada. He spent Holy Week the year before
(April 14–21, 1935) not in Granada but in Seville, at the invitation of
Joaquín Romero Murube, keeper of the Alcázar, a story he tells about
in an interview: "Murube rented a balcony, just for me, where I could
watch [the procession]. The gypsies, who are very fond of me, gave
me an intimate Holy Week with the best of their wines and their litur-
gies. They built an altar on top of ten huge casks of wine, with paper
roses and burning candles and the pictures of two bullfighters, Joselito
and Sánchez Mejías, and before that altar I read for the first time my
Lament for Ignacio Sánchez Mejías. After that they danced in bare feet
and didn't let even my best friends into the room. The only non-gypsy
there was me. And that night I slept at the house of *La Malena* [gypsy
dancer] in a huge, lovely white bed that smelled sweetly of apple."
Later, he sat in the gardens of the Alcázar, chatting with the gardener
and gathering material for his comedy *Doña Rosita, or The Language of
the Flowers*. Spanish text: *OC*, III: 271–274.

Casida of One Wounded by Water (p. 91)
From *Divan of the Tamarit*, published posthumously in 1940. The
Huerta del Tamarit, from which the book takes its name, was a coun-
try house owned by one of Lorca's uncles. With its ghazals and
casidas, the "Divan" (collection of verse) was a poetic tribute to Arab-
Andalusian poetry. Spanish text: *OC*, I: 600.

Casida of the Boughs (p. 92)
From *Divan of the Tamarit*. In his lecture "Play and Theory of the
Duende" (1933), Lorca says of artistic inspiration: "The duende does
not come at all unless he sees that death is possible. The duende must
know beforehand that he can serenade death's house and rock those
branches we all wear: branches that do not have, will never have, any
consolation" (*Deep Song*, pp. 49–50.) Spanish text: *OC*, I: 601–602.

Ghazal of the Love Which Hides from Sight (p. 93)
Lines 1–2 are from the lyrics of a flamenco piece, a *tanguillo*: "I want to
live in Granada / only to hear / the bell of the Vela / when I go to
sleep." In his *Handbook for Travellers in Spain* (1:303), Richard Ford

explains that the "*torre de la Vela is* so called, because on this watch-tower hangs a silver-tongued bell, which, struck by the warder at certain times, is the primitive clock that gives notice to irrigators below. It is heard on a still night even at Loja, 30 miles off, and tender and touching are the feelings which the silver sound awakens. This bell is also rung every January 2, the anniversary of the surrender of Granada; on that day the Alhambra is visited by crowds of peasantry. Few maidens pass by without striking the bell, which ensures a husband, and a good one in proportion as the noise made, which it need not be said is continuous and considerable. The fete is altogether most national and picturesque." The crown of vervain (*verbena*) in line 3 would be appropriate for a future husband or wife. The rhyme *verbena / Cartagena* was suggested by a children's song. Spanish text: *OC*, I: 594.

Ghazal of the Dead Child (p. 94)
From *Divan of the Tamarit*. Spanish text: *OC*, I: 594–595.

Ghazal of the Morning Market Place (p. 95)
The "Gateway of Elvira," once the principal entrance to Granada, leads to the gypsy (formerly Moorish) quarter of the Albaicín. Spanish text: *OC*, I: 644.

How a City Sings from November to November (p. 97)
Lecture given in Buenos Aires, October 16, 1933. "My lectures will be illustrated by music, and I am going to sing," Lorca told a journalist in Buenos Aires in October 1933. "I won't sing very loudly, but yes, I will sing, because I believe I'm the only person who can illustrate – no matter how badly I do so – my comments on the origins of Andalusian music."

Throughout his adolescence – until around 1917 – music seemed far more important to Lorca than literature. In a letter to a friend he says that he "took the Holy Orders of music" long before he began to write poetry. By 1918 he was a fine classical pianist, and was making a collection of "the splendid inner polyphony of the folk music of Granada." This songbook, which was to be titled *Tonadas de la Vega* is one of five works said to be "in preparation" on the last page of his first book of prose, *Impresiones y paisajes*. *Tunes of the Vega* was never published, perhaps never even compiled, though in the 1930s Lorca boasted to the musician Marcelle Schweitzer that he had collected over 300 folksongs from Granada and could play them by heart. He had gathered many of them in the company of his beloved mentor Manuel de Falla, with whom he collaborated on puppet plays, a great festival of *cante jondo*, and an unfinished musical play entitled *La comedianta (The Actress)*.

Lorca's love of folk music inspired several of his lectures, among them the famous defense of *cante jondo*, first given in 1922, revised in 1930 and read "as a polemic" in different cities of Cuba, Argentina and Spain. In January, 1928 he announces to a friend that he is writing a lecture about the pathos of the Spanish cradle song, and when he read it the following December to his friends at the Residencia de Estudiantes, Madrid, he himself sang the lullabies. Federico de Onís, who taught Spanish literature at Columbia University when Lorca studied there in 1929–1930, tells us that "His voice was not an extraordinarily good one for singing; it might almost be called defective; a little hoarse and weak, though when he was speaking or reading aloud it acquired expressiveness and personality."

Like the singers of *cante jondo*, Lorca relied on *duende* – on his own dark personal charm – rather than on polish and style. Whom else could he trust to sing his favorite songs, neither embellishing them nor falsifying their rhythms? "Songs," he said, "are creatures, delicate creatures whose rhythm one must take pains not to alter. Each one is a miracle of equilibrium, like a silver coin on the point of a needle. Songs are like people. They live and perfect themselves. Some degenerate and crumble away until they are nothing but palimpsests, full of lacunae and things that make no sense."

In "folksongs worn down by time" he found poetic mystery, a quality he sought for his own works. "How a City Sings…" is not only an attempt to define the lyrical essence of Granada, or, defeating time and space, to evoke its beauty for others; as in almost all of his lectures, Lorca is revealing the forces that nurtured his own art, and trying to capture the essence of Granada.

First published by Mario Hernández in his edition of Federico García Lorca, *Federico y su mundo*, 2nd ed. (Madrid: Alianza Editorial, 1982), pp. 471–485. Published for the first time in English in this translation in a limited edition (San Francisco: Cadmus Editions, 1982).

p. 97   Wolf notes are known as *gallos* (roosters) in Spanish.

p. 97   In his story "Santa Lucía y San Lázaro" Lorca writes: "St. Lucy was a beautiful maiden of Syracuse. In paintings she is shown holding her two magnificent ox-like eyes on a tray. She suffered martyrdom under the consul Pascasian...". *OC*, I:488. The story of her life is told by Jacobus de Voragine in *The Golden Legend*.

p. 97   *Alfajor, torta alajú, mantecado*. There are no English equivalents for these Spanish pastries, two of which are mentioned in Lorca's 1928 lecture on Spanish cradle songs: "To know the Alhambra of Granada..., before touring its rooms and courtyards, it is very useful, of great pedagogical value, to sample the delicious *alfajor* of Zafra or the *tortas alajú* made by the nuns. The taste and fragrance of these sweets give us the authentic temperature of the palace when it was alive – the ancient light, the cardinal points of its courtly temperament." *Deep Song*, p. 8.

p. 98   *Songs that cannot fly*. In the earlier lecture on lullabies, Lorca had distinguished between folksongs that stray from their native regions to other parts of Spain, e.g., the *bolero*, and songs which do not. See *Deep Song*, p. 22.

p. 99   "*What pain and what despair...*". Titled "Generalife" and dedicated by the great Spanish poet Juan Ramón Jiménez to Lorca's sister Isabel. Isabel and Federico had accompanied Jiménez to the Alhambra when he visited Granada in summer 1924.

p. 100   *The prose of Bécquer*. Gustavo Adolfo Bécquer (1836–1870), Spain's greatest Romantic lyric poet.

p. 100   In his youth Lorca witnessed a revival of Renaissance Spanish music for the *vihuela*, including that of Luis de Narvaez, a native of Granada (1530–1550), who published a collection of pieces for that instrument.

p. 100   *Debussy*. In his lecture on *cante jondo* (1922), Lorca writes that in Debussy's "Vague, tender *Soirée en Grenade*... one can find all the emotional themes of the night in Granada: the blue remoteness of the Vega, the Sierra greeting the tremulous Mediterranean, the enormous barbs of the clouds which sink into the distance, the admirable rubato of the city, the hallucinating play of its underground waters." *Deep Song*, pp. 29–30.

p. 101   *Don Pedro* is the protagonist of Calderón's *The Surgeon of*

His Honor and the subject of Lorca's "Romance con lagunas" (Ballad with Lagoons) in *The Gypsy Ballads*. Don Alonso is the hero of Lope de Vega's *El caballero de Olmedo*. Duke Octavio of Naples is one of the characters in Tirso de Molina's play about Don Juan. *Miguel de Mañara*, the seventeenth-century Spanish sinner and mystic, has often been compared to Don Juan.

p. 101 The *zambomba* is a sort of friction drum used in Christmas festivities: its membrane is pierced with a stick which the player moves up and down.

p. 101 "The Four Muleteers" was one of the songs Lorca recorded with *La Argentinita* in 1931 (now available on CD from Sonifolk, Madrid). He told a journalist in Buenos Aires, "it is the typical Christmas carol of the Albaicín. It is only sung at Christmas, when the weather is cold. It is a pagan carol, like almost all of the ones sung by the people. The religious carols are only sung in the churches and to put children to sleep. It is very strange, this pagan carol, which reveals Andalusia's Bacchic sense of the Nativity" (*OC*, III: 484).

p. 102 *From Granada to Africa*. The musicologist Theodore Grame writes that this *músiquí andalusí*, which still flourishes in Northern Africa, "was originally the court music of Muslim Andalusia and was carried from there to North Africa by the many intellectuals, artisans and musicians who fled after the fall of the Kingdom of Granada in 1492." See *The New Grove Dictionary of Music and Musicians*, ed. Stanley Sadie, vol. 12 (London: Macmillan, 1980), p. 588.

p. 102 *Tambourines and chicharras*. The *pandereta* is a tambourine with jingles, and the *chicharra* a tube, one end of which is covered with a parchment membrane pierced by a piece of waxed thread. When the thread is moved it makes a cricket-like sound. *Carrañacas*: Two notched pieces of wood rubbed together. The "copper mortars" are turned upside down and played like bells.

p. 102 *Joyous Christmas ballad*. One of the songs recorded by Lorca with *La Argentinita*. Lorca remarks in an interview in Buenos Aires that he knew two versions of this song: "One has a gay rhythm and is sung in the Vega; the other is melancholy and comes from the Sierra" (*OC*, III: 483).

p. 105 *Uyuí*. The word is illegible in the manuscript; perhaps *uyuiy*. Lorca seems to be referring to the stylized shout of joy that ends certain folksongs.

p. 106 *San Nicolás*. A square in the northern part of Granada commanding a view of the Alhambra and the Sierra Nevada.

p. 106 *I come from the poplars, mother...* Lines 5–6, on Granada, do not appear in the version of this song found in Juan Vázquez's *Recopilación de sonetos y villancicos a cuatro y cinco voces* (Seville, 1560). Did Lorca invent them? *Miguel de Fuenllana* and *Diego Pisador* are sixteenth-century composers of *vihuela* music. *Juan del Encina* is remembered for his plays, and *Francisco de Salinas* for his theoretical work on music, *De musica libri septem*.

p. 108 *Comadre* is the form of address used by two women from the same village.

p. 108 *The church bells of San Juan de Dios*. In this church, dedicated in 1759, is a reredos of gilded wood "of such singular style that the most delirious imagination would, today, be quite incapable of conceiving it". Manuel Gómez Moreno, *Guía de Granada*, 1892, p. 358.

p. 109 *Elvira Street*. The poet's brother tells us that this is a local folksong, a *fandanguillo* (*Federico y su mundo*, p. 364). The *manolas* – women dressed in typical costume – are mentioned in "St. Michael" and brought to life in the last act of Lorca's play *Doña Rosita*.

p. 109 *The last firecracker*. On p. 17 of the manuscript Lorca crossed out the following words: "Last summer I had gotten together with some friends, popular types, who were singing. A firecracker went off nearby and no one was the least bit perturbed. One of them simply said: 'That was just a clap that came in at the wrong time.'"

p. 109 *Under the leaf...* Another of the songs recorded by Lorca and *La Argentinita*.

p. 112 *St. Michael*. See above, p. 77. The "sea of fruits" mentioned in the next paragraph refers to those sold at the stands set up on Michaelmas in the vicinity of the shrine.

p. 113 *Knock, knock...* Lorca's poem imitates traditional children's rhymes.

p. 114 *Candles for the deceased*, on All Souls Day, November 2.

EL CAFE DE CHINITAS

Recogida y armonizada por Federico García Lorca

Allegro moderato

En el Ca - fé de Chi - ni tas di - jo

Pa - qui ro a su her - ma no en el Ca - fé de Chi -

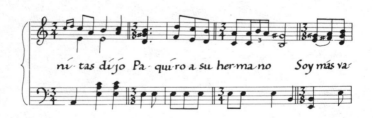

ni - tas di jo Pa - qui ro a su her - ma no Soy más va -

lien - te que tú más to - re - ro y más gí -

126

ta - no, soy más va - lién - te que tú más to -

re - ro y más gi ta - no.

LAS TRES HOJAS

Recogida y armonizada por Federico García Lorca

De - ba - jo de la ho - ja de la ver,
ten-go a mi a - man - te ma - lo, Je - sús qué

be - na de - ba, de - ba - jo, de - ba - jo, de la
pe - na

ho - ja de - ba - jo, de - ba - jo, de la ho - ja

de - ba - jo de la ho - ja de la ver - be - na.

FROZEN TRACKS

FROZEN TRACKS

AN INSPECTOR ERIK WINTER NOVEL

Åke Edwardson

TRANSLATED FROM THE SWEDISH BY LAURIE THOMPSON

VIKING

VIKING
Published by the Penguin Group
Penguin Group (USA) Inc., 375 Hudson Street, New York, New York 10014, U.S.A. ▪ Penguin Group
(Canada), 90 Eglinton Avenue East, Suite 700, Toronto, Ontario, Canada M4P 2Y3 (a division of Pearson
Penguin Canada Inc.) ▪ Penguin Books Ltd, 80 Strand, London WC2R 0RL, England ▪ Penguin Ireland,
25 St. Stephen's Green, Dublin 2, Ireland (a division of Penguin Books Ltd) ▪ Penguin Books Australia
Ltd, 250 Camberwell Road, Camberwell, Victoria 3124, Australia (a division of Pearson Australia Group
Pty Ltd) ▪ Penguin Books India Pvt Ltd, 11 Community Centre, Panchsheel Park, New Delhi – 110 017,
India ▪ Penguin Group (NZ), 67 Apollo Drive, Rosedale, North Shore 0745, Auckland, New Zealand (a di-
vision of Pearson New Zealand Ltd.) ▪ Penguin Books (South Africa) (Pty) Ltd, 24 Sturdee Avenue, Rose-
bank, Johannesburg 2196, South Africa

Penguin Books Ltd, Registered Offices:
80 Strand, London WC2R 0RL, England

First American edition
Published in 2007 by Viking Penguin,
a member of Penguin Group (USA) Inc.

10 9 8 7 6 5 4 3 2 1

Copyright © Åke Edwardson, 2001
Translation copyright © Laurie Thompson, 2007
All rights reserved

Originally published as *Himlen är en plats på jorden* by Norstedts Forlag, Stockholm.

LIBRARY OF CONGRESS CATALOGING-IN-PUBLICATION DATA
Edwardson, Åke, ———.
    [Himlen är en plats på jorden. English]
    Frozen tracks : an inspector Erik Winter novel / Åke Edwardson ;
translated from the Swedish by Laurie Thompson.
    p.   cm.
    ISBN 978-0-670-06323-9
    I. Thompson, Laurie, ———.   II. Title.
    PT9876.15.D93F7613   2007
    839.73'74—dc22   2007009222

Printed in the United States of America
Set in Dante with Eras
Designed by Daniel Lagin

FROZEN TRACKS

ONE OF THE CHILDREN JUMPED DOWN FROM THE JUNGLE GYM into the sandbox below, and he laughed out loud, suddenly, briefly. It looked like good fun. The man wanted to join in, but that would mean getting out of his car, walking around the fence and in through the gate, and climbing up the structure, which was red and yellow.

A drop of rain fell on the window, then another. He looked up and could see the sky was darker now. He turned his attention back to the playground and the trees beyond it and along the left-hand side. There were no leaves on the branches; the trees were bare. Things you couldn't see in the summer were visible now. The city was naked. That thought had struck him as he drove there through the wet streets. This city is naked again. He didn't like it. It was almost worse than before.

Now another child jumped down. He could hear the boy laughing as he lay in the sand; he could hear that even when the radio was on, as it was now. He wasn't listening to it. He was listening to the boy's laughter. He was laughing himself now. He wasn't happy, but he was laughing because hearing the child laughing, it sounded like so much fun to be a child getting up to climb the jungle gym and jump down once more.

It stopped raining even before it had really started. He rolled down the window a bit more. There was a smell of autumn turning into winter. Nothing else smelled like it. Leaves lay on the ground and had turned black. People were walking along paths through the park. Some were pushing strollers. A few people were standing around in the playground, grown-ups. There weren't many of them. But lots of children, and many of them were laughing.

He had also laughed, not now, but when he was a child. He could remember laughing once when his mom had lifted him up high and his head had bumped the ceiling lamp and the light up there had gone out when she put him down again.

Somebody said something on the radio. He didn't hear what as he was still in a land where he was a small boy who'd come down to the ground again and his mom had said something that he could no longer remember; he couldn't remember any of it, but she had said something, and afterward he had spent a long time thinking about what she had said, how important it was to him, those last words she had said to him before walking out of the door never to come back.

She never ever came back.

He could feel his cheek was wet, like the windshield would have been if it had continued raining. He heard himself saying something now but didn't know what it was.

He looked back at the children.

He could see the room again, it was later but he was still a small boy; he sat looking out of the window and there was rain on the windowpane, and he'd made a drawing of the trees outside that didn't have any leaves left. His mom was standing beside the trees. If he drew a car, she was inside it. A horse, and she was riding it. A little child, and she was holding its hand. They were walking on grass where red and yellow flowers were growing.

He drew the fields. He drew an ocean on the other side of the fields.

Every night he made a bed for his mom. He had a little sofa in his bedroom and he made her a bed on it, with a blanket and a pillow. If she suddenly appeared she'd be able to sleep there. Just lie down without him needing to get the bed ready, it would be all done.

Now he rolled down the window and took a deep breath. Rolled it up again and started the engine and drove around the playground so that he could park right outside the entrance. He opened the door. There were several other cars around. He could hear the children's voices now, as if they were sitting in his car. As if they'd come to his car, to him.

There was music on the radio now, and that voice he recognized came back and said something. It was a voice he'd heard several times. It spoke when he drove home from work during the day. Sometimes he drove at night.

He could feel how wet the ground was under his feet. He was standing beside his car but didn't know how he'd gotten there. It was strange; he'd thought about the radio and then suddenly he was standing beside the car.

Children's laughter again.

He was standing by the playground that was next to the trees that no longer had any leaves, only bare branches.

The video camera in his hand was hardly any bigger than a pack of cigarettes. A little bit bigger, perhaps. Amazing what they could make nowadays.

He could hardly hear the faint hiss when he pressed the button and filmed what he could see.

He moved closer. There were children all around but he couldn't see a single grown-up. Where were all the grown-ups? The children couldn't be left alone, they might get hurt when they jumped down from the red and yellow jungle gym or leapt from the swings.

The jungle gym was right here, next to the entrance. He was standing by it.

A leap.

"Wheee!"

Laughter. He laughed again himself, jumped, no, but he could have jumped. He helped the little boy to his feet. Up again, up, up! Lift him up to the sky!

He took it from his pocket and held it out. Look what I've got here.

It was three paces to the entrance. Then four more to the car. The boy's steps were shorter, six to the entrance and eight to the car.

Children, children everywhere, it struck him that he was the only one who could see the boy now, keep an eye on him. The grown-ups were standing over there with their coffee cups steaming in the air that was cold and damp, just like the ground.

More cars. The boy couldn't be seen at all now, not from any direction. Only *he* could see him, he was holding his hand now.

"There we are. Yes, I've got a whole bag full, how about that? So, let's open the door. Can you climb in all by yourself? You *are* smart."

———

The back of the student's head had been struck in such a way that the wound looked like a cross, or something very similar. His hair had been shaved off, making the wound all the more visible. It was horrific, but he was still alive. Only just; but he had a chance.

As they left the hospital Bertil Ringmar's face looked blue in the lights of the front entrance.

"I thought you should see this," said Ringmar.

Winter nodded.

"What kind of weapon would make a wound like that?" wondered Ringmar.

"Some sort of pick-ax. Maybe a farm tool. A kitchen utensil. A gardening tool. I don't know, Bertil."

"There's something about it, I don't know. It reminds me of something."

Winter zapped the doors of his Mercedes. The parking lot was deserted. The car lights flashed like a warning.

"We'd better have a word with Old MacDonald," said Winter as they drove down the hill.

"Don't joke about it."

"Joke about it? What is there to joke about?"

Ringmar made no reply. Linnéplatsen was just as deserted as the parking lot had been.

"This is the third one," said Ringmar.

Winter nodded, loosened his tie, and unfastened the top two buttons of his shirt.

"Three kids more or less beaten to death with something, but we can't figure out what," said Ringmar. "Three students." He turned to look at Winter. "Is there a pattern?"

"You mean the fact that they're all students? Or that we think the wounds look like a cross?"

"That they're all students," said Ringmar.

"Students are a big group," said Winter, continuing west. "There must be thirty-five thousand of them in this city."

"Mmm."

"Quite a circle of friends, even if they only mix with their own kind," said Winter.

Ringmar drummed his fingers on the armrest. Winter turned off the main thoroughfare and drove north. The streets grew narrower, the houses bigger.

"A pick-ax," said Ringmar. "Who wanders around with a pick-ax on a Saturday night?"

"I don't even want to think about it," said Winter.

"Did you go to school here in Gothenburg?"

"Briefly."

"What did you study?"

"Prudence. Then I dropped out."

"Prudence?"

"Introduction to jurisprudence. But I quit, like I said."

"Imprudence follows prudence," said Ringmar.

"Ha, ha," said Winter.

"I was a student of life myself," said Ringmar.

"Where do you study that? And when do you qualify for a degree in it?"

Ringmar gave a snort. "You're right, Erik. A student of life is tested all the time. Continuous judgment."

"By whom?"

Ringmar didn't reply. Winter slowed down.

"Turn right here, you'll avoid the intersection," said Ringmar.

Winter did as he was told, threaded his way past a couple of parked cars, and pulled up outside a wood-paneled detached house. The lights from the house cast a faint glow over the lawn and through the maples that looked like limbs reaching up to the sky.

"Want to come in for a sandwich?" Ringmar asked.

Winter looked at his watch.

"Is Angela waiting up for you with oysters and wine?" wondered Ringmar.

"It's not quite the season yet," said Winter.

"I expect you'll want to say goodnight to Elsa?"

"She'll be fast asleep by now," said Winter. "OK, I'll have a bite to eat. Do you have any south Slovakian beer?"

Ringmar was rummaging in the fridge as Winter came up from the cellar, carrying three bottles.

"I think I only have Czech pilsner, I'm afraid," said Ringmar over his shoulder.

"I'll forgive you," said Winter, reaching for the bottle opener.

"Smoked whitefish and scrambled egg?" Ringmar suggested, examining what was in the fridge.

"If we've got time," said Winter. "It takes ages to make a decent scrambled egg. Got any chives, by the way?"

Ringmar smiled and nodded, carried the ingredients over to the counter, and got to work. Winter sipped the beer. It was good, chilled without being cold. He took off his tie and hung his jacket over the chair. His neck felt stiff after a long day. A student of life. Continuous judgment. He could see the student's face in his mind's eye, then the back of his head. A law student, just like he'd been once. If I'd stuck with it I could have been chief of police now, he thought, taking another sip of beer. That might have been better. Protected from the streets. No bending over bodies with shattered limbs, no new holes, no blood, no wounds in the shape of a cross.

"The other two don't have an enemy in the world," said Ringmar from the stove, where he was stirring the egg mix with a wooden fork.

"Who?"

"The other two victims who survived with the cross-shaped wounds on their heads. Not an enemy in the world, they're saying."

"That goes with being young," said Winter. "No real enemies."

"You're young yourself," said Ringmar, lifting up the cast-iron pan. "Do you have any enemies?"

"Not a single one," said Winter. "You make enemies later on in life."

Ringmar put the finishing touches to the open sandwiches.

"We should really have a drop of schnapps with this," he said.

"I can always take a taxi home."

"It's settled, then," said Ringmar, going to get the hard stuff.

"The same man was responsible for all the attacks," said Ringmar. "What's he after?"

"Satisfaction from causing injury," said Winter, draining the last of his second schnapps and shaking his head when Ringmar lifted the bottle questioningly.

"But not any old way," said Ringmar.

"Nor any old victim."

"Yeah, maybe."

"We'll have to hear what this kid has to say tomorrow," said Winter.

"Attacked from behind in an unlit street. He saw nothing, heard nothing, said nothing, knows nothing."

"We'll see."

"Pia Fröberg will have to put in some extra effort to help us with the weapon," said Ringmar.

Winter could see the forensic pathologist's pale, tense face in his mind's eye. Once upon a time they'd been an item, or something pretty close to that. All forgotten and in the past now. No hard feelings.

"Always assuming that will help," Ringmar added, gazing down into his beer glass.

They heard the front door open and shut, and a shout from a female voice.

"We're in here," Ringmar informed her.

His daughter came in, still wearing her anorak. As dark as her father, almost as tall, same nose, same eyes, focused on Winter.

"Erik needed some company," said Ringmar.

She reached out her hand. Winter shook it.

"You still recognize Moa, don't you?" asked Ringmar.

"Haven't seen you for ages," said Winter. "Let's see, you must be . . ."

"Twenty-five," said Moa Ringmar. "Well on the way to being a senior citizen, and still living at home. What do you say to that?"

"You could say that Moa's in-between apartments at the moment," Ringmar explained.

"It's the times we live in," said Moa. "Fledglings always return to the nest."

"That's nice," said Winter.

"Bullshit," said Moa.

"OK," said Winter.

She sat down.

"Any beer left for me?"

Ringmar got her a glass and poured out what was left of the third bottle.

"So there's been another assault," she said.

"Where did you hear that?" wondered Ringmar.

"At the department. He's a student there. His name is Jakob, I'm told."

"Do you know him?"

"No, not personally."

"Do you know anybody who knows him?" asked Winter.

"Hey, what's all this?" she protested. "I see you're back at work again." She looked at Winter, then turned to her father. "Sorry. It *is* serious. I didn't mean to joke."

"Well?" wondered Winter.

"I might know somebody who knows somebody who knows him. I don't know."

Vasaplatsen was quiet and deserted when Winter got out of the taxi. The streetlamps lit up the newspaper kiosk at the edge of Universitetsplatsen. A student of life, he thought as he punched the code to the front entrance.

There was a faint smell of tobacco in the elevator, a lingering aroma that could have come from him.

"You smell like alcohol," said Angela when he bent down to kiss her as she lay in bed.

"Ödåkra Taffel Aquavit," he said.

"I figured as much," she said, turning over to face the wall. "You're dropping off Elsa tomorrow morning. I have to get up by half past five."

"I just looked in on her. Sleeping like a log."

Angela muttered something.

"What did you say?"

"Just wait until tomorrow morning," she said. "Early."

He knew all about that. After six months' paternity leave? He knew all there was to know about Elsa, and she knew all about him.

It had been a terrific time, maybe his best. There was a city out there that he hadn't seen for years. The streets were the same, but he'd been able to view them at ground level for a change, in his own time, not needing to be on the lookout for anything more than the next café where they could pause for a while and he could sample some of that other life, real life.

When he went back to work after his paternity leave, he felt a sort of . . . hunger, a peculiar feeling, something he almost felt ashamed of. As if he were ready for battle again, ready for the war that could never be won but had to be fought well, regardless. That's the way it was. If you chopped an arm off the beast, it promptly grew another one, but you just had to keep on chopping.

As Winter fell asleep he was thinking yet again about that remarkable wound on the back of the student's head.

2

IT WAS A QUIET NIGHT AT THE EMERGENCY DESK, AND IT FELT LIKE the calm before the storm. But there won't be any storm tonight, thought Bengt Josefsson, the duty officer, gazing out at the trees that were also still, like they are before an autumn gale. But it's too late for autumn gales now, he thought. Soon it'll be Christmas. And after that maybe we won't be around anymore. They're talking about closing down this station, and Redbergsplatsen will be handed back to the enemy.

The telephone rang.

"Police, Örgryte-Härlanda, Josefsson."

"Ah, yes. Well. Er, good evening. Is this the police?"

"Yes."

"I called the police switchboard and they said they'd connect me to a station close to Olskroken. Er, that's where we live."

"You've got the right number," said Josefsson. "How can I help you?"

"Well, er, I don't really know what to say."

Josefsson waited, pen at the ready. A colleague dropped something hard on the floor in the locker room at the end of the corridor.

"Just tell me what it's about," he said. "Who am I talking to?"

She gave her name and he wrote it down. Berit Skarin.

"It's about my little boy," she said. "He, er, I don't know . . . He told us tonight, if we understood him correctly, er, that he's been sitting in a car with a 'mister,' as he put it."

Kalle Skarin was four, and when he got back home from the nursery school he'd had a soft-cheese sandwich and a cup of hot chocolate—he'd mixed the cocoa and sugar and a splash of cream himself, and then Mom added the hot milk.

Shortly afterward he'd said he'd been sitting in a car.

A car?

A car. Big car, with a radio. Radio talked and played music.

Did you and your friends go out on a trip today?

Not a trip. Playground.

Are there cars there?

The boy had nodded.

Toy cars?

Big car, he'd told her. Real car. Real, and he'd moved his hands as if he were holding a steering wheel. Brrrrm, brrrrmm.

Where?

Playground.

Kalle. Are you saying you went for a ride in a car at the playground?

He'd nodded.

Who did you go with?

A mister.

A mister?

Mister, mister. He had candies!

Kalle had made a new gesture that could have been somebody holding out a bag of candy, or maybe not.

Berit Skarin had felt a cold shiver run down her spine. A strange man holding out a bag of candy to her little boy.

Olle ought to hear this, but he won't be back until late.

And Kalle was sitting there in front of her. She'd held him when he'd jumped up to go and watch a children's program on TV.

Did the car drive away?

Drove, drove. Brrrrrrmm.

Did you go far?

He didn't understand the question.

Was your teacher with you?

No teacher. Mister.

Then he'd run off to the TV room. She'd watched him go and thought for a moment, then gone to get her handbag from a chair in the kitchen and looked up the home telephone number of one of the nursery-school staff, hesitated when she got as far as the phone, but called anyway.

"Ah. Sorry to disturb you in the evening like this, er, it's Berit Skarin. Yes, Kalle's mom. He's just told me something that I have to ask you about."

Bengt Josefsson listened. She told him about the conversation she'd had with one of the nursery school staff.

"Nobody noticed anything," said Berit Skarin.

"I see."

"Can that kind of thing happen?" she asked. "Can somebody drive up in a car and then drive off with one of the children without any of the staff seeing anything? Then bring the child back again?"

Much worse things than that can happen, thought Josefsson.

"I don't know," he said. "The staff didn't notice anything, you say?"

"No. Surely they would have?"

"You'd think so," said Josefsson, but in fact he was thinking something else. Who can be on the lookout all the time? Thinking who's that man standing under the tree over there? Sitting in that car?

"How long does your boy say he was away?"

"He doesn't know. He's a child. He can't distinguish between five minutes and fifty minutes if you ask him afterward."

Bengt Josefsson pondered this.

"Do you believe him?" he asked.

No reply.

"*Fru* Skarin?"

"I don't know," she said. "I just don't know."

"Does he have, er, a lively imagination?"

"He's a child. All children have lively imaginations if there's nothing wrong with them."

"Yes."

"So what should I do?"

Bengt Josefsson looked down at the few sentences he'd jotted down on his notepad.

Two colleagues came racing past his desk.

"Robbery at the newspaper kiosk!" one of them yelled.

He could already hear the siren from one of the cars outside.

"Hello?" said Berit Skarin.

"Yes, where were we? Well, I've noted down what you said. Anyway, nobody's missing. So, if you want to report it, then, er—"

"What should I report?"

That's the point, thought Josefsson. Unlawful deprivation of liberty? No. An attempted sexual offense, or preparation for one? Well, perhaps. Or the imagination of a very young man. He evidently hadn't come to any harm be—

"I want to take him to a doctor now," she said, interrupting his train of thought. "I take this very seriously."

"Yes," said Josefsson.

"Should I take him to a doctor?"

"Have you, er, examined him yourself?"

"No. I called right after he told me."

"Oh."

"But I will now. Then I'll see where we go from there." He heard her shouting for the boy, and a reply from some distance away. "He's watching TV," she said. "Now he's laughing."

"Can I make a note of your address and phone number?" said Josefsson.

There were the sirens again. It sounded as if they were heading east. Chasing the robbers. A couple of thugs from one of the ghettos north of the town, drugged up to the eyeballs. Dangerous as hell.

"OK, thank you very much," he said, his mind miles away, and hung up. He made his handwriting clearer in a couple of places, then put the page to one side, ready for keying into the computer. Later on he'd put his notes into the file, if he got around to it. Filed under . . . what? Nothing had happened. A crime waiting to be committed?

There were other things that had already happened, were happening right now.

The phone on his desk rang again, phones were ringing all over the station. Sirens outside, coming from the south. He could see the flashing blue light on the other side of the street, whirling around and around as if the officers in the patrol car were about to take off and fly over to where all the action was.

Jakob, the student, was conscious but very groggy and in a world of his own. Ringmar by his side, wondering what had happened and how. There were flowers on the bedside table. Jakob was not alone in this world.

Somebody entered the ward behind Ringmar. Could that be a flash of recognition in Jakob's eye? Ringmar turned around.

"They said it was alright for me to come in," said the girl, with a bunch of flowers in her hand. She seemed to be about the same age as his own daughter. Maybe they know each other, he thought, getting to his feet as she walked over to the bed, gave Jakob a cautious little hug, and then put the flowers down on the table. Jakob's eyes were closed now; he'd probably nodded off again.

"Even more flowers," she said, and Ringmar could see that she would have liked to take a look at the card with the other bouquet but couldn't bring herself to do it. She turned to face him.

"So you're Moa's dad, are you?"

Good. Moa had done her job.

"Yes," he said. "Maybe we should go to the waiting room and have a little chat."

———————

"I suppose he was just unlucky," she said. "Wrong man in the wrong place, or however you put it."

They sat down by a window. The gray light of day outside seemed translucent. The room was in a strange sort of shadow cast by a sun that wasn't there. A woman coughed quietly on a sofa by a low wooden table weighed down by magazines with cover photos of well-known people, smiling. Well-known to whom? Ringmar had wondered more than once. Visiting hospitals was part of his job, and he'd often wondered why *Hello* and similar magazines were always piled up in dreary hospital waiting rooms. Maybe they were a kind of comfort, like a little candle burning on the tables of these huge wards. All of you in that magazine, who are photographed at every premiere there is, maybe used to be like us, and maybe we can be like you if we get well again and are discovered in the hectic search for new talent. That search was nonstop, never ending. The photos of those celebrities were proof of that. There was no room for faded Polaroids of crushed skulls.

"It wasn't bad luck," said Ringmar now, looking at the girl.

"You look younger than I expected," she said.

"Based on Moa's description of me, you mean," he said.

She smiled, then turned serious again.

"Do you know anybody who really disliked Jakob?" Ringmar asked.

"Nobody disliked him," she said.

"Is there anybody he dislikes?"

"No."

"Nobody at all?"

"No."

Maybe it's the times we live in, Ringmar thought, and if so it has to be a good thing. When I was young we were always mad at everything and everybody. Angry all the time.

"How well do you know him?" he asked.

"Well . . . he's my friend."

"Do you have more mutual friends?"

"Yes, of course."

Ringmar looked out of the window. Some fifty meters away two kids were standing at the bus stop in the rain, holding their hands up to the sky as if giving thanks. Not an enemy in the world. Even the damned rain was a dear friend.

"No violent types in your circle of friends?" asked Ringmar.

"Certainly not."

"What were you doing when Jakob was attacked?"

"When exactly was it?" she asked.

"I'm not really allowed to tell you that," he said, and proceeded to do so.

"I'd been asleep for about two hours," she said.

But Jakob wasn't asleep. Ringmar could see him in his mind's eye, walking across the square named after Doktor Fries. Heading for the streetcar stop? There weren't any streetcars at that time of night. And then somebody appeared out of nowhere, and one hell of a bash on the back of his head. No help from Dr. Fries. Left there to bleed to death, if the guy who'd called the police hadn't passed by shortly after it had happened and seen the kid lying there.

Jakob, the third victim. Three different places in town. The same type of wound. Could have been fatal, really. But none of them actually had died. Not yet, he thought. The other two victims had no idea. Just a blow from behind. Saw nothing, just felt.

"Do you live together?" he asked.

"No."

Ringmar said nothing for a moment. The two kids had just jumped aboard a bus. Maybe it was getting a bit brighter in the west, a slight glint of light blue. The waiting room was high up in the hospital, which itself was on top of a hill. Maybe he was looking at the sea, a big gray expanse under the blue.

"You weren't worried about him?"

"What do you mean, worried?"

"Where he was that night? What he was doing?"

"Hang on, we're not married or anything like that. We're just friends."

"So you didn't know where Jakob was that night?"

"No."

"Who does he know out there?"

"Where?"

"In Guldheden. Around Doktor Fries Square, Guldheden school, that district."

"I don't have the slightest idea."

"Do you know anybody around there?"

"Who lives there, you mean? I don't think so. No."

"But that's where he was, and that's where he was attacked," said Ringmar.

"You'll have to ask him," she said.

"I'll do that, as soon as it's possible."

Winter had taken Elsa to the nursery school. He sat there for a while with a cup of coffee while she arranged her day's work on her little desk: a red telephone, paper, pencils, crayons, newspapers, tape, string. He would get to see the result that afternoon. It would be something unique, no doubt about that.

She barely noticed when he gave her a hug and left. He lit a Corps in the grounds outside. He couldn't smoke anything else after all those years. He'd tried, but it was no use. Corps were no longer sold in Sweden, but a colleague made regular visits to Brussels and always brought some back for him.

It was a pleasant morning. The air smelled of winter but it felt like early autumn. He took another puff, then unbuttoned his overcoat and watched children hard at work: building projects involving digging and stacking, molding shapes; every kind of game you could think of. Games. Not much sign of games in the sports grown-ups indulge in nowadays, he thought, and noticed a little boy running down the slope toward a gap in the bushes. Winter looked around and saw the two staff members were fully occupied with children who wanted something or were crying or laughing or running around in all directions, and so he strode swiftly down the hill and into the bushes where the boy was busy hitting the railings with his plastic shovel. He turned around as Winter approached and gave him a sheepish grin, like a prisoner who'd been caught trying to escape.

Winter shepherded the little boy back to the fold, listening to some story he couldn't quite understand but nodding approvingly even so. One of the ladies in charge was standing halfway up the slope.

"I didn't know there was a fence there," said Winter.

"It's a good thing there is," she said. "We'd never be able to keep them on the premises otherwise."

He caught sight of Elsa on her way out into the grounds: She'd clearly decided it was time to take a rest from all that paperwork.

"Hard to keep an eye on all of them at the same time, eh?" he said.

"Yes, it is now." He detected a sort of sigh. "I shouldn't stand here complaining, but since you ask, well, it's a case of more and more children and fewer and fewer staff." She made a gesture. "But at least we've got them fenced in here."

Winter watched Elsa playing on the swings. She shouted out when she saw him, and he waved back.

"How do you manage when you take them out for trips? Or take the whole class to the park, or to a bigger playground?"

"We try not to," she said.

Ringmar was with the student, Jakob Stillman. The latter had been living up to his name, but now he seemed able to move his head slowly, and with some difficulty he could focus on Ringmar from his sickbed. Ringmar had introduced himself.

"I'd just like to ask you a few questions," he said. "I suggest you blink once if your answer is yes, and twice if it's no. OK?"

Stillman blinked once.

"Right." Ringmar moved the chair a bit closer. "Did you see anybody behind you before you were hit?

One blink.

"Ah, so you did see something?" Ringmar asked.

One blink again. Yes.

"Was it far away?"

Two blinks. No.

"Were you alone when you started walking across the square?"

Yes.

"But you were able to see somebody coming toward you?"

No.

"So somebody was behind you?"

Yes.

"Could you make anything out?"

Yes.

"Did you see a face?"

No.

"A body?"

Yes.

"Big?"

No blinking at all. This boy is smarter than I am, thought Ringmar.

"Medium-size?"

Yes.

"A man?"

Yes.

"Would you recognize him again?"

No.

"Was he very close when you saw him?"

Yes.

"Did you hear anything?"

Yes.

"Did you hear the sound before you saw him?"
Yes.
"Was that why you turned around?"
Yes.
"Was it the sound of his footsteps?"
No.
"Was it the sound of some object scraping the ground?"
No.
"Was it a noise that had nothing to do with him?"
No.
"Was it something he said?"
Yes.
"Did it sound like Swedish?"
No.
"Did it sound like some other language?"
No.
"Was it more like a shriek?"
No.
"More like a grunt?"
Yes.
"Something deeper?"
Yes.
"A human sound?"
No.
"But it came from him?"
Yes.

3

HE DROVE THROUGH THE TUNNELS THAT WERE FILLED WITH A darkness denser than the night outside. The naked lights on the walls made the darkness all the more noticeable. The cars coming toward him made no noise.

He had the window open, letting in some air and a cold glow. There was no light at the end of the tunnel, only darkness.

It was like driving through hell, tunnel after tunnel. He was familiar with them all. He would drive around and around the city through the tunnels.

Music on the radio. Or had he put a CD in? He couldn't remember. A beautiful voice he liked to listen to when he was driving under the ground. Soon the whole city would be buried. The whole road alongside the water was being sunk into Hell.

He sat down in front of the television and watched his film. The playground, the jungle gym, the slide the children slid down, and one of the children laughed, and he laughed as well because it looked like so much fun. He pressed rewind, watched the fun once again, and made a note on the sheet of paper on the table beside him, where there was also a vase with six tulips, both of which he'd bought that same afternoon.

Now the boy was there. His face, then the car window behind him, the radio, the backseat. The boy told him what to film, and he filmed it. Why not?

The parrot hanging from his rearview mirror. He'd picked out one that was red and yellow, just like the climbing frame at the playground that needed another coat of paint, but his parrot didn't need repainting at all.

The boy, who'd said his name was Kalle, liked the parrot. You could see that in the film. The boy was pointing at the parrot, and he filmed it even though he was driving. That called for a fair amount of skill, and he was good at driving while thinking of something else at the same time, doing something else entirely. He'd been good at that for a long time now.

Now he heard the voices, as if the volume had suddenly been turned up. "Rotty," he said.

"Rotty," echoed the boy, pointing at the parrot, and it almost looked as if it were about to fly away.

Rotty. It was a trick. If anybody else were ever to see this film, which wouldn't happen, but if, it would seem as if Rotty was the parrot's name. But that wasn't the case. It was one of his tricks like all the other tricks he had when he was little and his voice suddenly g-g-g-ot s-s-st-st-st-st-st-stu-stu-stu-stuck in midstride, as it were, when he first st-st-started stuttering.

It started when his mom walked out. He couldn't remember doing it before. Only afterward. He had to invent tricks that would help him out when he wanted to say something. Not all that often, but sometimes. The first trick he could remember was Rotty. He couldn't say parrot, pa-pa-pa-pa—no, he could stand there stuttering for the rest of his life and still not get to the end of that word. "Rotty" was no problem, though.

He heard a sound that he recognized. It was coming from him. He was crying again, and it was because he'd been thinking about the parrot. He'd had a red and green parrot when he was a little boy, and for a while when he was older. It was a real one, and it could say his name and three other funny things, and his name was Bill. He was sure that Bill had been real.

The film had finished. He watched it again from the beginning. Bill was there in several of the scenes. Bill was still there for him because he hung a little parrot from his rearview mirror every time he went out in the car. They might be different, with different colors, but that didn't matter because they were all Bill. He sometimes thought of them as Billy Boy. His favorite Rotty. The boy was laughing again now, just before everything went black. Kalle Boy, he thought, and the film ended, and he stood up and fetched all the things he needed for copying, or whatever you called it. Cutting. He liked doing that job.

"Sounds like the Incredible Hulk," said Fredrik Halders.

"This is the first of the victims who's seen anything," said Ringmar. "Stillman's the first."

"Hmm. Of course, it's not certain that it was the same hulk who carried out all the attacks," said Halders.

Ringmar shook his head. "The wounds are identical."

Halders rubbed the back of his neck. It wasn't all that long since he himself had received a savage blow that had smashed a vertebra and paralyzed him temporarily, but he'd managed to get the use of his limbs back. For what that was worth, he'd thought a long time afterward. He'd always been clumsy. Now it was taking him time to get back to his former level of clumsiness.

To get back to his old life. His former wife had been killed by a hit-and-run driver. A nasty word. Former. Lots of things had been different formerly.

He lived now in his former house, with his children who were anything but former.

He rubbed the back of his neck.

"What kind of a pick did he use, then?" he asked.

Ringmar raised both his hands and shrugged.

"An ice pick?" suggested Halders.

"No," said Ringmar. "That's a bit passé nowadays."

Halders examined the photos on Ringmar's desk. Sharp colors, shaved scalps, wounds. Not the first time, but the difference now was that the victims were still alive. The most common head in the archives is generally a dead one. Not these, though, he thought. These are talking heads.

"Never mind the damn picks," he said, looking up. "The important thing is to catch the lunatic, no matter what kind of weapon he uses."

"But it's significant," said Ringmar. "There's something, something odd about these wounds."

"Yes, no doubt, but we've got to put a stop to it all."

Ringmar nodded his agreement and continued perusing the photos.

"Do you think it was somebody he knew?" asked Halders.

"That thought had occurred to me," said Ringmar.

"What about the other two guys? The other two victims?"

"Eh. Saw nothing, heard nothing. A relatively open space. Late. No other witnesses. You know how it is. Had a few, but not completely blotto."

"And then wham."

"The same attacker every time. Do you think so too?" asked Ringmar.

"Yes."

"Mmm."

"We'd better dig a bit deeper into the victims' circle of friends and acquaintances," said Halders.

"They're all separate circles," said Ringmar. "They don't know each other, and they don't have any friends in common, as far as we've been able to find out."

"OK, so they don't move in the same circles," said Halders, "we know that. But then again they're all students in departments located in the town center, and they might have bumped into each other without realizing it. A nightclub, the student union, a political party, handball, bird-watching, any damn thing. Fraternities with strippers jumping out of cakes and giving a few blow jobs. Maybe that's what it is, and so they think they've got a good reason to lie about it. Or a student disco. No doubt they still have them at the union. It's got to be more likely than not that they'd run into each other somewhere or other."

"OK," said Ringmar. "But so what? Was their attacker there as well?"

"I don't know. But it's a possibility."

"So he was specifically out to get these three?"

"It's a hypothesis," said Halders.

"But you could just as well say he was ready to attack anybody at all he happened to come across," said Ringmar. "Late, deserted, a drink or two to dull their wits."

Halders got to his feet and walked over to the wall map of Gothenburg. He stretched both arms back over his shoulders, and Ringmar could hear his colleague's joints creak. Halders glanced at him with what might have been a little grin, then turned to the map again and put his finger on it.

"Linnéplatsen the first time." He moved his finger to the right. "Then Kapellplatsen." He ran his finger downward. "And now Doktor Fries Square." He turned around and looked at Ringmar. "A pretty limited area." He looked back at the map. "Like a triangle."

"Not all within walking distance, though," said Ringmar.

"There's such a thing as public transportation."

"Not much of it late at night, though. No streetcars, for instance."

"Night buses," said Halders. "Or maybe the Hulk has a car. Or he just walks. The attacks weren't all on the same night."

"But why change location?" asked Ringmar.

"He probably thinks we have enough resources to keep an eye on the previous place," said Halders. "So he doesn't go back there."

"Mmm."

"But we don't."

"There's something about these places," said Ringmar. "It's not just coincidence." Then he added as if talking to himself: "It rarely is."

Halders made no comment, but he knew what Ringmar meant. The location of a violent assault was often significant. The attacker, or the victim, nearly always had some kind of link with that particular spot, even if it wasn't obvious from the start. The location is always key. Always start off with the location. Spread your search out from there.

"I've had a word with Birgersson," said Ringmar. "After the Guldheden incident. We're probably going to get a few more officers so that we can knock on a few more doors."

Halders could see the superintendent in his mind's eye. As scraggy as the vegetation in the far north where he grew up, chain-smoking after yet another failed attempt to quit.

"What about the triangle?" asked Halders. "The triangle theory? Add the third line and you've got a right triangle." Halders ran his finger over the map from Doktor Fries Square to Linnéplatsen.

"No. You're the first to come up with that fascinating link."

"Cut the sarcasm, Bertil. You're too nice a guy for that kind of thing." Halders grinned. "But Birgersson has a soft spot when it comes to math, I know that, especially geometrical shapes."

Halders grinned again. Maybe it was Sture Birgersson who did it. Nobody could fathom the man. Once a year he would disappear, nobody knew where. Winter maybe, but maybe not. Maybe Sture was wandering around the streets in a black cloak, wielding the mechanical cloudberry picker he'd had as a kid and using it to draw crosses on students' heads. Halders could picture his silhouette in the light from the street lamp: Doctor Sture. Afterward, Mister Birgersson. One might ask which of them was worse.

"So you think we'd get more officers because we can see a geometrical shape here?" wondered Ringmar.

"Of course."

"And the more it changes, the more men we'd get?"

"Obviously. If the triangle turns into a square, it means that the Hulk has struck again."

"I'll stick with the triangle," said Ringmar.

Halders went back to the desk.

"If they give us a few more detectives we might be able to do a proper check on what buses were running those nights," he said. "Talk to the drivers. There can't be all that many of them."

"Taxis," said Ringmar.

"Are you crazy? Our dark-skinned friends are all operating without a license. When's the last time we got any useful information from a cabbie?"

"I can't remember," said Ringmar.

The sun made everything look even more bare. Yes, that was how it was. You could see what it was really like. Nothing existed anymore, just the trunks and branches of trees, and the ground.

The sun isn't serving any useful purpose here, he thought. It belongs somewhere else now. Take off.

The children had spilled off the streetcar at Linnéplatsen. It was always the same, day after day. They always walked in a long line over the dead grass of the soccer field in the middle of the square.

Sometimes he followed them.

He'd parked his car on the other side, where the children were headed.

It was the first time he'd driven to this place.

He'd talked to the boy in his car. That had happened once.

He wanted to do it again. No. No. No! He'd shouted out loud during the night. No!

Yes. Here he was. Just because he wanted to . . . see, get . . . close. No big deal.

The long procession of children broke up, and they spread out in all directions. One little girl disappeared into some bushes, emerged on the other side, then turned back again, going around the bushes this time. He looked at the two women in charge and could tell they hadn't noticed her.

Just think if some stranger had been standing behind the bushes when the little girl emerged on the other side?

There she was again, around the bushes once more, and then back to the other children.

He carried her in his arms; she was as light as a feather. Nobody noticed him; the trees were leafless, but they were densely packed. The surprise when he lifted her up and carried her off. Is this really me doing this? His hand placed so gently over her mouth. It all went so quickly. There's the car. You can drive in and park here, but nobody ever thinks of doing that. Probably think it's not possible, or not allowed.

This is just something I draped over here. Let's lift it up and go into the tent. Yes, this is a tent. Let's pretend!

We've got a radio. Listen, the nice man's saying something. Did you hear that? They're going to play some music.

Now, let's see what we've got here. You can take whatever you like. There's lots of interesting things here.

What lovely hair you have! What's your name? You don't know? Yeees, of course you do!

This is Bill. That's his name. Bill. Billy Boy. He can fly. See that? Fly fly fly.

Ellen? Is your name Ellen? That's a lovely name. A splendid name. Do you know what my mom was called? No, how could you know that?

What do you think, wasn't it a marvelous name, my mom's?

Have some more. Take the whole bag.

He . . . he . . . here it co-co-co-co-comes . . .

He moved his hand lightly over the girl's head. Her hair was like the down on a baby bird, a little fledgling whose heart you could feel beating when you touched it. He'd felt that once on a little bird that was even smaller than Bill. He was just as small as a bird too, in those days.

He touched her again. The man on the radio was saying something. He found it difficult to breathe, rolled down the window, and found some air he could breathe. He touched the girl again, that down, all those tiny bones. She said something.

Evening was closing in. Clear outlines. The sun lingered there between the houses, like a memory that Winter breathed in. He could feel the late autumn air between drags as he stood smoking. Winter was closing in. He looked down on Vasaplatsen, and watched people heading off, gradually leaving the square deserted. Everybody was going home, by bus, streetcar, or car, and leaving him and his family behind, here where they belonged.

Angela hadn't said anything about buying a house for ages, and he knew she felt as he did, always had. They were city dwellers, and the city was for them. The city of stone, the heart of the city. The heart of stone, he thought, taking another pull on his cigarillo. A beautiful heart of stone. It was easier to live here. In the classy suburbs down toward the sea you became worn out more quickly, past it, over the hill. For God's sake! He'd turned the corner already. Forty-two. Or forty-three. He couldn't remember right then, and that was just as well.

He shivered, standing on the balcony in his shirtsleeves, the cigarillo in his hand fading away just like the evening out there. A few young people sauntered past down below, full of self-confidence. He could hear them laughing even at this distance. They were all set for a good time.

He went back in. Elsa saw him coming and presented him with the drawing she'd made. A bird flying in a blue sky. These last few weeks all her drawings had been of blue skies and yellow sands, green fields and then lots of flowers in every color in her crayon box. Nonstop summer. Autumn hadn't sunk in for Elsa yet. He'd taken her down to the park and helped her to collect fallen leaves, carried them back home, dried them. But she'd put off depicting autumn till the very end. Just as well.

"A bird!" she said.

"What kind of a bird?" he asked.

She seemed to be thinking it over.

"A gull," she said.

"Let's let the bird have a laugh," he said to Elsa, and burst out laughing himself. "Ha-ha-*ha-ha*." She looked a bit frightened at first, but then she couldn't stop herself from giggling.

Winter picked up a crayon and a blank sheet of paper, and drew something that could just possibly be construed as a seagull laughing. There was even a name for this gull, and he announced it in the top right-hand corner of the picture. "Blackie the Blackhead." His bequest to posterity. The first drawing he'd made for thirty years.

"It looks like a flying piglet," said Angela.

"Yes, isn't it amazing? A pig that can laugh and fly as well."

"But pigs *can* fly," Elsa said.

They were sitting at the kitchen table with a glass of red wine each. Elsa was asleep. Winter had made some anchovy sandwiches, which they'd just finished eating.

"Those things make you thirsty," he said, getting up for some more water.

"I bumped into Bertil on our ward today," said Angela.

"Yes, he was there."

Angela rubbed the base of her nose with her finger. He could see a faint shadow under one of her eyes, only the one. She was tired, and so was he. Not excessively so, but the way you feel after a day's work. She couldn't always relax at home and forget about her job as a doctor, but she was better at it than he was. Still, he was better than he used to be—not good, but better. He often used to sit with his laptop, working on a case until he fell asleep in his chair. He was no longer that solitary, and he didn't miss the old ways.

"That boy got a nasty blow," she said. "He could have died."

"Like the other two."

She nodded. He could see the shadow under her eye deepen when she bent forward. When she leaned back it almost disappeared.

Their . . . everyday work overlapped. He wasn't sure what to call it. Their professional activities, perhaps. Was that preordained? He sometimes thought so. When they first met Angela had just decided to study medicine. He'd recently joined the CID as a raw recruit.

Nowadays she saw right into his world, and he into hers. The injured and dying and sometimes even the dead came from his world into hers, and he would follow them, and then everybody would move back and forth between the two worlds, just like Bertil earlier that day, who'd bumped into Angela when he'd been trying to extract some words from a battered body that Angela was simultaneously trying to heal. Fucking hell. He drank the remains of his red wine. She poured some water into his glass. The radio was mumbling away on the counter. It was almost night.

"They seem to be in a bind at the nursery school," he said.

"What do you mean?"

"Oh, I don't know. Lots of children and not many staff."

"More and more of one, and fewer and fewer of the other."

"Yes."

"Is there something in particular that made you think of that just now?"

"Well, this morning I suppose, when I dropped off Elsa. They didn't seem to be able to keep an eye on all the children."

"Is that the police officer in you talking?"

"If it is, doesn't that make it all the more important? All the more serious? The police officer in me sees the shortcomings in the security."

"Shortcomings in the security? You sound like you're responsible for President Bush's safety."

"Bush? He can look after himself. It's those around him that need protecting."

"You know what I mean."

"And what I mean is that you can't risk a child wandering off. There was a little boy who ran through a gap in a hedge and would have disappeared if it hadn't been for the fence on the other side."

"But Erik, that's why the fence is there. So that the children can't get out. Can't disappear."

"But nobody noticed him wandering off through the bushes."

"They don't need to worry about that. The staff knows there's a fence on the other side."

"So there's no problem, is that it?"

"I didn't say that. I seem to remember saying a couple of minutes ago that there are more and more children and fewer and fewer staff. Of course that's a problem, for heaven's sake." She took a sip of water. "A big problem. In lots of ways."

"And that brings us back, well, to security again," he said. "What a responsibility it is for the ridiculously few staff. Keeping an eye on all those kids as they go toddling off in all directions."

"Hmm."

"When they go out on a trip. If they dare to go on outings at all. They don't seem to want to risk it anymore." He stroked his chin, making a rasping noise. "And they have good reason not to."

He fingered the wine bottle, but resisted the temptation to pour himself another glass. She looked at him.

"You know too much about all the dangers lurking out there," she said.

"So do you, Angela. You know all the things that can make people sick."

"Is it anything in particular, this business of security at the nursery school?" she wondered.

"It's really a matter of children and their safety in general," he said. "OK, maybe I do know too much about the potential dangers. So would you if you stood outside a children's playground and took a careful look at what was going on. Maybe you'd notice somebody walking around and devoting an unusual amount of attention to the kids. Types like that often hang around a nursery school as well. Or outside a school at dismissal. Or they might be sitting in their cars watching the girls play handball or volleyball. Gentlemen who get into their fancy cars after work or the latest board meeting and park outside the schoolyard with the morning paper over their knee and their hands around their cocks when the girls jump up under the basket."

"You sound cynical, Erik."

"Cynical? Because I'm telling it like it is?"

"What do you do, then?"

"Eh?"

"What do you do about these fancy men in their fancy cars? And the others lurking around these places?"

"Try to keep an eye on them in the first place. You can't arrest someone for sitting in his car reading a newspaper, can you? That's not a crime in a democracy."

"For God's sake!"

"But don't you see? We have to wait until a crime is committed. That's the frustrating thing about it. We know, but we can't do anything."

"Why can't you . . . caution them?"

"How?"

"Erik, it's not—"

"No, but I'm being honest and serious now. I'd love to hand out loads of cautions, but I also want to keep my job. You can't just march up and fling a car door open. Or arrest somebody for looking shady and standing under a tree next to a children's playground."

"But you think about it."

"It struck me this morning at the nursery school just how vulnerable little kids are, and older ones too, come to think of it. All that watching, and all that goes with it. And what it leads to. But the danger as well. Real danger."

"Yes."

"I'd love to hand out no end of cautions, but it's difficult. And we need more police." He poured himself some more wine after all. "In that respect we're in the same position as the staff at the nursery school," he said with a smile.

She gave a shiver, as if the window looking out over the courtyard was wide open instead of just a narrow crack letting in a little wisp of night air.

"You know, Erik, you give me the creeps with all this."

He didn't reply.

"Elsa goes to a nursery school," she said. "Elsa's one of a group of children with too few staff to look after them properly. I can't get that out of my mind now."

"I'm sorry."

"No, no. It's just as bad for you too." She suddenly burst out laughing, short but loud. "God, it's ridiculously easy to be worried when you are a parent." She looked at him. "What should we do? Send her to a different nursery school? Get a nanny? Hire a bodyguard for Elsa?"

He smiled again.

"There is a fence around the place, as you pointed out a few minutes ago. And Elsa loves her nursery school."

She drank up the rest of the water in her glass. "You've certainly gotten me thinking, Erik."

"Oh hell, it was stupid of me to go on about all the dangers."

"At least about all those sick weirdos hanging around outside schools," said Angela. "What's going to happen when she starts school?" She stood up. "No, that's enough for one night. I'm going to take a shower."

4

INSPECTOR JANNE ALINDER ANSWERED THE FIRST CALL OF HIS
evening shift three seconds after it had started. He hadn't even sat down.

"Police, Majorna-Linnéstaden, Alinder," he said, flopping down onto his
swivel chair. It creaked under his weight.

"Hello, is that the police for Linnéstaden?"

Come on, didn't I just say that? he thought. It was always the same. No-
body ever listened. Was it his fault, or the caller's? What did they want con-
firming? It would be better just to say "hello" since the question was bound to
come anyway.

"This is the police station in Tredje Långgatan," he said, spelling it out in
detail.

"It's my little girl," said the voice: it could belong to a young woman, or
a middle-aged one. He was not very good with voices. Especially women's
voices. He'd often spoken to somebody on the phone who sounded like
what's-her-name, that sexy newsreader on channel 4, only to find out when
he met her, the caller that is, that she looked like Old Mother Hubbard and
had been using a bus pass for years. And vice versa. A voice like gravel and a
body like Marilyn Monroe.

"Who am I speaking to?" he asked, pen poised. She introduced herself as
Lena Sköld.

"Something odd has happened," said Lena Sköld.

"Start from the beginning and let's hear all about it," said Alinder, the
usual routine.

"I can't understand it."

"What happened?"

"It's my little daughter . . . Ellen . . . She told me she met somebody this
afternoon."

"Go on."

"When she was out in the woods, a nursery-school outing. At Plikta. The children's playground. It's at the inter—"

"I know where it is," said Alinder.

Only too well, he thought. He'd spent years there when the children were little. He'd stood there, usually feeling frozen stiff, sometimes hungover, but he'd gone there with the kids even so because Plikta was closest to their apartment in Olivedalsgatan and he couldn't think of any reason to say no. He was glad he hadn't said no. Those who don't say no get their reward in due course. Those who do say no get their punishment from the children later on when they flee the nest without so much as a backward glance.

"She says she met a man there. A mister, as she put it. She sat in his car."

"What do the staff say?"

"The nursery-school staff? Well, I called one of the girls who was with them but she didn't notice anything."

Alinder waited.

"Is it normal for them not to notice anything?" asked Lena Sköld.

It depends if anything has happened, thought Alinder.

"Where is your daughter now?" he asked.

"She's sitting at the table here in front of me, drawing."

"And she told you she was in a car with a man. Have I understood that correctly?"

"That's how I understand it, in any case," said Lena Sköld.

"So she went off with somebody? Without the staff noticing?"

"Yes."

"Is she injured?"

Straight to the point. It's better to come straight to the point.

"No, not as far as I can see. I have actually looked. Just now. It was only an hour ago that she mentioned it."

"An hour?"

"Well, two maybe."

"How does she seem?"

"Well, happy, I suppose. As usual."

"I see," said Alinder.

"I didn't have anybody to ask about what I should do," said Lena Sköld. "I'm a single parent and my husb . . . er, my ex is not somebody I'd turn to about anything at all."

I'll take your word for it, Alinder thought. This town was full of real bastards, and their exes were better off keeping as many miles away from them as possible. The children as well.

"Do you yourself believe what Ellen says?" he asked.

"Er, well, I don't really know. She has a vivid imagination."

"Children do. So do a lot of adults."

"Are you referring to me?"

"No, no, it was just something that slipped out. A throwaway comment."

"I see."

"What did you say about Ellen's imagination?"

He could hear the girl now. She must be sitting right next to her mother at the table. He heard the word "imagination" and heard Lena Sköld explaining what it meant, and then the girl asked another question he couldn't catch. Then the mother's voice was back on the line.

"Sorry about that, but Ellen was listening to what I said. She's gone to her room now to get some more paper."

"Her imagination," said Alinder again.

"She makes up quite a lot, to be honest. Imaginary things, or imaginary people. People she says she's been talking to. Even here, at home. In her room. It's not unusual for children, I suppose."

"But you decided to call here."

"Yes, I suppose that does sound a bit odd. But it was different somehow. As if she hadn't made it up this time. I don't really know how to explain it. But I sort of believed it. Not that she said much, though."

"And the 'it' you say you believed was that she'd been in a car with a strange man, is that right?"

"Basically, yes."

"Anything else?"

"Candy, I think. I think she was given some candy."

"How old is Ellen?"

"Four."

"Does she speak well?"

"Pretty well."

"Has she said any more about the car? Or about the man?"

"No. But then we haven't spent the whole evening talking about it. She said something when she came home, after I picked her up, and then I asked her something, and I started thinking, and then I called the woman from the nursery school, and then I phoned the police and . . . Well . . ."

Alinder looked at the sheet of paper in front of him. He'd noted her name and address and her day and evening phone numbers, and a summary of what she'd said. There was nothing else he could do now. But he took it seriously, as much as he could. The girl might well have been with somebody, in a real car. That was possible. Or she might just have been in a big wooden car. There was one like that at Plikta. Perhaps she'd suddenly enlarged one of her friends at the nursery school ten times over. Perhaps she'd been dreaming about candy, millions of bags of candy, just like he could dream about marvelous meals and dishes, now that eating was more important to him than sex.

"If she says anything else about, er, about the meeting, write it down and let us know," he said.

"What happens now, then?"

"I've noted down everything you've said, and I'll write a report on our conversation and file it."

"Is that all?"

"What do you think we ought to do, Mrs. Sköld?"

"I'm not 'Mrs.' anymore."

"What should we do?"

"I don't know. I'll talk to the staff at the nursery school again, and I might get back to you."

"Good."

"But, well, I suppose it is possible she's made it all up. I mean, she's not nervous or anything like that. Doesn't seem to be frightened or worried or anything."

Alinder didn't respond. He glanced at his watch. He jotted down another note.

"What did you say your name was? Did you say?"

"Alinder. Janne Alinder."

"Oh yes, thank you."

Something occurred to him. Might as well do this properly, now that they'd started.

"Just one other thing. Check to see if there's anything missing. If Ellen has lost anything."

The city swished by on the other side of the big windows, just as naked this evening as this morning and yesterday and tomorrow. He was more or less in a dream, but he was doing his job perfectly. Nobody could have grounds for complaint about what he was doing.

Good afternoon, good afternoon.

Yes, I can open the center doors again, no problem.

Of course I can wait for half a minute while you come running from over there even though we should be on our way now if we're going to stick to the schedule, but I'm not some kind of a monster who just drives off.

There were drivers like that, but he wasn't one of them, certainly not.

People like that ought to get themselves another job. They certainly shouldn't be driving passengers around, he thought, as he increased the speed of the windshield wipers. The rain was getting worse.

He enjoyed this route. He'd been driving it for so long, he knew every curve, every corner, every cranny.

He could drive buses as well. He also had his favorite bus routes, but he wasn't going to tell anybody what they were. Not that anybody ever asked, but he had no intention of telling them even if they did.

Maybe he'd told the girl what they were. It was funny, but he couldn't remember. Oh yes, he remembered now. He'd touched her, and it had felt like the down on a little bird, with the tiny bones just underneath, and he'd left his hand there, and he'd looked at his hand and it was trembling, and he knew, he knew at that very moment, as if he'd had second sight, could see into the future, what he could do with the g-g-g-girl if he left his hand there, and he'd hidden it then, hidden it inside his jacket and his pullover and his shirt, hidden it from himself and from her, and then he'd hidden his face so that she couldn't see it. He'd opened the door for her and helped her out, and then he'd driven off. When he got home he had—

"Are we ever going to move, or what?"

He gave a start, and in his rearview mirror he could see a man almost leaning into the streetcar driver's cab. That wasn't allowed. The driver mus—

"It's been red and green and purple and white ten times, so when are you going to move your fucking ass?" said the man, and he could smell the stench of alcohol through the protective glass shielding him from the horrible creature on the other side.

"*Get moving!*" screamed the horrible creature.

Horns were sounding from behind.

Horns were sounding from the sides. He looked ahead and the lights changed and he—

"*Get moving for fuck's sake!*" yelled the horrible creature, grabbing hold of his cab door handle, and he took off faster than intended and something happened to the lights that shouldn't have happened, and he went along with the streetcar as it moved forward, he wasn't the one driving anymore, it was as if the other man was at the controls, the horrible creature smelling of alcohol, a smell seeping through into his cab, and he was suddenly scared that the police would come and stop them right here and smell the liquor, and would think he was driving while under the influence, that *he* of all people, but he never touched a drop, and if they thought that, that he was driving while under the influence, he'd never be allowed to drive again. That would be disastrous.

He accelerated through the intersection as if to get away from the threat hanging onto his glass door, but the lights had already changed for traffic coming from the east and north and south and he ran straight into the back of a Volvo V70 that had just turned off the main road, and the Volvo rammed into an Audi that had stopped for a red light. Another Volvo drove into the right-hand side of the streetcar. A BMW rammed into the Volvo. He let the streetcar stop of its own accord. He couldn't touch the controls, he couldn't move. He could hear the police sirens in the distance, coming closer.

"*Get moving!*" screeched the horrible creature.

5

IT WAS ONLY IN EXCEPTIONAL CIRCUMSTANCES THAT JANNE ALINDER went out in a patrol car, but this was one of those occasions, and typically all hell broke loose as he drove sedately along the beautiful boulevard. The streetcar ahead of him suddenly ran amok and almost *bounced* over the intersection and became a sort of hard air bag for the cars that crashed into it from all directions.

"*Saatana perkele,*" said Johan Minnonen, who was born in Finland and became a Swedish citizen and then a police officer, and seldom spoke a word of Finnish.

Alinder immediately called for reinforcements. It looked bad. Cars had gone up the sides of the streetcar and then fallen back down again. They didn't need much speed for that to happen. He could hear somebody screaming. He could hear an engine that wouldn't shut up despite being in its death throes. He could hear sirens. He could see the lights. Somebody screamed again, a woman. An ambulance appeared. It must have been just around the corner when he sent out the emergency call. A squad car raced up, and another, and a patrol car fitted with the new roof lights that spattered light out in circles over the whole county.

Nobody had died. It turned out that there was one broken arm and a few sprains and bruises caused by air bags inflating. A drunk who had been standing next to the streetcar driver's cab had been thrown against the windshield without smashing it. On the other hand, the drunk's forehead had been smashed, but none of his brains had run out as far as they could see.

He'll soon be able to start enjoying life again, Alinder thought as the drunk was carried off to the ambulance.

Alinder had been the first to enter the streetcar once he'd persuaded the shocked driver to open the doors. Alinder had looked around: the man bleeding at the front; a woman sobbing in a loud howl; two small children crammed into a seat beside a man with his arm still around them to protect them from the crash that had already happened. Two young men in the seats behind. One was black and the other white and looking pale in the various lights streaming in. The black man might also be pale.

The driver had been sitting motionless, staring straight ahead, in the direction he would have been driving in peace and quiet if only he'd done his job properly and obeyed the traffic lights. There was a smell of liquor, but that might have come from the man lying on the floor and blocking the way into the driver's cab. Yes, that was no doubt the source; he looked like a real mess. But then again, the driver might have had a drop or two, it was known to happen.

The driver had slowly turned to look at him. He seemed calm and uninjured. He had picked up his briefcase and placed it on his knee. Alinder hadn't been able to see anything unusual about the cab. But what do they normally look like? That wasn't his strong suit.

There had been something hanging from a peg behind the driver. Alinder thought it was some sort of toy animal, or a little bird perhaps, green in color and almost the same as the wall. It had a beak. Looked like a mascot.

The driver had swung around on his chair, raised his left hand, taken down whatever it was, and stuffed it into his briefcase. Hmm. A mascot. We all need some kind of company, Alinder thought; or protection, perhaps. To ward off bad luck. But that bunch of feathers hadn't been much use on this occasion.

The streetcar had been half full. When he looked around he saw that people had started to get off. His fellow officers whose job would be to stop them hadn't arrived yet.

"I'd appreciate it if you could stay inside the streetcar until we've got the situation under control," he said.

Two young men with half their heads covered in piercings had looked around but continued on their way out through the door. Not that I blame them, Alinder had thought. Or intend to stop them. I can't stop them, there's no time for that.

There was no sign of the black man nor the white man any longer.

The driver was sitting in front of him. He was in some kind of shock, but it wasn't bad enough to prevent him from saying something, now that he was about to start the interview.

At least he was sober.

He was fair-haired and about forty years old, and his eyes had a piercing sharpness that almost made Alinder want to turn around and see what the man was looking at straight through his head.

His uniform was badly cut and ill fitting, more or less like the one Alinder was wearing. He held his cap in his hand, twirling it around like the earth around the sun, around and around and around. He had a tic in his left eye. He'd hardly spoken, just mumbled and nodded when they'd finally managed to worm their way out of the circle of curious bystanders at the scene of the accident.

Alinder had noted his name and address.

"Let's start from the beginning," said Alinder, switching on the tape recorder and testing his pen by drawing a little peaked cap on the sheet of paper in front of him. "Looks like you got a little out of sync with the traffic lights, is that right?"

The driver nodded, almost imperceptibly.

"Why?" asked Alinder.

The driver shrugged, still twirling his cap around and around.

"Come on now," said Alinder. "Was the drunk putting you off?" A leading question, but what the hell, he thought.

The driver looked up at him, those remarkable eyes.

"The man lying at the side of the driver's cab had quite a few in him," said Alinder. "What was he doing there? When the crash happened?"

The driver's mouth moved, but no words came out.

Is he a mute, Alinder wondered. No, Gothenburg Tramways wouldn't employ a mute driver. A driver has to be able to communicate. Is he still in shock? Can that make people mute? Huh! What an ignorant bastard I am.

"You have to answer the question," he said.

The man twirled his cap.

"Can't you talk?"

The cap, around and around.

OK, thought Alinder. Let's try this. He slid forward a glass of water, but the man didn't touch it.

His briefcase was standing by his chair, the kind all the streetcar drivers have. Alinder had always wondered what was inside them whenever he saw a driver walking toward his streetcar, like a pilot on his way to his aircraft. Alternative routes? A bit more difficult in a streetcar than up in the air. Harder to drive around and around Brunnsparken while waiting to approach your stop than to circle over the airport at Landvetter.

He knew one thing that was in the briefcase, but that had nothing to do with the accident.

"Was there something wrong with the lights?" he asked.

The driver didn't reply.

"But you drove through a red light," said Alinder.

The driver nodded.

"It's a very busy intersection," said Alinder.

The driver nodded again, somewhat hesitantly.

"Things could have turned out a lot worse than they did," said Alinder.

The driver was looking elsewhere now. Ex-driver, Alinder thought. He's not going to be driving anymore streetcars until this incident has been thoroughly investigated by the tramways people as well.

"We can help you," said Alinder.

"H-h-h-h-h-h," said the man.

"I beg your pardon?"

"Ho-ho-ho-ho-how?"

So you're a stutterer, poor bastard, thought Alinder. Is that why? Or is it the shock after the crash?

"We can help you by going through exactly what happened," he said.

"Th-th-th-th . . ."

"Yes?"

"Th-th-th-the o-o-o-oth-oth-other," said the driver.

"The other? You mean the other man?"

The driver nodded.

"The other man. Which other man?"

The driver jerked his head as if he were looking down at something on the floor.

"The man lying on the floor? Is that who you mean?"

The driver nodded. Alinder looked at the tape recorder, and the tape spinning around and around. All the nods and head shakes are duly recorded, he thought. All the st-st-st-st-stutters.

"Am I to interpret that as meaning the man distracted you while you were driving?"

They were preparing for a party. They had invited mainly recent parents from the prenatal group they used to attend, looking trim and fit after all those relaxation exercises. Angela had kept in touch with several of the girls, and he was surprised to discover he got on well with several of the men. Despite a considerable age difference.

"That's because you are still so immature," Angela said.

"And I'm so used to always being the youngest," he retorted, opening another bottle of wine.

"Is that something worth striving for?"

"No, but that's the way it's always been."

"Not anymore," she said.

"Still."

"Phone your mom," she said. "You're still the youngest in her family."

"The youngest detective chief inspector in Sweden."

"Is that still true?"

"Ask my mom!" he said, and the phone rang and they both guessed it was his mother calling direct from Nueva Andalucía: It was typical of her timing. He picked up the receiver, but it wasn't her.

He recognized the voice, though.

"Long time no see, Erik."

"Likewise, Steve."

DCI Steve Macdonald had been his partner in a difficult case some years previously. Winter had been over in London, in the suburbs around Croydon where Macdonald's homicide squad operated, and the pair had become friends. Long-distance friends, but still.

Macdonald had been in Gothenburg for the dramatic climax of the case. They were the same age, and Steve had a set of teenage twins.

"We're coming over," Steve Macdonald announced. "The kids want to see the land of the midnight sun."

"More likely the land of the midday moon at this time of year," Winter replied.

"Anyway."

"When are you coming?"

"Let's see, where are we now? Er, late November. They have a long holiday starting early in December, and so we thought: Why not? Otherwise it'll never happen."

"Good thinking. But that's very soon."

"Gothenburg's almost commuting distance from London."

"Mmm."

"Do you think you could arrange a good hotel in the center of town? By 'good' I mean one that comes up to my modest standards. Not yours."

"You must stay with us, of course," Winter said.

"No, no. Beth'll be coming as well, so there'll be four of us."

"You've been here before," Winter reminded him, and pictured Steve, glass in hand, on the balcony one warm evening in May, very nearly falling over the railing to the ground twenty meters below. They'd been trying to relax after all the awful happenings of the previous weeks. "You know we have plenty of room."

"What I saw was mainly the kitchen and the balcony, and to tell you the truth, I don't remember many details."

"It's so big that my modesty prevents me from telling you just how big. And I don't suppose you're planning to stay for six months."

"Of course we are."

"That's OK."

"Three days."

"That's also OK."

"Well . . ."

"You know our address," Winter said. "We can sort out the practical details a couple of days before you arrive."

"I shall be on holiday," Macdonald said. "I don't intend to be practical."

"I was thinking of the beer and whiskey."

"I'll bring that with me. A thirty-year-old Dallas Dhu plus a Springbank that's out of this world, I can promise you. Older than we are, as well."

Macdonald grew up near Inverness on a farm, not far from the village of Dallas in Speyside.

"I think I'd better take vacation as well," Winter said.

"How about that! The DCI's getting more cooperative."

"Or lazy."

"In that case I'll be happy to impose on you. How are Angela and Elsa?"

"Just fine."

"Well, then—"

"See you later, alligator," Winter said, then wondered why on earth he'd come out with such a corny expression. Maybe because he was feeling cheerful.

But there wouldn't be a reunion in fact, no Dallas Dhu and no Springbank. Not this time. Before the end of November Steve Macdonald would phone to say that one of his twin daughters had had an attack of bronchitis that was threatening to develop into pneumonia, and they'd have to cancel their trip.

There were more people in the flat than he could remember ever having seen there before. Men and women and children. It was a good party. Nobody talked shop, and as far as Winter was concerned that was the main criterion for a successful occasion. He'd prepared two sides of lamb that he carved for the buffet, and nobody complained about the taste of the lamb nor that of the oven-baked potatoes with herbs nor the salsa with roast chili served in order to warm the guests up.

Nor the cherry pies for dessert. The espresso. The calvados and grappa and the bottle of marc that more guests wanted to taste than he'd expected when he put it out.

It took him three tries before he finally managed to open his briefcase, but Bill was lying on top and hadn't been damaged at all. Now Bill was hanging from his peg and he could almost hear his Rotty doing those funny voice imitations. He could hear him now! It was such fun!

The policeman had talked for ages, and he'd also started talking after a while, when the band around his throat had loosened and everything calmed down.

The girl laughed straight at him and he could see her holding her arms out and Bill swinging backward and forward. The film ended, and he rewound it and watched it again. They'd had so much fun. He watched her putting some candy into her mouth. He saw his own right hand touching her, then pulling back quickly, quickly. Like stroking down.

You're so soft, Uncle had said. You're so soft to touch.

He'd been sitting on the train. A lady had asked him where he was going. He'd laughed.

Mom!

Mom!

She'd been waiting for him at the station, and the town was very big. Where he lived with his dad wasn't a town at all, but this one was big. Enormous.

Mom!

My little boy, Mom had said.

You can call this man Uncle, she'd said.

Uncle had taken him by the hand, and touched his head.

My little boy, Uncle had said.

Uncle lives here with me, Mom had said.

Or you with me, Uncle had said, and they'd laughed, and he laughed as well.

They'd had a marvelous dinner.

This is where you'll sleep, Mom had said.

The next morning she'd gone to work in town, a long, long way away.

Do you want to go for a little walk? Uncle had asked.

They'd gone for an enormous walk in one direction, and just as far back again.

I can feel that you're cold, Uncle had said when they got back home.

Come here, my boy, and I'll warm you up. You're so soft. You're so soft to touch.

6

THIS WAS HOW HE RECOUNTED WHAT HAD HAPPENED. HIS TONE was almost exhilarated.

He couldn't remember why he had decided to cut across the soccer field when that meant he would actually have farther to walk back to the student dorm where he lived, but maybe he'd noticed a forgotten soccer ball lit up by the streetlights and suddenly felt a strong desire to shoot the damn thing into the back of the net, and show some of those jokers on the national team how it was done. Let the world know that he'd quit too soon, simply given up before his career had really taken off.

That could have been it. But it might just have been that he'd been to a party. In any case, he'd walked over the playing field at Mossen on the way home, and it had been well into the night, or rather the morning. Half past four. He'd noticed a poor newspaper delivery boy trudging around, back bent, among the high-rise apartment buildings soaring heavenward behind him. Poor kid. Lugging newspapers up to the fortieth floor. Morning after morning, no thanks. Good for keeping fit, no doubt, but you should work out at a sensible time of day. Newspaper boys are the bottom of the heap, he'd thought, and grinned as he tried to adjust his footsteps that were leading him off course to the left when he didn't look where he was going, the student dorm that was lying in wait for him over there, gloomy and cheerless, dormant until the murky gray light of dawn signaled time for more cramming and more hassle. But not for him, no thank you very much. He would be fast asleep the whoooole day long. No cramming, no hassle, no rain down his collar, no lousy lunch, no long-winded lectures, no slushy corridors, no aggressive women throwing their weight around.

That's what was going through his head when he staggered to his left again and heard something *swiiiishing* past his head that had been in a different position a quarter of a second before, and something thudded into the ground in front of him and seemed to be *stuck* there, and he turned his head and saw the guy tugging and heaving at something with a long handle.

"What the hell . . ." he had managed to mutter in a shaky voice, and the other person was still tugging at the handle or whatever it was and it had dawned on him now, he'd been slow on the uptake, but now he realized that this wasn't some old guy digging up potatoes two months late, and in a strange place at that. The guy had jerked whatever it was out of the ground, and then presumably had looked at him, but he wouldn't have seen much, as his intended victim had fled over the soccer field at a pace that would have forced Maurice Greene and Ato Boldon and all the other wooden-legged Olympic sprinters to give up. All the potato man would have seen was his back and his legs, on the way to anywhere that would provide protection. He hadn't heard any footsteps following him, but he hadn't listened for any either. He had raced across the road and in among the little houses and across the street on the other side of the block and down the hill, eventually slowing down because his rib cage would have burst otherwise.

His name was Gustav Smedsberg, and he was sitting in front of a police officer in a thick woolen sweater who had introduced himself as Bertil Ringsomething.

"You did the right thing, getting in touch with us, Gustav."

"I remembered reading something about some guy going around bashing people on the head."

Ringmar nodded.

"Was it him?"

"We don't know. It depends what you remember."

"What I remember is more or less what I told the guy I spoke to on the phone. The duty officer or whatever you call it."

"Let's run through it once again," said Ringmar, and they did.

"Odd that I didn't hear him," said Smedsberg.

"Were there any other noises at the time?"

"No."

"No traffic in the street?"

"No. Only a newspaper delivery boy."

"Somebody was delivering newspapers at that hour?"

"Yes. Or just before. As I was crossing the street before you get to the sports field. Gibraltargatan."

"Did you see this delivery boy?"

"Yes."

"How do you know?"

"Know what?"

"That it was a newspaper delivery boy?"

"Somebody carrying a pile of newspapers early in the morning," said Smedsberg. "That's what I call a newspaper delivery boy."

"Just one? Or two? Three?"

"Just one. I didn't see any others. He was just going into one of the apartment buildings as I passed by." Smedsberg looked at Ringmar. "That's a tough job. So early in the morning."

"Did you speak to him? To the newspaper boy?"

"No, no."

"Did you see him again?"

"No."

"Are you sure?"

"Yes, of co—" Smedsberg looked up at Ringmar again, and sat up straighter on the chair, which creaked.

"Do you think that—"

"Think what?" said Ringmar.

"Do you think it was the newspaper boy who tried to kill me?"

"I don't think anything," said Ringmar.

"Why are you asking so much about him, then?"

"Describe how he was dressed," said Ringmar.

"Who? The newspaper boy?"

"Yes."

"I have no idea. No idea at all. It was dark. It was raining a little and I was sort of looking down."

"Did he have anything on his head?"

"Er, yes, I think so."

"What exactly?"

"A wool hat, I think. I'd have remembered if it was a baseball cap, I think, a Nike cap or something like that." He looked out of the window, then back again at Ringmar. "I'm pretty sure it was a wool hat."

"The person who attacked you. Did he have anything on his head?"

No answer. Smedsberg was thinking. Ringmar waited.

"I really don't remember," said Smedsberg eventually. "Not right now, at least." He ran his hand over his forehead, as if trying to help his memory along. "Isn't that the kind of thing I should be able to remember?"

"It depends on the circumstances," said Ringmar. "Maybe you'll remember in a little while. Tomorrow maybe, the day after. It's important that you get in touch with us the moment you remember anything. Anything at all."

"Anything at all? Shouldn't it have something to do with the case?"

"You know what I mean."

"OK, OK. I feel a little, well, a little tired right now." He was thinking about his bed, and his plans for today, which weren't exactly ambitious.

"I think it might have been an iron," said Gustav, after they'd had a short break.

"An iron?"

"A branding iron. The thing you mark cattle with."

"Would you recognize a thing like that?"

"I grew up on a farm."

"Did you have branding irons there?"

He didn't answer. Ringmar wasn't certain he'd heard the question, and repeated it. The boy seemed to be thinking about his answer, or perhaps about the question. It was a simple question.

"Er, yes, of course. They're old things, been around for a long time."

"Is that normal?" Ringmar asked.

"What do you mean, normal?"

"To brand your animals that way?"

"People do it. But it's not like in Montana or Wyoming," Smedsberg said. He looked at Ringmar. "American prairies."

"I know."

"I've been there."

"Really?"

"Cody. Terrific place."

"Were you a cowboy?"

"No. But maybe one day. When I've graduated from Chalmers."

"The cowpokin' engineer."

Smedsberg smiled.

"There are jobs there. Engineering jobs, I mean."

"How were you able to see that it was a branding iron?" Ringmar asked, abandoning Montana for Mossen.

"I didn't say it was, definitely. But I think so. Then again, I didn't hang around, if you know what I mean."

"Was it the handle that looked familiar?"

"I guess it must have been."

"What did it look like?"

"I can try to draw it for you. Or you can visit a farm and see one for yourself."

"Do they all look the same, then?"

"I know what they looked like at home. This one was similar to them. But I didn't see the branding part itself."

Ringmar stood up.

"I'd like you to take a look at some photographs," he said.

He walked over to a cabinet, took out one of the folders, and produced the pictures.

"Oh shit," said Smedsberg when he saw the first photograph. "Is he dead?"

"None of these pictures are of dead people," Ringmar said. "But they could easily have been."

Smedsberg was shown several pictures from various angles of the three young men who had been attacked with what seemed to be the same weapon.

"And I was supposed to be the fourth victim, is that it?" Smedsberg said.

"Assuming it's the same attacker, yes."

"What kind of a lunatic is this?" Smedsberg looked up at Ringmar, then back down at the photograph of the back of Jakob Stillman's head. "What is he trying to do?" He looked again at the photograph. Ringmar observed him closely. "Looks like he's just out to bash somebody in the head." Smedsberg looked up again. "Anybody at all."

"Do you know any of these guys?" Ringmar asked.

"No."

"Take your time."

"I don't know any of them."

"What can you say about the wounds, then?" Ringmar pointed to the photographs.

Smedsberg scrutinized them again, held some of them up to the light.

"Well, I guess he could have been trying to mark them."

"Mark them? What do you mean by that?"

"Like I said before. It could be a marking iron. A branding iron."

"Are you sure?"

"No. The problem is that you often brand farm animals with some characterizing mark on their skin. But these are not that kind of wound, as far as I can see."

"There's something I don't understand," Ringmar said. "A branding iron is used for branding cattle. But in this case it's been used as a club. Would there still have been a brand mark?"

"I really don't know."

"OK. But an ordinary branding iron must be pretty heavy, you need to be on the strong side to use one, is that right?"

"Yes, I would say so."

"You'd need an awful lot of strength, in fact?"

"Yes."

"The man who attacked you—did you get the impression that he was big?"

"Not particularly. Normal."

"OK. Let's assume he's determined to club you on the back of the head with a branding iron. He creeps up behind you. You don't hear him and ha—"

"Why didn't I hear him? Shouldn't I have?"

"Let's not worry about that for the moment," Ringmar said. "He's behind you. He attacks you. At that very moment you veer to one side."

"Stagger to one side, I'd say. I wasn't stone cold sober, to be honest."

"Stagger. You stagger to one side. He attacks you. But all he can hit is thin air. He hits thin air. His weapon thuds down into the ground and gets stuck. He tugs at it, but it doesn't come loose. You see him standing there, and then you take off."

"Yes."

"Why did this weapon, whatever it was, get stuck in the ground?" Ringmar wondered. "It wouldn't have if he'd jabbed at you in a straight line."

"So he didn't do that, I guess," said Smedsberg.

"Really?"

"He took a swing at me with the branding iron."

"If that's what it is," Ringmar said.

"Whatever it is, you've got to catch him pretty damn quick," Smedsberg said. "Will he come after me again?"

Ringmar made no comment. Smedsberg looked away. He seemed to be thinking something over again.

"Maybe he's trying to brand people, really brand them." He was looking at Ringmar now. "Maybe he wants to show that he owns them, these people he's branded?"

Ringmar listened. Smedsberg looked as if he were concentrating, as if he'd already accepted a job as a CID officer and was now on duty.

"Maybe he didn't want to kill us. The victims. Maybe he just wanted to show that, er, that he owned us," said Gustav Smedsberg.

"Fascinating," said Halders. "We should give the kid a job here. Start at the bottom and work his way up to the top."

"And where's the top?" asked Aneta Djanali.

"I'll show you when we get there," said Halders. "We'll make it one fine day."

"It's a fine day today," said Djanali.

She was right. The sun had returned after a prolonged exile. The light outside made your eyes hurt, and Djanali had shown up at the police station in black sunglasses that made her look like a soul queen on tour in Scandinavia. At least, that's what Halders had told her when they met outside the entrance.

They were in Winter's office now. Winter was sitting on his desk chair, and Ringmar was perched on the edge of his desk.

"Shall we consult the farmers' union—what do they call themselves, the Federation of Swedish Farmers? FSF?" Winter wasn't quite sure if Halders was joking.

"Good idea, Fredrik," he said. "You can start with all of Götaland."

"Certainly not," said Halders, looking at the others. "I was only joking." He turned to Winter again. "What if it is a bumpkin, then? What do we do? How will we be able to pinpoint every clodhopper in the area?"

"Officer Plod in search of a clod," said Winter.

"They're a dying breed," said Ringmar.

"Officer Plods?" said Djanali.

"Farmers," said Ringmar. "Soon there won't be any Swedish farmers left. The EU will see to that."

"There'll always be tough little Portuguese olive growers, though," said Halders. "The Swedish national dish will become olives, whether you want the crappy things or not."

"Olives are good for you," said Djanali. "Unlike baked pig's feet."

"For Christ's sake," screamed Halders. "Why did you mention pig's feet? You've made *my* feet hurt."

At last the banter is getting back to normal, Winter thought. About time too.

"Maybe he wants to brand pigs," said Halders. He sounded serious now. "Our attacker. Branding people he regards as swine."

"*If* it is a marking iron, or whatever it's called," said Winter.

"We'd better start making comparisons," Ringmar said. "We'll have to get hold of a branding iron."

"Who's going to volunteer to have their head bashed in so that we can make comparisons?" Halders wondered.

Everybody stared at him.

"Oh no, no, not me. I've already been bashed on the head, that's enough for this life."

"Maybe it wasn't enough, though?" said Djanali.

Have I gone too far? she thought. But Fredrik asks for it.

Halders turned to Winter.

"The answer could be in the victims. Maybe there is a link between them after all. They don't have to be random choices."

"Hmm."

"If we can find a common denominator we'll have made a start. We haven't checked up on the first two in detail yet. Not enough detail, at least," Halders continued.

"Well," said Ringmar.

"Well what? I can think of ten questions they weren't asked but should have been. But I must say I think this last kid's story is a bit odd. Gustav. The farmer's boy."

"What do you mean, odd?" asked Djanali.

"Confused, muddled."

"Perhaps that makes it more credible," said Winter.

"Or even incredible," said Halders. "How can you fail to notice somebody creeping up on you in the middle of a soccer field?"

"But the same thing goes for the others, in that case," said Djanali. "Are you seriously suggesting that they're all in it together? That the victims allowed themselves to be injured? Or at least knew what was going to happen to them?"

"Maybe there's something important he wants to tell us but doesn't dare," said Ringmar.

Everybody understood what Ringmar was getting at. A lot of people tell lies, and often because they are scared.

"We'll have to ask him again," said Djanali.

"Nothing surprises me anymore," said Halders. "But OK, maybe they weren't all aware of what was going to happen to them. But maybe they were, to some extent at least. This Gustav, though, he might have other reasons for telling us this story."

Nobody spoke. Winter contemplated the sunlight blazing in through the window. We need some light, he'd thought as he raised the blinds shortly before the others arrived. Let there be light.

The trees in the park outside had been pointing at him, black fingers glinting in the sun. The sky was as blue as it's possible to be in late November.

"He also said something about a newspaper delivery boy. We'd better check up on that," Winter said, still staring into the heavens. "Bergenhem can look into that when he gets back from lunch. Somebody was working there that morning, and might have seen something."

"Or done something," said Ringmar.

"Even better if that's the case. We'll have solved it."

"What about the other attacks?" asked Djanali. "Were there newspaper boys around then too?"

Winter looked at Ringmar.

"Er, we don't actually know yet," Ringmar said.

"Is that code for we haven't looked into it yet?" asked Halders.

"Now we have a time pattern that is becoming clearer," said Winter, getting to his feet. "All the attacks took place at about the same time—in the hours before dawn."

"In the wee hours of the morning," said Halders.

"We're trying to interview everybody who might have been around the areas where the incidents took place, and now it's the delivery boys' turn," said Winter.

"That's hard work," said Halders.

"Interviewing newspaper boys?" said Djanali.

"I've worked as a newspaper boy," said Halders, ignoring her.

"Good," said Winter. "You can give Bergenhem a hand, then."

"I'll take another look at the locations first," said Halders.

7

HE WAS AT KAPELLPLATSEN, STANDING ON THE EDGE OF THE square. The high-rise buildings concealed the sun that would remain up in the northern sky for a bit longer.

Halders turned his head, and felt how stiff it was. He couldn't swivel his head around anymore. The blow to the vertebrae at the back of his neck had left behind this physical reminder. He could just about manage to turn his head to the right, to the left was worse. He'd had to learn to turn his body instead.

Other memories were worse. He had once run all the way across this very square with Margareta when they were very young and very hard up and very happy. The number 7 streetcar had already left and he had stood in the way and nearly been run over. But it had stopped. And Margareta had nearly died laughing once she'd gotten over the shock. And now she really had died, not just nearly died—hit by a drunk driver, and it was debatable whether or not he'd gotten over the shock, or ever would. God only knows. They'd been divorced when it happened, but that didn't mean a thing. Their children were still there, as a reminder of everything that life stood for. That's the way it was. If there was a meaning at all, that was it. Magda's face when lit up by the sun at the breakfast table. The spontaneous joy in the little girl's eyes that turned into diamonds in that flash of light. The feeling inside him. At that moment. Happiness, just for one second.

Still, despite everything he was on the way back to some kind of normality. The banter that morning had been a positive sign. He was glad about that. Therapy? Could be.

He was glad that Aneta had caught on, and played along.

Maybe the two of them were going somewhere together. No, not maybe. We are going somewhere together. Very slowly, very carefully.

He turned around, slowly, carefully. The student had come up the steps from Karl Gustavsgatan. Maybe he was tired. Certainly a bit drunk. Beer. Aryan Kaite, as black as could be, like Aneta; and what a name! Aryan. Perhaps a plea from his parents, it had struck Halders when he talked to the kid after he'd come around. An Aryan black man. Weren't they the first humans? Africans?

This one was studying medicine,

A horrible wound to the head. Could have killed him. The same went for the others. He thought about that as he stood by the steps looking down at the paving stones sparkling in the sunlight. All of them could have been killed, but nobody had died. Why? Was it a coincidence, a stroke of luck? Was that the intention? Were they meant to survive?

This is where the blow had been delivered, in the square, Kapellplatsen. Then darkness.

Linnéplatsen was surrounded by tall buildings that were new but meant to look old, or at least in time blend in with the century-old patrician mansions.

Jens Book had been clubbed down outside Marilyn's, the video store. Halders was standing there now. There were five film posters in the windows, and all of them depicted people brandishing guns or other weapons. *Die Fast! Die Hard III! Die and Let Die! Die!*

But not this time either. Jens Book was the first victim. Studying journalism. The Aryan, Kaite, was the second. Jakob Stillman the third. In the same department as Bertil's daughter, Halders remembered, and moved to one side to avoid a cyclist who came racing down from Sveaplan. Gustav Smedsberg was the fourth, the yokel studying at the university of technology, Chalmers. Branding iron. Halders smiled. Branding iron my ass.

Book was the one with the worst injuries, if it's possible to grade them like that. The blow had affected nerves and other things, paralyzing the kid on his right side, and it was not clear if he would recover mobility. Maybe he wasn't as lucky as I was, Halders thought as he backed out of the way of a cyclist evidently determined to ride straight ahead. Halders very nearly fell through the door of the video store.

He thought about the blows again. First the one he'd received. Then the ones that had injured the young men.

It had all happened so quickly. Wham, no warning. Nobody noticed anything in advance. No footsteps. Just wham. No chance of defense, of protecting themselves.

No footsteps, he thought again.

He watched the cyclist ignoring a red light and riding straight over the crossroads, displaying a splendid contempt for death. Die? Pfuh!

The cyclist.

Have we asked about a possible cyclist? Have we thought about that?

He had interviewed the Aryan himself, but there had been no mention of a bicycle.

Had the attacker been riding a bike?

Halders stared down at the pavement, as if there might still be some visible sign of bicycle tracks.

Lars Bergenhem had some news before lunch. Winter was smoking a Corps. The window overlooking the river was open a couple of centimeters, letting in air he thought smelled more distinctly than his cigarillo smoke did. The Panasonic on the floor was playing *Lush Life*. Only Coltrane today, and in recent weeks. Winter had unfastened two buttons of his Zegna jacket. Anybody coming into his office now who didn't know any better would think he wasn't working. Bergenhem came in, saying:

"There was no newspaper delivery boy there."

Winter stood up, put his cigarillo down on the ashtray, turned down the music, and closed the window.

"But the kid saw him," he said as he was doing this. "Smedsberg."

"He says he saw somebody with newspapers," said Bergenhem, "but it wasn't a newspaper delivery boy."

Winter nodded and waited.

"I checked with Göteborgs Posten delivery office and on that particular morning, the day before yesterday, their usual employee for that round called in sick just before it was time to start delivering, and it took them at least three hours before they could find a replacement. So that would have been at least two hours after Smedsberg was attacked."

"He could have been there anyway," Winter said.

"Eh?"

"He could have called in sick but showed up anyway," Winter said again. "He might have started to feel better."

"She," said Bergenhem. "It's a she."

"A she?"

"I've spoken to her. There's no doubt. She has an awful cold, and a husband and three children who were all at home that morning and give her an alibi."

"But people received their morning papers?"

"No. Not until her replacement showed up. According to GP, in any case."

"Have you checked with the subscribers?"

"I haven't had time yet. But the girl at GP says they had lots of complaints that morning. As usual, according to her."

"But Smedsberg says he saw somebody carrying newspapers," Winter said.

"Did he really say that he'd seen the actual newspapers?" Bergenhem wondered.

Winter sorted through the pile of papers in one of the baskets on his desk and read the report on the interviews Ringmar had submitted.

Ringmar had asked: How do you know it was a newspaper boy?

Because he was carrying a bundle of newspapers and went into one of the buildings, and then I saw him come out again and go into the next one, Smedsberg had replied.

Was there a cart outside with more newspapers? Ringmar had asked.

Good, Winter thought. A good question.

No. I didn't see a cart. There could . . . No, I didn't see one. But he was definitely carrying newspapers, that was obvious, Smedsberg had answered.

"Yes," said Winter, looking at Bergenhem. "He said that this person was carrying newspapers and went in and out of apartment buildings in Gibraltargatan."

"OK."

"But there was no cart—don't they usually have one?" Winter said.

"I'll check," said Bergenhem.

"Check who the replacement was as well."

"Of course."

Winter lit his cigarillo again and exhaled smoke.

"So, we might have a fake newspaper boy here, hanging around the area at the time of the attack," he said.

"Yes."

"That's interesting. The question is: Is it our man? And if it isn't—what was he doing there?"

"A mental case?" Bergenhem suggested.

"A mental case pretending to be a newspaper boy? Well, why not?"

"A mild form."

"But if he is our man, surely he must have planned it. A bundle of newspapers etcetera. On the spot at that particular time."

Bergenhem nodded.

"Did he know that Smedsberg would go that way? Or did he know that somebody or other would come by? That students often stagger over Mossen in the early hours? In which case it could have been anybody?"

"Why go to the trouble of lugging newspapers around?" Bergenhem said. "Wouldn't it have been enough simply to hide?"

"Unless he was using that disguise or whatever we should call it, that *role*, to establish some kind of security," Winter said. "Melt into the background, create an atmosphere of normality. What could be more normal at that hour than a hardworking newspaper boy?"

"Maybe he even made contact," Bergenhem said.

Winter drew on his cigarillo again and watched it growing murkier outside. The sun had wandered off again.

"That had occurred to me too," he said, looking at Bergenhem.

"Can't I ever have a thought of my own?" Bergenhem wondered.

"Well, you said it first," said Winter with a smile.

Bergenhem sat down and leaned forward.

"Maybe they spoke to each other. It's pretty harmless to exchange a few words with a newspaper boy."

Winter nodded, and waited.

"Maybe they did make some sort of contact."

"Why didn't Smedsberg say anything about that?" Winter asked.

"Why do you think?"

"Well, it's possible. Everything's possible. They exchanged a few words. The guy continued on his way. The newspaper boy went on delivering."

"Come on, Erik. That can't be what happened. Smedsberg would have told us about it if it was."

"Give me another theory, then."

"I don't know. But if they made contact and exchanged more than a few words, Smedsberg must be concealing something from us."

"What would he be concealing from us if that's the case?"

"Well . . ."

"Does he want to hide the fact that he spoke to a stranger? No. He's an adult, and we are not his parents. Does he want to hide the fact that he was a bit drunk and doesn't want us to remind him and others of that fact? No."

"No." Bergenhem repeated Winter's word, knowing where he was heading.

"If this hypothetical reasoning leads us to wonder what he wanted to hide, it might have to do with his orientation," Winter said.

"Yes," Bergenhem agreed.

"So what is he trying to hide from us?" Winter inhaled again and looked at Bergenhem.

"That he's gay," said Bergenhem. "He made some kind of contact, this fake newspaper boy responded positively, maybe they were heading for Smedsberg's dorm, and all hell broke loose on the way there."

"But we're living in the twentieth century in an enlightened society," Winter said. "Or in the twenty-first, actually. And why would a young man want to conceal his orientation to the extent of shielding a person who tried to murder him?"

Bergenhem shrugged.

"Well, why would he?" asked Winter again.

"We'll have to ask him," said Bergenhem.

"We will. Why not? It would explain a lot."

"One other thing," Bergenhem said.

"Yes?"

"It's connected." Bergenhem looked at Winter. "Where are the newspapers?"

"Yes."

"He was carrying a bundle of papers, but not a single subscriber received one and we haven't found any."

"We haven't looked," Winter said. "We've assumed that the papers were delivered."

"That's true, of course."

"They might be around there somewhere. A pile of them. It would be useful if we could find them, wouldn't it?"

"Yes."

"But when we spoke to the newspaper delivery people, we'd taken Smedsberg's word for it that he'd seen a newspaper boy at that particular time." Winter scratched his nose. "Why do we believe that if we have reservations about other parts of his story?"

"So we need to find other witnesses who saw a fake newspaper boy at that place and at that time," said Bergenhem.

"Yes, and we've already started on that."

Bergenhem stroked his hand across his forehead, from left to right. His four-year-old daughter had already acquired the same habit.

"This line of reasoning could shed new light on the other attacks," he said.

"Or cast a shadow over them," Winter said. "Maybe we should backpedal, not get ahead of ourselves."

Pedal, he thought the moment he'd said it. A bicycle. Perhaps the attacker had ridden up on a bike. That would explain the speed, the surprise. A silent bike. Soft tires.

"But just think," Bergenhem continued. "Four attacks, no witnesses of the actual violence, no trace of the attacker. The victims didn't see or hear anything, or not much at least."

"Go on," Winter said.

"Well, maybe they all made contact with the person who clubbed them down."

"How? Did he pose as a newspaper boy every time?"

"I don't know. Perhaps he posed as something else, somebody else, so as not to scare them."

"Yes."

"Have we checked this newspaper boy business in connection with the other cases?" Bergenhem asked.

"No. We haven't gotten that far yet," said Winter.

"It would be worth following up," Bergenhem said. "We haven't asked the people living in the areas concerned about newspapers."

Yes, Winter thought. You don't get answers to unasked questions.

"And then," Bergenhem said, "there's the business of the other victims' sexual orientation."

"All gay?"

Bergenhem made a gesture: Could-be-a-possibility-but-how-do-I-know.

"Young gays who spotted an interesting possibility and paid dearly for it?" asked Winter.

"Could be," Bergenhem said.

"So they fell victim to a gay basher? Or several? A homophobe?"

"It's possible," said Bergenhem. "And I think there's just one attacker."

"And what's the orientation of the culprit?" Winter asked.

"He's not gay himself," Bergenhem replied.

"Why not?"

"I don't know," said Bergenhem. "It doesn't feel right."

"Are gays nonviolent?"

"Gay bashers aren't homosexual, are they?" said Bergenhem. "Is there such a thing as a gay gay basher?"

Winter didn't respond.

"This attacker isn't gay," said Bergenhem. "I know we can't rule anything out, but I already have a very strong feeling that it isn't the case here."

Winter waited for Bergenhem to say more.

"But it's too early to think anything about anything," Bergenhem said.

"Not at all," said Winter. "This is the way we make progress. Talking it over. Dialogue. We have just talked ourselves into a possible motive."

"And that is?"

"Hatred," said Winter.

Bergenhem nodded.

"Let's assume for the moment that these four young men don't know one another," said Winter. "They have no common background, nothing like that. But they are linked by their sexual orientation."

"And the attacker hates gays," said Bergenhem.

Winter nodded.

"But how did he know that his victims were gay? How could he be so sure?"

"He didn't need to wait long," said Winter. "Only long enough to be invited to go home with them."

"I don't know . . ."

"You were the one who started this line of reasoning," Winter said.

"Was I?"

"Yes."

"OK. But maybe the attacker knew all four of them."

"How could he?"

"It could be that he has the same predilections. Maybe they knew each other from some club. The Let's All Be Gay Club, I don't know. A pub. Confidential contacts. In any case, it developed into a drama of passion."

"With quite a lot of people involved," Winter said.

"There could still be more," said Bergenhem.

Winter scratched his nose again. It was possible that they were on entirely the wrong track. Then again, they might have made progress. But this was just a conversation, just words. Words were still the most important tools in existence, but everything they'd been talking about now needed to be followed up with questions and more questions and actions and visits to streets and staircases and new interviews and telephone interviews and reading after reading after reading after run-through after run-through.

"There's another one as well," said Winter, "and it has nothing to do with sexual orientation."

"What's that?"

"If there really was a fake newspaper boy there, if we can get Smedsberg's claim corroborated by others, how could this person have known that he would be able to operate that morning undisturbed?"

Bergenhem nodded.

"He must have known the real one was indisposed. Otherwise the real one and the fake one might have bumped into each other. But she didn't show up. How could he have known that?"

8

RINGMAR WAS STANDING BY THE WINDOW, LOOKING OUT AT HIS November lawn that no longer needed mowing; he was grateful for that. It was large, and lit up by the lantern over the front door of his house and the streetlights on the other side of the hedge.

The rain falling onto the garden covered it like a shroud. Wind was whistling through the three maples whose crowns he had watched developing over the twenty years they had lived in the house. For twenty years he had been able to stand by this same window, watching the grass grow, or resting, as now. Luckily enough, he'd had other things to do. But still. He was thirty-four when they bought the place. Even younger than Winter. Ringmar took a swig of the beer glittering in its thin glass. Younger than Winter. For a while, quite a long while, before even Winter grew older, that had been an expression in the Gothenburg CID, even the whole force, in fact. Nobody was younger than Erik. A bit like the slogan "Cooler than Borg," which he'd seen in one of the newspapers when he was a UN police officer in the buffer zone in Cyprus eons ago. That was before Moa's time, even before Birgitta's time. Before Martin's time.

He took another drink, listened to the wind, and thought about his son. Strange how things could turn out. His twenty-five-year-old daughter lived at home with them, temporarily; but it could take some time for her to find a new apartment. His twenty-seven-year-old son hadn't even sent them his current address. Martin could be in a buffer zone, for all he knew. Aboard a ship on the other side of the world. Drinking life away in a bar in Vasastan. Gothenburg was big enough for Martin to hide himself away in if he wanted to. If nobody looked for him. And Ringmar didn't look for him. No active search for a son he'd heard nothing from for almost a year. No looking for somebody who didn't want to be found. Moa knew that the little brat was alive but that's all.

But he did search for him inwardly instead, tried to figure out why.

Surely he'd treated him well? Tried to be there when needed. Was it because of his damned job, when all was said done? His peculiar working hours? The traces of post-traumatic stress that were not always just traces?

The memory of a dead child's body wasn't something you could rinse off in the shower the same night. The little face, the gentle features that could no longer really be made out. Younger than anything else, and that's the way it would always be. Finished, finished forever.

Ringmar emptied his glass. I'm rambling, he thought. But the children have been the worst.

Now I'm longing for a conversation with my only son.

The telephone on the wall by the kitchen door rang. At the same time a little flock of small birds took off from the lawn, as if frightened by the noise.

Ringmar walked over to the telephone, put his glass down on the counter, and lifted the receiver.

"Hello, Bertil speaking."

"Hi, Erik here."

"Good evening, Erik."

"What are you doing?"

"Watching the lawn rest. Drinking a Bohemian pilsner."

"Do you think you could have a word with Moa?" Winter asked.

"What are you talking about, Dad?"

"To tell you the truth, I don't really know."

"This isn't something you've thought up yourself."

"Not in that way," he said.

He was sitting in the armchair in her room that had been there as long as the room had been hers. Twenty years. She usually sat by the window, looking at the lawn, just like her father.

"Not in that way?" she said from her bed. "What does that mean?"

"To tell you the truth, I don't really know," he said again, with a smile.

"But somebody has dreamed up the suspicion that Jakob Stillman is gay, is that it?"

"I don't know that I'd use the word 'suspicion.'"

"Call it whatever you like. I'm just wondering what all this is about."

"It's about this job I have, among other things," said Ringmar, shifting his position in the puffy armchair that was starting to sag after all these years. A bit like me, he thought. "We're testing various theories. Or hypotheses."

"Well, this one is way off base," she said.

"Really?" he said.

"Completely wrong."

"But you said you didn't know him," Ringmar said.

"He has a girlfriend. Vanna. I sent her to see you, didn't I?"

"You did."

"Well, then."

"Sometimes it's not that straightforward."

She didn't respond.

"Well?" he said.

"What would it mean, anyway?" she asked. "If he did turn out to be gay."

"To tell you the truth, I don't really know," Ringmar said.

"What exactly do we know?" asked Sture Birgersson, who was just about to light a new John Silver from the stub of his old one. The head of CID was standing in his usual place, in front of the window, behind his desk.

"I thought you quit," Winter said.

"My lungs feel better," Birgersson said, inhaling. "I thought I'd better reconsider."

"A healthy approach," said Winter.

"Yes, glad you think so." Birgersson held the cigarette in front of him, as if it were a little carrot. "But we have other questions to consider here, methinks."

"You've read the notes," said Winter.

"Do you need more people?"

"Yes."

"There aren't any more."

"Thank you."

"If things get any worse, I might be able to dig a few more out," said Birgersson.

"How can things get any worse?"

"Another victim, for Christ's sake. If someone dies."

"We could easily have had four dead bodies," said Winter.

"Hmm." Birgersson lit his cigarette using the glowing butt. "Bad, but not bad enough."

"Four murders," said Winter. "That would be a record, for me at least."

"And for me." Birgersson walked around his desk. Winter could smell the tobacco. As if the old tobacco factory down by the river had come back to life. "But you're right. It's nasty. What we're stuck with might be a serial killer who hasn't actually killed."

"Assuming it's the same person."

"Don't you think it is?"

"Yes, I suppose I do," said Winter.

Birgersson leaned backward and picked up three pieces of paper from his desk. Apart from them, it was empty, clear, shiny. There's something compulsive about him, Winter thought, as he always did when he was standing there, or sitting, as he was at the moment.

Birgersson read the documents again, then looked up.

"I wonder if this gay theory is valid," he said.

"It's only you and me and Lars and Bertil who know about it," said Winter.

"That's probably just as well."

"You've taught me to investigate through a bifocal lens," said Winter.

"Have I really? That was pretty well put." Birgersson stroked his chin. He looked Winter in the eye, possibly with just a trace of a smile. "Can you remind me what I meant by it?"

"Being able to look down and also forward at the same time. In this case, investigating several parallel motives."

"Hmm."

"It's obvious, really," said Winter.

"I didn't hear that."

"Like all great thoughts."

"Hear, hear," said Birgersson.

"The gay theory might give us a motive," said Winter.

"Have you managed to interview any of the kids again? With this idea in mind?"

"No, we've only just thought of it," said Winter.

Birgersson didn't respond, which meant that the discussion was over for the time being. Winter picked up his pack of Corps and removed the cellophane from one of the slim cigarillos.

Birgersson held out his lighter.

"You quit too," he said.

"It hurt too much," said Winter. "Now I feel better again."

———

Halders stood in the middle of Doktor Fries Square. Time stood still here, in this square that had been built during the era of the Social Democrats, when Sweden's welfare state was strong, when everybody was cared for from the cradle to the grave and looked into the future with confidence, anticipating the fulfillment of their dreams. In this square I'm a little boy again, Halders thought. Everything here is genuine; this is what it looked like then.

Flags, stone, concrete. But everything in the square was lovely then, dammit. Concrete soaring high over the ground. Not bad, not bad at all.

A few people were wandering around between the library, the community center, and the dentist's office that Halders knew Winter used. There was a pizza parlor, of course. A closed-down bank, of course. A newstand, post office (but not for much longer). A self-service store—a name that fit the square's appearance and age. For me this shop will always be a self-service store. That's a 1960s term.

Halders sat down on one of the benches outside Forum and drew a map in his notebook.

Stillman had passed by here, after climbing up the steps that lead down to the city center. He'd walked through the bushes, which must have been pitch black. There were other routes he could have taken. This had been the most awkward one. Perhaps the boy was a bit of an adventurer. Halders drew a line that Stillman must have walked, from where he was sitting to the point where the attacker had clubbed him down.

Almost the dead center of the square. He looked in that direction. Somebody might have been standing in the covered passageway in front of the self-service store. Or by the tobacconist's. Or the delicatessen on the other side. Crept forward with his club. A seven iron. Or a different iron. Or swished up on a bicycle. Or run like the devil on silent soles, and the young man who was tired and tipsy hadn't heard a thing. Too bad the victim didn't have a Walkman with Motörhead filling his brain at full volume. That would have explained a lot.

Perhaps they weren't alone. Halders kept thinking that when he made this follow-up visit to the various locations. Maybe they were with somebody but didn't want to say who, even though whoever it was had tried to kill them. Could that be the case? Were they protecting their own attacker? Huh. Halders had learned a lot in this job. It was a mistake to believe that people will behave rationally. The human psyche was an interesting piece of reality in that respect. Or frightening, rather. You had to take things as they came.

Not alone. Shielding somebody. Or ashamed of something? He looked down at his sketch again. Drew a dotted line to the bus and streetcar stop. Stillman had been on his way there, he'd said.

From where? He still hadn't been able to explain what he'd been doing here. Halders didn't buy all that stuff about just strolling around, going nowhere in particular. It was a long way from here to Olofshöjd and his dorm room. It's true that it's possible to go there from Slottskogen via Änggården and Guldheden, just as it's theoretically possible to stroll east from Gothenburg to Shanghai.

Had he been visiting somebody around here? In which case, why the hell didn't he say so? Did they go for a moonlit walk? We'll have to have another chat with him. And with the other students, a student from Uppsala-la-la-la-la, la-la-la-la-la, la-la-la-la-la. Halders hummed the tune as he got up from the bench and made his way to the delicatessen to buy lunch.

Winter lingered on the grounds after dropping off Elsa at the nursery school and waving to her through the window. She had turned away immediately and vanished, and it dawned on him that he and Angela were no longer the only ones in her life.

A lot of children were running around the grounds. Two supervisors, as far as he could see. There was a lot of traffic passing by—the second stage of the morning rush hour. I'll be joining the rush shortly.

A little boy was making his way through the bushes. Maybe the same one as last time, hoping to escape to freedom outside the fence.

Winter watched him disappear into the undergrowth. He'd soon be out again. Maybe he had a secret den among the bushes that he went to every day.

Winter walked down to the gate and looked to the right, expecting to see the boy on the other side of the bushes and inside the fence. But there was nobody in sight. He walked toward the bushes but still could see nothing, hear nothing. He approached closer still, noticed a loose bit of the thick steel wire, pulled at it, and felt the whole length open like a swinging door.

He turned around, but there was no little boy in brown overalls and a blue cap standing in the bushes, waving.

What the hell . . .

The opening was too small for him to clamber through. He jogged quickly to the gate and out into the street, but he still couldn't see the boy anywhere.

He walked the ten or so meters to the intersection, which was partially hidden from view by the evergreen bushes surrounding the nursery school, turned right, and saw the boy some twenty meters ahead of him, marching purposefully away.

By the time Winter got back to the nursery school with the boy, they had already called the register.

"We were going to have a snack," said the deputy manager, who was standing at the gate, looking worried.

"There's a hole in the fence," said Winter, putting down the boy who had allowed himself to be carried back without protesting.

"Good Lord," she said, squatting down in front of the boy. "Have you been out for a walk, August?"

The boy nodded.

"But you mustn't go outside the fence," she said.

The boy nodded again.

She looked up at Winter.

"I've never seen anything like this before." She looked in the direction of the juniper bushes. "How on earth can the fence have broken?"

"I don't know," said Winter. "I didn't have time to examine it. But you'd better have it fixed right away."

"I'll call this very minute," she said, standing up. "We'll keep the children indoors in the meantime."

Winter went back to the fence and secured the loose strand of wire. Another length came loose when a few rusty staples gave way. He was stronger than August, but nonetheless, the boy had managed to open up the gap, even if it was rusty to start with. Not encouraging. Winter thought of Elsa. Had she ever been to this hole in the fence with August before? Never go with strange men.

The whole group was playing some kind of hide-and-seek, the children were laughing and looked delightful. He'd have loved to run forward and stand against the wall and count to a hundred, then shout "Ready or not, here I come!" and then start looking and see somebody emerge from their hiding place and make a dash for it, but he would be faster and touch base first, and then they'd do it all over again with the same result, and everybody would say that he was the fastest and the best and then, when it was his turn to hide, nobody would find him, and he would dash out and touch base and win again. He would win every time.

He was crying now.

It was raining; he could see drops on the windshield.

The same voice on the radio again, always the same voice when he was out driving, when he felt as he felt now. When he wanted to be where the children were. Talk to the children, that's what he wanted to do. That was all.

The same voice, the same time, the same program, the same light in the sky. The same feeling. Would any of the children want to go with him, a bit farther? Go home with him? How would he be able to turn them down? Even if he wanted to?

The voices out there sounded like a swishing noise, just like the rain. He liked both sounds, the way in which they blended so softly and gently that made him want to sit there forever and ever and listen to them.

Then came that feeling that was a new feeling, and he knew that it made him feel frightened, and he tried to shake his head so that it would sink back down inside him like it had done before, but it didn't. It made him stretch and open the car door and step out onto the ground that was covered in rotting leaves that smelled more strongly than they had the previous time, and now he was standing at the side of the car and the feeling was getting even stronger, and it was like a band of steel across his chest. He could hear his own breathing, and it was so loud that he thought everybody else must be able to hear it as well. But nobody heard. Everybody ran. Everybody laughed. Everybody was happy and he didn't want to think about when he was that little and maybe had run and laughed just like they were doing. With Mom. Mom had always held his hand and the ground had been covered in leaves of many colors.

There was a little girl, running.

A good hiding place.

He followed her.

Here's a better one.

Yes. I'm playing with them as well. Now they're looking this way! What if they see you!

Here, here.

This is a better hiding place.

In here.

He'd seen this path before, a sort of corridor between the boulders and the trees where he'd left the car. Behind the hill. He was almost surprised by how easy it was to drive there from the parking lot.

This is the best place, over here. Nobody will find you here.

He felt the rain on his tongue when he realized it had been sticking out.

He'd thought the police would want to talk to him again, but why should they? He hadn't done anything. It was the other one. Everybody had understood that. They'd understood that at work. Have a rest for a few weeks, and we'll take a good look into what happened.

I don't need a few weeks. I need my work. That's what he'd told them. He'd answered their questions about what had happened, he'd told them everything.

Have you never had anybody like that in your streetcar? Somebody like that! Gothenburg is full of them, in the streetcars, in the buses. It was dangerous for the public, and dangerous for the drivers. Just look at this mess! Isn't this proof of what can happen? What *caused* the accident?

Yes, this is my car. Who'll be able to find you in here? This is the best place.

JANNE ALINDER STRETCHED OUT HIS ARM IN AN ATTEMPT TO EASE
the pain in his elbow. He raised it to an angle of about forty-five degrees, palm down, and it occurred to him that if anybody were to come into his office now it might look a little odd.

Johan Minnonen came in and stood behind him.

"Don't worry, I won't tell anybody," said Minnonen.

"Tennis elbow," said Alinder.

"Unusually straight for that."

"You can believe whatever you like."

"My dad fought on their side."

"Whose side?"

"The Germans, of course. Against the Russians."

"Not all Germans were Nazis," said Alinder.

"Don't ask me." Minnonen's expression became more somber. "I was too little. And Dad never came back home."

"I'm sorry to hear that," said Alinder.

"Neither did I, actually. Come home again, that is. I was sent to Sweden, and I stayed here." Minnonen hadn't sat down. "A war child, as they called us. My real name was Juha, Johan in Swedish."

"What about your mother?"

"Oh yes, we met again after the war; but there were a lot of us brothers and sisters. Ah well . . ."

Alinder knew that was as much as Minnonen was going to let on. He had never been as forthcoming as this before.

Oh my God; he realized that he still had his arm raised.

The telephone rang. He lowered his right arm and picked up the receiver. Minnonen clicked his heels and saluted, then left and made his way toward the police cars.

"Police, Majorna-Linnéstaden, Alinder."

"Er, yes, hello. My name is Lena Sköld. I called a few days ago about my daughter, Ellen."

Sköld, Sköld, Alinder thought. Daughter. He had some vague recollection.

"It was about Ellen. She said she'd been with, er, with some stranger or other."

"I remember now. How is she?"

"She's fine. Everything's normal."

"Hmm."

"Anyway, you said I should get in touch again if I thought that . . . that something was missing. I think that's what you said?"

If you say so, Alinder thought. Hang on a minute, yes, I remember now.

"Yes, I remember saying that."

"Well, she always has a good-luck charm in a pocket in her overalls, but it's missing," said Lena Sköld.

"A good-luck charm?"

"Yes, you know, one of those—"

"Yes, I know what it is. I mean . . ." Hmm, well, what the hell do I mean? "A charm, you say?"

"An old good-luck charm, one that I used to have myself when I was a kid. It's a sort of superstition thing, from me. It's supposed to bring you good luck."

Silence.

"Yes?"

"She always has it in the left-hand chest pocket of her overalls. A special extra pocket. I can't understand how . . ."

Silence again.

"Yes?"

He waited for whatever she was going to say next.

"I can't understand how it could have fallen out," said Lena Sköld.

"Could Ellen have taken it out herself?"

"No, I don't think so."

"And this is the first time?"

"What do you mean?"

"The first time it's been lost?" Alinder asked. A daft question, but what am I supposed to do? This is the type of conversation I don't really have time for.

"Yes, of course."

"What do you think happened?"

"Well, if what Ellen says is true, then it could be that the man in the car took it."

"Have you asked Ellen about him again?"

"Yes."

"And?"

"She says more or less the same thing as before. Odd that she should re-member, don't you think?"

I have a file with notes on what was said before, Alinder thought. I guess I can add a few sentences.

"Can you describe that charm for me," he said, picking up his pen.

"It's a little bird, silver," she replied.

Just a little thing. A souvenir. He'd be able to take it out and look at it, and that would be enough.

For now at least. No. No! That would be enough. Enough!

He knew that it wouldn't be enough. He would have to make use of it.

He closed his eyes and looked toward the wall and the bureau that stood next to the bookcase with the videos.

He had that little drawer in his bureau, with the boy's car and the girl's lit-tle silver bird. The car was blue and black, and the bird glistened and showed off a color of its own that wasn't like anything else.

He had in his hand the little ball that the other girl had had in her pocket. It was green, like a lawn at the height of summer. Maja, her name was. That was a name that also suggested summer. Maja. It wasn't a name for this time of year. He didn't like the autumn. He felt calmer in the summer, but now—now he wasn't so calm anymore.

He would go out driving, driving around. He drove around, didn't want to, but he couldn't help it. Playgrounds. Nursery schools.

Being there and joining in the fun.

He dropped the ball and it bounced up as high as the top drawer in the bureau, then down again, and he leaned to one side and caught it in one hand. A one-handed catch!

When it was so dark outside that he didn't need to draw the curtains in order to watch the video recording, he switched on the television.

Maja said something funny. He could hear himself laughing on the film. He smiled. He could see the rain on the car window behind her. The empty trees. The sky, empty. It looked so miserable out there, on the other side of the car windows. Gray. Black. Damp. Rotten. A sky that was gray or black or red like . . . like blood. No. Nasty. The sky is a big, nasty hole that's bigger than anything else, he thought, and he squeezed the ball hard in his hand. Things fall from the heavens that we are afraid of, run away from, hide from. The heavens are empty, but rain comes down from there and we can't get away from that, and that's why heaven is just a place on earth. Heaven is a place on earth, he thought again. He used to think about that when he was a child. Uncle had come to him when he'd been crying. The light had been out, and Uncle had asked him various things and then gone away. But later, he'd come back again.

It had hurt so much. But who had it been? Had it been Dad? Or Uncle? Uncle had comforted him afterward.

Comforted him so often.

He turned to the television again. It had been warm and cozy in the car. He'd felt warm as he shot the film. He could hear the radio as well. Then came the voice, and a swear word. The child had heard it. Maja. Maja said that the man on the radio has used a bad word.

Yes indeed. It was a very bad word.

What a nice ball you have, Maja. Show it to me.

Winter was sitting on the floor by the door in the long, narrow hall with his legs spread out, and he was rolling the ball to Elsa, who was sitting at the other end. He managed to roll the ball all the way to Elsa, but she couldn't roll it all the way back again. He stood up and sat down again a bit nearer.

"Ball stupid," Elsa said.

"It's easier now," he said, and rolled it to her again.

"The ball, the ball!" she shouted as she succeeded in rolling it all the way to him. "The ball, Daddy!"

"Here it comes," he said, rolling it back to her.

Elsa was asleep when Angela got home after her evening shift. A long day on the ward. Morning shift. A short rest. Evening shift. He heard the elevator clattering up to the landing outside, and opened the door before she had even reached it.

"I heard the elevator."

"So did everybody else for miles around." She took off her raincoat and put it on a hanger ready for transportation to the bathroom. "That elevator should have been retired thirty years ago." She took off her boots. "It's scandalous that the poor thing has to keep on working."

"But Elsa likes Ella being here and working for us," said Winter.

Ella Vator was Elsa's name. Just think, all these years I've lived here and traveled up and down in this elevator without knowing its name, Winter had thought when Elsa christened the old girl. Ella Vator.

"How did it go today?" said Angela, heading for the kitchen.

"Another incident at the nursery school," he said, following her.

"What this time?"

"I think it was the same little boy as before who ran off through the bushes, but this time he got out."

"Got out? Where? Who?"

"August, I think his name is. Do you know who that is?"

"Yes, I think so."

"There was a hole in the wire fence, and he got out into the street."

"Oh my God."

"I managed to catch up with him before anything happened."

"How the hell could there be a hole in the fence?"

"Rusted away."

"Oh my God," she said again. "What are we going to do?"

"What do you mean?"

"What are we going to do about Elsa? You don't think I'm going to leave her there when there's a hole in the fence leading out onto one of northern Europe's busiest roads?" She looked at him and raised a hand. "It's like a hole straight into the cruel world outside."

"They've fixed it."

"How do you know?"

"I checked." He smiled. "This afternoon."

"Have they replaced the whole fence?"

"It looks like it."

"Looks? Are you not as worried as I am?"

"I called the lady in charge, but I couldn't get through."

"Well, I'm going to get through."

She marched over to the telephone and called one of the numbers on a Post-it Note stuck onto the refrigerator.

Angela bit his knuckle when she felt that he was as close as she was. He heard a spring complaining in the mattress underneath them, a noise that could in fact have come from Ella on the landing, but he didn't think of that until afterward.

They lay still in the silence.

"Could you get me some water, please?" she asked eventually.

He got up and went to the kitchen. Rain was pattering on the window overlooking the courtyard. The wall clock showed a quarter past midnight. He poured a glass of water for Angela and opened a Hof for himself.

"You won't be able to sleep now," she said, as he drank the beer on the edge of the bed.

"Who said anything about sleeping?"

"I can't come and go as I please like you," she said. "I have strict working hours."

"I can be creative at any time of day or night," he said.

She took a drink of water and put the glass down on the wooden floor that seemed to gleam in the glow coming in from the street lighting outside. A bus could be heard driving past, tires on water. Then another vehicle. No ambulance at the moment, thank the Lord. A voice perhaps, but it could also have been a bird, hoarse from having stayed too long in the North.

That thought triggered another: Have we stayed here too long? Isn't it time we moved out of this stone city?

She looked at him. I haven't brought it up with him again. Perhaps that's because I no longer want to move away myself. You can lead a good life in Gothenburg. We are not country people. Elsa isn't complaining. She's even made friends with somebody on our floor. The fence around the nursery school has been mended. We can always rent a house in the country for the summer.

She looked again at Erik, who seemed to be lost in thought. Things between us are better now than they used to be, a year or so ago. I didn't know for certain then. I didn't know for certain for some time. I don't think he knew for certain either.

We could have been in different worlds. I could have been in heaven, and Erik here on earth. I think I'd have gone to heaven. I'm not sure about him. Ha!

I've forgotten about most of the experience. It was just bad luck.

She thought about what had happened during the months before Elsa was born. When she had been kidnapped by a murderer. How she had been kept in his apartment. What thoughts had gone through her mind.

I don't think he ever intended to hurt me.

Things are different now. It's good. This is a good time to be on earth. A good place.

She heard another noise from the street down below, a brittle sort of noise.

"A penny for your thoughts," she said to Erik, who was still sitting in the same position with an introspective look on his face, which she could make out, even in the half light.

He looked at her.

"Nothing," he said.

"I was thinking that we have it pretty good, you and me," she said.

"Hmm."

"Is that all you have to say?"

"Hmm."

She grabbed a pillow and threw it at him, and he ducked.

"Elsa will wake up if we start fighting," he said, putting down his bottle of beer and throwing his pillow, which thudded into the wall behind her and knocked a magazine off her bedside table.

"Try this on for size," she said, hurling his pillow back at him. He saw it coming.

"We actually found a little decomposing pile of newspapers outside the entrance," said Bergenhem, the first time he'd spoken at the morning meeting. "It was underneath an even more unpleasant pile of leaves."

"How come you didn't find it earlier?" asked Halders.

"We weren't looking, of course," said Ringmar. "We didn't know we should be looking for newspapers."

"Have we found any fingerprints?" asked Halders.

He rubbed at the back of his head, which was feeling stiff again. Stiffer than normal, if you could call this goddamn stiffness normal. He'd been cold out in the square the previous day.

"Beier's team is looking into it now," said Ringmar. "They're also trying to see if they can make out the date on the newspapers. They should be able to."

The forensic officers had looked doubtful when they were handed the rotting bundle.

"Pointless," said Halders. "Just as pointless as trying to find specific bicycle tracks at the places where the boys were clubbed down."

"Bicycle tracks?" said Bergenhem.

"It's my own theory," said Halders, sounding as if he were preparing for a DCI examination. "The attacker zoomed in on them on a bike. Silent. Fast. Unexpected."

"Why not?" said Winter. He didn't say that the same thought had occurred to him.

"It sounds like such an obvious possibility that all of us must have thought about it," said Bergenhem.

"Go on, rob me of my idea," said Halders.

"A newspaper boy on a bike," said Aneta Djanali.

"It doesn't have to match up exactly," said Halders.

"Speaking of newspaper boys," said Ringmar.

"Yes, go on," said Djanali.

"It's a bit odd, in fact. The newspaper delivery person for the buildings around Doktor Fries Square phoned in sick the morning Stillman was attacked," said Ringmar. "Just like when Smedsberg was almost clubbed down on Mossen."

"But Stillman didn't say anything about seeing anybody carrying newspapers," said Halders.

"Nevertheless."

"Nevertheless what?" said Halders.

"Let's leave that for the moment," said Winter, starting to write on the white board. He turned to face the group. "We've been discussing another theory."

The evening had moved on when Larissa Serimov sat down at the duty officer's desk. Moving on was an expression her father liked to use about most things. He had moved on himself, moving from the Urals to Scandinavia after the war, and he'd managed to have a child at an age when others were having grandchildren.

We'll go back there one of these days, Larissa, he always used to say, as if she had moved there with him. And so they did when it finally became possible, and when they got there she had realized, genuinely *realized*, that they had in fact moved together all those years ago. His return had been her return as well.

He had stayed there, Andrey Ilyanovich Serimov. There were people still living there who remembered him, and whom he remembered. I'll stay on for a few months, he'd said when she left for Sweden, and she'd been at home for three and a half days when she received the message that he'd fallen off a chair outside cousin Olga's house, and his heart had probably stopped beating even before he hit the rough decking that surrounded the big, lopsided house like a moat.

The telephone rang.

"Frölunda Police, Serimov."

"Is this the police?"

"This is the police in Frölunda," she repeated.

"My name is Kristina Bergort. I'd like to report that my daughter Maja was missing."

Serimov had written "Kristina Bergort" on the sheet of paper in front of her, but hesitated.

"I beg your pardon? You said your daughter *was* missing?"

"I realize that this might sound odd, but I think my little daughter was, well, abducted by somebody, and then returned again."

"You'd better start again, at the beginning," said Serimov.

She listened to what the mother had to say.

"Are there any marks on Maja? Injuries? Bruises?"

"Not as far as I can see. We—my husband and I—have only just heard about this from her. I called right away. We're going straight to Frölunda Hospital to have her examined."

"I see."

"Do you think that's a bit, er, hasty?"

"No, no," said Serimov.

"We're going anyway. I believe what Maja told us."

"Of course."

"And, she also told us he took her ball."

"He stole it? Her ball?"

"He took her favorite ball, a green one. He said he would throw it to her through the car window once she got out, but he didn't. And she doesn't have it now."

"Does Maja have a good memory?"

"She is very observant," said Kristina Bergort. "Here comes my husband. We're off to the hospital now."

"I'll meet you there," said Larissa Serimov.

10

THE HOSPITAL WAS SUFFUSED WITH A LIGHT THAT MADE PEOPLE in the emergency waiting room look even more ill. There seemed to be lots of waiting rooms. It looks like half of Gothenburg is here, Larissa Serimov thought. Despite the fact that this is a welfare state. We're not in the Urals. She found it difficult not to laugh. Emergency treatment was not a term that existed in Russia anymore. Emergency, yes—but treatment, no.

At least there was a doctor here, even if the line to see him was long.

The Bergort family were on their own in one of the side rooms. The girl was rolling a ball backward and forward, but her eyes were heavy. She'll sleep her way through the examination, Serimov thought, and shook hands first with the mother and then her husband. She could see that people were staring at her uniform, which was black with the word POLICE in grotesquely large print on her back. What's the point of that, she had thought the first time she put it on. To avoid being shot in the back? Or to encourage it?

"Yes, here we are," said Kristina Bergort.

"How much longer before your turn?" asked Serimov.

"I have no idea."

"I'll see what I can do," said Serimov, and went over to the desk. Kristina Bergort saw her talking to the nurse, then vanishing through a door behind it. Then she saw her emerge again with a doctor, who gestured toward the little family.

The doctor examined the girl. He had considered sedating her, but didn't.

Serimov waited outside. It struck her how calm the Bergort family was. The husband hadn't actually said a word so far.

They emerged, and she stood up.

"The doctor would like a word with you," said the mother, looking at her daughter sleeping in her father's arms.

"What was the outcome? What did he find?"

"Nothing at all, thank God." Kristina Bergort started walking toward the big glass doors. "I'll have another word with Maja tomorrow morning."

"You're welcome to call me again," said Serimov.

The mother nodded, and they left.

Larissa Serimov went back to the doctor's office. He finished dictating his summary into the tape recorder, then looked up and rose to his feet. This wasn't the first time she'd been in there. Police officers and doctors met frequently, especially in Frölunda, where the hospital and the police station were practically next door, separated only by the service road. Just a stone's throw away, she had once thought; and stones had been thrown, but by citizens expressing their views on law and order in the city. Ah well. Perhaps it had helped to make her feel at home in a country she didn't come from, or in the other one that she hadn't asked to live in, but was grateful for having been born in.

She knew the doctor.

"What's this all about, Larissa?"

"I don't really know."

"Does anybody know?"

"The mother was worried, and that's hardly surprising," said Serimov.

"The kid has an imagination, and a pretty lively one at times," he said. "The mother told me what happened, and, well, I don't really know what to think."

"You don't have to think anything at all. An examination is all we need."

"Which showed that she hadn't been interfered with, at least."

"At least? Are you suggesting there's something else, Bosse?"

"A few bruises on her arm. One on her back. Hard to say what caused them."

"Somebody holding her too tightly? Or something worse?"

"I asked about them. Didn't get a convincing answer. At first."

"What do you mean?"

"The father seemed to look the other way." He looked at her. "But perhaps it was just a feeling I had."

"What did the mother say?"

"That the girl had fallen off a swing and crashed into the frame. But then she seemed to remember why they had come here and said maybe this stranger the girl had gone off with did it."

"Is that possible? Falling into the frame of the swing? Could that have left those marks?"

"Well . . . The bruises are fresh."

"You're being evasive."

"It just struck me that it's not all that unusual for parents who beat their children to report such incidents as accidents. Or to dream up stories that would seem to fit in, sometimes amazing flights of fantasy."

"Like a girl going off with a stranger."

"Yes. But that's more your field," he said, answering the telephone that had just rung. He looked up with his hand over the receiver. "But I have to say it is possible that it's true."

Winter and Ringmar were preparing for the afternoon's interrogations. They were in Ringmar's office, which Winter thought was even gloomier than usual. It wasn't due exclusively to the late autumn weather outside.

"Did you repaper the place?" he asked.

"Of course. Last weekend, all on my own. I can do yours for you next Sunday."

"It's just that it looks darker," said Winter.

"It's my mood. Reflected in the walls."

"What's the matter?"

Ringmar didn't answer.

"Is it the usual?" Winter asked.

"It's Martin, of course."

"Still no word from him?"

"No."

"But Moa knows?"

"Where he is? I don't think so anymore. If she did I think she would've told me." Ringmar snorted and raised his arm, sneezed once into it, then twice. He removed his face from his arm and looked at Winter. "He calls her now and then. I think so, at least."

Bertil's eyes were watery. Winter knew that was due to the sneezing attack, but Bertil's situation was enough to bring tears to anybody's eyes. Why didn't the boy get in touch? Bertil deserved better than this. Winter knew him well enough to be certain of that.

"Ah well, I'm still in contact with my other child," said Ringmar, looking past Winter at the window, which had a narrow band of condensation across the bottom of it. "I suppose that's not all that bad an outcome." He looked at Winter. "Fifty percent success in the breeding stakes. Or however the hell you describe it."

"He'll come back," said Winter. "He's just on a journey, trying to find himself. Young people go searching, more than others."

"A journey to find himself? That was nicely put."

"Yes, I'm glad you think so."

"But for Christ's sake, he's nearly thirty. You call that young?"

"You keep calling me young, Bertil. And I'm over forty."

"Are you also on a journey to find yourself?"

"I most certainly am."

"Are you being serious?"

"I most certainly am."

"Searching for the meaning of life?"

"Of course."

"Do you still have far to go?"

"What do you think?" said Winter. "You're past fifty. You've got further to go than I do."

Ringmar looked past Winter again, at the window that reflected the fading afternoon light.

"I think I've found it," said Ringmar. "The meaning of life, the whole point of life."

"Let's hear it, then."

"Dying."

"Dying? Is that the only point of living?"

"That's the only point."

"For God's sake, Bertil."

"That's the way it feels right now, at least."

"There's medicine you can take for this, Bertil."

"I don't think I'm suffering from clinical depression."

"Well, you're not suffering from manic optimism, that's for sure," said Winter.

"Everybody has the right to feel depressed now and then," said Ringmar. "There are far too many people running around with a grin on their faces."

"I couldn't agree more."

"Far too many," said Ringmar.

"Why don't you have a talk with Hanne?" Winter suggested.

Hanne Östergaard was the police vicar who worked part-time in the police headquarters, and she'd been a great help to a lot of officers. She'd been a solid rock of support for Winter in one of his cases that had caused him extreme anguish.

"Why not," said Ringmar.

Ringmar did have a talk later that afternoon, but it wasn't with Hanne Östergaard.

Jens Book was propped up by pillows and didn't look especially comfortable, but he shook his head when Ringmar offered to rearrange the bedclothes.

Here we go again, Ringmar had thought as he entered Sahlgren Hospital, which was swarming with people in both civvies and white coats.

We should have an office here. Why has nobody thought of that before? I should get a bonus for the idea. We spend lots of our time here. We need some kind of practical and convenient arrangement. Maybe our own secretary? A whole team of doctors with the word POLICE printed in black on the back of their white coats? Vehicles that are a mixture of ambulance and police van? Firing range in the basement? His head was full of ambitious plans when he stepped into the elevator. The boy had had his plans rudely interrupted. No journalism studies for him for a while, if ever. Halders had suggested he set his sights on the Paralympic Games, and that was a comment from somebody who had come close to being a prospective competitor himself. If he'd wanted to and had the ability.

But Jens Book had started to regain mobility, first in his right shoulder and then slowly down through the rest of his body. There was life and hope. He had recovered some movement in his face, which made it possible for them to talk, but Ringmar wasn't sure what they should talk about. You don't always get the answers you want from your questions.

"Do you think he crept up on you on a bicycle?" he asked now.

The young man appeared to be thinking. He had been walking along the pavement at Linnéplatsen, past the video store. Hardly any traffic, dim light, mist over the park veiling the night sky.

"Maybe," he said. "It happened so quickly." He turned his head toward the pile of pillows. "But I didn't hear, or see, anything to make me sure that he was riding a bike."

"Nothing at all?"

"No."

The kid moved his head again.

"How's it going?" Ringmar asked.

"Well . . ."

"I heard that you're on the mend."

"It seems so."

"Can you move your right hand?"

"A little bit, yeah."

"Soon you'll be able to wiggle your toes."

Book smiled.

"We're still not absolutely clear about where you'd been that night," Ringmar said.

"Er, what do you mean?"

"Where you were coming from when you were attacked."

"What difference does it make?"

"Somebody might have followed you."

"From there? No, I don't think so."

"From where, Jens?"

"Didn't I say that I'd been to a party in, er, Storgatan I think it is? Just past Noon."

"Yes."

"Well, then."

"But you weren't there the whole time," Ringmar said.

"What do you mean?"

Ringmar looked down at his notebook. The page was empty, but sometimes it was a good idea to look as if you were checking information you already had.

"You left that party about two hours before the attack at Linnéplatsen took place."

"Who said that?"

Ringmar consulted his notebook again.

"Several of the people we've spoken to. It wasn't a secret."

"It sounds almost like I'm being accused of something."

"I'm not saying that."

"It sounds almost like that."

"I'm only trying to establish what you were doing. Surely you can understand that? If we're going to find this attacker, we have to walk in your footsteps, so to speak," Ringmar said.

Pure bullshit, he thought. I'm thinking like my daughter speaks.

The boy didn't answer.

"Did you meet somebody?" Ringmar asked.

"Even if I did, it's got nothing to do with this."

"In which case there's no harm in telling, is there?"

"Telling what?"

"If you met somebody," Ringmar said.

"Yes and no," said Book. His eyes were wandering all round the room.

Ringmar nodded, as if he understood.

⸻

"What year are you in?" asked Winter.

"My second."

"My wife's a doctor."

"Really?"

"She's a hospital doctor. General medicine."

"I suppose that's what I want to be."

"Not a brain surgeon?"

"It would be useful to be one, after this," said Aryan Kaite, grimacing slightly and touching his head with his left hand: The big bandage had been replaced by a smaller one. "The question is whether I'll be able to go on studying." He took down his hand again. "Thinking. Remembering. It's not certain that everything will still work."

"How do you feel now?" Winter asked.

"Better, but not good."

Winter nodded. They were in a café in Vasastan, chosen by Kaite. I should come here more often, Winter thought. It's relaxing. Interviewing people over coffee. There should be a sign outside: Coffee and Questions.

"I live just around the corner," Winter said.

"Working within walking distance, then," said Kaite.

"Yes, again," said Winter, and told him about the case he'd worked on a few years previously, the couple in the apartment fifty meters down the street who had been sitting so still. The odd circumstances regarding their heads. But he didn't say anything about that particular detail.

"I think I read something about that," said Kaite.

"We got the call from a newspaper boy," said Winter. "A young kid who became suspicious."

"I guess they see a lot," said Kaite.

"You didn't see a newspaper boy that morning, did you, Aryan?"

"When I had my head bashed in? I couldn't see anything at all."

"When you came up to Kapellplatsen, or just before you were attacked. You didn't notice a newspaper boy around? Or on the other side of the square? Near the buildings?"

"Why do you ask?"

"Did you see anybody carrying newspapers?"

"No."

"OK. I'll tell you why I'm asking. I take it you've heard that another young man was, er, attacked, in the same way? At Mossen?"

"Yes."

"He says he saw a newspaper boy shortly before it happened, but there was no newspaper boy there that morning. The usual person was sick."

"So it must have been a replacement."

"No. The usual one called in sick at the last minute, and they didn't have time to find anybody else."

"How does he know it was a newspaper boy he saw, then?"

"There was somebody carrying newspapers up and down staircases at four-thirty in the morning."

"Sounds like a newspaper boy," said Kaite.

"Exactly," said Winter.

"But isn't there something a bit fishy there? How could he know the usual delivery person was sick?" he asked. "He could have bumped into her. How did he know?"

"That's what we are wondering as well," said Winter, studying the boy's face—it was as black as Aneta Djanali's, but with different features from another part of Africa.

"Very odd," said Kaite.

"Where do you come from, Aryan?"

"Kenya."

"Born there?"

"Yes."

"Are there a lot of Kenyans living in Gothenburg?"

"Quite a few. Why?"

Winter shrugged.

"I don't hang out with any of them," said Kaite.

"Who do you hang out with, then?"

"Not many people."

"Fellow students?"

"Some of them."

"Who were you with that evening?"

"Eh?"

"When you were attacked. Who were you with then?"

"But I told you I was on my own."

"Before you came to Kapellplatsen, I mean."

"Nobody. I was just wandering around the streets."

"You didn't meet anybody?"

"No."

"Not at all? All evening?"

"No."

"It was a long night."

"Yes."

"And you didn't meet anybody later on, either?"

"No."

"And you expect me to believe that?"

"Why shouldn't you?" He looked surprised. "Is it that strange?"

"So you didn't know the person who clubbed you down?"

"What kind of a question is that?"

"Do you want me to ask it again?"

"You don't need to. If I knew who it was, I'd say so of course."

Winter said nothing.

"Why on earth wouldn't I?"

11

"WHAT WOULD YOU SAY IF I SAID 'BICYCLE'?" ASKED HALDERS.

"Is this some kind of word association game?" wondered Jakob Stillman.

"—What?" said Halders.

Stillman eyed the detective inspector with the shaved head and rough polo-necked shirt and jeans and heavy shoes. Who was he? Was there a mix-up during the arrest of a gang of aging skinheads?

He rolled carefully to one side. His head followed his body, and hurt. He couldn't shake off this constant headache. And this conversation was not making things any better.

"Word association game," he said. "You say something and I associate it with something else."

"If you'd said 'bicycle,' I might have said 'hit in the head,'" said Halders.

"Yes, that's a natural association."

Halders smiled.

"Do you understand what I'm getting at?" he asked.

"Is this how you conduct all your interviews?" Stillman wondered.

"You're studying law, is that right?"

"Yes."

"Haven't you gotten to the chapter on cognitive interrogation methodology?"

Stillman shook his head, which was a mistake. It felt as if something was loose inside it.

"Let's go on," said Halders. "Do you think it's possible that whoever attacked you was riding a bicycle?"

"I saw just a body, as I said to your colleague. And it all happened too quickly."

"Maybe that's why?" said Halders. "He was riding a bike?"

"Well, I suppose that's a possibility."

"You can't rule it out?"

"No. I guess not."

Halders checked his notes, which were detailed and comprehensive. It seemed that after the blow to his head he'd become more inclined to make notes. As if he didn't really trust his own mind anymore. Before that he'd often managed with notes recorded on the inside of his eyelids; but now he needed a notebook and a pencil.

"When Bert . . . DCI Ringmar asked you about the noises you'd heard—it seemed obvious that you didn't think they were human sounds. What might they have been, then?"

"I really don't know."

"What would you say if I said 'bicycle'?" said Halders.

"I don't know what to say," said Jens Book.

"I asked you if you'd met anybody after you'd left the party and before you were attacked, and you answered yes and no."

Book said nothing.

"It's an answer you really ought to elaborate on," said Ringmar.

"I did meet somebody," said Book.

"Who did you meet?"

"It has nothing at all to do with this," said Book.

"Why do you find it so hard to tell me?" Ringmar asked.

"For Christ's sake, can't I be left in peace?"

Ringmar waited.

"It's as if I've committed a crime," said Book. "I'm lying here paralyzed and smashed up and . . . and . . ." His face contracted and he burst into tears.

Ease off now Bertil, Ringmar thought.

"If you tell me who you met, that can help me to find whoever it was who attacked you," he said, and had the feeling that he'd said precisely that before, many times, to many victims.

"OK, what the hell," said Book. "I met a guy, OK?"

"That's completely OK," said Ringmar.

"OK," said Book again.

"Why was it so difficult to say that?"

The boy didn't respond. He was studying something behind Ringmar's head but Ringmar knew that there was nothing there to look at, nothing but a blank wall covered in paint that had never glistened. Hospital wards are very

much like Lutheran assembly halls, he thought, or maybe chambers for asce-
tic sects: Life is but a journey to death, and this is an opportunity to get there
a bit quicker.

"Who was it?" he asked.

"A . . . just a guy."

"A friend?"

Book nodded, carefully. It seemed like a solemn moment, as if he were
about to reveal his big secret. Which was exactly what he did.

"A close friend?"

"Yes."

"I'm not going to ask you how close," said Ringmar. "But I must ask you
if you met him at his place."

"Yes."

"I need his address."

"Why?"

Ringmar didn't answer that question. Instead, he asked:

"Did he go with you when you left?"

"Go with me?"

"When you left his home."

"Yes. Just a short way."

"What time was that?"

"I can't remember."

"When was it? In relation to when you were attacked."

"Er . . . Half an hour before, maybe."

"He lives near there, does he?"

Book didn't answer.

"Were you still together when you were attacked?"

"No."

"Where did you part?"

"A bit . . . A bit farther up the street."

"In Övre Husargatan?"

"Yes."

"Where exactly?"

"Just past Sveaplan."

"When?"

"When, er, it was just before that bastard came and knocked half my
head off."

"I want his name and address," said Ringmar.

"Don't we all?"

"I mean your friend's," said Ringmar.

It was more or less dark when they assembled again in Winter's office. There wasn't enough light in there to fill the corners.

"Can't you put that bloody cigarillo out just for once?" said Halders.

"I haven't even opened the pack yet," said Winter, with a look of surprise on his face.

"Prevention is the best cure," said Halders.

Ringmar cleared his throat and spread some of his papers out on the desk that Winter had just tidied.

"It was hard for the kid to come out with it," said Ringmar. "For Book, that is."

"I hope you managed to convince him that in principle we couldn't care less about his sexual orientation," said Winter.

"It's that 'in principle' that could get in the way," said Ringmar.

"Was his friend at home?"

"No reply when I called him."

"We'll have to pay him a visit." Winter looked at Bergenhem. "Will you have time this evening, Lars?"

"Yes. Just a formal check, I take it?"

"No," said Halders. "Bring him in here and give him a good whipping."

"Is that an attempt to be sarcastic?" said Bergenhem, turning to face Halders.

"Attempt?" said Halders.

"The time is absolutely crucial, Lars," said Winter. "But you know that as well as I do."

"His pansy friend didn't do it, for Christ's sake," said Halders.

"But he might have seen something," said Ringmar.

"In which case he'd have come and told us about it already," said Halders.

"You don't understand what it's like," said Bergenhem.

"What what's like?" asked Halders.

"Having to be secretive about it," said Bergenhem.

"No—but you do, do you?" wondered Halders.

"It takes a lot of courage to come out, or whatever they call it," said Bergenhem without seeming to have heard what Halders had said.

"Really?" said Halders. "How come then that you can't open a newspaper nowadays without reading about how some celebrity fairy has just come out of the closet?"

"It's different for celebrities."

Ringmar cleared his throat again.

"Got a sore throat, have you, Bertil?" Halders turned to look at Ringmar.

"Fredrik," said Winter.

Halders turned to look at Winter.

"There's something these four kids have in common, and it's not their sexuality," said Winter. "Can you repeat what you told me earlier, Fredrik?"

"I did a bit of checking up," said Halders. "They've all lived in the Olofshöjd student dorm."

Bergenhem whistled.

"The same goes for about half of all Gothenburg students, past and present," said Halders.

"Even so," said Bergenhem.

"Kaite and Stillman still live there now," said Winter.

"Smedsberg moved to the Chalmers student dorm," said Ringmar.

"Why?" Bergenhem wondered.

Nobody knew at this stage.

"And Book shares an apartment in Skytteskogen," said Halders. "No doubt they'll have to make it handicapped accessible now."

"What are we going to do about Olofshöjd?" asked Winter. "Any suggestions?"

"We don't have enough personnel," said Ringmar.

"We can check their halls, though," said Bergenhem. "The one where Kaite and Stillman live."

"Their rooms are in different halls," said Halders.

"Kaite said something odd when I spoke to him," Winter said. He fumbled for his pack of cigarillos in his breast pocket, and noticed Halders staring hard at him. "We were talking about Smedsberg having seen a newspaper delivery boy, and Kaite was wide enough awake to ask how the fake one could have known that he wouldn't run into the real one."

"Maybe he just took a chance and risked it," said Bergenhem. "The fake one, that is."

"That's not the point," said Winter. "The thing is that Kaite said 'her' when he was referring to the usual delivery person. 'He could have bumped into her,' he said. How could he know that it was a woman?"

"Maybe a slip of the tongue," said Bergenhem.

"Don't you think that's a very odd slip of the tongue?" said Winter.

"It could be that in a guy's world, it's always women who deliver newspapers," said Halders. "In his dreams. He lies awake and hopes they are going to drop in on him in the wee hours."

"How does this fit in with the gay theory?" wondered Bergenhem.

"Don't ask me," said Halders. "That's yours and Erik's theory, isn't it?"

12

BERGENHEM CROSSED SVEAPLAN WITH A STRONG WIND BEHIND
him. A sheet of newspaper went flying past the corner shop.

The buildings around the square looked black in the dusk. A streetcar rattled past to his right, a cold, yellow light. Two magpies took off as he rang the bell next to the nameplate. He heard a distant answer.

"I'm looking for Krister Peters. My name is Lars Bergenhem, from the Gothenburg CID."

No response, but a humming sound came from the door and he pulled it open. There was no smell in the stairwell, as if the wind had blown in and cleansed it. The walls on each side were dark as the building's facade.

Bergenhem waited for an elevator that never appeared.

He walked up the stairs and rang the bell next to the door labeled Peters. The door opened a couple of inches after the second ring. The man peering though the crack could've been the same age as Bergenhem. Five or six years older than the students.

He stared at Bergenhem. His dark hair hung down over his forehead in a way that looked intentional, fixed with some kind of gel or spray. It looked as if he hadn't shaved for three or four days. He was wearing a white vest that stood out against his tanned and muscular body. Of course, Bergenhem thought. No, you shouldn't be prejudiced. The guy is just uncombed and unshaven and fit.

"Can I see your ID," said the man.

Bergenhem produced his card and asked, "Krister Peters?"

The man nodded and gestured toward Bergenhem's right hand holding the plastic pocket with his ID:

"That could be a fake."

"Can I come in for a few minutes?"

"You could be anybody," said Peters.

"Have you had bad experience with people knocking on your door?" asked Bergenhem.

Peters gave a little laugh, then opened the door fully, turned his back on apartment Bergenhem and went into his apartment, which opened out in all directions from the hall. Bergenhem could see the buildings on the other side of the square. The sky looked lighter from inside here, more blue, as if the apartment building soared up above the clouds.

He followed Peters, who sat down on a dark gray, expensive-looking sofa. A pile of magazines stood on a low glass table. To the right of the magazines were a glass and a bottle, and a misty little carafe containing what could have been water. Bergenhem sat down on an armchair that matched the sofa.

Peters stood up.

"I'm forgetting my manners," he said, left the room, and came back with another glass. He sat down again and held up the bottle. "A drop of whiskey?"

"I don't think I should," said Bergenhem.

"It's after twelve," said Peters.

"It's always after twelve somewhere or other," said Bergenhem.

"Hell, it's noon in Miami, as Hemingway said when he started drinking at eleven o'clock."

"I'll pass this time," said Bergenhem. "I came by car and I have to drive home when I leave here."

Peters shrugged, poured a couple of fingers into his glass, and topped it up with water.

"You're missing a pretty decent Springbank," he said.

"There might be other times," said Bergenhem.

"Perhaps," said Peters. He took a drink, put down his glass, and looked at Bergenhem: "When are you going to get to the point?"

"What time was it when Jens Book left you?" Bergenhem asked.

"Nasty business," said Peters. "Will Jens ever be able to walk again?"

"I don't know."

"It's unbelievable. Only a couple of blocks away from here." Peters took another drink, and Bergenhem could smell the alcohol. He could always leave the car here and take a taxi home. Hell, it's noon in Torslanda.

"You were in the vicinity when it happened," said Bergenhem.

"Yes, it appears so."

"Jens wasn't especially forthcoming about that," said Bergenhem.

"About what?"

"That he'd been to see you."

"Really."

"That he was with you shortly before the attack."

"Really."

Bergenhem said nothing.

Peters held his glass in his hand but didn't drink from it.

"I hope you don't think I beat him up?" he said. "That I crippled him and he knows I did but is protecting me?" Peters took a drink. Bergenhem couldn't see any sign of intoxication.

"Is that what you think?" Peters repeated.

"I don't think anything at all," said Bergenhem. "I'm simply trying to find out what actually happened."

"Facts," said Peters. "Always the facts."

"According to Jens you separated about half an hour before he was clubbed down."

"That could be," said Peters. "I don't know exactly when it happened, of course. When was he attacked?"

"Where was that?" asked Bergenhem. "Where did you separate?" He glanced down at his notebook, where it said "just past Sveaplan," as Book had told Ringmar.

"It was just outside here," said Peters, gesturing toward the window. "A little ways down the street from Sveaplan."

"Exactly where?"

"I can point it out to you later if it's important."

"Good."

Peters seemed to be racking his memory.

"What happened next?" asked Bergenhem.

"What happened next? You know what happened next."

"What did you do immediately after Jens had left?"

"What did I do? I smoked a cigarette, then came back in and listened to a CD, and then I took a shower and went to bed and fell asleep."

"Why did you go out into the street with him?"

"I needed some air," said Peters. "And it was a pleasant night. It was only blowing half a gale at that point."

"Did you see anybody else out there?" asked Bergenhem.

"No pedestrians," said Peters. "A few cars went by. In both directions."

"Were you watching Jens?"

"While I was smoking the cigarette, yes. He even turned around at one point and waved. I waved back, finished the cigarette, and went back in."

"And you didn't see anybody else in the street?"

"No."

"Nobody else walking down the street?"

"No."

Bergenhem could hear sounds from the street down below, which was one of the busiest in Gothenburg. Suddenly he heard an ambulance siren. The hospital was not far away. Then he recognized the music Peters was playing.

"The Only Ones," he said.

Peters bowed in acknowledgment. "Not bad. You should be too young for the Only Ones."

"Has Jens been here on more than one occasion?" Bergenhem asked.

"Yes."

"Have you received any threats?"

"I beg your pardon?"

"Has anybody ever threatened you?"

Peters said nothing. He took another drink, just a sip. Bergenhem could smell the high-quality malt again. The Only Ones continued their dark, 1980s journey through the world of drugs; a dark mass of music hovered over the room.

"Of course there have been threats," said Peters. "Once people find out that you're gay, you're always exposed to that risk."

Bergenhem nodded.

"Do you understand what I mean?" asked Peters.

"I think so," said Bergenhem.

"I'm not sure you do," said Peters.

"Do you understand what I'm getting at?" asked Bergenhem.

Peters thought it over. He held onto his glass but didn't drink. The music had finished. Bergenhem saw a black bird fly past the window, and then another. A telephone rang somewhere in the apartment, and again, and again. Peters didn't move a muscle. The music started again, something Bergenhem didn't recognize. The telephone kept on ringing. Eventually the answering machine picked up. Bergenhem could hear Peters's voice, but no message afterward.

"Surely you don't mean that whoever hit Jens was really after me?" said Peters in the end.

"I don't know."

"Or that he was after Jens because of, well, for some special reason?"

Bergenhem didn't reply.

"That he was being targeted? Because he's gay?"

"I don't know," said Bergenhem.

"Well, I suppose that could be the case." Peters held up his glass. It was empty now. "That sort of thing doesn't surprise me anymore."

"Tell me about when you've felt threatened," said Bergenhem.

"Where do I start?"

"The last time."

Aneta Djanali parked by the curb and they got out of the car. Halders was massaging the back of his neck as he watched Djanali lock the doors. She turned around.

"Does it hurt?" she asked.

"Yes."

"I could give you a massage this evening."

"I'd like that," said Halders.

Djanali checked her notebook, and they walked to the entrance of the student dorm. There was a bicycle in the stairwell. A noticeboard was plastered with layer upon layer of messages and a big poster at the top advertised the autumn ball at the student union—which had taken place ages ago.

There was a vague smell of food, an aroma that had accumulated over decades of inventive cooking skills applied to cheap ingredients. Halders had lived in a student hall while he was at police college in Stockholm. He recognized the smell immediately.

"It smells just like the hall I lived on as a student," he said.

"Toasted sandwiches and minced meat sauce," said Djanali.

"Baked beans," said Halders.

Aneta Djanali laughed out loud.

"What's so funny?" asked Halders.

"In the hall where I lived we had a girl whose diet consisted exclusively of baked beans, and she used to eat them straight out of the can, with a spoon, without heating them up. It made me feel sick."

"Don't baked beans always have that effect?" wondered Halders.

Djanali breathed in the aroma again.

"Isn't it strange how we have memory chips that kick in as soon as we come across a particular smell?" she said. "That smell is familiar, and so all the memories come flooding back."

"I hope it doesn't make you feel too ill," said Halders. "We're out on business."

"But do you know what I mean?"

"Only too well," said Halders. "There are things I thought I'd forgotten all about, but now they come tumbling out, just like you said."

"I hope they don't influence you too much," said Djanali with a smile.

"Speaking of that girl's diet," said Halders. "You should have seen what me and my friends used to eat."

"I'm glad I didn't," said Djanali, and she rang the bell of the hall where Gustav Smedsberg had lived before transferring to Chalmers. Jakob Stillman had a room on the floor directly above, when he wasn't in Sahlgren Hospital. He'd soon be back here again.

Aryan Kaite lived in the dorm next door. That didn't necessarily mean that the boys knew one another, or would even recognize one another if they met in the street. This is a pretty anonymous environment, Djanali thought. Everybody minds his or her own business and studies and occasionally slips out into the communal kitchen to fix a bite to eat, then slips back into their room with a plate, and the only time they look at anybody else is when there's a party. Then again, there's always a party. I remember in my day it was Saturday every day of the week, every week. Maybe it's still like that today. If it's always Saturday, good for them. For me nowadays it always seems to be Monday. Well, maybe not anymore.

Halders read the list of nameplates.

"Maybe one of these people has a grudge against his neighbor?" he said.

"Hmm."

"Here comes one of them," he said, as a girl appeared on the other side of the glass door. Halders held up his ID, and she opened it.

"I remember Gustav," she said.

They were sitting in the communal kitchen. Halders's and Djanali's memories were all around them, a swarm of baked beans. Everything was familiar, time had stood still in there just as it had in all other student halls in every city in the country. It smelled like it always had. If I opened the fridge door, I'd be back in my prime, Djanali thought.

"So he was clubbed down?" asked the girl.

"No," said Halders. "He was attacked, but he escaped uninjured, so he is a very important witness for us."

"But . . . why are you here, then?"

"He lived here not long ago."

"So what?"

It wasn't an impertinent question. She doesn't look the impertinent type, Halders thought.

"This whole business is so serious that we're trying to pin down everybody the victims might have come into contact with," said Djanali.

"But you said Gustav wasn't a victim?"

"He could easily have been," said Djanali.

"Why did he move out of here?" asked Halders.

"I don't know," said the girl, but he could see she wasn't telling the truth, the whole truth, and nothing but the truth.

"He didn't exactly trade up by moving to the Chalmers dorm," said Halders.

She shrugged.

"Did he have a dispute with anybody here?" Halders asked.

"A dispute? What kind of a dispute?"

"Anything from a minor difference of opinion to all-out war with air raids and antiaircraft fire," said Halders. "A dispute. Some sort of dispute."

"No."

"I'm only asking because this is such a serious case," he said. "Or series of cases."

She nodded.

"Is there any special reason why Gustav moved out of here?" Halders asked again.

"Have you asked him?"

"We're asking you. Now."

"Couldn't he tell you himself?"

Neither Halders nor Djanali said anything. They just kept on looking at the girl, who looked out of the window that was letting in the mild November light. She turned to look at them.

"I didn't know Gustav all that well," she said.

Halders nodded.

"Not at all, really."

Halders nodded again.

"But there was something," she said, and stared out of the window again, as if looking for that something so that she could show it to them.

"What, exactly?" Halders asked.

"Well, a dispute, to use your word." She looked at Halders. "Not quite antiaircraft fire, but there were a few occasions—several occasions—when he yelled into the telephone, and sometimes there was shouting, sort of, coming from his room."

"What kind of shouting?"

"Well, just shouting. You couldn't hear what they were shouting. It was just a few occasions."

"Who is 'they'?" asked Djanali.

"Gustav, and the person in there with him."

"Who was that?"

"I don't know."

"Was it a he or a she?"

"A he. A guy."

"Was there more than one?"

"Not as far as I could see."

"You mean you saw him?"

"I don't know for sure if it was the one who was shouting. But a guy did come out of his room shortly after I'd heard them shouting. I was on my way to the kitchen and he came out of the room and headed for the stairs." She nodded in the direction of the landing. "From the corridor."

"Did you see him on several occasions?"

"No. Just once."

"Who lives in Gustav's old room now?" asked Djanali.

"A girl," she said. "I've hardly met her either. She's only just moved in."

"Would you recognize the guy who came out of Gustav's room?" asked Halders.

"I really don't know," she said, looking at Aneta Djanali. "It's not so easy. It was just the color of his skin. Plus there are lots of them living here."

"Now you've lost me," said Aneta Djanali.

"Just because people have the same colored skin, that doesn't mean that they look alike," said the girl, and started gesticulating. "This has always both-ered me. The fact that people's appearance gets tied up with the color of their skin." She seemed to smile, briefly. "And it's not just us, in the so-called West-ern world. There are people in China who can't tell one white person from another." She nodded at Aneta Djanali. "I guess you're familiar with this. Or have thought about it, at least."

"So this guy who came out of Gustav Smedsberg's room—you're saying that he wasn't white?" asked Djanali.

"No, he looked like you. He was black. Didn't I say that?"

He saw a flash of sunlight as he emerged from the apartment building where he lived, a reflection. It was an ugly building, but the flash of sun was beautiful.

Other people said that the sun comes from the sky, but he knew better. The sun comes from somewhere else, where it's warm and quiet and every-body is nice to one another. A place where there's nobody who . . . who does things people shouldn't do. Where children dance, and grown-ups dance alongside them, and play and laugh.

He suddenly felt sweat on his brow, but it wasn't the sun—it wasn't warm enough.

Since he'd been . . . forced, yes, actually *forced* to stay away from work, things had gotten worse.

Pacing around and around the apartment.

The films? No, not now. Yes. No. Yes, yes.

Things had gotten worse.

He went to the chest of drawers and took out the things that had belonged to the children and held them in his hand, one after another. That amusing little silver thing that was a bird. He spent ages wondering what kind of bird it was. A canary, perhaps? It certainly wasn't a Rotty, ha ha.

The green ball was also fun, soft and terrific for bouncing. It didn't look like it would be a good bouncer, and felt very soft when you picked it up—but boy, could it bounce!

Now he was holding the car. The little blue-and-black car he'd gotten from the boy he'd chatted with that first time. It was the same car. No, it was the same make. He wasn't exactly an expert, but surely it was the same make as his own car? Yes. Kalle, that was the boy's name, and it had been such fun, sitting in the car and talking to Kalle. What's that you've got? Can I take a look? Hmm. Lovely, isn't it? I've got a car too. It looks just like this one. But a little bit bigger. No, not just a little bit. A lot bigger! Much, much bigger! It's the one we're sitting in now. We can go for a little drive in this car, and you can drive your car at the same time, Kalle.

But that isn't what had happened. Not that time.

He drove Kalle's car over the floor, through the living room and then over the threshold into the kitchen, brrrmmm, *Brrrmmm;* it echoed all round the room when he imitated the sound of the engine, *Brrrrmmmmm!*

And now he was opening the door of the big car. The sweat was still there on his brow. Worse than ever.

He drove. He knew where he was going. His face hurt because he was clenching his teeth so hard. No, no, no! He only wanted it to be fun. Nothing else, *nothing else,* but as he drove he knew that it would be different this time, and so it didn't matter that when he tried to turn left he actually turned right at the first intersection, and then at the second one.

He could have driven with his eyes closed. The roads followed the streetcar tracks. He followed the streetcar tracks. He could hear the streetcars even before he saw them. The rails glinted in the sun, which was still shining. He kept as close to them as possible, because when he did that he didn't feel so frightened.

13

THE LIGHT OVER THE FIELDS WAS AS SOFT AS WATER. IT SEEMED as if everything was sinking down toward the ground. Trees. Rocks. Fields glowing black, the soil plowed into furrows, like a sea that had stiffened and would not thaw and come to life until the spring.

What am I doing? What have I done? What *have I done*?

He could see a tractor in the distance. He couldn't hear anything, but saw that it was moving. It had been working out there in the fields for so long that its paint had rubbed off and disappeared, and so everything out there was the same color, the machine and the countryside, the same rubbed-off November glow that always seemed to be gliding through the day toward dusk.

He felt calmer now, after driving for an hour, but he knew that was only temporary, just as everything all around him was temporary. No. Everything around him was not temporary. It's eternal, he thought. It's bigger than anything else.

I wish I loved it, but I hate it.

He turned in through the gates that seemed to have acquired a new layer of rust on top of the old one. The farm road was almost the same as the fields out there, churned up by the tractor wheels that were still rotating out on the prairie.

He was standing in the farmyard now.

I once dreamed about the prairie. I could have had a horse and ridden through that glade and never come back.

I could have flown in the sky. Lots of people could have seen me.

I'll do that one day.

The wind was whipping pieces of straw and twigs into a circle in the middle of the yard.

There was a smell of dung, as always, and straw and seeds and soil and rotten leaves and rotten apples and rotting wood. The smell of animals lingered on even though there were no animals left.

Not even Zack. He walked over to the dog pen that seemed to be hovering above the ground, as if waiting for the wind to come and whisk it away over the fields and roads.

He missed Zack. Zack was a friend when he needed a friend, and then Zack had passed away and everything had been as it had always been.

He heard the tractor approaching down the road, and soon it would grunt its way in through the gate and stop more or less where he was standing now.

He turned around. The old man parked the tractor, turned off the engine, and clambered down in a way suggesting habit rather than agility. His body would keep on moving as per routine long after it had lost all its softness.

All its softness, he thought again. When you're a child everything inside you is soft and everything outside you is hard, and you eventually become hard as well.

The old man limped up to him.

"Been a long time," he said.

He didn't reply.

"I didn't recognize the car," said the old man.

"It's new."

"It don't look new," said the old man, staring at the hood.

"I mean it's one you haven't seen before."

The old man looked at him. There were specks of dirt on the old man's face. He'd always looked like that. It had nothing to do with age, didn't mean that he could no longer take care of his personal hygiene or anything like that.

"Shouldn't you be at work?" the old man asked. "It's the middle of the day, a weekday." He looked up at the sky as if to get confirmation of the time. Then he looked back at his visitor and snorted: "But you couldn't have driven your streetcar here." He snorted again. "That'd been something to look at."

"It's my day off," he said.

"A long way to drive."

"Not all that far."

"You might as well live at the other side of the globe," said the old man. "What could it be?" He looked up again at the Big Calendar in the Sky. "Is it four years since you were last here? Five?"

"I don't know."

"Typical."

He heard the beating of wings overhead. He looked up and saw a few crows flying from the cowshed to the farmhouse.

"Now that you're here you'd better have a cup of coffee," said the old man.

They went in. He recognized the smell in the hall, and suddenly he was back here again, but at a different time.

He was a little boy again.

Everything in the house looked just the same as before. There was the chair he used to sit on at that other time. She had sat opposite him, big, red.

She had been nice, at first she had, that was when he could still feel that his boyish body had softness in it, when it still wasn't too late.

Was that the way it was? Did he remember correctly?

It belonged to that other time. Then those misters and ladies had decided that he shouldn't live with his mom. He'd gotten a foster father, and the old man was fussing at the stove now and the water was bubbling away after a while, and the old man produced a couple of cups and saucers from the cupboard behind him.

"Yes, nothing's changed, as you can see," he said, and served up a little basket full of buns, still in their plastic wrapping.

"Yes."

"Not as neat and tidy as it used to be, but apart from that, nothing's changed," said the old man.

He nodded. Assumed it was a joke.

The old man served coffee, then sat down again and looked at him just as he used to do, with one eye sinking down and the other lifted up.

"Why did you come here?"

"I don't know."

He'd been back a few times. Perhaps because this was the nearest he'd had to anywhere that could be called home. And he'd liked the countryside, no doubt about that. All those smells.

"I wrote," he said.

"That's not the same thing."

He took a sip of coffee that tasted like the soil in the fields outside must taste, or the tar that had been used to upgrade the farm road when he used to live here. That was a smell to remember.

"What are you after, then?" said the old man.

"What do you mean?"

"What do you want?"

"I don't want anything. Do I have to want something?"

The old man drank some coffee and took a bun, but only held it in his hand.

"I've got nothing to give you," he said.

"Since when have I asked for anything?"

"Just so as you know," said the old man, who then took a bite of the bun and kept on speaking with his mouth full. "There's been a break-in here. In the cowshed, just imagine that. Somebody breaks into a cowshed where there's no animals and nothing to steal. For Christ's sake."

"How do you know there was a break-in, then?"

"Eh?"

"How do you know there was a break-in if there wasn't anything to steal?"

"You see that kind of thing if you've had the same cowshed all your life. You see if somebody's been in there." He washed the bun down with a mouthful of coffee. "You see that kind of thing," he said again.

"Really."

"Oh yes."

"But nothing was taken?"

"A few things, but that doesn't matter." The old man was staring into space now. "That's not the point."

He said nothing,

"The point is that you don't want anybody prowling around when you're not there. Or are fast asleep in bed."

"I can understand that."

The old man looked at him, his eyes pointing in different directions.

"You don't look all that well," he said.

"I've been, er, been sick."

"What's been up with you?"

"Nothing serious."

"Flu?"

"Something like that."

"So you came here to get a whiff of cow shit."

"Yes."

"Well, all you need to do is breathe in deeply," said the old man, who snorted again, although he might have been laughing.

"I have."

"Take as much as you like."

He raised his cup to his mouth again but couldn't bring himself to drink. The damp air in the kitchen made him shudder. The old man hadn't had time to light a fire after his work in the fields. God only knows what he'd been doing out there.

"I think I have a few things here still."

The old man didn't respond, didn't seem to have heard.

"I was thinking about it the other day, and I remembered a few things."

"What kind of things?"

"Toys."

"Toys?" The old man refilled his cup, the black sludge that could kill. "What do you want toys for?" He looked hard at his visitor. "Don't tell me you have a kid?"

No answer.

"Do you have a kid?" the old man asked again.

"No."

"I didn't think so."

"They are my . . . memories," he said. "My things."

"What are these toys you're on about?"

"They're in a box, I think."

"Oh Lord, for God's sake," said the old man. "If there's anything it's upstairs, and I haven't been up there since Ruth died. " He stared at his visitor again. "She asked about you."

"I'll go up and take a look," he said, getting to his feet.

The stairs creaked just like they used to.

He went into the room that was once his.

It smelled of nothing, as if this part of the house no longer contained any memories. As if everything had disappeared when the old man stopped using the upstairs and made up a bed in the small room behind the kitchen. But things hadn't disappeared, he now thought. Nothing disappears. They are still there, and they're getting bigger and stronger and more awful.

The faint afternoon light was trying to force its way in through the little window at the gable end. He switched on the light, which was a naked forty-watt bulb hanging from the ceiling. He looked around, but there wasn't much to see. A bed that he hadn't slept in. An armchair he remembered. Three wooden chairs. A wobbly table. Three overcoats were hanging on a rail to the right.

There was sawdust on the floor, in three little piles. There were a few cardboard boxes in the far corner under the window, and he opened the one on the left. Underneath a few tablecloths and handkerchiefs he discovered the two things he was looking for: He picked them up, tucked them under his left arm, and carried them down to his car.

The old man came out.

"So you found something?"

"I'll be going now," he said.

"When will I see you again, then?" asked the old man.

Never, he thought.

Winter parked behind the building that contained half the shops in Doktor Fries Square. It wasn't his first time here. Once he'd had a toothache so bad that he had had double vision for a few seconds before getting out of his car. When Dan, his dentist, had touched the tooth responsible Winter had felt for his gun. Not really. But the tentative touch by the dentist had almost made him lose consciousness.

This time he wasn't going to visit the dentist. That might have been better. Young men being viciously attacked was worse.

The square was practically deserted. This could be the 1960s, he thought. That's what it looks like here. I must have been four years old, maybe three. I must have been here as a three-year-old. Dad's dentist had his office here even then. It must have been around here, surely?

His mobile vibrated in the inside pocket of his overcoat.

He looked at the screen.

"Hello Mom."

"You saw my number, Erik?"

"As usual."

"Where are you now?"

"At Doktor Fries Square."

"Doktor Fries Square? Are you at the dentist's?"

"No." He stepped to one side to avoid two young women, each of them pushing a stroller. "This is where Dad used to go to the dentist's, wasn't it?"

"Yes, I think so. Why do you ask?"

"It doesn't matter." He could hear the rustling in the mobile all the way from Nueva Andalucía to 1960s Gothenburg. Perhaps she was reading a newspaper at the same time. "What's it like on the sunshine coast?"

"Cloudy," she said. "It's been cloudy all day, and yesterday as well."

"That must be awful," he said. "Cloudy on the Costa del Sol."

"Yes."

"What's the Spanish for Cloudy Coast?" he asked, taking out his pack of Corps and lighting a cigarillo. It tasted like a part of the early winter surrounding him, a dark taste filled with heavy aromas.

"I don't know," she said.

"You've been living down there for years and years and you still don't know the Spanish word for cloud?"

"I don't think there is one," she said.

He laughed out loud.

"Did you know that the Japanese don't have a word for blue?" he asked.

"Ah, I know the Spanish for that," she said. "It's *azul*."

"*El cielo azul*," said Winter, gazing up at the gray sky overhead.

"The sun is just beginning to break through over the sea," she said. "This very minute, as we're speaking."

He knew what it looked like. Some years previously he had spent a few days in a hot Marbella in early autumn while his father was dying in the local hospital.

One morning he'd left the breakfast table at Gaspar's and walked down to the beach under a leaden sky, and in the space of a few seconds the clouds over the Mediterranean had been torn apart and the sun swept over the water all the way to Africa.

"Was there something special you wanted to talk about?" he asked.

"Christmas," she said. "I've been thinking about it again. Will you be able to come here for Christmas? You know I've asked you before."

"I'm not sure if it will be possible."

"Think about Elsa. She'd enjoy it so much. And Angela."

"What about me?" he said.

"You too, Erik. You would too."

"I really don't know what the work situation is for both of us," he said. "It's not quite clear what will happen on Angela's ward."

"There must be other doctors, surely?"

"There are not many available when it's a big holiday."

"Make sure that Angela can get away," she said. "What does she say about coming to Spain?"

"Can't you come home instead?" he asked.

"I'll be coming in the spring. But it would be such fun to celebrate Christmas with you all down here. We've never done that."

"Have you asked Lotta?"

His sister made regular visits to his mother, with her two teenaged daughters.

"She and the girls are probably going to do something with some close friends."

"What's his name?" asked Winter, thinking about how his sister was trying to find a new man after her grim divorce.

"She didn't say anything about a him."

"OK, I'll look into it."

"Don't interfere in her life, Erik."

"I meant that I'll look into the possibility of getting time off so that we can visit you over Christmas."

"You should have done that already, Erik."

He didn't respond.

"I can make a Christmas ham," she said.

"No, no! If we come we want fish and shellfish."

Winter found it hard to picture his mother in front of a stove; she had never been that kind of mother. She could stoop over a counter in the kitchen, but that would be in order to cut slices of lemon for some drinks, or to prepare a cocktail shaker. A drink or two too many at times. But she had always been good. She had treated her children with respect. He had grown up to become a man who tried to do the same with the people he came across. He had a reason. Far too many people didn't have a solid base against which to brace themselves when the going got tough.

"It's almost December," she said. "You should be booking flights. It might be too late already."

"So you should have called earlier," he said.

She said nothing.

It suddenly dawned on him why. She had been waiting for as long as she could in the hope that he would ask her if they could visit her over Christmas. She'd only been hinting that they should before. Now she couldn't wait any longer.

"I'll look into reservations," he said.

Why not? Over twenty degrees, lots of places with good tapas, and a few extremely good restaurants. It was only one Christmas. He'd spent so many in Gothenburg wrapped up in a shawl of freezing cold winds from the sea. Long days between Christmas and New Year's when it never became fully light out but everything was enveloped by a mist that a poor detective was unable to see through as he staggered through the city in search of answers to riddles. Holmes. My name is Sherlock Winter Holmes.

They hung up. He stood there in the square for a moment without the slightest idea of why he'd gone there.

He drove back to town, leaving the plain behind him and all the smells associated with that world.

His head had been overfilled with memories, and now he tried to get rid of them, to let them blow away through the open window. The slipstream tugged at his hair and his cheeks. It felt good.

He followed a circular route he knew well. The network of highways sucked him slowly in toward the city center, like a spiral rotating inward. Or downward, he thought as he stopped for a red light in the Allé.

He parked at the same place as before. It might have been exactly the same spot. No. He used the maple tree as a marker, and that showed him it was a slightly different spot.

He touched his forehead and felt the sweat. The back of his neck was also wet, and the back of his head.

He touched the parrot hanging from his rearview mirror. Bill was with him. He touched the little bear on the seat next to him. Odd that he'd never given it a name. It was always Bear.

He touched the parrot lying next to Bear: It looked exactly the same as Bill. The colors were almost identical, maybe something red was yellow instead, but the difference was so slight that you could hardly see it.

"What do you want them for?" the old man had asked as he got into the car.

"They're mine," he'd said.

"That weren't what I asked. I asked what in hell's name you wanted them for now."

"They're mine" was all he'd managed to come out with.

The only things he had left from his childhood.

"You've always been an odd 'un," the old man had commented.

Those words had almost been enough to make him run the old man over. To make a big circle around the farmyard, then come back and really *show* that he didn't want people to talk about him like that.

He held up the bird so that it was looking past him and at the trees and the lawn and the playground where children were on the swings or running around and playing tag or playing hide-and-seek, and there were far too many of them and far too few grown-ups to keep an eye on the children and make sure that nothing happened to them.

He would have to help them.

He got out of the car and left his things behind, but he didn't lock the doors.

He'd positioned the car so that it was pointing toward the road back to the park, and he walked past the square and he found himself behind the high-rise buildings after only one or two minutes, and he could feel the sweat again and he suddenly felt sick, his head was spinning. He paused and breathed deeply, and that felt better. He walked a few more paces and somebody said something.

He looked down at the boy, who was standing beside a bush.

"What's your name?" asked the boy.

14

HE LOOKED AT HIS HANDS ON THE STEERING WHEEL. THEY WERE
shaking. He had to keep moving them to new positions, to make sure his driving wasn't affected. He didn't want that to happen.

All the parking places were taken, which was unusual. He drove around the block, and when he returned there was an empty space.

He drank a glass of water in the kitchen before taking off his shoes. He'd never done that before. He always left his shoes in the hall, so as not to bring grime and dirt into the apartment, as had happened now. He'd cleaned the apartment yesterday, and wanted it to be nice and tidy for as long as possible.

He put down his glass and looked at his hand, and at what was in his palm, and he turned his head away again and walked all the way through the kitchen and the hall to the bathroom, where he washed his hands with his face averted. He couldn't see properly what he was doing, so water splashed down onto the floor, but that couldn't be helped.

He dried his hands. The telephone rang. He dropped the towel. The phone was still ringing. He went into the hall.

"Hell . . . hello?"

"Is that Jerner? Mats Jerner?"

"Er, yes."

"Hello, this is Gothenburg Tramways, Järnström here. I'm calling in connection with that accident at Järntorget. I'm handling the inquiry."

Järnström and Järntorget, he thought. Did they select inquiry chairmen on the basis of their name? Or of the victim. My name fits in as well.

"It's almost finished, in fact," Järnström went on.

"Have we met?"

"No."

He heard the rustling of paper.

"We're basically done," said Järnström, "with all this. You can start again."

"Start work again, do you mean?"

"Yes."

"So there'll be no more interrogations?"

"Interrogations?"

"Questions about how I do my job."

"That's not what—"

"So it's not my, er, not my fault anymore?"

"Nobody ever said it was. You were—"

"I was suspended."

"I wouldn't call it that."

"What would you call it then?"

"It's just that we had to hold this inquiry and it's taken a bit of time."

"Whose fault was it, then?"

"I beg your pardon?"

"Whose fault was it, then?" he yelled into the telephone. The man was evidently a bit deaf and he had to speak more loudly. *"Who's going to take responsibility for everything that's happened?"*

"Calm down now, Jerner."

"I am calm."

"It's all over and done with now," said Järnström. "As far as you're concerned."

"Who isn't it all over for?"

"I don't follow."

"Is it the drunk it's not all over for? It was all his fault."

"That kind of thing is a problem," said Järnström.

"Who for?"

"For Gothenburg Tramways," said Järnström.

"For the drivers," he said. "It's a problem *for the drivers.*"

"Yes."

"That's what causes this kind of thing."

"Yes, I know."

"Was there anything else?"

"No, not at the moment. We might need to ask you about the odd detail later on, but tha—"

"So I just need to show up for work again?"

"That's precisely why I called you, to tell you that."

"Thanks a lot," he said, and hung up. His hand was starting to shake again. It was clean now, but it was shaking.

He went back to the kitchen and sat down, then stood up again immediately and went into the hall and felt in his right-hand jacket pocket and took out the souvenir he had of the boy.

He sat on the sofa and contemplated it. Then burst into tears.

It had never gone this far before. Never. He'd felt it coming on and had driven around in a big circle first in the hope of maybe being able to snap out of it, but instead he'd been sucked into the spiral, and he'd known it would end up like this.

What would happen next time?

No *no no no*!

He went to get the video camera from the hall, and continued arguing with himself.

He watched the film play on the television screen.

He heard the boy's voice asking what his name was. He heard himself replying without knowing *then* what he'd said. But he didn't say the name he had now. He said the other name he'd had when he was a boy, a little boy like him, no, bigger, but still little.

The film was flickering on the screen. Cars, trees, rain outside, traffic in the street, a set of traffic lights, then another, his own hand on the steering wheel. The boy. A glimpse of his hair. No voice now, no sound at all. His hand. A glimpse of the hair again, no face, not in this film.

Winter tried to think in time with the music, which was in tune with the November twilight outside. Car headlights on the other side of the river were stronger than the light from the sky.

He had taken the same route that Stillman, the law student, had walked that night. Climbed up the steps and passed Forum and his own dental office and the library and stood in the middle of the square where the attack had taken place. How could it happen? How could he not have seen what was coming? Bicycle, perhaps. But that was hard to believe. Somebody creeping up from behind? Hmm. No, he didn't think so. Somebody Stillman had arranged to meet? Who came sauntering up from behind or the side or in front? More likely. But Stillman should have noticed, for God's sake. Should have been able to say something about it afterward.

He might have met somebody he knew.

There was also the other possibility, that he was with somebody whose identity he didn't want to disclose. Why? *Warum? Pourquoi? Porqué?*

That was always the most difficult question, no matter what language you asked it in. "Who?" and "where?" and "how?" and "when?" were the immediate questions that required immediate answers, and when those answers were found, the case was solved. But there was always that "why?" often in the form of a little prick in his memory, long afterward. Something unsolved, or undiscovered. Always assuming there was an explanation. Not everything was wrapped up, with explanations as an extra bonus.

But nevertheless. If he could get a better idea of this "why," and soon, he'd be able to discover the answers to "who" and "where" and "how" and "when."

There was a knock on the door and in came Ringmar. Winter remained in his desk chair, and Ringmar perched on the edge of his desk.

"It's gloomy in here," said Ringmar.

"Are you referring to the light?"

"What else?"

"It's serene," said Winter.

Ringmar eyed the Panasonic on the floor under the window, and listened for half a minute.

"Serene music," he said.

"Yes."

"In tune with the light."

"Bobo Stenson Trio. *War Orphans*," said Winter.

"War victims."

"Not really. More like kids who have lost their parents thanks to war."

"War victims sounds better."

"If you say so."

Ringmar sat down on the chair in front of the desk. Winter switched on his desk lamp and the light formed a little circle between them. They had sat there many a time and slowly discussed their way forward to solving a riddle. Winter knew he wouldn't have gotten as far as he had without Ringmar. He hoped it was the same for his older colleague. No, he knew it was. Even so, there were things he didn't know about Bertil, of course. Large chunks of his life. The kind of things he didn't need to know, just as Bertil didn't need to know everything about him.

But at this moment he did want to know more about the older man opposite him, assuming Bertil wanted to tell him. Perhaps it was connected with Winter's own life, his . . . his development. His maturity, perhaps. His journey from being a lonely young man with a lot of power to something different that also encompassed others.

They needed each other, needed their conversations. The banter that wasn't always merely banter.

Ringmar's face seemed thinner than usual. There was a shadow behind his eyes.

"Why does everybody insist on telling lies all the time?" he said.

"It's part of the job," Winter said.

"Telling lies?"

"Listening to lies."

"Take these guys who've been attacked. It's becoming a real mess."

"Theirs first and foremost."

"But ours as well," said Ringmar.

"We can untangle their mess. That's our job. They can't do it themselves."

Ringmar nodded, but didn't say anything.

"Or else it's the truth and nothing but the truth."

Ringmar nodded again, but still didn't say anything.

"But that's not why you came to see me, Bertil. Is it?"

Ringmar said nothing.

"To be honest, you don't look all that good," Winter said.

Ringmar ran his hand over his forehead and his face, as if trying to wipe away the tiredness and the shadows. It looked as if he were moving his head in time with the jazz coming from the Panasonic without realizing it.

"Do you have a fever?" Winter asked.

"It's not that," said Ringmar.

Winter waited for what was coming next. The music stopped, the CD had finished. It was darker outside now. He could see the car headlights more clearly, and the sounds coming from outside were clearer as well. A few drops of rain tapped hesitantly at the windowpane. It could turn into snow, but that didn't seem likely. Snow was a rare gift to Gothenburgers. A surprise to the snow-clearing teams every other winter when chaos descended. Winter had always enjoyed that type of chaos. He liked to walk home over Heden in the eye of the snowstorm, and drink a glass of winter punch while looking out of the window.

"It's Martin, of course," said Ringmar.

Winter waited.

"Ah well . . . ," said Ringmar.

"There's something else you want to say," said Winter.

"I don't know how to put it," said Ringmar.

"Just say it," said Winter.

"It's about . . . about fathers and sons," said Ringmar.

"Fathers and sons," said Winter.

"Yes. I'm trying to figure out what the hell he's thinking," said Ringmar. "How things could have gotten this bad. What could have caused it." He ran his hand over his brow again. "What I've done. What he's done. No, what I've done above all else."

Winter waited. Took out his pack of Corps but didn't touch the cigarillos. He raised his head and Ringmar looked him in the eye.

"That's why I thought about you," said Ringmar. "About how it was for you, with your father. How things got to the state they did. Why you two . . . why you . . . didn't have any contact."

Winter lit a cigarillo and inhaled deeply. The smoke drifted through the circle of light from the desk lamp.

"That's a complicated question you're asking, Bertil."

"You saw how hard it was to ask."

Winter smoked again. He could see himself standing on a slope overlooking the Mediterranean when his father was buried after a funeral in a church as white as snow. Sierra Blanca. No possibility of contact anymore.

"He took off, and took his money with him," said Winter.

"I know," said Ringmar.

"I didn't approve."

"That's it?"

Winter didn't answer, took another draw on his cigarillo, stood up and walked over to the window, opened it, and saw that it had stopped raining. He tapped the ash from his cigarillo after checking to make sure nobody was marching around on the lawn below. He turned around.

"I don't know," he said.

"How much did you actually know about . . . Bengt's financial affairs?" asked Ringmar.

"Enough to disapprove."

"You are a moral person."

"He did something wrong," said Winter. "He could have stayed in Sweden and, well, helped out. He could afford it. And he could have had his house in the sun." Winter smiled. "If he'd paid his taxes we might have had an extra CID officer."

He went back to his desk. He suddenly felt weary. All the things he'd just said to Bertil. What was the point? Everything could have been resolved if only they'd spoken to each other. The only thing that helps is communication with words. That's the only thing that enables us to make progress. Silence begets more silence, and eventually causes a muteness that is like cement.

"By the end it became impossible to say anything," he said. "It was as if we'd lost the ability to talk to each other." He sat down. "I don't know. Sometimes I think there must have been something else, further back in time. Something unconnected with—with that money business. Something different."

Ringmar didn't answer. The shadows behind his eyes had deepened.

"Jesus, Bertil, I shouldn't be sitting here telling you this."

"That's why I came here."

"I don't think you're a masochist. And you're not like him."

"We're all different," said Ringmar, "but even so, we all make the same damned mistakes."

"What mistakes have you made?"

"I must have done something. I have a grown-up son who doesn't want to meet me. He doesn't even want to talk to me."

"He'll regret it. He'll change his mind."

"Are you speaking from experience?"

Winter didn't reply. Rain was pattering against the windowpane again, coming from a sky that had turned black. It's not even five o'clock, but night is upon us.

"I'm sorry, Erik. It's just that . . . Oh, damn . . ."

"I could try to talk to him," said Winter.

"I don't even know where he is."

"But your daughter has some kind of contact with him, doesn't she? Moa?"

"I don't actually know exactly how much," said Ringmar.

"Should I talk to her as well?"

"I don't know, Erik. I've tried to talk to her, but she . . . respects her brother's wishes."

"What about Birgitta?"

"It's even worse for her. He seems to have decided that since he doesn't want to talk to me, that includes her as well." Ringmar sat up straight and smiled, just as Winter had done a couple of minutes previously. "A sort of package deal, you might say."

"Should I give him a good beating if I find him?"

"At last we're getting down to the nitty-gritty. I thought you were never going to ask that."

"Violence is the most extreme form of communication. When words are not enough, it's time for a good thump." Winter held his fist up in the mixture of light and smoke. "It's not an uncommon way of communicating." He took down his fist. "Not in the force, either."

"Still, perhaps we ought to try verbal methods first," said Ringmar.

There was a knock on Winter's door and Winter shouted in response. Bergenhem came in and walked up to the desk that was lit up by a circle of light while the rest of the room was in darkness.

"Are you interrogating each other?" Bergenhem wondered.

"When you don't have a suspect, you have to make do with what you do have," said Winter.

"Count me out," said Bergenhem.

"But you're in," said Winter. "You knocked on that door and came into this office."

"I checked up on that marking iron or whatever it's called. Smedsberg's farm-union babble."

"I noticed we don't have any details about that," said Winter.

"They're coming now." Bergenhem sat down on the chair beside Ringmar. He seemed to be exuding an air of excitement. Winter switched on a standard lamp next to the Panasonic. It was all so cozy. All that was missing was a few candles.

"I spoke to a woman at the Ministry of Agriculture," said Bergenhem. "Prevention of cruelty to animals section."

"Where else?" said Ringmar.

Winter couldn't help laughing.

"It's about to get even funnier," said Bergenhem.

"Sorry, Lars," said Ringmar. "The interrogation I just went through has exhausted me."

"Branding irons like that actually exist in Sweden, not just in Wyoming and Montana." Bergenhem had a notebook open in front of him but didn't need to consult it. "But it's no longer allowed in Sweden to burn symbols onto animals. Not with hot irons, that is."

"What do they do, then?" asked Ringmar.

"They use so-called freeze branding," said Bergenhem.

"Carbon dioxide snow, also known as dry ice," said Winter.

Bergenhem looked at him. He seemed almost disappointed.

"Did you know about that?"

"No, just a lucky guess."

"That wasn't guesswork, come off it."

"Go on," said Winter.

"Anyway, they can freeze the branding iron using dry ice, or liquid nitrogen, and then brand the animals."

"And that still happens today?" asked Ringmar.

"Yes, apparently. It's used mostly on trotting horses, as a sort of ID. And the woman at the ministry figures it's also used on cattle."

Ringmar nodded. Bergenhem eyed him acidly.

"You knew that already, didn't you, Bertil?"

"Farmers aren't satisfied with a number clipped onto a cow's ear," said Ringmar. "If they're milking a lot of cows at a time, they can't see the label on the ear when they're busy down at the udder."

"Good God, what is this?" Bergenhem wondered. "Did I walk in on a boardroom meeting at the Federation of Swedish Farmers?"

"The new EU regulations are a pain in the ass," said Winter.

"Why is it forbidden to brand cattle with a hot iron?" Ringmar asked, looking serious again.

"Well, I suppose it's for humanitarian reasons, if you can use that expression in this context. In any case, the cruelty to animals law was revised in 1988, and as a result it was legal to brand cattle with a cold iron, but it says nothing about hot ones, which means that it's forbidden."

"But you can use the same branding iron for both methods?" asked Winter.

"It seems so."

"Did you ask about that specifically?"

"Yes."

"OK. Go on."

"The most interesting part is the symbol itself," said Bergenhem. "They use a combination of numbers." Now he was reading from his notebook. "It's usually three digits, but it can be more."

"What do the numbers mean?" Ringmar asked.

"It's a number allocated to a particular farm, and applied to each product."

Ringmar whistled.

"Does this apply to every farm in Sweden?" Winter asked.

"Every farm with cattle and sheep and goats and pigs."

That could apply to the police station we're in at this very moment, Ringmar thought. The staff—and our clients.

"What about the ones who don't?" asked Winter.

"What do you mean?"

"The ones who no longer keep animals? That's not exactly uncommon nowadays. Are they still on the list? Or have they been removed?"

"I don't know yet. I couldn't get through to anybody from the registration department."

"So our young men might have a combination of numbers underneath their scabs," said Ringmar. "A sort of tattoo."

"Is it possible to accelerate the healing process?" Bergenhem wondered.

"I'll have a word with Pia," said Winter.

"In which case we've solved the case," said Ringmar.

Bergenhem looked at him.

"Are you being serious, Bertil?"

"I certainly am."

"So," said Winter, "we have an attacker who dipped his weapon into dry ice before launching his attack."

"And where could he have done that?" asked Ringmar.

"He might have been carrying the dry ice in a thermos," said Winter. "For instance."

"Would it leave any traces afterward?" asked Bergenhem.

"I wouldn't have thought so," said Winter. "Who would know about this kind of thing? Animals and dry ice and that kind of stuff?"

He looked at Ringmar.

"Inseminators," said Ringmar. "They keep sperm in a deep freeze."

Winter nodded.

These guys are in the wrong business, Bergenhem thought.

15

THE CHILDREN WERE ASLEEP. HALDERS AND ANETA DJANALI WERE
on the sofa, and Halders was listening to U2. *All That You Can't Leave Behind.*

He had flashes of black memories.

He didn't know if Aneta was listening. She was contemplating the rain
lashing the glass door leading out onto the patio. *It's a beautiful day*, sang
Bono. He could hardly be heard above the noise of the rain that was getting
louder now. Perhaps this is an Irishman's idea of a beautiful day, Halders
thought. Or a Gothenburger's.

He felt Aneta's hand around his neck.

"Do you want that massage now?"

He bowed his head slightly; she got up and stood behind him and started
massaging his damaged vertebrae.

He could feel himself relaxing as she massaged away. *Stuck in a moment
you can't get out of,* sang Bono. Exactly. That was a good thing right now.

Was it a year ago that his ex-wife was killed? It was in the beginning of
June, he remembered that. The school final examinations had taken place in
mid-May, so the seniors had graduated already, but his children still had a few
days left in the term. It had been hellishly hot, and hell had continued for him.

They caught up with the bastard eventually. Halders had tried to track
him down himself, but failed. Then he'd been injured in the course of duty.
An idiotic injury. Caused by an idiot—himself. No, he thought, as Aneta
kneaded the back of his neck like a professional, it wasn't me, then. It was some-
body else.

The bastard hit-and-run driver was a pathetic type who was not worth
pummeling to death. When Halders saw him, long afterward, the cretin meant
nothing to him anymore. He felt no hatred. He had neither the time nor the
strength for that. He'd needed all his strength for the children, who had been
slowly beginning to understand what had happened to their lives. Nothing

would ever be the same as before. Margareta's voice had gone, her body and her movements. They had been divorced, he and Margareta, but that didn't matter.

"Mom's in heaven now," Magda would sometimes say.

Her big brother would look at her without comment.

Maybe he doesn't believe her, Halders sometimes thought, as he sat with them at the breakfast table. Doesn't believe in heaven. Heaven is up there in the sky, just something we can see from the earth. It's the same up there as it is down here. Mainly air and rain, and big distances between everything.

"How's it feel now?" asked Aneta.

Slow down my beating heart, sang Bono, in a voice that could have been black, as black as Aneta's hands that he could see on his shoulders. One hand on his chest. *Slow down my beating heart.*

"Let's go to bed," he said.

Angela drove through the rain. It was really evening now, even if the transformation had been barely noticeable. She smiled. December was almost here, and she was looking forward to the Christmas holidays. Her work with her patients was getting more arduous. They grew more tired as the year drew to a close, and she too became more tired. She had managed to get time off between Christmas and New Year's. Erik had muttered something earlier on about going to the Costa del Sol. She had hoped that Siv would call. She got along well with Siv. She also got along well with a blue sky and some sun and a glass of wine and charcoal-grilled langoustines.

But first she had a few errands to run in Haga. The shopping mall would be open until eight this evening.

She crossed over Linnéplatsen and down Linnégatan, checked her rearview mirror, and saw the blue light rotating, suddenly, silently, as if a helicopter had landed behind her, soundlessly.

The police car was still there. She wondered why they'd been called out. I can't pull over here to let them pass. Now they've switched on the siren. Yes, yes, all right, I *will* pull over as soon as I can.

She saw a spot outside a pub and pulled into it.

The police car parked behind her. The light was still spinning, as if they'd just reached the scene of a crime. She couldn't see anybody lying on the pavement.

She looked in the mirror again and saw one of the officers get out of the car, and she turned icy cold, totally mute, completely *filled with terror,* as everything she had been through not so very long ago came back to her, the memories were there, like beams of light spinning around in circles. She had been . . . kidnapped by a man in a police uniform. She had been stopped by somebody she thought was a police officer, and Elsa had been in her stomach . . .

There was a tap on the window, and she could see his black glove. She didn't want to look. More knocking, and she looked, quickly. She saw his gesture: Roll down this window.

She felt for the panel on the door but couldn't find the button. Now. The window rolled down in a series of nervous jerks.

"Didn't they teach you at driving school that you're supposed to stop when a police car tells you to?" he said, and there was brutality in his tone.

She didn't answer. She thought: Didn't they teach you the basics of politeness and civility at police school? Have you even been to school? Primary school?

"We've been behind you for ages," he said.

"I . . . I didn't think . . . it was me you were after," she said.

He looked at her, seemed to be studying her face. His own face was in shadow, flecked with the evening's electric lights. There was hardness in his eyes, perhaps even something worse than that. A desire to hit something or somebody. A calculated provocation. Or maybe he's just tired. Everybody gets tired by work. She was tired out herself at the moment. Even so she could still behave in a civilized manner.

She knew a few police officers by sight, but this wasn't one of them. She glanced in the mirror to see if there was anybody else in the police car, but she couldn't see anything through the rain streaming down the rear window of her Golf.

Her first week in a small car, and this happens.

"Are you feeling all right?" he asked.

She didn't answer.

"Driver's license," he said.

She found it eventually. He checked it and said: "Angela Hoffman?" and she nodded.

He took a couple of steps back. She assumed he was running a check on her name. For a moment she wished she had Erik's surname. Mr. Brutal Face would recognize it. Mumble something and give her back her license and drive off with his fucking blue light and harass some other victim.

She calmed down. She could have made her irritation obvious. Or her fear. But that might only make things worse.

Maybe we should get married? I could add Winter after Hoffman.

I might feel safer in the streets then.

A wedding by the sea.

Admit that you have thought about that.

The officer returned and handed back her license, muttered "Angela Hoffman" again, and returned to his car and the blue light that had been spinning around nearly the whole time and attracted a little group of people on the sidewalk, curious to see the criminal whose papers were being examined by the long arm of the law. Curious to catch a glimpse of the criminal's haggard face, she thought, as she made a racing start and headed north, having forgotten what pointless errands she was going to run in these parts, and she turned eastward into the first street she could find and was home five minutes later and outside the apartment door from the basement parking lot in another four, and shortly afterward her boots ended up in two corners of the hall.

"I thought you'd brought guests home with you," said Winter coming out of the kitchen with Elsa in his arms. "It sounded like the SWAT team busting through the door."

"Hold on while I count to ten," she said.

"Hard day at the office?"

"Only afterward," she said. "I was stopped by one of your colleagues on the way home."

"A roadblock?"

"No. Sheer harassment."

Elsa was struggling in his arms, wanting both to greet Angela and to finish her evening meal.

"Just a minute," said Winter, going back to the kitchen, sitting Elsa on her chair, and letting her continue eating. There was food all over the table.

"I think I'm going to be sick," said Angela, who had come into the kitchen still wearing her overcoat.

She left the room.

Shortly afterward he heard her crying somewhere else in the apartment.

He picked up the telephone and called his sister.

"Hello, Lotta. Is Bim or Kristina at home this evening?"

"Bim's here. What's up?"

"Do you think she could baby-sit for us on extremely short notice?"

"There are bastards in every job," said Winter.

"Somebody like that is not fit to be a police officer," she said. "You can't behave like that." She was holding her wineglass in her hand.

"I can easily find out who it was," he said.

She had seen the furrow between his eyes. He *would* be capable of doing something drastic. There was a dark streak inside him that could turn him into—anything at all. For one brief, horrific moment.

"And do what?" she asked.

"You'd rather not know," he said, and took a sip of their Puligny-Montrachet.

"Let's forget about it," she said, taking a drink and looking out of the window. "We're here now." She looked at him and nodded her head toward the white functionalist building on the other side of Lasarettsgatan. "I like the curtains in my old place." She looked at the balcony and the window beside it, up on the fifth floor. There was a light on.

There was a good view from the apartment, in all directions, from the top of Kungshöjd.

He nodded.

"I miss it, sometimes," she said.

He nodded again.

"I was there for quite a few years," she said.

"So was I," he said.

"For you it was more like an overnight place," she said with a smile. "Although you seldom stayed all night."

"I miss the view," he said.

"This place didn't exist then," she said, looking around the restaurant.

Bistro 1965 was new, and this was the second time they'd been there, and it wouldn't be the last. Perhaps they would be the first regular customers.

Angela's pilgrim mussels grilled with coriander came with pumpkin purée. After all, it had been Halloween not long ago, she'd thought as she ordered it. Winter's slightly smoked goose fillet came with eggplant and vanilla oil.

"It's good," she said.

"Hmm."

"Should we feel bad for leaving Elsa?" she said, taking a sip of water.

"We can take the menu with us and read it out loud to her tomorrow evening," he said.

"I might want to read it myself," she said, looking at the gastronomic glossary attached to the back of today's menu. "Do you know what *escalavida* is, for instance?"

"It's a purée made from paprika and onions and eggplant and lemon, among other things."

"You've already read this."

"Of course I haven't." He took a sip of wine and smiled.

"What's *gremolata*?"

"That's too easy."

"Good Lord." She looked up. "Get off your high horse."

"Come on, give me a real challenge."

"*Confit?*"

"Too easy."

"*Vierge?*"

"*Vierge?*"

"Yes, *vierge.*"

He glanced down at the menu he had on his knee. "That's not on the list."

"Eh! I knew you were cheating."

A car passed by in the street outside. The evening had cleared up. There were stars visible in the sky above Angela's former home.

When he'd gone there for the first time, he'd been in uniform. It wasn't while he was on duty. Are you mad? she'd asked him. The neighbors will think I'm a crook.

I forgot, he'd said.

How can you forget a thing like that? she'd asked.

"What are you smiling at?" she heard him say.

"That first time," she said, nodding in the direction of the apartment building that was gleaming in the light from the streetlamps. A car was coming up the hill from Kungsgatan. "You came in uniform."

They continued the conversation. It calmed them down. There's always a feeling of absolute privacy when you're sitting in a public place surrounded by strangers, Winter thought. A strange paradox.

He took a sip of wine. His glass now contained Fiefs de Lagrange, to accompany the rack of lamb with *gremolata,* ragout with lima beans, and artichokes, and this *vierge* that he hadn't thought about when he ordered: a light sauce made of virgin olive oil, tomato, lamb stock, garlic, and herbs. He'd had a taste of Angela's red wine risotto.

The waitress changed the candle. There were fewer people in the restaurant now. Winter's mobile rang in the inside pocket of his jacket.

Elsa, Angela thought.

"Hello?" said Winter.

"It's Bertil. Sorry to disturb you."

16

WINTER COULD SEE THE BOY THROUGH THE DOOR. HE WAS ASLEEP.
Or more likely mercifully anesthetized. Angela was standing beside Winter.
They'd taken a taxi from the bistro. I want to be there this time, she'd said.
You shouldn't have to face everything on your own. Besides, it's my work-
place. Even my ward. And Elsa's asleep.

"He could have frozen to death," said Ringmar, who was standing on the
other side of Winter.

"That, or some other awful fate," said Winter. He'd read the reports, not
that there were many of them so far. One by the hospital doctors, and one by
Pia Fröberg, the pathologist.

"When did the call go out?" Winter asked.

"It couldn't have been long after he disappeared," said Ringmar.

"When was that? When did he disappear?"

"Just after four." He checked his notes. "About a quarter past four. But
that timing hasn't been confirmed."

"Is that information from the nursery-school staff?"

"Yes."

"What exactly happened? What did they do? What did he do?"

"Nobody can say for sure."

"So he was wandering around on his own?"

Ringmar didn't respond.

"Is that what he was doing?"

"I don't know, Erik. I haven't interrogated the—"

"OK, OK. Anybody determined to kidnap a child can do it, no matter
what."

Angela gave a start.

There was a woman dressed in white sitting beside the boy. Machines

were humming away. Sounds that didn't sound natural. Lights that were any-
thing but pretty.

"Let's go to that other room," said Winter.

A room had been set aside for them.

"Where are the parents?" Winter asked as they walked down the corridor.

"With one of the doctors."

"I expect they'll be staying overnight?"

"Of course."

"I'm going home now," said Angela.

They embraced, and Winter kissed her. He looked Ringmar in the eye
over Angela's shoulder. Ringmar's face looked hollow.

The room was as bare as the trees outside the window and the streets below.
Winter leaned against the wall in a corner of the room. The three glasses of
wine he'd drunk had given him a headache that he was now trying to rub
away from his forehead with his left hand. A radio in the distance was playing
rock music. He could just about hear it. *Touch me,* he thought he heard. And
something that sounded like *take me to that other place.* But there was no other
place. It was here, everything was here. He didn't recognize the tape. Halders
would have recognized it immediately, as would Bergenhem. And Macdon-
ald. When was Steve supposed to be visiting them? *Take me to that other place.*
Reach me. It's a beautiful day.

The boy in that other room wasn't that much older than Elsa.

"What happened next?" Winter asked.

"They sent out a car, and then another one," said Ringmar.

"Where to?" Winter asked.

"First to the Plitka playground at Slottskogen Park. Then, well . . ."

"Grasping in the dark," said Winter.

"They were six miles apart," said Ringmar.

Six miles between Plitka and the place where he was eventually found.

"Who found him?"

"The classic setup. A dog, and then the dog's owner."

"Where is he? The dog's owner, I mean."

"At home."

Winter nodded.

"So four hours had passed," he said.

"Just over."

"How much do we know about the injuries?" he asked.

Ringmar made a gesture that suggested everything and nothing. It was as if he could barely raise his hand. The guitars had stopped resounding in the corridor. Who the hell was playing rock music in the hospital?

"There are obvious injuries to the boy's torso," said Ringmar. "And his face. Nothing under, er, below his waist."

"I saw his face," said Winter.

"I saw one of his arms," said Ringmar.

"Does anything surprise you anymore?" Winter asked, prying himself away from the wall and massaging his forehead again.

"There are questions you can't answer with a yes or a no," said Ringmar.

"Where were the parents when the alarm was raised?"

"The man was at work—he has lots of colleagues—and his wife was drinking coffee with a friend."

And I was drinking wine in a restaurant, Winter thought. A brief moment of calm and warmth in a protected corner of life.

"He must have had a car," he said. "Don't you think? Driving through the rush hour traffic when everybody else is staring straight ahead and looking forward to getting home."

"He parked inside the park," said Ringmar. "Or close by." He scratched his chin and Winter could hear the rasp from the day-long stubble. "The crime-scene boys are out there now."

"Good luck to them," said Winter, without conviction. A million tire tracks one on top of the other in a parking lot. With some luck a soft and wet patch of grass; otherwise there would be no chance.

We'll have to check up on the usual suspects, he thought. To start with. Either we find him there, or we don't. This could be a long journey.

"I'll have to talk to the nursery-school staff as well," he said. "How many of them are there now? Or rather, how few?"

But first, the parents. They were sitting in an office that Winter recognized. It was Angela's. She'd arranged for them to be settled there before going home. There was normally a photograph of himself with Elsa on her desk, but she had removed it before Paul and Barbara Waggoner arrived, bringing their desperation in with them. Good thinking. Angela was sensible.

The man was standing, the woman seated. They radiated a sort of restrained restlessness that Winter knew all too well from all his other meetings with the relatives of victims, who were also victims, of course. A restlessness that was a sort of tangible desire to reach back in time and preserve the past forever. Of course. The victims of crimes were always searching for a life in the past. Perhaps they were not the only ones. He himself would have liked to remain in Bistro 1965, an hour ago, which could easily have been in another era in another world. The protected corner. *Take me to that other place.* Strictly speaking Bertil didn't need to call him, but Bertil knew that Winter would want to be there. Bertil's intuition on this occasion had scared Winter, but his colleague was never wrong in such matters: This was going to be a long, dark road and Winter needed to be there from the very beginning. It wasn't the sort of thing you could explain to others. He noticed that Ringmar was standing beside the woman, who was sitting on the little visitor's sofa. It's something between Bertil and me. He rubbed his forehead again. My headache has gone.

"Will he be able to see again?" asked Barbara without looking up.

Winter didn't respond, nor did Ringmar. We are not doctors, Winter thought. Take one look at us and you'll see that.

"They are not doctors, Barbara." The words came out more like an exhalation. "We've just finished speaking to the doctor." Winter detected a slight but unmistakable foreign accent, possibly English. His name suggested that.

"He couldn't say anything about that for sure," she said, as if she were transferring her hope to the new specialists who had just entered the room.

"Mrs. Waggoner," said Winter, and she looked up. Winter introduced himself and Ringmar. "May we ask you a few questions?" He looked at her husband, who nodded.

"How could anyone do that to a child?" she said.

Winter couldn't answer that. He asked the hardest question first: Why?

"Isn't that your job? Isn't that what you are supposed to find out?" Paul asked, with the same intonation as before, an aggressiveness lacking in energy. Winter knew it could become much more forceful if he didn't play his cards right. He must be an Englishman, he thought.

"We're going to do everything we can to find whoever did this, you can count on it," he said.

"What kind of a fucking monster did this?!" Yes, Englishman.

"We'll—"

"Don't you have a register of scumbags like this? All you have to do is look him up?" His accent had suddenly become more marked.

"We'll do that," said Winter.

"Why are you sitting here, then?"

"We have to ask some questions about Simon," said Winter. "It will—"

"Questions? We can't say any more than what you've seen for yourself."

"Paul," she said.

"Yes?"

"Please calm down."

Paul looked at her, then at Winter, and then looked away.

"Ask your questions, then," he said.

Winter asked about times and routines and clothes. He asked if Simon had had anything with him. Things he couldn't talk to the boy himself about.

"What do you mean, anything with him?"

"Have you noticed anything missing? Something he had before but doesn't have now?" Winter asked.

"A toy or something similar," Ringmar said. "A stuffed animal. A charm, anything at all that he used to have with him or on him."

"A keepsake?"

"Yes."

"Why do you want to know that?"

"I understand why," said Barbara, who was sitting up straight now. Winter could hear a slight accent when she spoke now, very slight. He wondered if they spoke English when they were at home together, or Swedish, or both for Simon's sake.

"Oh yes?" her husband said.

"If he's lost something," she said. "Don't you see? If he . . . if the one that . . . if he took something from Simon."

"Was there anything to take?" Winter asked.

"We haven't thought about that," said Paul. "We haven't checked it."

"Checked what?" asked Winter.

"His watch," said Mrs. Waggoner, raising her hand to her mouth. "He never took it off." She looked at her husband. "I didn't see it."

"It's blue," said the father, looking at his wife.

"A kid's watch," said the mother.

Ringmar left the room.

"Would you like me to fix some coffee or something?" Winter asked. "Tea?"

"We've already had some, thank you," said Barbara.

"Is this a common occurrence?" asked Paul. "Does this happen to many children?"

Winter didn't know if his question referred to the city of Gothenburg, or to Sweden, or to child abuse in general, or the type of crime they were up against now. There were various possible answers. One was that it was common for children to be abused by adults. Children and young people. It was most common within families. Nearly always within families, he thought, and looked at the Waggoners, who seemed to be about thirty, or possibly even younger, aged by the sharp lines and hollows that marked their faces in their distress. Fathers and mothers beat their children. He'd come across a lot of children who'd been beaten by their parents. He'd been in many such homes and tried to hide the experience away in his memory until the next such occasion. Children who were handicapped for life. Some of them could no longer walk. Or see, he thought, thinking of little Simon lying in the ward with eyes that were no longer like they used to be.

Some of them died. The ones who lived never forgot it. God, he had met victims who had become adults, but the damage was still present, always there in their eyes, their voices.

In their actions. Sometimes there was a pattern that carried on, a terrible inheritance that wasn't really an inheritance but something much worse.

"I mean here in Gothenburg," said Paul. "That children can be abducted by somebody just like that, and abused, and dum . . . dumped, and maybe . . . maybe . . ." He couldn't bring himself to go on. His face had collapsed a little bit more.

"No," said Winter. "It's not common."

"Has it happened?"

"No. Not like this."

"What do you mean? Not like this?"

Winter looked at him.

"I don't really know what I mean," he said. "Not yet. First we need to learn more about what actually happened."

"Some unknown madman kidnapped our son when he was at a playground with his day care people," said Paul Waggoner. "That's what happened." He looked at Winter, but there was more resignation than aggression in his eyes. "That's what actually happened. And I asked you if anything like that had actually happened before."

"I'll know more about all this soon," said Winter.

"If it's happened before it can happen again," said Waggoner.

"*Isn't it enough for you to know that it's happened, Paul?*" said his wife, getting to her feet and walking over to them and putting her arm around her husband's shoulders. "It's happened to us, Paul. It's happened to Simon. Isn't that enough for you? Can't we . . . can't we concentrate on trying to help him? Can't you understand? Can't you just let the police do what they have to do while we do what we have to do? Paul? Do you understand what I'm saying?"

He nodded, abruptly. Perhaps he did understand. Winter heard Ringmar open the door behind him. Winter turned around. Ringmar shook his head.

"Did you find the watch?" asked Paul Waggoner.

"No," said Ringmar.

Larissa Serimov adjusted the strap and felt the weight of her gun against her body. Or perhaps it was more the knowledge of what it could do that she felt. A SigSauer wasn't heavy, anything of a similar weight could be forgotten about; but not a gun.

This early December day was mild, almost as if they were farther south. Signs of Christmas everywhere but a temperature of eleven degrees, maybe twelve. Brorsson was driving with his window more than half down.

"You'll get a stiff neck," she said.

"I only get that in summer," he said. "For some reason."

"I know the reason," she said as they turned off toward the sea. She could hear seabirds through Brorsson's open window.

"What?"

"You get a stiff neck in the summer because you drive with the window open," she said, and saw the glint of water beyond the field that appeared to be almost as full of water as the sea.

"But it's not summer now," he said.

She laughed loudly.

"Although it's pretty warm," he said. "From a purely statistical point of view the average temperature today is high enough for it to count as summer."

"In that case it must be summer, Billy," she said.

"Yes, you're right," he said, turning to look at her.

"And so it follows that you'll soon get a stiff neck," she said, looking out at the rocks and the sea, both of which were totally motionless.

Brorsson rolled the window up.

"Straight ahead," she said at the roundabout.

They drove to a turning space and parked, and stepped out of the car. The modern terraced houses on the right were built-in steps, like some of the rocks. There were hills behind them. The bay was open here, and the ocean lay in wait beyond the archipelago. There were sailboats still moored to jetties as if to confirm what Brorsson had just said: Summer had refused to die this year. No snow this year, and Larissa Serimov liked snow. Snow on the ground and snow on the ice. That's my heritage. A white soul in a white body.

"It's open," said Brorsson.

They could see the interior of the restaurant through the glass doors. It looked inviting. The horizon appeared to cut right through the building, making it seem like a tower, or a lighthouse. The placidity of the coast this newly born December felt as restful as it was. But not for them.

"We just had lunch," she said. "Have you forgotten?"

"Yes, I know, but I thought we could get the customers to blow into the bag when they come out." She noticed his eyes, apathetic and exhilarated at the same time. "I need to book a few more drunks before Christmas." He looked at her. "The statistics are important as far as I'm concerned."

"So I've gathered."

"What do you say, then?" he said, checking his watch.

"Can't you leave poor people alone just for once?"

"What do you mean?"

"Like that poor woman yesterday afternoon in Linnégatan. We wouldn't have needed to be there at all if it hadn't been for your statistics."

"She didn't stop," he said.

"She tried to let you pass."

"She was lucky she got away with it," he said.

"Got away with what?" asked Serimov.

He didn't answer.

"Got away with what?" she asked again.

"Arrogant bitches," he said.

"You have a problem, Billy," she said.

"So, should we wait here for a while and see what we can do?" he said.

"Certainly not. They live up there, and that's where we're going," she said, pointing.

"In that case there was no need for me to drive down here first," he said.

"I wanted to see the sea," she said.

"The sea, the sea! I could kiss the sea!" he said.

Kiss my ass, she thought: She was good at swearing. She had a Russian background, after all. The Russian language is world champion when it comes to swear words. In Sweden people call them "bad words," but a lot of the Russian swear words are beautiful, she thought, gazing out to sea again.

They got back into the car and drove up the steeply sloping streets.

"Here we are," she said, and he pulled up.

"I'll wait out here," he said.

"Don't harass the neighbors," she said. She got out of the car and rang the doorbell.

Kristina Bergort answered after the second ring. Larissa could see Maja peeping out from behind her mother.

"Come in," said Mrs. Bergort.

"I hope this isn't too inconvenient for you," Larissa said, aware of how silly it sounded. She had called in advance and Kristina Bergort had said that it was OK.

The girl was clinging to her mother.

"Magnus called to say that he couldn't get away from work," said Bergort.

You are the one I want to talk to anyway, Larissa thought, feeling awkward in the kitchen wearing her police uniform.

The girl looked at her belt and the gun sticking out like . . . like a . . . well, sticking out. Larissa realized that she hadn't spoken to the girl yet.

"Hello, Maja," she said.

The girl looked up, shyly, smiled quickly, and then looked down again.

"You can go back and play," said her mother.

Maja turned around and Larissa could see a scratch on her upper arm, like a line of chalk. Larissa watched her walk away. She crossed over the threshold. Larissa was still watching. There was something odd. But what? There was something about the way she moved. What was it? Her leg? It was . . .

Maja was out of sight now.

"Is there something wrong with her leg?" Larissa asked.

"What? Her leg?"

"Maja's leg. She seemed to be limping."

"Limping? Maja? I haven't noticed anything." Kristina Bergort looked at her with an expression that could have been one of concern. "Surely I would have noticed?"

Larissa Serimov wondered what to say next. She ought to know. She knew why she'd come here.

"Would you like a cup of coffee?" asked Mrs. Bergort.

Larissa thought about Billy Brorsson waiting outside, said "yes please," and then her mobile rang.

"Are you going to be in there long?" asked Brorsson.

"Ten, fifteen minutes."

"I'll go for a little drive."

She hung up and thought about the plight of humanity exposed to assault by Brorsson, and turned to Kristina Bergort.

"I've been thinking a bit more about that story Maja told you," she said.

THEY WERE SERVED COFFEE, CHEESE ROLLS, AND THREE KINDS OF cookies. The rooms were full of Christmas decorations, an excess of them. The children had been given free rein. Angela recognized Elsa's paintings because Elsa had shown them to her before. There were lines and circles that could symbolize most things. Or just represent them. Not everything was symbolic.

There was a smell of candle wax and hot punch. Parents were circulating and discussing the Christmas atmosphere that had arrived here about three weeks early.

There were no children present this evening. No overtime for them, Angela thought. Elsa can relax at home with Erik. Rolling the ball across the floor until he's too stiff to stand up again. No, it wasn't that bad. But obviously, being a father at forty is not the same as being a father at twenty-five.

She looked around. She was at a sort of middle age when it came to parenting, not too young and not too old. Waiting until you were thirty before having a child was no big deal nowadays. Lots of women waited. But she wouldn't have wanted to wait any longer. Nevertheless, Erik had waited until she couldn't take it any longer. And she hadn't taken it any longer. No more waiting.

The future was not over. Just wait and see, Erik.

They assembled in the big hall. The nursery-school manager welcomed them to the annual Christmas get-together. This nursery school is a bit special, she said. Inner-city dwellers and inner-city children.

Angela could see the house by the sea in her mind's eye. An avenue, trees on all sides, gravel paths, and a kitchen garden.

The future was not over.

But the apartment at Vasaplatsen wasn't something you just got rid of. At the moment it seemed to be the best place for Elsa. Big, shiny floors. They were easy to roll a ball over.

It was afterward, when there were fewer parents still present, that the matter came up. Lots of them had been thinking about it all evening, the staff as well of course, but one of them said:

"We didn't really know how to bring it up."

"Which nursery school was it?" somebody asked.

"Hepatica."

"Where's that?"

"In Änggården."

"But that's not very far from here."

"They were in Slottskogen."

"It's terrible."

"Yes, awful."

"Has anything like this happened before?"

"Not to my knowledge."

"How's the boy?"

"I don't know."

Angela listened, but said nothing. She had seen the boy the evening it happened, and then again today. One day later. Simon. His parents. His father had said "fuck" at one point, maybe a couple of times.

Angela was sitting on the edge of the group, next to the window, on a chair that was intended for a much shorter and younger person. A street lamp illuminated the swings and the slide. Car headlights lit up the street down the slope. She thought about the hole in the fence. Had it really been mended?

She could see the church tower in the park on the other side of the street; that was lit up as well.

A woman sat down on the other little chair.

"Who knows if we'll be able to stand up again," she said.

"I'm afraid to try," said Angela.

"Lena Sköld," said the woman, reaching out her right hand.

"Angela Hoffman."

Angela had never met Lena Sköld before. It was usually Erik who took Elsa to the nursery school, and collected her. But come to think of it, she did recognize her after all. And she thought she could remember what her child looked like. A girl with dark hair.

"I'm Ellen's mom," said Lena Sköld.

"I'm Elsa's mom," said Angela.

"Yes, of course." She picked up her cup. "We—Ellen and me—haven't been here for very long." She took a sip of coffee. "We used to go to a different nursery school before."

"I think I can remember what Ellen looks like," said Angela.

"She's in the picture behind you."

Angela turned to look at the little photograph behind her, stuck onto a bigger sheet of paper. The girl was standing on a beach, laughing out to sea. It was windy. The photograph was framed by all the colors of the rainbow. Arrows with the girl's name pointed at the picture. A little exhibitionist.

"She wanted to make it clear that she was the one in that picture and nobody else," said Lena Sköld with a smile.

"She's got plenty of self-confidence," said Angela.

"Hmm . . . I don't know about that." She took another sip of coffee. "We'll find out about that eventually, I suppose." She looked at Angela. "I'm a single parent." She put down her cup and smiled.

Angela nodded. Through the window she could see people leaving the nursery school on their way home. She checked her watch.

"Yes, I suppose it's time to make a move," said Lena Sköld. "If we can stand up." She made an effort with her legs. "Eh, I failed at the first attempt."

"I don't think I'm even going to try," said Angela.

Lena Sköld also stayed put, looking through the window in which her face was mirrored.

"I keep thinking about what we were talking about earlier," she said.

"About the boy who, er, disappeared?" said Angela.

"Yes." She looked as if she wanted to say more, and Angela waited.

"Something odd happened to me not long ago. Or rather, to Ellen." She looked at Angela. "It feels almost creepy. Yes, it definitely does. What with what happened to the boy and all that. But I mean this incident with Ellen. Given the rest of it."

What on earth is she talking about? Angela wondered.

"It was very strange," said Lena Sköld. "What happened to Ellen. She came home and, well, I suppose you could say she told a story. About how she'd met somebody while her group was on an outing."

"What do you mean, met somebody?"

"A man. A mister, as she called him. She said she met this mister and sat with him for a while. In a car. If I understood it correctly they were sitting in a car."

"That's what she told you?"

"That's how I understood it, at least," said Lena Sköld. "And there was another thing. Something disappeared that day."

"What was it?" Angela asked.

"A little silver charm that she had in her overall pocket. It vanished. The police asked me to check if there was anything missing, and it was that charm."

"The police?"

"That evening when Ellen came home, I mean, when she said she'd met somebody, I called the police about it."

"The police where?"

"What do you mean?"

"Did you call the local police station, or the communications center?"

"I don't know what it's called. I looked up a number in the phone book and got through to a call center, and they passed me on to another number." She put her cup down on the floor. "It was a police station close to where I live."

"Your local station," said Angela.

"Yes." She looked at Angela. "You seem to know about these things. Are you a police officer?"

"No."

"I think they said it was the Majorna and Linnéstaden police."

"What else did they say?"

"The man I spoke to wrote down what I said. At least, it sounded like he did. And then he said that stuff about me checking to see if anything was missing and I did and I phoned back to tell him about the charm."

"Have they been in touch with you again? The police, I mean?"

"No."

"How's Ellen?"

"Same as ever. I expect it was just her imagination." She looked around the playroom, which was neat and tidy. All the toys were in big boxes along the walls. There were Christmas drawings all over the walls.

There was still a smell of candle wax and hot punch, in anticipation of Christmas. There was a sound of voices from the other rooms, but fewer now. "But when you hear what happened to that poor boy, it makes you wonder."

Angela said nothing.

"What do you think?" asked Lena Sköld.

"Have you tried talking to Ellen about it again?"

"Yes, several times."

"What does she say?"

"More or less the same thing. I've been thinking about that. She doesn't seem to have forgotten about it. It's the same little story. Or maybe it's just a . . . fairy story. A fantasy."

18

ANGELA WALKED HOME DEEP IN THOUGHT. SANTA CLAUS WAS IN most of the shop windows, but there was no snow on the ground. The pavements glistened damply in the electric light from the streetlamps and windows. She thought about the injured boy and his parents. She thought about Lena Sköld and her life as a single parent. No man in her life now, and no father for Ellen. Maybe later.

She paused outside the front door. Vasaplatsen was quiet this evening, but the wind was picking up from the north and blowing along the Allé. She raised the collar of her overcoat and paused to take in the scene. A streetcar stopped on the other side of the street, then trundled off again in the same direction as the wind. She could see two people in the front car, but nobody at all in the second one. A way of traveling for someone who wanted to be alone. She noticed the driver looking at her as he drove past.

Driving a streetcar was one way of seeing Gothenburg. Anyone who drove the same route for a long time would get to know all the surrounding streets and the intersections and the parks. And the streetcars didn't go fast, either. In fact, they were annoyingly slow, and she was glad she had her Golf; but then again, she also had the usual guilty conscience about ruining the quality of the air that everybody was forced to breathe, whether they wanted to or not.

She would leave the car at home. Occasionally.

Elsa has to breathe this air. Vasaplatsen isn't the best place to be, from that perspective. Elsa is still a tender rosebud. What do we do? Do we have any choice but to move? We'll have to discuss it again, Erik and I, seriously. She had shouted from the hall but there was no reply, so she'd gone to the bedroom. They'd fallen asleep in the double bed. There were about ten picture books scattered around them in a rough circle.

Elsa mumbled in her sleep when Angela picked her up and put her to bed in her own room, where the light was on.

Winter was in the kitchen now, and had put the kettle on.

"How about a cup of tea?"

"Yes, please. I need that after all the coffee at the meeting."

"Would you like a slice of pie?"

"No thank you."

"Half a baguette with brie and salami?"

"*Non, merci.*"

"Smoked mussels."

"Erik, I'm not hungry."

"How did it go?"

"There was some talk about that . . . that incident. The Waggoner boy."

"We're going to try to speak to him tomorrow."

"Any leads?"

"We're checking all the local loonies now. Nothing yet."

"What does Pia say?"

Angela had met Pia Fröberg, the forensic pathologist, several times.

"She can't see any signs of sexual assault," he said. "It's probably just your usual assault."

"Just?"

"Didn't you hear the quotes? I prefer not to write them in the air."

"Where'd that tea go?"

The wind was blowing rain all over the big windshield. There was something wrong with one of the wipers: It was out of sync with the other one. Or perhaps it was the other one that was faulty. In any case, it was like watching somebody with a limp, dragging one leg. He'd have to report it.

Gothenburg glittered as he drove around the city. It would soon be Christmas again. The old man had asked him. He'd said no.

Hardly anybody in the streetcar, but he wasn't complaining. Somebody got off at Vasaplatsen, but nobody got on. There'd been a woman standing in a doorway, watching him. Didn't people have anything better to do? There was a restaurant on the corner to her left. She could have gone there.

Several people got on at the Central Station, on their way to the northern wildernesses that he was also heading for, of course. Wastelands with high-rises so tall they looked as if they were trying to fly up to heaven, but they could ask him about heaven and he would've told them the truth about it. There's nothing there.

He drove alongside the river, which was as black as it always was. He could see the other bridge to the west that was bigger and more beautiful.

You could see a lot of beautiful things from here. There were fir trees decorated with a thousand Christmas candles.

The boy had put up a fight.

He bit his hand so hard it hurt.

Bill was dangling on his string beside him. The parrot was positioned in such a way that nobody getting on would be able to see it unless they sort of bent around the driver, and why would anybody want to do that? Besides, it wasn't allowed.

He stopped the streetcar, and lots of people got on. Why on earth did they want to be out at this time? It was starting to get late.

Why hadn't he driven the boy back to where he'd found him?

He'd intended to do that. He always did that. Assuming that he'd driven *away* in the first place.

I don't understand why I didn't take him back. Perhaps because he put up a fight. That was no doubt why. He didn't want to be nice when I was being nice. I tried.

Somebody to his right said something. The doors were open. He could feel the wind coming in from the outside. This could create a sort of spiral of wind in the streetcar.

"Why aren't we moving?"

He turned to look at the man standing next to his cab.

"Sixteen kronor," he said.

"Eh?"

"A ticket costs sixteen kronor," he said. People should know that if they were going to take a streetcar ride. Some didn't pay at all. Cheated. Some of them got caught when an inspector came onboard. He never talked to the inspectors, who were known as the Tenson gang because they always wore ugly Tenson jackets. They did their job and he did his.

"I don't want a ticket," said the man. "I've already got one and I just got it stamped."

"No ticket?"

"Why are we standing here? Why don't you start moving?"

"This is a stop," he said. "I have to stop so that people can get on and off."

"They've already done that, for Christ's sake!" said the man, who appeared to be drunk. There were always drunks on the streetcars. He could tell you all about that!

"We got on and off about a hundred years ago, and now we want to go," said the man, leaning forward. "Why the hell don't you start moving?"

"I'll call the police!" he said, without having intended to say that the second before he did so.

"Eh?"

He didn't want to say it again.

"Call the police? That's a fucking brilliant idea. Then we might finally get moving. They can give us an escort," said the drunk. "I can call them myself, come to that." He produced a mobile.

Now I'm off.

The streetcar started with a jerk, and the man with the mobile was flung backward and almost fell over, but managed to hang on to one of the straps. He dropped his mobile and it crashed to the floor.

They were off.

"You're a fucking lunatic," yelled the man. His posture was most peculiar. A drunk who couldn't stand up straight. Now he was bending down. He was visible in the mirror. "I dropped my mobile." It was impossible to hear what he said next. Now he was back by the driver's cab again. It was forbidden to talk to the driver while the streetcar was in motion.

"If it's busted I'll fucking report you to the fucking police, you fucking idiot."

He decided to ignore the drunk. That was the best way.

He came to a halt at the next stop. People were waiting to get on. The drunk was standing in the way. The newcomers forced him back. He had to make way. A lady got on. A ticket? Of course. That'll be sixteen kronor, please. Here you are, a ticket and four kronor change.

He took off, stopped, took off again. It was quiet now. He stopped once more. Opened the doors.

"Consider yourself lucky that my mobile's still working, you fucking idiot," yelled the drunk as he got off. Good riddance.

Unfortunately there would be more of them. Some more would get on after he'd turned around and started on his way back. It was always the same. They were a traffic hazard. He could tell the authorities all about that. He had, in fact.

"It's as if I've lost all my enthusiasm for Christmas," said Angela. "It was a sort of sudden feeling I had in the elevator. Or an insight."

"An insight into what?"

"You know."

"You shouldn't have come with me the first time we saw the boy," said Winter.

"Yes, it was important for me to be there."

He didn't reply, listened for a moment to the fridge, and to the radio mumbling away in its corner.

"Is it the twenty-third our flights are booked for?" Angela asked.

"Yes."

"It'll be nice."

"I expect so."

"A warm Christmas," she said.

"I don't think it will be all that warm."

"No, there's bound to be subzero temperatures on Christmas Eve in Marbella." She continued warming her hands around the cup she hadn't yet finished. "Stormy, freezing cold, and no central heating."

"There might be snow," said Winter.

"There *is* snow," she said. "On top of Sierra Blanca."

He nodded. The trip would work out. His mother would be pleased. There would be sun there. Five days on the Costa del Sol, and then it would be New Year's again, and the weather would turn and spring would begin to advance, and then summer, and there was no need to look any further ahead than that.

"I met a woman at the nursery-school meeting who had something interesting to tell me," she said, looking at him. "It was a bit strange."

"Go on."

"It made me think about that boy. I mean, we had been talking about it during the evening."

"We can't keep everything secret," said Winter.

"That might be for the best."

"What did she have to say?" he asked.

"That her daughter had . . . met a stranger. Apparently she'd been sitting in a car with some grown-up. That's all."

"What do you mean, that's all?"

"I don't know. The girl came home and told her mother about it. That she'd been sitting in a car, I guess, with somebody else for a little while. That was all."

"She came home and told her mom about it?"

"Yes. Ellen. The girl's name is Ellen. She goes to the same nursery school as Elsa. Ellen Sköld."

"I recognize the name."

"That's who it was. Her mother's called Lena."

"And she believed it?"

"She didn't really know what to believe. Nothing had happened."

"What did she do next? After hearing about this?"

"She reported it. She spoke to somebody at the local police station in Linnéstaden."

"What did the staff say?" he asked. "The nursery-school staff, I mean."

"She spoke to them but nobody had noticed anything."

Winter said something she couldn't hear.

"What did you say?"

"They can't see everything," he said.

She stood up, went to the sink, and put her mug on the draining board. Winter remained seated. She went back to the table. He was staring into space.

"A penny for your thoughts."

"This all sounds strange."

"Her mother thinks so, too. Lena."

"But she reported it to the police. So there should be a record of it." He looked at her. "At the station, I mean."

"There must be. The police officer she spoke to seemed to take it seriously, at least. He asked her to check if the girl had lost anything, and it turned out that she had."

"Something disappeared? When?"

"The day it happened."

"Children lose things all the time. That's not unusual, you know that."

"But this seems to have been something she couldn't just lose. Ellen, I mean. It was a charm that was fastened down somehow."

"Lena Sköld," said Winter. "You said the mother was called Lena Sköld?"

"Yes. What are you going to do?"

"Talk to her."

"I didn't tell her that I lived with a detective chief inspector."

"Well, she'll find out now. Does it matter?"

"No."

"I think I've probably exchanged a few words with her when I've dropped Elsa off. I recognize the girl's name. But I don't think her mother knows what my job is."

"Does it matter?"

Winter smiled, and stood up.

"You knew exactly what you were doing when you told me this, didn't you?" he said.

She nodded.

"Have you ever heard of anything like this before?" she asked.

"I'll first have to find out exactly what it is that I've heard about," he said.

He went to the bathroom and brushed his teeth. He thought he would probably be able to recognize the girl when he saw her.

He allowed the darkness to linger on in his apartment after he closed the door. He knew his way around it so well, it wouldn't have mattered if he'd been blind. In his apartment, that is. He wouldn't have managed so well outside.

Darkness was more attractive indoors than out. A small amount of light trickled in through the venetian blinds even though he had closed them as tightly as possible.

He sat in front of the television screen. The boy in the video was laughing. At least, it looked like he was laughing. But something was wrong.

Why had he stopped? Suddenly he didn't want to touch the boy anymore. What was it? Should he go to the doctor and tell him what happened and ask if it was normal or abnormal?

He watched all the videos. He had a little collection. Similar videos, but slightly different. He was familiar with all the details now. You could see. A little extra step each time. He knew that now. And yet, he didn't really. He was on the way to . . . to . . . He refused to think about it. Refused. I refuse!

Don't think about the boy. That was something different. No. It was *not*.

Mom never heard him when he shouted. He had moved in there and didn't need to make a bed for his mom every evening in the house a thousand miles away. Mom was there. He used to shout.

She never heard.

Once he emerged *afterward* and he shouted and she sat there with her head averted, and she didn't hear him then either. It was as if he wasn't there. He didn't dare stand in front of her. Maybe she really hadn't heard him before, but if he stood in front of her and she didn't see him, he wouldn't exist anymore. He knew that she wasn't blind, and so he wouldn't exist. He didn't exist.

Then she wasn't there anymore.

And then came all the rest of it.

The telephone rang. He jumped and almost dropped the remote control. He let the phone ring, ring, ring. Five times, six. Then it stopped. He didn't have an answering machine. What was the point?

It rang again. He wasn't there. Or he was there but he didn't hear the telephone, and so he wasn't there. It stopped eventually, and he could busy himself with the videos for a bit longer and then get ready for bed. All this without switching on a single light. Anybody passing by outside would definitely think there was nobody at home, or that someone was in bed, asleep. And that was what he was going to do now.

19

HALDERS AND DJANALI WERE BACK AT THE STUDENT DORM, IN A
different hall. The girl who had heard the argument in Smedsberg's room had
identified Aryan Kaite as the young man who had come rushing out. No
doubt about it, despite Halders's provocations: Don't you think all black peo-
ple look the same? Aneta Djanali hadn't moved a muscle. How does he treat
her? the girl had wondered, looking at Djanali.

They were sitting in Kaite's room. There was a picture of a winter land-
scape on the wall behind the desk, a white field. The room had been cleaned
recently. The desk was tidy: penholder, notepad, computer, printer on a stand,
books in two neat piles next to the penholder, more books in two low book-
cases. A Discman, two small speakers on the ledge of the window looking out
onto the street where cars were flitting past in the half light.

"Would you guess that this kid was studying medicine simply by looking
around this room?" Halders asked.

"The anatomy poster would suggest that," said Djanali, pointing to the
wall where the bed was located.

"Everybody has something like that these days," said Halders. "People
are so interested in themselves that they hang X-rays of themselves next to
the china cupboard in the living room."

"Even so, that's a little odd," said Djanali.

"Odd? It's standard practice."

"Hmm."

"Don't you believe me?"

"Why hasn't Kaite come back yet?" Djanali wondered.

"Good question," said Halders, looking at his watch. "Maybe he's the
nervous type."

Aryan Kaite had excused himself after he'd let them in and gone back
into the hall. He needed to go to the bathroom.

They hadn't called ahead and fixed a meeting time before stopping by.

Kaite still had a bandage on his head when he opened the door. What was hidden underneath? Halders wondered. They would probably be able to find out the next day. The kid looked like a black prince in a turban. Maybe his whole tribe looked like that in the savannah back home. He feels homesick when he sees himself in a mirror.

Maybe he's on his way there now. Halders looked at his watch again, and then at the room's little hallway.

"What's that door?" he asked, pointing.

"It must be a closet," said Djanali.

Halders walked over to the door and opened it. He was confronted by a toilet, sink, and shower curtain.

The kid *was* on his way home.

"He's taken off," he said, and opened the door to the hall.

"What the hell for?" Djanali wondered.

Winter called the police station in Tredje Långgatan.

"Police, Majorna-Linnéstaden, Alinder."

Winter explained who he was and what he wanted.

"It sounds vaguely familiar," said Alinder.

"Do you know who took the call?"

"Lena Sköld, did you say? The little girl who said she'd been with a 'mister'? I recognize that. It was me."

"OK. Do you have time to check the details on that call right away?"

"Give me five minutes to rummage through the files. What's your number?"

Alinder phoned back seven minutes later.

"I've got the notes in front of me."

"OK."

"The girl's name is Ellen, and her mother, who's a single parent, wasn't sure if it was just a figment of her daughter's imagination."

"What did the girl say happened?"

"Hang on, let's take a look. She'd been sitting in a car with a man she didn't know. That's all."

Winter could hear the rustle of paper.

"No, just a minute," said Alinder. "The girl said she'd been given candy as well."

"Did the mother say she'd spoken to the staff at the nursery school?"

"Yes. Nobody had noticed anything."

"Is that what they said?"

"Yes."

"Was she upset?"

"When?" said Alinder. "When she called me, you mean?"

"Yes."

"No."

"Is there anything else?" Winter asked.

"Yes. I'm reading it now. I asked her to check if anything had disappeared, and she called back later to say the little girl had had a little silver charm in a secure pocket in her overalls, and that it was no longer there."

"And this coincided with when she met this man?"

"I asked the same question and she said it did. And that it would have been impossible for the charm or whatever it was to fall out by accident, and that the girl wouldn't have been able to take it out herself."

"Maybe the girl didn't even know it was there," said Winter. I must ask Lena Sköld about that, he thought.

"No. Her mother said it was supposed to bring her good luck or happiness or something. It was hers from when she was a little girl."

"And now it's gone."

"That's what she said. I can't confirm that, of course."

"I'll ask her," said Winter.

"Why are you asking me all this?" Alinder asked. "And how did you know she called me?"

"My partner met her at a parents' meeting," said Winter. "We use the same nursery school."

"Well, I'll be damned!"

"Thanks for your help," said Winter.

"Why the interest in the first place?" Alinder wondered.

"I'm not sure really," said Winter. "It was just a thought."

"I heard about that business with the little boy," said Alinder.

"What did you hear?"

"That he was abducted and dumped somewhere else. I just read about it on the intranet. Nasty business. How is he?"

"He's been struck dumb," said Winter. "Hasn't said a word yet. But his eyes will be fine."

"Can you really see a link here? Between this woman's phone call and what happened to that little boy?"

"What do you think, Alinder? How do you see it?"

"Well . . . I've only just heard about your case. But I suppose I might have started to put two and two together after a while. I don't know. I might well have been in touch with you after a while. But then again, I might not. Anyway, the notes are here on file."

"You haven't had any similar calls to your station, I take it? You or any other officer?"

"I haven't. And none of the others have said anything. I'll check in with them."

"OK, many thanks for your help," said Winter, and hung up.

He called Lena Sköld. They met half an hour later at her home. Ellen was sitting at the table, drawing a snowman.

"Has she ever seen any snow?" Winter asked.

"When she was one. It lasted for three days," said Lena.

The west coast climate—although now it's milder than ever, Winter thought. Soon there'll be palm trees along the avenue.

"That looks like a real snowman," he said. "My Elsa's a bit younger, of course, but I'll be proud of her when she can draw as well as that."

"Would you like a cup of coffee?"

"Yes please."

"You can ask me your questions while I'm making it."

She stood up. Winter remained seated at the kitchen table opposite Ellen, who was starting a new drawing. He saw something that looked like a car, only upside down from where he was.

Children and drawings. He thought about a case he'd solved a few years earlier, about Helene, the dead woman who had remained anonymous for so long. Her face in the ditch near Lake Delsjö at dawn, her teeth exposed, as if she'd uttered a cry from the far distance that had echoed down through time; the past had cast shadows over the future, and the truth was hidden in the darkness. The only clue he'd had was a child's drawings. The child saw what it saw, and then drew her memories.

Memories could be revisited like wide-open gates, enabling him to go in, or allowing somebody else to enter. Somebody else might get there first, and that could be the equivalent of falling into the abyss. He had seen it before. When memories were opened up the result could be catastrophe, the ultimate one.

If he wasn't there at the time.

Why am I having such thoughts right now? The drawing, yes. But something else as well. Is all this linked to a memory?

"A car," he said to Ellen.

She nodded.

"A big car."

She nodded again. Drew the wheels.

"She drew a similar one when she came home and told me about the stranger," said her mother, who had come back with two mugs of coffee and a little jug of milk.

"Do you still have it?"

"Of course. I save all her little works of art."

"I'd like to take a look at it later."

"Why?"

"I'm not sure. It might contain something I can use."

"For what?"

"I'm not sure of that either," he said, and smiled.

"What do you think about all this, then? What Ellen said?"

The girl looked up.

"I think it's important enough for me to come here and talk to you," he said, taking a sip of coffee.

"What happens now, then?" asked Lena.

"I don't know that either."

"What's your next move?" She looked at him. "Isn't that what you say?"

Winter looked at the girl, who looked up again and smiled.

"Surely you're not going to interrogate her?" She looked first at Winter, then at her daughter.

Winter gestured as if to say: I don't know.

"Has this happened in other places? What might have happened to Ellen?"

Same gesture from Winter.

"You don't know?" she asked.

"We'll check it out and see if we can find any links," he said.

Winter was sitting in Ringmar's office that afternoon. It was the same standardized design as his own, but the window faced another direction.

The city outside was at its most electric now. Dusk was closing in and Gothenburg was starting to glitter in sheer joy at the approach of Christmas.

"Have you bought any Christmas presents?" asked Ringmar, who was in the window watching the lights come on.

"Of course," said Winter, untruthfully.

"Books?"

"Yes. For Elsa so far."

At least that was true.

"Hmm," Ringmar grunted.

"Then there'll no doubt be some last-minute shopping, as usual," said Winter.

"When's your flight to the sunshine coast?"

"The day before the day." Winter rolled a cigarillo between his fingers without lighting it. It smelled good even so. "But I don't think I'll make it."

"Really?"

"Well, do you?"

Ringmar turned around.

"You mean you think we'll still be looking for him?"

Winter didn't reply.

"Maybe we'll have cracked it by then, so that we can enjoy some peace and quiet like everybody else," said Ringmar, turning back to look out of the window.

"Did you send out the CID appeal?"

"Half an hour ago."

They'd also sent messages to all their police colleagues, but who got around to reading all those e-mails that flooded in every day? The CID information sheet was a better bet. Were there any more like Alinder? And Lena Sköld? Worth a try.

They got no information at CID headquarters. If something came to them specifically, they would hear. But otherwise, they didn't have a clue as to what was going on. Nobody coordinated information coming into individual stations and departments anymore.

"Nobody coordinates stuff anymore," Ringmar had said to young Bergenhem. "Nobody calls CID direct nowadays. In the old days, before the reorganization, everything was sent to the head of CID, who read it all and kept duplicates—about pedophiles, for instance. Suspicions, or even unusual things people noticed." Ringmar had nodded at his own words. "A lot of people think they see child molesters everywhere all the time, but it's important not to ignore their reports. Don't you think? We should collect all the documentation so that we can sift through it when we are looking for a really nasty specimen."

Winter was still on the chair, rolling his cigarillo.

"It seems like the boy has lost the ability to speak," said Ringmar. "I was there an hour ago."

"Nothing new?"

"No."

"We'll have to see what we've got so far," said Winter.

"The Sköld girl? Could be imagination. The nursery-school staff didn't notice anything."

"We'll have to see," Winter said again.

The neighbor had set up his Christmas lights when Ringmar got back home. Every sleeping aspen and maple in the garden on the other side of the skeletal hedge was laden with hundreds of little glittering lights that were reflected in the dull paint of his unwashed Audi.

Each of the next-door windows was lit up by a set of electric Advent candles. That's the home of somebody who's not short on cash, Ringmar thought. A private illuminations warehouse. A plethora of light.

The disgust was still visible in his face when he entered the hall.

"What's eating you?" asked Moa, who was on her way out.

"Where are you going?"

"What kind of tone is that?"

"I'm sorry."

"I'm going to buy a Christmas present, if I can find what I'm looking for," she said. "Which reminds me, I haven't seen a wish list from you yet."

"A wish list? I haven't written one of those for years."

"But now I'm living at home, temporarily, and so you need to write a wish list," said his daughter, pulling the other boot over her heel.

"You should know already what's at the top of my list," he said.

She looked up from the stool under the light that illuminated her hair and made her look like one of the handmaidens in a queen of light procession. Or even Lucia herself.

"Do you think I don't know?" she said.

"Hmm."

"Do you really think so? Do you think I haven't spoken to him?"

"What did he say?"

She didn't answer, stood up.

"When did you last speak to him?"

"It's a while ago now."

"What do you mean by that?"

She opened the door.

"When's the next time going to be?" Ringmar asked. "For God's sake, Moa, this is crazy."

"Give it some time, Dad."

"Some time? What the hell am I supposed to give some time to?"

20

"FRÖLUNDA WANTS TO SPEAK TO YOU," SAID MÖLLERSTRÖM AS Winter was passing. The registrar waved the telephone receiver at him.

"I'll take it in my office," Winter said.

He picked up the receiver in his office without taking off his overcoat.

"Winter."

"Hi, this is Larissa Serimov from Frölunda police station."

Somebody he'd never heard of before.

"Hi Larissa."

"I read your appeal in the CID information circular."

"And?"

"On the intranet as well, incidentally."

"So what do you have to say?"

"I've had something similar here as well."

"Tell me."

"A woman called the station and I took the call, and she said that her daughter had been with a stranger."

"How did she know?"

"The girl told her about it."

"Told her about what?"

"As I just said. An encounter of some sort."

"Any injuries?"

"No . . ."

"There's hesitation in your voice."

"It might be more complicated. I have my suspicions. About the possible injuries the girl has. But it might have nothing to do with the stranger business."

"I see."

"But then again . . ." Winter could hear the rustling of papers. "The girl also lost a ball, by the way. According to her mother. It could have happened at any time, of course, but the mother says she lost it the same day."

"Where are you now?"

"At the station."

Winter checked his watch.

"I'll be there in half an hour. I'm leaving right away."

The Frölunda police station was not small, but it was dwarfed by the furniture store next door. There were no vacant places in the store's parking lot. A procession of cars drove away with sofas and armchairs strapped to the roof. Beds and headboards were balanced precariously on open trailers. Sticking out like crosses on which an unwary driver might well find himself suspended. It's a good thing the rain has stopped, at least, Winter thought. A wet bed is not exactly uplifting.

Larissa Serimov was waiting for him at reception.

"I went with them to the hospital," she said. "The mother was worried. The girl's father was there as well."

"So the name of the family is Bergort?"

"Yes. The girl's name is Maja."

"What did the doctor have to say?"

"He found no injuries in the lower part of the body, nothing of that kind. But he said something else."

"Yes?"

"The girl, Maja, had a few bruises."

"Had she been abused?"

"He couldn't say."

"What did they look like?"

"Swelling. Bruises. Not big."

"But he had an opinion, no doubt?"

"The mother said that Maja had fallen off a swing and hit the frame. She thought that's what had happened. Maja had been crying, she said. And the doctor said that was possible."

"The alternative?"

She looked down at the computer printout. The order of events, Winter thought. That could be of crucial significance.

"What he said was more or less exactly this: 'I just thought that it's not totally unheard of for parents who beat their children to report it to the police as an accident. Or to invent stories that might fit the bill, some of them absolute fantasy.' I assume he was referring to the situation with the stranger."

"But he didn't want to make an official report."

"No. Nothing like that."

"What about you, though?"

She looked at him, as if she'd been expecting that question at any moment.

"I haven't been able to let go. I went to see them and met the mother and the girl again."

Winter waited. They were still in reception. He still had his overcoat on. He'd thought briefly that Inspector Larissa Serimov's blouse was the same color as the sky out there. In summer the blouse might have looked overwashed against the aggressive brightness of the clear sky, but now it was a part of the winter world, a sort of camouflage uniform the police were obliged to wear when outdoors in December without a jacket.

"There was something about the child. Something had happened again," said Serimov.

"Are you sure?"

"No. But yes."

"How did the mother react?"

"As if nothing had happened."

"But she reported the incident with the stranger," Winter said.

"And the obvious question is: Why?" said Serimov.

"Do you want to file a report?" Winter asked. "Against the parents?"

"I'm still not a hundred percent sure," she said. "Everything seems to be so . . . normal. So . . . as it should be. The harmonious little family. A family just like every other."

Like mine, Winter thought.

"Have you met the father aside from at the hospital?" he asked. "What was his name again?"

"Bergort. Magnus Bergort. But to answer your question: No—he wasn't at home when I stopped by."

Winter looked out through the door and noted that the light was faint but nevertheless brighter than it had been for several months.

"Let's step outside for a couple of minutes." He held up his cigarillo by way of explanation.

They were standing in front of the parked police cars. Larissa Serimov wasn't shivering without her jacket. It was so mild. Her blouse was the same color as the sky. Camouflage. Winter smoked his cigarillo. It was only his fourth today. Daily consumption was going down, but there was a lower limit.

"What's your impression of this situation?" he asked.

"It's all based on what the child says, of course. The mother doesn't know what to think. The most concrete evidence she has is that the ball has disappeared, and that Maja says that this mister, or whatever we should call him, took her favorite ball and said he would throw it to her through the car window, but didn't."

"And where was the car parked?" Winter asked.

"Outside one of the nursery schools in Marconigatan. There's a little hill. They were playing on it."

"So there's somewhere to park there?"

"Yes. And it's sort of hidden. I checked."

"But the staff didn't notice anything?"

"No, nothing."

"Should they have?" Winter asked.

"I really don't know."

They drove to Marconigatan. The traffic had intensified along with the gathering darkness. The enormous parking lot behind Frölunda Square was starting to fill. Some people were going to the Arts Center, the library, and the swimming pools, but most to the shops. Streetcars clattered past in a constant stream. Windows in the high-rise buildings were lit up like broad smiles, row upon row of them. The moon was stronger than the sun now. There were stars up there, a reminder that the sky hadn't shut down for good. Winter suddenly felt hungry, and thought about food for dinner. He looked at his watch. He would have time to get to the market later in the afternoon, but buying food wasn't the most important of today's jobs.

Some children were digging in the sand. Two women were standing among them. Two staff members for three children, Winter thought. I'm assuming that's not a normal statistic.

The nursery-school manager was still there. She looked tired, like most people who were trying to hang on until the holidays finally arrived. There were jam stains on her apron. A little child was sitting on her knee, and smiled when Winter stuck his finger into his mouth, puffed up his cheeks, and made a little popping noise to amuse all present.

"Now I guess I'll have to keep doing that in the future," said the manager, putting down the little boy who had only just learned to walk.

She took off her apron and revealed a dress that looked like the apron. Her eyes were wide apart, and she gave the impression of being more than competent.

Winter had already introduced himself.

"Let's go outside," said the woman, whose name was Margareta Inge-marsson.

"We've met before," she said to Serimov.

She's ambitious, Winter thought, looking at his colleague. But she didn't contact us. If she had I wouldn't have had anything to say. Not then. We would've had a memo of the call, just like she had.

They stood diagonally behind the U-shaped nursery school. The traffic had fused to form a continuous beam of headlights. There was a fence, and beyond it a hill and some trees. A narrow paved road ran around the hill linking the parking lot in front of the nursery to the one belonging to the housing estate on the other side.

"Just a moment," Winter said, and walked higher up the slope in order to look down at the narrow road, partly hidden by the trees. He went back to where the two women were standing.

"Well, I really don't know what else I can say," said the nursery manager.

"Did you speak to Maja's mother?" Winter asked.

"Yes." She glanced up at the top of the hill, then looked back at Winter. "We don't know what to think here."

"Could it have happened?"

"What exactly do you mean?"

"What the girl said. That she sat in a car with somebody for a little while. Somebody she didn't know," Winter said. "That it happened here."

"It sounds incredible to me," said Ingemarsson. "But what can I say? We didn't notice anything. And I would maintain that we keep a close eye on our children here."

"Do they come up here to play?" asked Winter, gesturing toward the slope and the trees.

"Sometimes. But never alone."

"What's the staffing situation?"

"In relation to the number of children? Catastrophic."

That was one way of answering the question, Winter thought. Nothing new to me. I'm a detective chief inspector, but I'm also a father.

Police headquarters was warm and pleasantly welcoming as always. My second home. Winter walked down the corridor, which would shortly be decorated with a Christmas tree. He could hear the rhythmic tapping of a computer keyboard. The last report of the day was being written in the front office. He could see a hunched back. A few more lines, then home, home, home. He thought about a venison steak with sliced oven-baked potatoes. Or mashed root vegetables. Mushrooms, perhaps. I didn't use to think like this. Does it have to do with turning forty? No. It has to do with the fact that I haven't had any lunch.

He heard his telephone ringing before he reached his office. It stopped, then started again when he was inside.

"Erik? Hello. We have a problem here at the hospital. Car accident victims. Multiple ones. Could you pick Elsa up, please?"

Angela sounded stressed.

Another nursery school. Yes, of course.

"What time?"

"Half past five. It's Thursday today." .

Winter looked at the clock hanging on the wall over the sink. Half past four. He might have time to fit in the market as well.

"What time will you be home?" he asked.

"I don't know. I have no idea, and I have to go now."

"OK, I'll pick her up. There'll be . . ."—but she had whispered a quick "love you" and hung up before he had time to inform her about dinner.

He turned on his computer. There were several messages in his in-box. He selected one of them and phoned the direct number.

"Police, Örgryte-Härlanda, Berg."

"Hello, Winter here, CID. Can I speak to Bengt Josefsson, please?"

"He left an hour ago."

"Do you have his home number?"

"How do I know you are who you say you are?"

"Look, I have to pick up my daughter from the nursery school in less than an hour and go to the market before then, and before that I need to talk to Josefsson about a message he left me, so be a good boy and give me his home number now."

"I can see on the display here that you are one of us; or at least you are calling from police headquarters," said Berg.

This Berg idiot is a piece of work, Winter thought. He got the number, and called it.

"Josefsson."

"Hello, Erik Winter here."

"Ah, yes."

Winter heard him swallow, and what sounded like ice cubes in a glass of whiskey. Blended. Josefsson was enjoying his free time.

"It's about that business with the young children," said Josefsson.

"I'm all ears," said Winter.

"I saw your appeal, and I've got something that might be relevant." Winter heard another clink, fainter now as the ice cubes melted and grew smaller. "I made a note of a phone call I received," said Josefsson. Winter heard his voice rather thicker and milder now, from the smoke in the spirits.

He found a parking space for the Mercedes by the canal. There were more customers in the market today than there had been the day before, but not as many as there would be the next day. Winter bought his venison steak and some langoustines for a possible appetizer, and some ripe goat's cheese. The market was beginning to acquire the heavy aroma of fresh pork that was so central to the Swedish Christmas. Winter's mind turned to shellfish tapas on a coast farther south. He'd soon be there.

But back in the car he wasn't sure. He had a nagging worry. He recognized it as an old enemy that kept coming back.

Elsa already had her jacket on. He had arrived just on time.

When they were in the car, she asked about dinner.

"Are you hungry?"

"I'm really really hungry."

"Did you have any lunch today?"

"No," she said, nose in the air.

"Nothing at all?"

"No!"

"I can understand why you're hungry, then."

"What's for dinner?"

He didn't have the heart to tell her it was venison. Bambi. He just didn't have the heart.

"A lovely little steak that won't take long in the oven, and there'll be sauce, and I can make you some mashed potato and some mushrooms."

"Yes!"

"And before that you can help me to make a salad with some langoustines and whatever else we can find."

"Find *where*?!"

"Inside your nose," he said, turning around.

"Ha ha ha!" She was jumping up and down in her car seat. "Really really hungry."

But that was when she could still talk. In the kitchen she very nearly fell asleep with her arm around a langoustine that looked as if it were her cuddly toy. He picked it up, prepared it, and added it to the others.

Elsa couldn't wait. An unusually hard day at the office. She ate a claw and he quickly prepared a small portion of mashed potato and heated up what was left of yesterday's salmon and cod au gratin. It smelled good, but Elsa's interest had faded somewhat.

He read to her.

"Are you tired tonight, sweetie? What have you done today?"

She was asleep. He closed his eyes and thought about the Waggoner boy who didn't want to talk and couldn't raise one arm, but could still see.

He lifted her into her bed and left the door ajar. He went back to the kitchen, checked the steak, and peeled some more potatoes and took some more mushrooms out of the freezer. He happened to think about that clinking noise over the telephone, and poured himself a Rosebank with a small glass of water on the side.

The sky was clear. Winter stood in the balcony doorway and drank and enjoyed the fresh, dry taste of herbs, and the whiff of a lowland breeze. He rejected the idea of a Corps. He left the balcony door open for a while, went to his desk, switched on his laptop, and spent a quarter of an hour thinking while the big room filled up with music.

If he had described that scene to anyone, they would have understood it as peaceful. He didn't feel at peace. He was trying to work out a pattern on the basis of what he'd heard that day, and there was no trace of peace in that pattern.

Angela came home while he was setting the table.

"Will you pour me a drop of wine?" she said, before coming anywhere near the kitchen. He had heard her briefcase thud on the floor from a great height. "Mmmm. It smells good."

She went in to see Elsa as he was adding a lump of butter to the sauce. The final touch before they sat down to eat.

"Ah yes, of course" said Angela, when she came into the kitchen and saw the deep dishes with the shellfish salad. "It's Thursday after all."

"Elsa was tired out."

"I'm more hungry than tired now," she said. "And thirsty." She held her wineglass up to the light and studied the contents. "I declare as the house doctor that wine is good for you after a hard day's work."

They sat down at the table. The music was Mingus, drifting in from the living room.

"I hope you didn't tell Elsa what we're eating for the main course?" she said.

He shook his head.

"It's very good even so. Everything is good."

"Better than Bistro 1965?"

"There are questions you can't answer with a simple yes or no," she said.

Such as, have you stopped beating your children? he thought.

21

THE MORNING MEETING WAS HELD BY CANDLELIGHT. TWO ADVENT candles were burning on the table, and hundreds of similar ones dotted the building. Coffee and Lucia buns were on the table, as well as a plate of ginger cookies that Halders was working his way through. Before Winter had the opportunity to say anything, the door burst open. Birgersson had a strange grin on his face, and was beckoning:

"Come and look at this."

They could hear the singing in the corridor. It was December 13, St. Lucia's Day, and the traditional procession was approaching, led by Lucia, dressed in a white robe and with a crown of burning candles on her head. She was accompanied by her maids, looking like angels gliding through the catacombs. Winter recognized Lucia as a girl from reception, and some of her maids. At the back of the procession were two "star" boys, both with the same strange grin as Birgersson had worn a minute ago, and still had, as Winter saw when he looked at him. The two star boys, wearing conical white hats and carrying sticks with a silver star on the end, were a couple of experienced officers from the cells. One of them was notorious for his violent temperament.

Halders tried to trip him as he walked past. His colleague responded with an internationally recognized gesture.

"You can shove that where the sun don't shine," said Halders with a smile, pointing at the star boy's stick.

"That could be anywhere at all in this town," mumbled Birgersson next to Halders. "At this time of the year."

The procession continued along the corridor, singing Saaantaa Luuciiiia in keys unknown to musicologists, amplified by the acoustics of the tiled walls. Bergenhem held his hands over his ears.

"Did you know it was Lucia Day today?" asked Winter, turning to look at Birgersson.

"I'm the boss here, aren't I? I know everything."

"And now we'll have to wait until next year," said Aneta Djanali. "Another year before we can see anything like this again."

"Maybe they'll make you Lucia," said Halders. "It would be modern and politically correct to have a black Lucia, don't you think?"

"Yes, that has always been my dream. It would be a dream come true."

"Besides, Lucia came from Africa," said Halders.

"Sicily," said Djanali. "Southern Italy."

"Southern Europe, North Africa, what's the difference?" said Halders.

"The coffee's getting cold," said Winter.

The candles were still burning on the table, but they had turned on the overhead light. Goodbye cozy atmosphere, Djanali thought.

"We'll make another attempt to talk to the boy," said Ringmar.

"How much does he understand?" said Halders. "He's barely four years old."

"According to his parents he speaks well," said Ringmar. "Besides, he's bilingual."

"That's more than you can say for us," said Halders.

"Speak for yourself," said Djanali.

"He's still in a state of shock," said Winter, "but they haven't found any injuries to his head."

Is this Halders we're talking about? Bergenhem thought.

"His ability to move his limbs is improving, and he probably won't suffer any permanent damage." He looked up. "Physical damage, that is."

"How's your search through the records going?" asked Halders, looking at Möllerström.

"There are a lot of names," said Möllerström. "Pedophiles, child abusers, other sex offenders, you know the types. It's a long list."

"Let's go through it slowly and carefully," said Winter.

"All we've come across so far are alibis," said Bergenhem. "They all seem to be behaving themselves."

"Any chance of more staff to help with the door-to-door?" Halders wondered.

"Possibly," said Winter.

"What's the matter with Birgersson?" said Halders. "This could have led to murder, for Christ's sake. People living in the area might have seen the bloody lunatic when he picked up the boy."

"For now we have to work with the resources we have," said Winter.

"Why wasn't the boy abused sexually?" asked Djanali. She looked around at her colleagues. "I've been asking myself that, you've been doing the same. He's injured, but not in that way. Why? What does the man want? Why did he hurt the boy at all? Do these injuries mean something particular? Did he plan to do that from the start? Did something happen in the car? Had he actually intended to rape the boy? Why did he leave him like he did?"

"That's a lot of questions," said Halders.

"But all ones we have to ask ourselves," said Djanali.

"Of course," said Winter. "And it gets worse." Everybody looked up. "Or maybe better. Listen to this. This is from the last twenty-four hours."

He told them about the other children who had met this unknown mister. Ellen Sköld. Maja Bergort. And Kalle Skarin, the boy in Bengt Josefsson's memo at the Härlanda police station.

"Hmm, what can you say to that?" said Halders.

"Anything at all," said Winter. "We're a team and this is all about teamwork, and I want to hear your views now."

"Is there actually a link between these three?" asked Halders, of nobody in particular.

"We don't know yet," said Winter. "We'll have to speak to the children."

Everybody looked at him.

"Do you really mean that?" asked Sara Helander.

"I'm not a hundred percent sure what I mean yet," said Winter. "Let's continue the discussion."

"Links," said Djanali. "We were talking about links. What could they be?"

"Three children, or four if you include young Waggoner. One difference: The other three were not abducted."

"Why not?" asked Helander.

"He wasn't ready yet," said Halders. He looked at Ringmar and Winter on the other side of the table. "It's basic psychology. The guy wasn't ready the first few times. He was testing and maybe went a step further each time, and in the end he was up for it. But it is not necessarily anything sexual. Or maybe that will come later."

"Instant analysis," said Djanali.

"I'll be proved right," said Halders. He looked at Winter again. "Which means that he's going to strike again. Fuck, fuck, fuck." He shuddered. "And always assuming, of course, that we establish a connection. And that some of this did actually happen. Well, we know about the Waggoner boy. But what about the others? They might just have been telling stories."

"They might have," said Winter.

"Four small kids find their way into a weirdo's car without anybody notic-ing? Is this credible?" wondered Sara Helander.

"Maybe he wasn't what we normally call a weirdo," said Halders. "Didn't you hear my analysis?"

"But is it credible?" insisted Helander. "That none of the staff noticed anything?"

"What staff?" said Halders. "They don't have any damn staff anymore," said Halders. "That's the way it is nowadays. Bigger and bigger groups of chil-dren, and less and less staff to take care of them."

"So you're suggesting that this actually could happen? That these kids could vanish, presto, just like that?"

"Absolutely."

"I doubt it," said Helander.

"I think you should take that doubt of yours to any playground you like where there are lots of kids running around, and take a second to think about how you might be able to kidnap one," said Halders. "Or at least arrange a private meeting with one of them."

"Are you being serious?"

"You'd be surprised, Sara. At how easy it is."

"Shouldn't we check out these places properly?" asked Bergenhem. "The children's playgrounds and nursery schools or wherever it was that these things happened?" He looked at Winter. "Apart from Plikta, that is, where Simon was abducted."

"That applies to Ellen Sköld as well," said Winter. "According to her, it also happened at Plikta."

Even as he said that Winter could picture Elsa's face. His daughter on the swings, in the middle of the playground, next to the parking lot.

Would the man they were hunting be there now? Had he already been there twice and achieved what he wanted to do? Would it happen again? In the same place? It was possible. Possibly more than possible.

"Anyway," said Bergenhem, "should we put some resources into it?"

"Yes," said Winter, picturing Elsa's face. "But I don't know the best way to go about it yet. I'll think it over, and have a word with Sture."

"Do it now while Lucia is still on his mind," said Halders, causing Sara Helander to giggle.

"Was that funny?" said Halders, with a surprised expression on his face.

"One other thing," said Winter. "Three of the children lost something after meeting this man. Maja Bergort lost a ball."

"Good God," said Halders. "When *don't* children lose balls?"

"Do you mind if I finish?"

Halders nodded and said nothing.

"Her favorite ball," said Winter, "She always had it with her. Ellen Sköld had a little silver bird charm zipped into an overall pocket. Gone. And Simon Waggoner lost his watch." He looked up. "All this is according to the parents."

"What about the fourth child?" asked Aneta Djanali. "What was his name?"

"Skarin. Kalle Skarin. I'm drawing a blank there so far. I spoke briefly to his mother yesterday, and she is going to look into it," said Winter.

"What's the chronological order of the incidents?" Halders asked.

"In the order of the phone calls we received it started with Skarin, then Sköld, then Bergort, and lastly Waggoner."

"If he is the last," said Halders.

"Do we have any doctors' reports?" asked Djanali.

"In two cases. Waggoner, obviously, and the Bergort girl."

"And?"

"No sexual abuse, if that's what you are wondering. We know about Waggoner's injuries, and in the case of Maja Bergort there's a suspicion of injuries."

Everybody looked at him.

"A colleague in Frölunda, Larissa Serimov, took the call and was also at the hospital where the parents took the girl immediately after she told her story. The doctor found some bruises. Serimov visited their house a few days later and thought she could see more."

"So maybe it's got nothing to do with our case," said Halders. "They beat their kid and drive to the emergency room with their hearts in their mouths to have the injuries checked, and seem to be innocent." He looked at Helander. "Happens all the time."

"But the mother's story is almost exactly the same as what the other mothers have said," said Winter.

"Why is it only the mothers?" wondered Halders.

"It fits," said Winter.

Nobody spoke for a while. The candles were still burning as the daylight outside grew brighter. Winter had a clear view out the window and watched the concrete pillars of the Nya Ullevi stadium slowly acquiring the same wispy gray mist as the air around them. Everything was part of a whole, everything seemed to be hovering. There were no borders, no lines. Now he could hear the patrol cars down below, more traffic than usual. It was Lucia morning and Gothenburg was different, thousands of young people needed assistance after the night of partying. They were lying in bunches all over town, as Halders had put it when he arrived. The railway stations were full of teenagers sleeping off their intoxication and preparing to cope with their hangovers, which would be awful but not as deadly.

"I've been trying to find some kind of pattern in the locations," Winter said. "Why those particular spots? Why those nursery schools, or those playgrounds?"

"Have you drawn a map of them?" asked Djanali.

"That's what I'm going to sit down and do this morning."

It will only raise more questions, Halders thought; but he didn't say so. Instead he said: "Are you intending to talk to the parents?"

"Yes."

"All of them?"

"Yes."

"I'd like to come with you when you go to the Bergorts out at Önnered."

"If you get a grip on yourself."

"You need me," said Halders.

The morning wasn't over. Work wasn't over. They never worked on one isolated case at a time. That might have been the situation in an ideal world, but that wasn't where they were living. In an ideal world they wouldn't have existed at all as a profession. In an ideal world there was no such thing as CID detectives, no uniformed police officers. Law and order took care of itself. Everybody lived in a land of milk and honey.

But who the hell would want to splash around in that muck? as Halders said when the topic came up for discussion some time ago.

Fredrik did his best to keep the banter going, but Winter could see the shadows behind his eyes, even deeper than those behind Bertil's.

Do you need to take time off? Winter had asked him casually not that long ago. Halders had taken time off, but not enough. I listen to what my children have to say, he'd said, and Winter might just have understood him. Fredrik had been condemned by fate to abandon the individual life he'd embarked upon and assume new responsibilities as the single parent of two children. How serious was it with Aneta? He didn't know. Did she?

"There's still no sign of our black medical student," said Halders, looking at Djanali. "Have you put the word out on the home front?"

"They're on red alert on the savannahs, from Kenya to Burkino Faso," she said.

"Are there any savannahs in Burkina Faso?" asked Bergenhem, who was interested in geography.

"No," said Djanali. "That's the point."

"It's a matter of interpretation," said Halders with a smile.

"I don't get it," said Bergenhem.

"You're not the only one," said Djanali.

"While you guys are bickering our man has escaped to South Africa," said Winter.

"OK, we'll nail him there, then," said Halders.

"Come on now, Fredrik."

Halders sat up straight. Winter could see how the pressure on the back of his neck was reflected in his face.

"We nailed Smedsberg late last night before he set off to visit his manure specialist buddies out in the flatlands. He confirmed that he'd fallen out with the Aryan, Mr. Kaite."

"Over what?" Winter asked.

"A girl."

"A girl?"

"That's what he said. Kaite thought he had something going with a girl who thought she had something going with Smedsberg."

"What did Smedsberg think?" Winter wondered. For Christ's sake . . .

"He remained neutral, as he put it."

"Does this girl exist?"

"We have a name and a telephone number." Halders gestured with his arms. "We called, but nobody answered. We checked the address and went there, but nobody was in. We managed to get into the apartment. But Kaite wasn't there, nor was the girl."

"Were you involved in this, Aneta?" Winter asked, but she shook her head: "I was in the car."

Winter looked at Halders.

"Did you leave a note on the hall table asking her to call you when she got back home?" Winter asked, with acid in his voice.

"That didn't occur to me!" said Halders, raising a finger to the skies.

"Do you believe Smedsberg?"

"I don't believe anybody," said Halders, "but he did give us her name. Josefin. Josefin Stenvång."

"Smedsberg is the only one of these four guys who wasn't injured," said Ringmar.

"Do you see a connection there, Bertil?" Halders wondered.

"Eh? . . . What?"

"Four students and three injured. Four children and three uninjured. Do you see a connection?"

"What did you have for breakfast today, Fredrik?" Ringmar asked. "You're just a little bit on overdrive."

"Doesn't the job we do depend on links, connections?" Halders said. "Or have I completely misunderstood everything?"

"Fredrik," said Winter.

Halders turned around.

Is this the moment when the crisis is going to kick in? Winter thought. Fredrik has managed to keep going until now. Oddly enough. Is there madness in his eyes? No. Has he started to hyperventilate? Not yet. What can I say now, when I have his full attention? What direction can I point him in?

"Please let Bertil finish what he has to say," said Winter.

"OK, OK," said Halders.

"Anyway, we have Smedsberg," said Ringmar. "He avoids the blow to the head. He's not marked by a branding iron or whatever the damned thing is. He saw a newspaper delivery boy. He grew up on a farm. He suggests that the wounds might reveal a number that could lead us to a particular farm, or some kind of code or symbol that would do the same. He lives in the same student dorm as two of the other victims, Kaite and Stillman. Book as well, come to think of it. So far he has denied knowing any of them, including Book."

"He's also a Chalmers student," said Halders.

"Oh, come on Fredrik, can't you keep your comments to yourself for once?" said Helander. Halders didn't seem to hear.

"We mentioned Jens Book," Ringmar continued. "Studying journalism, but not at the moment. He's still in Sahlgren Hospital. He's gotten some mobility back on his right side. The latest report is positive, very positive in fact, and it looks like he'll be able to walk again eventually."

"If the blow stops him from working as a journalist in the future, the report certainly is very positive," said Halders. He turned to Helander. "I don't like journalists, you see."

"Jens Book had been with his friend Krister Peters about half an hour before he was attacked in Linnéplatsen outside Marilyn, the video store."

"His homosexual friend," said Halders.

"Do you have a problem with that, Fredrik?" Ringmar had looked up from his file.

"Not at all. I only mentioned it for clarification."

"Peters is gay," said Bergenhem. "I've met him, as you know. He makes no attempt to hide the fact."

"Why was he secretive about his meeting with Book, then?" asked Djanali.

"It wasn't Peters who was secretive. It was Book himself," said Ringmar. "We had to drag it out of him. It took time."

"Not unusual behavior," said Bergenhem. "If he doesn't want to tell any-body, that's up to him. Don't you think? There are lots of people who don't want to. We've talked about it before." Bergenhem could see that Halders wanted to say something but was holding back. "Do you have a comment to make about that, Fredrik?"

Halders shook his head.

"So Book's possible relationship with Peters doesn't necessarily have any-thing to do with this," said Bergenhem.

"But Peters doesn't have an alibi," said Ringmar.

"Then again, the plain fact is that Book is the one we know most about when it comes to what they were doing immediately before they were at-tacked," said Bergenhem. "If we believe Peters, we know more or less what Book was up to all evening, apart from a short time before he was bashed."

"Yes," said Winter, who hadn't spoken for some time, had just listened and made a few notes.

"But it's quite different when it comes to Kaite, for instance. What was he doing in the hours before he was attacked in Kapellplatsen?"

Nobody answered.

"Kaite is very vague about that, and now he's run off to God only knows where," said Bergenhem. "He's also had an argument with Smedsberg, who lived in the dorm next door. There's a link for you, Fredrik." Halders gave a start. As if he'd woken up out of a short coma, Winter thought.

"And our friend the law student, Jakob Stillman, is no longer as silent as he was forced to be at first, but he doesn't have a very good memory either," said Bergenhem. "Unless it's the blows that have knocked the memories out of his head. Which I don't believe. I think he was somewhere that he doesn't want to tell us about, and then he walked across Doktor Fries Square and was attacked in the same way."

"What took him to Doktor Fries Square?" said Djanali.

"What took Kaite to Kapellplatsen?" said Bergenhem.

"Is there a link?" wondered Halders.

"Perhaps nothing more than the fact that they were on their way home," said Winter.

"On their way to the same place but from different directions," said Ringmar.

"At different times," said Bergenhem.

"Stillman seems to be a full-blooded heterosexual," said Halders. "If you can believe Bertil's daughter's friend, that is." He looked at Bergenhem. "Talking of nonlinks."

"The link here is that three of them were attacked by the same person," said Ringmar. "Or all four, in fact, since the intention was that Smedsberg should get the same treatment."

"If we can believe him," said Halders.

"He reported it to the police," said Djanali.

"So did that family out at Önnered," said Halders. "Possibly for the same reason as Gustav Smedsberg." Halders looked at Winter. "By the way, shouldn't we be on our way there now?"

"Soon."

"Speaking of getting under way, perhaps we should pay a visit to the Smedsberg family farm," said Bergenhem. "Out in the flatlands, as Fredrik put it."

"Why?" asked Winter.

"The weapon. The branding iron. If we follow through with the hypothesis that all of the victims actually did the opposite of what they said they did, it's Gustav Smedsberg who clubbed down the other three, and he did it with a branding iron like the one he said was back at home on the farm."

"Hang on," said Djanali. "If we shortly get hold of the identity number or whatever it's called, and on that basis can find the farm the weapon comes from, well, if Smedsberg half kills people with a weapon that can be traced back to him, and he puts us on the right track . . . Do you see what I'm getting at?"

"You're suggesting that people's actions are rational and based on sound logic," said Halders. "That we should use that as our starting point. The day we start doing that we might just as well pack up here and start selling roasted almonds in Slottsskogen." He looked at Bergenhem.

"We'll see," said Winter. "Perhaps we ought to drive out to the flatlands."

"It occurred to me that Kaite might be there," said Bergenhem. "And the girl, perhaps." He looked at Halders. "Bearing in mind what you just said about logic. Smedsberg and Kaite might have fallen out, so what could be more natural than Kaite relaxing at Smedsberg's home?"

"Precisely," said Halders. "But he won't be able to hide away from us out there in the Wild West."

"Who said he's trying to hide away from us?" asked Ringmar.

"He ran off when we tried to have a chat with him, didn't he? We were in his room, and he vanished."

"Hmm."

"What are you getting at, Bertil?"

"He might be more afraid of something else than you, Fredrik."

Halders said nothing.

"You as a police officer, I mean."

"Yes, I'm with you. You could have a point there."

"How long was he gone?" asked Ringmar. "When you were sitting in his room, waiting?"

"He still hasn't come back," said Djanali with a smile.

"I'll rephrase my silly question," said Ringmar.

"We understand it even so," said Halders. "We waited for ten minutes, and then it dawned on us that he couldn't be in the john all that time and we found he was gone with the wind. Gone with the monsoon." Halders pointed at the window, where the pale light of morning had turned into the darkness of aggressive winter rain. "Listen to that. I'll be damned if we don't have a northern monsoon up here at the edge of the universe."

"Have you questioned all the others living in the corridor?" asked Bergen-hem.

"Of course. And we didn't leave until we'd checked all the rooms to make sure he wasn't there."

"There is one thing," said Djanali.

Everybody waited.

"We've been waiting for the wounds on the boys' heads to heal suffi-ciently for us to see if there is a brand of some kind. But it didn't work with Stillman and Book. The scab has fallen off, but we haven't seen anything. We were waiting for Kaite, or however one should put it." She looked up but not at anybody in particular. "Was there somebody else waiting? Or who couldn't wait?"

22

HE FRIED TWO EGGS, PUT THEM ON A PLATE, LOOKED AT THEM, and decided that he wasn't hungry anymore. He stood up, scraped them into the trash can, and realized that he would have to throw them down the chute later.

He had collected eggs, turned his sweater into a carrier bag, and taken them to the kitchen. But that was then. They'd had a special smell, which seemed to force its way through the shell. Put them in the dish, the old man used to say. You could break them, carrying them like that.

The smell was no longer there when he put them in the dish. One of the eggs had broken even though he'd been as careful as he could possibly be.

What the hell are you doing, you little bastard!? Come here. Come here, I said!

We'd better send you back to where you came from.

He opened the cupboard door again and sniffed at the trash bag. Fried eggs didn't smell like raw eggs in the country, certainly not. It seemed that they were still warm, and that made the smell even stronger.

He tied the trash bag and sent it sliding down the chute on the landing. The resulting thud below was muted, which meant that they would soon be coming to empty the big bin down in the cellar.

It was sunny outside.

He went back in, put on his jacket, and emerged into the sunshine, which was less bright than it had seemed through the window. The sun was hidden behind the high-rise buildings—it didn't have the strength to rise above them at this time of year.

It was different out in the fields. There were no buildings there for the sun to hide behind. The neighboring farms were so far away that they seemed to be just a minor blot on the landscape. He could have been standing in the middle of an ocean. There was no end to it. The plain was as boundless as the ocean, and he was standing in the middle of it next to the island he lived on. It was a desert island that he longed to escape from, but no ships passed by to take him away. He could swim, but not that far. He wasn't big enough. When he grew up.

He walked around the high-rise building and saw the sun: He could look straight at it without going blind; it was like a low-voltage bulb up there in the heavens.

A streetcar clattered past down below. He raised a hand in greeting. Perhaps the driver was somebody he knew who would recognize him.

The streetcar stopped a bit farther on, and people got off carrying bags of Christmas presents. Packages wrapped in fun, colorful paper. They had to be Christmas presents.

He shook his head.

The old man had shaken the iron in his face. Shaken, shaken. He could detect the smell of singed hair, and something more. Singed flesh.

Great stuff, these irons, the old man had said. Look out! he'd said, and the iron had only just missed him.

The cow started sizzling. Another sizzling cow.

Once the burn heals nobody will be able to claim that she's not ours. The old man had held up the iron again. Should we brand you as well while we're at it, my boy? To make sure you don't wander off and can't remember where you live. That's the way they used to do things. Right? He'd backed off and felt a rake underneath his right foot. Come here, I said! Out there the sea swelled. He rushed out into the water.

Winter drove. Ringmar kept an eye on the road signs. The flatlands were black and enveloped by a damp breeze. A tractor in a rectangular field was doing God only knows what.

"Maybe they're sowing," said Ringmar, pointing. "Spring seems to have arrived before winter this highly peculiar season."

It was a different world. That was why Winter had wanted to pay a brief visit. He could see the horizon the way you could normally only see it from a ship.

I should get out of town more often. You walk up and down the city streets and the years go by. It's not far away, and it's something completely out of the ordinary.

"It's not easy to hide out here," said Ringmar.

"There are houses," said Winter.

"Everybody knows everything about everybody else," said Ringmar.

"If only we did."

"You should turn off here," said Ringmar.

The side road wasn't visible until they came to it. There was a signpost, but it was as insubstantial as the breeze, which was blowing from all directions. They couldn't see a road that might lead to a house.

"Where is this farm, then?" said Ringmar.

They kept going. The landscape curved away, and they saw the house.

A dog barked as they drove into the farmyard.

A man was clambering out of some kind of vehicle.

They got out of their car.

"Good afternoon," said Ringmar, and introduced himself and Winter. The man was over sixty and dressed in waterproof clothing and solid-looking boots. Winter could feel the rain now, like soft gravel. The man said "Smedsberg" and dried his hands on a rag that had been draped over the hood of what could have been a power mower but was presumably something else. Winter looked up at the farmhouse, which was two stories high. He didn't see any sign of a Swedish Kenyan peering out of a window.

"We're looking for somebody," said Ringmar.

Among other things, Winter thought.

"Is it some' to do with Gustav?" said the man, with a strong local accent.

"Didn't he tell you?" asked Ringmar.

"Told me what?"

Two cats were sitting beside the iron wood-burning stove. The farmer opened a hatch and inserted two logs. A modern electric range stood next to it. There was an unmistakable smell of old-fashioned heating that Winter had no personal experience of but recognized immediately. He could see from Bertil's expression that he remembered this kind of thing.

There were rag carpets on the floor. Winter and Ringmar had not been asked to take off their shoes. The farmer, Georg Smedsberg, had exchanged his boots for some kind of slippers that appeared to be homemade.

There were samplers on two of the walls: East West, Home's Best. God is the truth and the light. This earth is the creation of our Lord God. Honor thy father and thy mother.

Is there a Mrs. Smedsberg? Winter wondered.

They told the old man about what had happened to his son.

"You'd a thought he'd a said something," said Smedsberg, putting a coffeepot that seemed to be a wartime model onto the stove. "But nothin' happened to 'im, eh? He's alright, ain't he?"

"He wasn't injured," said Winter, taking a mouthful of the asphalt-black coffee that also seemed to be from another world. It would banish every bacterium in his body, good and bad.

"Good coffee," said Ringmar.

"It's how I like it," said Smedsberg.

To ask for milk would have been a mistake. Winter sipped at the hot liquid. Anybody wanting to create a surrealistic scene could have introduced an espresso machine into this kitchen.

"I don't suppose you've had any visitors recently? Friends of Gustav's?" he asked.

"When might that've bin?"

"In the last couple of days."

"No."

"Before that, then?"

"Nobody's bin 'round here since Gustav was home last."

Smedsberg scratched at his chin, which was shaven and shiny and didn't fit in with his clothes and general appearance. They hadn't announced their visit in advance. Perhaps he knew about it all the same. Out here everybody knows about everything, as Bertil had said. An unfamiliar car from Gothenburg. A Mercedes. A conversation with his son. Or smoke signals. Maybe the boy had called and told him what was going on. Even tillers of God's good earth could tell lies.

"When was that?" Ringmar asked.

"Let's see, it's nearly Christmas. It would'a been potato time."

"Potato time?" Ringmar wondered.

"When we took in the taters. Late. Beginning of October."

More than two months ago, Winter thought. Ah well. How often did Winter see his mother? There were direct flights from Gothenburg to Malaga almost every hour for all the retirees and golfers and all those who were a combination of the two, which was most of them.

There was a framed photograph on a desk on the other side of the kitchen table. A middle-aged lady with permed hair smiled timidly in black and white. Smedsberg saw that Winter was looking at it.

"That's my wife," he said. "Gustav's mom. She left us."

"Left you?"

"I'm a widower," said the man, standing up. He walked to the iron stove and put in some more birch wood. There was a sizzling sound as the dry wood reached the flames. Winter noticed that smell again.

"Has Gustav ever brought a friend home with him from Gothenburg?" asked Ringmar.

"When would that be?"

"Whenever. Since he started studying at Chalmers."

"Yes," said Smedsberg, remaining by the stove and warming his mis-shapen and discolored hands on the hotplates. "When 'e came around to give us a hand with t' potatoes 'e brought a friend with 'im." Smedsberg seemed to be smiling, or he might have been grimacing from the heat that he must be feeling in his palms. "A black one." He removed his hands and blew into them. "As black as the soil out there."

"So his friend was a black person, is that right?" asked Ringmar.

"Ya, a real blackie," said Smedsberg, and now he was smiling. "First time for me."

My first black man, Winter thought. There's a first time for everything.

"He'd a come in useful to scare the cows in," said Smedsberg.

"Was his name Aryan Kaite?" Winter asked.

"I don't recall a name," said Smedsberg. "I don't even know if I ever heard 'is name."

"Is this him?" Winter asked, showing him a copy of a photograph of Kaite they had taken from his student room. Smedsberg looked at the photograph and then at Winter.

"Hell's bells! They're all alike, aren't they?"

"You don't recognize him?"

"No," he said, handing the photograph back.

"Has he been here again since then?"

"No. I ain't seen 'im again since then, you can bet yer life I'd a remembered if I had." He looked from Winter to Ringmar. "Why are you asking all this? Did he disappear?"

"Yes," said Winter.

"Is 'e one of them others that was attacked?"

"Why do you ask?"

"Well, why else would you come 'ere?"

"Yes, he's one of them."

"Why would anybody want to take a shot at Gustav and this blackie, then?" asked Smedsberg.

"That's what we're trying to find out," said Winter.

"They mebbe deserved it," said Smedsberg.

"I beg your pardon?"

"They mebbe got what they deserved," said Smedsberg.

"What do you mean?" asked Ringmar, looking at Winter.

"What was they up to?" said Smedsberg.

"What do you mean by *that*?" asked Ringmar.

"They must a been up to sumthin'. It can't just be a coincidence that somebody took a shot at both of 'em, can it?"

"It didn't happen at the same time," said Winter.

"Still," said Smedsberg.

"And Gustav hasn't said anything to you about this?"

"He ain't been here since October, like I said."

"There's such a thing as the telephone," said Winter. There was even one in this house. Winter had seen it in the hall. An old-fashioned rotary, of course.

"We ain't spoken for a month or so," Smedsberg said, and Winter noticed how his face changed, clouded over.

Ringmar leaned forward.

"Do you have any other children, Mr. Smedsberg?"

"No."

"You live here all alone?"

"Since my Gerd left us, yes."

"Was Gustav still living at home then?"

"Yes." Smedsberg seemed to be looking into space. "He was little, and then 'e grew big. Did 'is national service as well. Then . . . Then 'e moved to Gothenburg and started 'is studies."

"So he doesn't want to take over the farm?" said Ringmar.

"There's nuthin' to take over," said Smedsberg. "I can barely scrape together a living 'ere, and when I go the crows can 'ave it."

They made no comment.

"You want some more coffee?" asked Smedsberg.

"Yes, please," said Ringmar, and Winter looked at him. Bertil must have a death wish. It will be a painful farewell. "If we have time."

"I'll just stir up the dregs," said Smedsberg, and went over to the stove. Winter gave Ringmar the thumbs-up.

"Gustav told us something else," said Winter. "The injuries those boys suffered might have been caused by an iron of some kind. That's what Gustav thought. Some sort of marking iron used on cattle."

"A branding iron, you mean? Are we supposed to have a branding iron here?"

"I don't think he said that. But the boys might have been beaten with a branding iron."

"I never heard of anythin' like that," said Smedsberg.

"Like what?"

"That anybody clubs folk down with a branding iron. Never heard of it."

"That's what Gustav suggested."

"Where'd 'e get that idea from? We never had a branding iron here."

"But he could have been familiar with one all the same, could he?" asked Ringmar.

"I suppose 'e could," said Smedsberg. "I wond . . ." but he didn't finish. The coffeepot was starting to rattle on the stove. He fetched the coffee and came back to the table.

"No, thank you," said Winter. Smedsberg sat down.

"I've just used ear tags on the cows 'ere," he said. "If I ever needed to mark 'em. But in the old days we had the number from the cooperative that we used to mark cattle with."

"What exactly do you mean?" Winter asked.

"Like I said. We marked 'em with a number for this district."

"For the district? Not the farm?" Winter asked.

"No. For the area."

"But we were told that there are special numbers that indicate the precise location the animals come from."

"That came later, ninety-five, with the EU."

"And there's one of those for every farm?"

"Yes."

"So there's one for your farm, then?"

"Yes. But I got no cows nowadays. No animals at all, apart from dogs and cats and a few chickens. I might buy a couple of pigs."

"But you still have the number?"

"It's always there. It goes with the farm."

Winter saw Ringmar take a drink of coffee, and his face suddenly split down the middle and a black stream of coffee gushed forth from his eyes . . . Well, not quite, but he made a face.

"So you've never had one of these marking irons, branding irons, at this farm?"

"No. It's more or less unheard-of. It's in America where they got such enormous ranches and they brand their cattle so that they can keep track." He smiled. "I bet they steal cattle over there as well." He took a swig of asphalt. "I reckon they brand horses in Germany as well."

"But not here?"

"Horses? There ain't no horses in these parts."

"Do you know anybody who might have used that method of marking cattle?" Winter asked.

Smedsberg didn't answer immediately; he seemed to be searching for the answer in the depths of his mug of coffee; then he looked up again. He looked across the room and out of the window, where the view was curtailed by the rain.

"Somewhere where Gustav might have seen it?" said Winter.

"Didn't you asked 'im?"

"Not directly," said Winter, although that wasn't really true. Gustav Smeds-berg had said that he couldn't remember. "But it's sort of become more rele-vant now."

"Become hotter?" A smile twinkled in Smedsberg's left eye. A farmer with a sense of humor, as black as his coffee and as the night outside, in an-other hour or two.

"So you've never seen an iron like that?" Winter asked.

"There is a farm in the upper parish, as we call it." Smedsberg looked Winter in the eye. "I don't come from around these parts, but my Gerd did. When 'er parents were still alive we sometimes used to visit."

He scratched his right cheek again, and his forehead, as if to massage the memory.

"There was a farm—I don't know if it's still there—him who ran it was a bit odd. Did things 'is own way, you might say." Smedsberg did some more massaging. "In the next village. We needed to go there once for some or other, and I think 'e . . . That 'e used to mark some of his animals like that. Come to think of it." He peered out from inside his memories, turned to look at them. "I remember the smell, in fact," he said. "Odd, ain't it? A sound as well. Yes. When we got back home I asked Gerd and she said . . . she said he used to brand 'is mark into 'is animals."

"You mean that number he was given by the cooperative?" Ringmar asked.

"No. He 'ad 'is own. I remember asking and Gerd said so."

"You remember a lot, Mr. Smedsberg," said Winter.

"It's the smell," he said. "Odd, ain't it? You remember this smell and then you remember loads of other things. All you gotta do is think of a smell, and memories start to come back."

Open the floodgates, Winter thought.

"What was the name of this farmer who had these unusual methods?"

"I don't remember, I can tell you that now. Don't have enough memory for that." It sounded as if he gave a chuckle. "There are limits."

"Do you remember where the farm was? Or is?"

"It's in the next parish."

"As far as we're concerned that could be in another province," said Winter.

"It is in another province, in fact," said Smedsberg.

"Could you show us where it is?" Ringmar asked.

"Do you mean now?"

"Is it far?"

"Yes. It's over twenty kilometers, I reckon. Depends on what route you take."

"Do you have time to show us now? We can go right away. We'll bring you straight back, of course," Winter said.

Smedsberg changed the waterproof trousers he'd been wearing. He somewhat hesitantly got into Winter's Mercedes. Winter noticed the Escort rusting away peacefully by the big barn.

The road was as straight as an arrow. Black birds circled overhead, followed them like seagulls shadowing a ship. The light sank down again, into the earth and over remote farms where lamps were starting to glimmer in the windows. They drove through a little village with a gray church and a hall next to it, with a dozen or so cars parked outside.

"Advent coffee meeting," said Smedsberg.

"Feel like a cup?" said Winter to Ringmar, who didn't reply.

"We don't got time, surely," said Smedsberg.

They passed two girls riding horses that looked as big as houses. So there are in fact horses around here. Winter gave them as wide a berth as he dared, and the girls waved in acknowledgment. The horses looked even bigger in the rearview mirror. It was a different world out here.

"We're getting close," said Smedsberg.

At a small crossroads he told them to turn left. The road surface was uneven and patchy asphalt that seemed to have survived both world wars. Fields were enclosed by rickety, broken-down fences, and the village seemed to have been abandoned. Which it no doubt has, Winter thought. They drove past two farmhouses that were in total darkness. A depopulated area: Everybody's moving into the cities nowadays.

"People've started moving out of this place," said Smedsberg, as if to confirm Winter's thoughts. "There used to be lots of young kids in them two farms."

They came to another crossroads.

"Left," said Smedsberg. It was a dirt road now. Smedsberg pointed. "That's where my Gerd came from."

Winter and Ringmar looked at the house, which was wood-built, still red in the fading light: a cowshed, a smaller cottage, a fence. No electric light.

"Her nephews and nieces use it as a country place, but they aren't there very often," said Smedsberg. "They ain't there now, for instance."

The forest became more dense. They came to a clearing, then more trees, another clearing. There was a gloomy-looking log cabin at the side of the road.

"That used to be a village store once upon a time," said Smedsberg.

"This really is a depopulated area," said Ringmar.

The forest suddenly opened up and they found themselves driving through fields that seemed endless, compared with the concentration of trees they'd just passed through. There was a big house on the other side, set back some fifty meters from the road.

"That's it," said Smedsberg, pointing. "That was the house."

There were lights on.

23

"HOW ARE WE GOING TO EXPLAIN THIS?" RINGMAR ASKED AS THEY walked toward the house.

"We don't need to explain anything," said Winter.

The wind was gusting in circles around the house. Winter could see only one single light, in the distance, like a lighthouse at the edge of the plain. Darkness was closing in fast. It also felt chillier, as if winter was approaching at last. If he were to come back here a month from now, everything would be white all around, and it really would look like an ocean. It would be even more difficult to see the difference between sky and land, between heaven and earth.

As he raised his fist to hammer on the door, he had the feeling that he would in fact be coming back here. It was a feeling he couldn't explain, but in the past it had led him deep down into the depths of darkness. It was a premonition that foreboded terrible things. Once it appeared, it wouldn't go away.

Everything is linked.

He kept his hand raised. Gusts spiraling, a strange hissing in his ears. A faint light in the window to the left. An acrid smell of soil. His own breath like smoke signals, Bertil's breath. Another smell, hard to pin down. He thought of a child on a swing, he could see it. The child turned to look at him and laughed, and it was Elsa. A hand was pushing the swing, and another face appeared and turned to look at him and it was not himself. He didn't recognize it.

"Aren't you going to knock?" Ringmar asked.

After the third salvo of hammering they could hear somebody moving inside, and a voice said: "What do you want?"

Yes, what did they want? Ringmar looked at Winter. Two stupid chief inspectors banging on the door of an isolated house in the middle of nowhere. In the backseat of our car is a hillbilly who has tricked us into coming here with his cock-and-bull story. Inside the house his psychopathic brother is waiting with an elk rifle. Our bodies will sink down under all the pig shit and never be recovered. Our coats will keep the brothers warm on their tractors.

You've got me covered, Erik?

Uh . . . sorry, no, Bertil boy.

"We're from the police," said Winter. "Can we come in and ask you a few questions?"

"About what?"

The voice was gruff and seemed to be in several layers, an old man's voice.

"Can we come in?" Winter said again.

"How do I know you're not thieves?" The voice was muffled by the door, which looked battered but substantial.

"I have my ID in my hand," said Winter.

They heard a mumbling and a clanking of bolts. The door opened and the man inside appeared as a silhouette, illuminated by a low-octane light from the hall and perhaps also the kitchen. Winter held out his ID. The man leaned forward and studied the text and photograph with his eyes screwed up, then looked at Winter and nodded at Ringmar.

"Who's he?"

Ringmar introduced himself and showed the man his ID.

"What do you want?" asked the man once more. He was slightly hunched but still of average height, his head shaved, wearing a whitish shirt, suspenders, trousers of no particular style, and thick woolen socks. Classical rural attire from head to toe. Winter could smell a wood-burning stove and recently cooked food. Pork. It was damp and chilly in the hall, and that was not entirely due to the air coming from the outside.

"We just have a few questions we'd like to ask," said Winter again.

"Are you lost?" asked the man. He appeared to be pointing at the ceiling. "The main road's that way."

"We'd like to ask you about a few things," said Winter. "We're looking for somebody." Best to start there.

"There's a search party out, is there?"

"No. Just us."

"What's your name?" Ringmar asked.

"My name's Carlström," said the man, without offering to shake hands. "Natanael Carlström."

"Could we sit down for a minute, Mr. Carlström?"

He made a sort of sighing noise and ushered them into the kitchen, which was reminiscent of Georg Smedsberg's but smaller and darker and much dirtier. Winter thought about Smedsberg sitting in the backseat of his Mercedes as it got colder and colder, and regretted leaving him there. They had better make this short.

"We're looking for this young man," said Ringmar, handing over the photograph of Aryan Kaite. It was simple, probably taken in a photo booth. Kaite's face looked like soot against the shabby background wall. Nevertheless, he had gone to the trouble of having it enlarged and framed, and had hung it in his room, Winter had thought earlier.

"You'd better get a move on before it gets dark out there, or you'll never see him," said Carlström, and the sighing noise dissolved into a rattling breath that could well have been a laugh.

"Have you seen him?" Winter asked.

"A black man out here on the flats? That's a sight worth seeing."

"So he hasn't been seen around here?"

"Never. Who is he?"

"Nobody else you know has mentioned him?" Winter asked.

"Who could that be?"

"I'm asking you."

"There is nobody else here," said Carlström. "Couldn't you see that for yourselves? Did you see any other houses near here?"

"So you haven't spoken to anybody else about a stranger in the vicinity?"

"The only strangers I've seen for a very long time are you two," said Carlström.

"Do you know Gustav Smedsberg?" Ringmar asked.

"Eh?"

"Do you know anybody named Gustav Smedsberg?"

"No."

"His mother grew up around here," said Winter. "Gerd." He hadn't asked Smedsberg senior about her maiden name. "She married Georg Smedsberg from the neighboring parish." Although it's hardly the right name for it, Winter thought. It's too far away.

"I've never heard anything about it," said Carlström.

"The Smedsberg kid knows this Aryan Kaite who has disappeared," said Ringmar.

"Really?"

"And these boys have both been violently attacked," said Winter. "That's why we're here."

He tried to explain about the branding iron. They were very curious to see what one looked like. And they'd heard that he might have one. It would help them to decide on the plausibility.

"The plausibility of what?"

"Of the assumption that it was used as a weapon."

Carlström looked as though he very much doubted that.

"Who said that I mark my animals with an iron?"

"We asked around a bit in the village."

"Was it Smedsberg?"

Does he mean the young one or the old one? Ringmar and Winter looked at each other. He remembered the name he'd never heard of before.

"Georg Smedsberg thought he'd seen you using one of those irons ages ago," said Winter.

"Is that him in the car outside?"

The old man sees more than you'd think. Winter was very tempted to turn around and look out of the window to see if Smedsberg's silhouette could be seen in the car.

"Why doesn't he come in?" said Carlström.

"He only showed us how to get here," said Winter.

Carlström muttered something they couldn't catch.

"I beg your pardon?" said Winter.

"Yes, that might well be," said Carlström.

"What might?" asked Winter.

"That I branded a few cattle." He looked up, straight at Winter. "It wasn't illegal." He gestured with his hand. "They don't like it nowadays, but nobody said anything then."

"No, no, we only wanted to see what—"

"I don't have the iron anymore," said Carlström. "I had two at one time, but not now."

"Did you sell them?"

"I sold one twenty-five years ago to an auctioneer, so you can try and track that one down." One of his eyes glinted, as if the very thought amused him.

"What about the other one?"

"Thieves."

"Thieves?" said Winter. "You mean it's been stolen?"

"This autumn," said Carlström. "That was why I was asking questions when you came knocking at my door. I was going to ask if that's what you'd come for, but then I thought it was better to be careful."

"What happened?" asked Ringmar. "The theft."

"I don't know. I went out early one morning and tools were missing from the shed."

"Several tools?"

"Quite a few. New and old."

"Including your marking iron?"

"Who would want that?"

"So the marking iron was stolen?"

"That's what I just said, isn't it?"

"When exactly did this happen?"

"This autumn, like I said."

"Do you know what day it was?"

"I think probably not. I was going to go into the village that day, I think, and it's not every day I do that . . ."

They waited.

"I'm not sure," said Carlström. "I'll have to think about it."

"Have you had any break-ins before?" Winter asked.

"Never."

"Did you report it to the police?"

"For a few old tools?" Carlström looked surprised, or possibly just bored stiff.

"How many tools?"

"Not many."

"Do you know exactly?"

"Do you want a list?"

"No," said Winter. "That's not necessary yet." Ringmar looked at him but said nothing.

"Have you heard of anybody else being burgled?" Ringmar asked.

"No," said Carlström.

We'll have to check with the neighbors, Winter thought. The problem is, there aren't any neighbors.

"Do you live alone here, Mr Carlström?"

"You can see that, can't you?"

"But we can't know for sure," said Ringmar.

"All alone."

"Do you have any children?"

"Eh?"

"Do you have any children?" Winter asked again.

"No."

"Have you been married?"

"Never. Why?"

"Thank you very much for your time, Mr. Carlström," said Winter, getting to his feet.

"Is that it, then?"

"Thank you very much for your help," said Winter. "If you hear anything about your tools I'd be grateful if you could let us know." He handed over a business card. "My number's on the card."

Carlström handled it as if it were a thousand-year-old piece of china.

"Especially if you hear anything about that branding iron," said Winter.

Carlström nodded. Winter asked his last question, the one he'd been waiting with.

"Do you happen to have a copy of your mark, by the way?" he asked in an offhand tone. "That symbol, or number combination, or whatever it was."

"Eh?"

"What did your mark look like?" Winter asked.

"I don't have a copy, if that's what you want to see," said Carlström.

"But you remember what it looked like?"

"Yes, of course."

"Could you draw it for us?"

"What for?"

"In case it turns up."

"If it turns up, it'll turn up here," said Carlström.

"But we'd be grateful if you could help us all the same," said Ringmar. "Then we could exclude your iron if we find the one that was used in the attacks."

"Why on earth would my iron have been used?" Carlström asked.

"We have no idea," said Winter, "and we don't think it was, of course. But it would still be helpful to know what it looked like."

"Yes, yes," said Carlström. "It's a square with a circle in it and a C inside the circle." He looked at Winter. "C stands for Carlström."

"Could you possibly draw it for us?"

Carlström made that strange sighing noise again, but stood up and left the room without a word. He returned a minute later with a sketch that he handed to Ringmar.

"Have you had it long?" Ringmar asked.

"As long as I can remember. It was my father's."

"Many thanks for all your help," said Winter.

They went back through the hall and stood in the doorway. The darkness was compact now; there was no sign of any stars or moon in the sky. The only light Winter could see was the lighthouse on the horizon, brighter now.

"What's that over there?" he asked, pointing. "The light."

"Television tower," said Carlström. "Radio, television, those stupid computer contraptions, God knows what else. It's been there for some time."

"Anyway, many thanks," said Ringmar, and they went back to the car and got in. Carlström was still in the doorway, a hunched silhouette.

"Are you cold?" asked Winter as he started the car.

"No. You weren't very long," said Smedsberg in the darkness.

"We took longer than we meant to."

Winter turned the car around and headed for the main road.

"Were we on the veranda long enough for you to recognize him?" Winter asked as they turned right.

"A few years've passed, but I've seen 'im now and again," said Smedsberg. "While I was sitting there I remembered 'is name as well. Carlström. Natanael Carlström. The kind of name you should remember."

"Is he religious?" asked Ringmar. "Or rather, his parents?"

"Dunno," said Smedsberg. "But there were a lot of God-fearing folk 'round here in the old days, so it ain't impossible."

They drove in silence. Winter wasn't familiar with the road. It was all darkness and narrow roads and trees lit up by his powerful headlights. Gloomy houses came and went, but they could have been different from the ones he'd seen earlier that afternoon.

They drove over the plain, the mother of all plains. Flickering lights like solitary stars anchored to the earth. Another crossroads. No traffic.

"Had a boy," said Smedsberg without warning from the darkness of the backseat.

"I beg your pardon?" said Winter, turning right toward Smedsberg's farm.

"Carlström. He had a boy at the farm for a few years. I remember now. Nothin' to do with it, I reckon, but I remembered just now as we turned in."

"What do you mean by 'a few years'?" asked Ringmar.

"A foster son. Had a foster son living with 'im. I never seed 'im misself, but Gerd said somethin' about 'im once or twice."

"Was she sure?" asked Ringmar.

"That's what she said."

No children, Winter thought. Carlström had said no when asked if he had any children, but maybe he didn't count a foster child.

"She said 'e was fed up with the boy," said Smedsberg. They'd arrived. Smedsberg's house was in darkness. "The old man was fed up with the boy and then 'e grew up, and I reckon 'e never came back again."

"Fed up?" said Winter. "Do you mean Carlström treated him badly?"

"Yes."

"What was his name?" asked Ringmar. "The boy?"

"She never said. I don't think she knew."

They drove home on roads wider than the ones they'd made their way along earlier in the day.

"Interesting," Ringmar said.

"It's a different world," said Winter.

They continued for a while in silence. It was almost exciting to see lit-up houses and villages and towns passing by, to see other cars, trucks. Another world.

"The old man was lying," said Ringmar.

"You mean Carlström?"

"I mean Natanael Carlström."

"That's the understatement of the day," said Winter.

"Lied through his teeth."

"That's a little bit closer to the truth," said Winter, and Ringmar laughed.

"But it's not funny," said Ringmar.

"I had bad vibes out there," said Winter.

"We've stumbled on a secret here," said Ringmar. "Maybe several."

"We'd better check up on burglaries in the area."

"Is it worth the effort?" Ringmar asked. They were approaching Gothenburg now. The sky was a fiery yellow and transparent, lit up from underneath.

"Yes," said Winter. He couldn't forget the feeling he'd had when he was about to hammer on the old man's front door. There was a secret. He'd sensed it. He had sensed the darkness that was deeper than the heavens that fell down over the earth around the big farmhouse.

24

THEY WERE INSIDE THE CITY LIMITS NOW. WINTER COULD STILL
detect the rotten smell of the countryside in the car. If he was lucky it would
accompany him up to Angela and Elsa. Or unlucky. Angela would say some-
thing about the house in the country. Or lucky. She might be right.

Coltrane was playing away on the CD player. A pickup truck passed by,
driven by a man wearing a Santa Claus hat. Coltrane's solo vibrated through
the Mercedes and Winter's head. Another person wearing a Santa Claus hat
drove past.

"What the hell's going on?" said Ringmar.

"Parade of the Santa Clauses," said Winter.

"Don't you have any carols?" Ringmar asked, nodding toward the CD
player.

"Why not sing along?" said Winter. "Make up your own words."

"While coppers watched their crooks by night too thinly on the ground,
a villain slipped past with his swag and didn't make a sound."

He fell silent.

"Encore," said Winter.

"Fear not, said Winter, we shall make your life a living hell. We'll track
you down and sort you out and lock you in a cell."

"The best carol I've heard in years," said Winter.

"And it isn't even Christmas yet," said Ringmar.

Winter stopped at a red light. The opera house was glittering like its own
solar system. The river behind it was red in the self-confident glow. Well-
dressed people crossing the road in front of him were on their way to see
some opera or other he didn't even know the name of. Not his kind of music.

"It's not going to be much fun this Christmas," said Ringmar softly as
they set off again.

Winter glanced at him. Ringmar was staring ahead, as if hoping to see more Santa Clauses who might put him in a better mood.

"Is it Martin you're thinking about?"

"What else?" Ringmar was gazing out over the water that had lost the glitter from the opera house by now, and instead was reflecting the motionless cranes on the docks on the other side, rising skyward like the skeletons they were. "I'm only human."

"I'll have a word with Moa," said Winter. "I've said that before, but I really will this time."

"Don't bother," said Ringmar.

"I mean that I'll speak indirectly to Martin. First Moa and then perhaps Martin."

"It's between him and me, Erik."

"From him to you, more like," said Winter.

Ringmar made a noise that could have been a quick intake of breath.

"I sometimes lie awake at night and try to figure out what particular incident caused all this," he said. "When did it happen? What started it? What did I do?"

Winter waited for him to continue. He exited the highway in order to take Ringmar home. Mariatorg was the same small-town square it had always been. Young people were loitering around the hotdog stand. Streetcars came and went. There was the drugstore, as in all little towns, the photo shop, the bookshop that he sometimes stopped in to buy the occasional book for Lotta and the girls on the way to Långedrag.

It had been Winter's own local square when he was growing up in Haga, in the same house his sister and her children now lived in.

"I can't find it," said Ringmar. "That incident."

"That's because it doesn't exist," said Winter. "Never did."

"I think you're wrong. There's always something. A child doesn't forget. Nor does a teenager. Adults can forget, or regard whatever happened as something different from what it was. In the child's eyes, at least."

Winter thought about his own child. All the years in store for them both. All the individual incidents.

He drove up to Ringmar's house. It was illuminated by the neighbor's Christmas lights in the same way that the river had seemed to be ablaze with the gleam of the opera house.

Ringmar looked at Winter, whose face looked like it had been caught in searchlight beams.

"Pretty, isn't it?" said Ringmar with a thin smile.

"Very. And now I understand the real reason why you can't sleep at night."
Ringmar laughed.

"Do you know him well?" Winter asked.

"Not well enough to march into his garden with my SigSauer and shoot out all the lights and be confident he'd get the message."

"Want me to do it for you?"

"You're already doing enough for me," said Ringmar, getting out of the car. "See you tomorrow." He waved goodbye and walked up the path that was lit up by the luminous forest outside the neighbor's house. You can get all the light therapy you need here, Winter thought. Light therapy. About ten more days and they would be lounging back in the Spanish garden with the three palm trees, overlooked by the White Mountain, and listening to the rhythmic music created by his dear mother as she mixed the second Tanqueray and tonic of the afternoon in the kitchen bar. Some tapas on the table, *gambas a la plancha,* and *jamón serrano,* a dish of *boquerones fritos,* perhaps *un fino* for Angela and maybe one for him as well. A little cloud in the corner of his eye, but nothing to worry about.

In an ideal world, he thought as he drove past Slottsskogsvallen on the way home. I'm not sure that's the world I'm living in right now. I'll have to be sitting back in the plane before I believe anything at all.

He drove back onto the highway. This morning he'd been driving in the opposite direction. Good Lord, was it just this morning? He and Halders had been sitting in silence, staring straight ahead.

"How are things, Fredrik?"

"Better than last Christmas. That wasn't much fun."

Winter had noticed that Bertil had used the same expression as Fredrik: not much fun. Well, they have a point, perhaps. When things were good it was fun.

Halders had spent last Christmas alone with his two children, Hannes and Magda, six months after Margareta had been killed in a hit-and-run accident.

Aneta Djanali had spent a few hours with Halders that Christmas Eve. Winter had never discussed that with Fredrik, but Aneta had stopped by Winter's home one autumn day similar to today, but about a month earlier. She hadn't come to ask for Winter's blessing, but she wanted to talk just the same.

They had talked for a long time. He was glad to have her on his team. He was glad he had Fredrik Halders, and he thought Fredrik and Aneta were glad they had each other, even if he didn't know exactly how they had managed it.

"Are you staying at home this year?" Winter had just negotiated the new roundabout east of Frölunda Square. There was not much traffic.

"Eh?"

"Will you be celebrating Christmas at home?"

Halders hadn't answered. Perhaps he hadn't heard, or preferred not to.

They drove along the coast road, where seaside vegetation had stiffened in yellow and brown, belts of reeds like a forest of spikes. Birds circled overhead, searching for food. There had been very few people in the fields or in the streets. They hadn't seen many cars.

Later the same day Winter would compare this countryside with the more remote solitude away from Gothenburg, where everything was so flat.

"Have you bought a Christmas tree?" Halders asked out of the blue.

"No."

"Neither have I. It feels like such a production, a little job like that." He looked up from out of his thoughts. "But the kids want a tree."

"So does Elsa," said Winter.

"What about you? And Angela?"

"If it's a little one," said Winter.

"All the dropped needles are a major nuisance," said Halders. "I always manage to get a tree that sheds its needles before you can say Merry Christmas. By Boxing Day the whole living room has turned into a green field. All you need is twenty-two men and a referee's whistle."

"Did you see the Lazio match yesterday?" Winter asked as they turned right by the jetty. The houses seemed to have been carved out of the cliff. It was a long time since he'd last driven along here.

"No, but I saw Roma."

Winter smiled.

"Lazio's an old fascist team with neofascist fans," said Halders. "They can go to hell as far as I'm concerned."

"Here we are," said Winter. His house was near the end of a cul de sac. There was a Christmas tree on the front lawn, but the lights were not on.

"The house on the right," Winter said.

"Looks very nice. Is Daddy at home now, do you think?"

"Keep calm when we get inside, Fredrik."

"What do you mean? I'll be the good cop and you can be the bad one."

———

Magnus Bergort shook hands, firmly and warmly. There was a look of confidence and curiosity in his eyes, as if he had been looking forward to this visit. His eyes were blue, the transparent variety. Mentally unbalanced was Halders's reaction. Pretty soon he'll make a chain saw out of food-processor parts and mete out justice to his family.

Bergort was wearing a black suit, dark blue silk tie, and shoes that shone more brilliantly than stainless steel. His hair was straight and blond, with a perfectly straight parting. Führer style, thought Halders, and said: "Thank you for taking the time to meet us."

"No problem," said Bergort, "as long as I can get to the office by half past ten."

The kitchen had been cleaned recently and smelled of perfumed detergent. A seagull could be seen circling around through the open window. Pans and knives and other kitchen utensils were hanging from hooks on the walls. Stainless steel.

The girl was at her nursery school. Winter had said that would be the best time to come.

"What's your work, Mr. Bergort?" Halders asked.

"I'm an economist. Analyst."

"Where?"

"Er, in a bank. SEB." He ran his hand through his hair, without a strand falling out of place. "Please call me Magnus."

"So you advise people on what to do with their money, is that right, Magnus?" asked Halders.

"Not directly. My work is more, how can I put it—working out a long-term financial strategy for the bank."

"So you advise your firm on what to do with its money?" Halders asked. Winter looked at him.

"Well . . . Ha ha! I suppose you could say that, yes."

"Is there any other strategy for a bank apart from the financial one?" asked Halders.

"Er . . . Ha ha! Good question. Obviously it's mostly about money."

"That's a problem I recognize; I have a similar problem myself," said Halders. "Money. Before you have a chance to sit down in peace and quiet and analyze your finances, they've disappeared. *Putz weg. Verschwunden.*"

"Yes . . ."

"Do you have any standard tips, Magnus? How the hell a man can hang on to his cash before it's all gone? *Verschwunden?*"

"Er, I'm sure I can—"

"Maybe we should hold off on that," said Winter. "Magnus has to get back to work soon, and so do we." Winter thought he could detect a look of relief on Bergort's face. Just wait, my friend. "What we're mainly interested in is what might have happened to Maja."

"Yes, it's a very strange story," said Bergort without hesitation.

"What do you think happened?" Winter asked.

Is Magnus Führer aware of what we're really talking about? Halders asked himself.

The man looked at his wife. Kristina Bergort looked as if she were going to explain everything now, for the first time. Explain what?

"Kristina told me and we, er, well, I spoke to Maja and she says that she sat in a car with a mister."

"What do you think about that yourself?"

"I really don't know what to think."

"Does the girl have a lively imagination?" asked Halders.

"Yes," said Bergort. "All children do."

"Has she said anything like this before?"

Bergort looked at his wife.

"No," said Kristina Bergort. "Nothing quite like this."

"Anything similar?" Winter asked.

"What do you mean by that?" asked Bergort.

"Has she mentioned meeting a strange man in different circumstances?" said Halders.

"No," said Kristina Bergort. "She tells us about everything that happens, and she would've mentioned it."

Everything, Halders thought. She tells them about everything.

"She lost a ball, is that right?" Winter asked.

"Yes," said the mother. "Her favorite ball that she's had God only knows how long."

"When did it vanish?"

"The same day she . . . talked about that other business."

"How did it happen?"

"How did what happen?"

"Losing the ball."

"She said that this man was going to throw it to her from the car, but he didn't. He said he was going to throw it."

"What did he do, instead?"

"He drove away with it, if I understand it correctly."

"What does she say now? Does she still talk about the ball?" Winter asked.

"Yes. Nearly every day. It wasn't all that long ago."

Halders sat down on a chair and seemed to be looking out of a window, but then he turned to face her.

"You decided very quickly to take her to Frölunda Hospital."

"Yes."

"What made you reach that decision?"

He noticed Kristina glance at her husband, "Magnus Heydrich," who seemed to be standing at attention in the doorway. Heydrich hadn't sat down at all during the interview, but had checked his watch several times.

"We thought it would be best," he said.

"Did she seem to be injured?"

"Not as far as we could see."

"Did she say that somebody had hit her?"

"No," said Kristina Bergort.

"You know that we are working on a case in which a stranger abducted a little boy and later injured him?"

"Yes. You explained that when you called yesterday," said Kristina Bergort.

"I haven't read anything about that," said Magnus Bergort. "Haven't heard anything either."

"It has been reported in the press, but without any exact details. You understand? This is a conversation in strictest confidence. We have spoken to some other parents who have been through something similar."

"What's going on?" asked the mother.

"We don't know yet. That's why we're asking."

"Did Maja have any injuries?" asked Halders, just beating Winter to it.

"No," said Mrs. Bergort.

"Weren't there a few bruises?"

"How do you know that? And if you knew, why did you need to ask?" said Kristina.

"The inspector who met with you previously told us about it. But we wanted to hear it from you."

"Yes, of course. Bruises, yes. She fell off the swing. On her arm, there." She held up her own arm, as if that were proof of what she was saying. "They're better now."

"They couldn't have had anything to do with this . . . encounter with the stranger?" Winter asked.

"No."

"How can you be so sure?"

"As I said, it was the swing." She was sitting on the chair, but only just. "Like I said." She looked at her husband, who nodded and checked his watch again. He was still standing in the doorway, like a tin soldier in uniform. "She fell off the swing." She held up her arm again. "Fell!"

There's definitely something wrong here, Winter thought.

25

MEMORIES LIKE NAILS BEING HAMMERED INTO HIS SKULL. BANG, bang, bang, in deep, and did it hurt? *Did it hurt?!*

There were no dreams out on the flats. Everything was emptiness and wind. He didn't want to look heavenward, but where else was there to look? The filthy dome covered everything up above and at the sides.

It's different here. I can see without things splitting inside my head.

He lay on the sofa. He looked up at the ceiling on which he had painted two scenes side by side. If he looked left he could see a starry sky, bright and radiant. He had painted the constellations from memory. If he looked right, the sun was shining from a blue sky that was the most beautiful one he'd seen. He'd made it himself, hadn't he?

Sometimes he would draw a curtain that ran along a runner in the middle of the ceiling. He could go from night to day, and vice versa, as it suited him.

He felt a jab inside his head, and another. Memories again. "That couldn't have hurt very much?!" The shadow above him, a peal of laughter. Several shadows, a circle around him. He could see only soil. It was raining. There were boots in front of his face. "Do you want to get up?" A boot. "He wants to get up."

Was there anybody else there? He couldn't remember.

He got up now, went into the other room, and sought out the new memories that didn't hurt when he touched them: the car, the ball, the charm, and the watch. He held the watch up to the light coming from the street lamps as if it were dark in the room. The watch had stopped now and he tried to wind it up again, but nothing moved. It had stopped back then. It had been pulled off the boy's arm and hit against something hard.

How had it been pulled off?

No, no, they were not good memories and he didn't want to see pictures like that inside his head where there were already wounds from all the other stuff.

The boy hadn't behaved as he should have. That's what had happened, he hadn't acted like the others to whom he'd shown things and who understood and who were nice and wanted him to be nice to them. The boy wasn't like that, and it was a big disappointment when he realized it. He could think about that and remember. The disappointment.

He twirled the charm around in his hand. Rolled the ball on the floor. Pushed the car between the chair and the coffee table. A lap around the table leg.

It wasn't enough. He let go of the car and stood up.

It wasn't enough.

In front of the television screen he felt the relief; for a moment there were no memories. He had closed his eyes.

He could see now. The children were moving back and forth without knowing they were being filmed. Just think if they had known! Everything would have been different then. Not good.

He saw the girl's face, the zoom on the camera worked. She seemed to be looking straight at the camera, but she couldn't know.

He knew where she lived. He had waited and watched when they picked her up. He didn't like them. Who were they? Did the girl belong to them? He didn't think so. He would ask her. He would . . . and he started to sing a song in order to keep the thought of what he would do next time out of his mind. There was once a little girlie, tra la la la la, and a little boy, da da da da da.

There would be a next time, and it would be . . . bigger then. Bigger.

Next time he would do what he would've liked to do right from the start, but hadn't been . . . brave enough. Cowardy cowardy custard!

You could hold hands. That would do.

He closed his eyes, looked, closed his eyes. Now all the children were there, as if they'd been given an order by the ladies who were standing like soldiers. He smiled. Like soldiers!

They were looking in his direction, straight into the camera that they couldn't see. Nobody could see it or him. He'd left his car and stood hidden, just as everything else had disappeared into itself among the bushes and woods and trees. Grass. Stones, rocks, everything else there. Soil.

The children set off walking, in a long line. He followed them. Here at home on the sofa he could see how his hand was shaking as he emerged from the bushes; a branch came swooping toward the lens.

They were in the street. He was in the street. He was a long way away

from them, but this was a good camera. One of the supervisors turned around
and looked at it.

He leaned forward. She was still looking at the camera. He had zoomed
in a bit closer. She turned away. She turned back again.

Buildings in the picture now. Uninteresting buildings that simply grew
and grew upward and sideways. Cars in front of the picture, making it blurry.

He had turned the camera away to avoid that stare. It wasn't *her* staring
he wanted. Why was she there?

The buildings had gone now. He was somewhere else. He knew where.
There were rocks behind the house. The girl was on a swing. Somebody was
standing behind her. The girl swung higher and higher. He followed her up
and down, up and down.

He sat there, following her with his head. The swing, the girl, the hands
pushing from behind the girl. It looked to funny.

Somewhere else. A family, and he'd followed them until they grew
smaller and smaller and no zoom in the world could have helped anymore.

Hours later, who could say how many. He drove past all the familiar places.
Everything was the same as usual, but the light was brighter and dazzled him,
must have dazzled others as well. Fir trees as if the forest had come walking
to the roadside and left a deserted plain behind them. Then, when it's all over,
there will be no forest left anywhere at all. Only the fields where you couldn't
escape. Nowhere to hide.

There's that park, and here's this one. He knew them all so well. Every-
thing was familiar.

"I'd like a monthly ticket, please."

A woman sticking her face into his cab as if she wanted to squeeze her fat
body through the opening and force him out through the window on the
other side. That wouldn't surprise him. They're all the same. Pressing, forcing
their big fat bodies against me, *pressing* up against me, their big fat bodies.

"Don't you have monthly tickets onboard?" she asked.

"Er, yes, that'll be one hundred twenty kronor please."

"A hundred and twenty? They only cost a hundred at the newsstand."

Buy one there, then, get out of here and buy a ticket there. At the news-
stand. He didn't want her here, in his streetcar. She was pressing. A man behind
her was pressing. They wanted to get into here, into his cab. They wan—

"Why should I pay a hundred and twenty?"

"Because it costs a hundred and twenty."

"But why?"

"I have to go now. Do you want a ticket or not? I have to get going now, you stupid bitch."

"Wh . . . what did you say?"

"I have to get going now."

"Wha . . . what did you call me?"

"I didn't call you anything. I said I have to take off now because I have to meet a deadline at Söbergsgatan."

"Söbergsgatan?"

"Söbergsgatan."

"Söderbergsgatan?"

"Söbergsgatan."

"Give me that ticket, then. I can't stand here all day."

"A hundred and twenty kronor."

"Here."

At last he was able to move again. The stupid bitch had disappeared toward the back of the streetcar. He could still smell her perfume. It was enough to make you sick. Imagine if she's got children. No, no, no.

He was just about to get into his car.

"Do you have a second, Jerner?"

It's already gone, he thought. I had it, but now it's gone.

He got into the car without answering.

"Jerner?"

What did he want—another second? Here you are, out through the window—now that one's gone as well.

"Turn the car off for a minute, Jerner. What the hell's the matter with you? Didn't you hear that I'd like to have a word with you?"

Have a word. What word would you like? How about asshole?

"If you don't listen to what I have to say you could find yourself in deep trouble," said the man who was still there beside the car. Jerner had turned off the engine. But the one who called himself the boss was still there. What did he want? He was babbling on. "The woman called HQ right away on her mobile and they passed the message on to me. She says you called her disgusting names and, well, were acting strange."

Disgusting names? Whose behavior had really been disgusting?

He drove off, didn't even bother to glance in the rearview mirror.

26

WINTER KICKED OFF HIS SHOES AND DROPPED HIS OVERCOAT ON the floor where he stood. Angela was watching.

"Pick it up!" he said, pointing to the coat.

"Not so loud. Elsa's asleep. She had a stomachache and was being a handful." Angela looked at the overcoat, then at him. "You don't have the voice of a bully."

He headed for the kitchen.

"Are there any leftovers?"

"You'll have to go sleuthing in the pantry."

"We don't have a pantry."

They were sitting at the kitchen table, as usual. Winter was thinking about Smedsberg's kitchen, not to mention Carlström's combination: cowshed and kitchenette.

"What was it like out on the flats?"

"Flat."

"Did that surprise you?"

"Yes, it did, in fact. Sometimes it was like being at sea."

"There's an illness you can get out on the prairies," said Angela. "Simply by living there."

Winter thought about the men they had met that day.

"That doesn't surprise me."

"In the USA they call it 'the sickness.' "

"Not bad. Why can't all illnesses have nice simple names like that?"

"People go mad in states like Wyoming and Montana. In those enormous prairies there are no reference points. All you can see is a vast flat plain and the horizon."

"Like being at sea, like I said."

Angela poured out more tea.

"There's nothing to look at, no trees, no houses, no roads with cars or buses. People lose their sense of direction. Lose their senses in the end."

"So all you'd need to stay sane would be an outhouse within sight?" said Winter.

"That would be enough, certainly."

"The people living where we were today certainly seem odd, but there are a few outhouses scattered around," said Winter.

"Did you find the boy? The medical student?"

"No. And nobody expected we would."

"Why did you go there, then?"

He didn't answer, poured out some more tea, buttered another slice of rye bread, placed a piece of Stilton on it, cut a wedge from his apple.

"Did you just need to get away for a while?" Angela asked.

"Something happened out there," said Winter.

"What do you mean?"

He took a sip of tea and a bite of his open sandwich. The radio on the countertop was churning out the latest weather forecast: colder, clearer, a chance of snow for Christmas.

"Something happened out there," Winter said again, sounding serious. "I had a strange feeling in one of the houses we visited."

"What are you basing that feeling on?"

"The sickness," he said, grinning over his teacup.

"Are you pulling my leg?"

"Of course."

But he wasn't pulling anybody's leg. Angela had seen that, and later, much later, he said so, after they made love and he got up to fetch two glasses of mineral water. He'd longed for a Corps, but didn't have the strength to go out onto the balcony.

"You know that I have a sort of intuitive ability," he'd said. "You know that."

"What was it, then?"

"When Bertil and I drove home, we agreed that one of those elderly men, the older one, was lying through his teeth. You can tell. I mean, it's our job to decide if people are telling the truth or lying."

"Does it always matter?"

"What do you mean?"

"People lie for different reasons. I can see that myself. Some just come out with a lie, without knowing in advance that they're going to lie. But it doesn't change anything. It doesn't turn them into criminals. It doesn't necessarily mean that they are concealing something horrific."

"No, but that was precisely the feeling I had out there. That there was something—something major that was being concealed. Something horrendous has happened. Do you understand? The old man we spoke to had something in his past that he didn't want us to know about." Winter took a drink of the mineral water. "But I also think the other one, Smedsberg's father, was lying. I don't know what to think. I don't even know if it's relevant."

"He probably got nervous when two snobby chief inspectors from the big city showed up."

"We're not snobby."

"Really? Were you wearing overalls?"

"Of course. Bought them in the village general store."

He emptied his glass. He could see her profile.

"Do you think he had that boy Kaite shut up somewhere?"

"Hidden away? No."

"What, then?"

"I don't know, like I said. But I do know we need to talk to the other old man again, Carlström. Before that, though, I need to speak to Smedsberg."

He noticed that she nodded slightly.

"At the same time we need to talk to these children, and have another word with their parents."

"It's awful," she said.

"It could be even worse than we think," he said.

She didn't answer.

"I've tried to think this one through, looking for a possible pattern that might become clearer if we get some more facts, memories. Pictures. Objects. Things. If there is a pattern, it probably won't make matters any easier. And if it gets more complicated it will also become . . . more horrendous." He stretched out his hand, rubbed her shoulder that was firm but soft. "Can you see the way my thoughts are going?"

"That it will get worse," she said.

"Yes."

"That it could go on and on."

"Yes."

"But what can be done, though?" she asked. "Lock up the children? Have armed guards posted at nursery schools and children's playgrounds, and schools?"

"It might be enough if there were more staff."

"Ha!"

"But there's no hundred percent certain way of stopping anybody who's determined to hurt somebody."

"So all you can do is wait?"

"Certainly not."

"What would happen if the press announced that there was somebody out there. Waiting. Or preparing himself."

"It wouldn't be good," he said.

"But what if you *have* to? What if you're forced to inform the public?"

"There are various ways of doing that."

"I've seen that little boy, Waggoner." He could hear her breathing. "How is that possible? Eh? What makes a person do something like that?"

How is it possible to be rational and clear in reply to a question like that, he thought.

"I know there simply isn't a rational and clear answer to that kind of question, but it has to be asked, don't you think?" He could see that she was looking at him now. He could see a glint in her eye. "Don't you think? Why? You have to ask why?"

"The answer to that question is what we're always looking for," he said.

"Is it enough?"

"Discovering why? I don't know. Sometimes there is nothing."

"No reason, you mean?"

"Yes. Why does somebody commit a serious crime? Is there only *one* reason? Is there a series of different reasons? Are they linked? Is it possible to analyze them logically? Should one even try to think logically if the crime, or crimes, are driven by chance and a lack of logic?" He looked at her again. "There could be so many possibilities. It could be pure lunacy, acute mental illness. Bad memories. Revenge."

"Is that common? Revenge?"

"Yes. Revenge against somebody who has treated you badly. Directly or indirectly. Yes, it certainly is common. It can go a long way back."

"A long way back in time?"

"A long way back," said Winter again. "The past casts shadows. You know that. It happens so often. To find the answers now you have to pin down a *then*. What happens now has its origins in that then."

"So that could apply in this case as well? With the assaults on those students? As well as to the abuse of the boy?"

"Yes, certainly."

"They are two different things, but still."

"Hmm."

"Aren't they two different things?"

"Well . . ."

"You're hesitating."

"No, I'm thinking about this searching backward through time. Digging. Looking for answers."

"You and your colleagues are acting like investigative journalists, you mean?"

"No. More like archaeologists. Archaeologists of crime."

27

THE "WANTED" MESSAGE SENT OUT IN CONNECTION WITH ARYAN
Kaite attracted a big response, but none of the tips led them to him, nor him
to them.

"Anything new from the African clubs?" asked Fredrik Halders as they
drove up through the hilly eastern suburbs to his house.

"No," said Aneta Djanali. "He's not a member. They knew who he was,
of course, but he's not on the membership rolls."

"Are you a member?"

"Am I a member of what, exactly?"

"The Ougadougou Club."

"What if I were to take you to Ougadougou, Fredrik? I sometimes think
you dream about Ougadougou. You're always talking about the place."

"Isn't everybody?" asked Halders.

Aneta Djanali was born in Eastern General Hospital in Gothenburg to
African parents, immigrants from Burkino Faso, who had left their homeland
when it was still called Upper Volta. Her father had trained in Sweden as an
engineer, and they'd returned home when Aneta was about to become an
adult. She had chosen to stay in Sweden. Of course. Her father now lived
alone in a little house in the capital, and his house was the same bleached
color as the sand surrounding the city. Everything there was hot, biting air (or
blue frozen air), and people always cherished the same dreams about water
that never came. Aneta had been back, if that was the right expression. It was
a foreign country as far as she was concerned. She had immediately felt at
home, but that was it—as if the expression "Home is where the heart is" had
lost its meaning. She knew that she would never be able to live there: But,
nevertheless, it would always be home.

She parked outside Halders's house, where Advent candles were illumi-
nating one of the windows.

"I can pick up Hannes and Magda, if you like," she said, as he got out of the car.

"I thought you had a lot to do."

"That can wait." She gave a laugh. "I was going to get some tapioca root and dried bananas, but I've got enough to last me."

"But what if your club throws a party tonight?"

"And what if people start taking your racist jokes seriously, Fredrik?"

"I don't even want to think about that," he said.

"Would you like me to pick them up, then?"

"Yes, please. I can make dinner for you." She turned around with the door half open. "I've got sand cakes."

"Yes, OK," said Djanali, and drove off.

━━━━━━

Winter was in Birgersson's office. His boss was smoking in the semidarkness.

The pillars holding up Ullevi Stadium were splayed out behind him, against a clear evening sky. Winter could see a star.

"What are you doing for Christmas, Erik?"

"Spain. Costa del Sol. If I can get away."

"I hope you can't."

"I know what you're saying, but even so I don't understand."

Birgersson grunted and tapped the ash off his cigarette.

"When are you going to start interrogating the children?" he asked.

"Tomorrow."

"It's going to be hard."

Winter didn't answer. He leaned forward and lit a Corps with a match, which he let burn for a few seconds. Birgersson smiled.

"Thank you for the Christmas atmosphere," he said.

"They speak pretty well," said Winter, letting the smoke float up. "More or less like adults."

Birgersson grunted again.

"We've got quite a lot to go on," said Winter.

"In the old days, which were not so long ago, we'd have said that a child was burned out after one interrogation," said Birgersson. "It wouldn't be possible to extract any more information after that." He studied the smoke from Winter's cigarillo. "But now we let the memories ripen. The images."

"Hmm."

"Let's assume for the moment that all this actually occurred," said Birgersson. "That what the children say is true. That these incidents did happen as described."

"Simon Waggoner hasn't said anything," said Winter.

"But in his case, we know," said Birgersson. "There's no doubt about it." Winter thought.

"He has something that entices them," he said.

"Is it just one thing? The same thing every time?"

"Let's assume that for the time being," said Winter.

"Go on."

"And they have something that he wants."

"What do you mean by that?"

"He's out to get something from these children. A thing. A souvenir he can take with him."

"He wants them for himself, is that it? He wants . . . the children."

"Let's leave that for the moment," said Winter. He drew on his cigarillo again. He could still see the star, and another one. It was as if he could see more clearly when he thought as he was thinking now. "He takes something from them. He wants to take it home with him. Or to have it in his possession."

"Why?" asked Birgersson.

"It's got something to do with . . . with himself. With the person he once was."

"The person he once was?"

"When he was like they are now. When he was a child."

"We know what he's taken," said Birgersson. "A watch, a ball, and some kind of jewelery."

"And perhaps also something from the Skarin boy. Probably."

"Are they trophies, Erik?"

"I don't know. No. Not in that way."

"Are the things he's taken similar to things he has himself?" said Birgersson, putting down the cigarette and rocking backward and forward in his swivel chair, which emitted a whining sound.

"That's a very good question," said Winter.

"That somebody could answer, if only we could find a somebody," said Birgersson.

"There are the children."

"True. But I was thinking of other grown-ups. Grown-up witnesses." He contemplated Winter, Winter's Corps, Winter's shirt unbuttoned at the neck, and his tie that looked like a noose. "Are we dealing with a grown-up here, Erik?"

"That's a very good question."

"A child in a grown-up body," said Birgersson.

"It's not that simple," said Winter.

"Who said it was simple? It's damned complicated," said Birgersson. He suddenly turned around, as if he could feel the beams on the back of his neck from the two stars that seemed to be nailed to poles towering up over Lunden behind Ullevi Stadium. He turned back again.

"This is an ugly mess," he said. "You know I think such expressions are unprofessional and I don't like them, but I'm going to use it in this case all the same." He lit another cigarette and pointed it at Winter. "Nail the bastard before something even worse happens."

28

ANGELA CALLED AS WINTER WAS LEAVING BIRGERSSON'S OFFICE.
He saw his own home number on the display.

"Yes?"

"Erik, the nursery-school manager just called. Our nursery school, that is."

"Is Elsa at home?"

"Yes, yes, thank God."

"What did she want?"

"They saw a strange person hanging around."

"OK, do you have her phone number handy?"

He called immediately on his mobile, still only halfway to his office.

He was sitting in her office, which was decorated with children's Christmas drawings. It wasn't the first time he'd been in this room, but the first time on business like this. The only people in the nursery school were the cleaning staff. The silence was strange, almost unnatural for rooms that were normally echoing with children's voices. He'd been here before in the evening, for parents' meetings, but then the quietness had been different, a grown-up murmur.

"Somebody filming them," Winter said.

"Yes. A delayed reaction, you might say. Lisbeth started to think about it when one of the fathers picking up his kid started taking video footage," said the manager, Lena Meyer.

"Where exactly was it?"

"As they were crossing the soccer field."

"Where was he standing?"

He heard a timid knock on the door behind him.

"This should be her now. Come in!"

Lisbeth Augustsson opened the door. She nodded to Winter—she'd spoken to him many times, but they'd only exchanged a few words. She was about twenty-two, possibly twenty-five, hair in thick brown plaits, red ribbons. She sat down on the chair beside Winter.

"Where exactly was he standing when he was filming?" Winter asked.

She tried to describe the spot.

"He followed us too," she said.

"Still filming?"

"Yes, it looked like it."

"Did you recognize him?"

"No."

"How can you be sure?"

"Well, I can't be certain, obviously. I didn't see him for all that long either. And he had a camera in front of his face." She smiled.

"Nobody you'd seen before?"

"No."

"What made you report this to Lena?" Winter asked.

"Well, there was this business about the girl who said she'd, er, spoken to somebody. Ellen Sköld. That makes you a bit suspicious." She looked at Lena Meyer. "We're always careful, of course."

She knew nothing about the other children. Not much about Simon Waggoner, not yet. Winter and his colleagues wouldn't be able to keep that secret for much longer.

"Have you ever seen anyone filming you before?" Winter asked. "When you were out on an excursion somewhere? Or here at the nursery school?"

"No, I can't say I have. It was just today."

"Please tell me exactly what happened, as accurately as you can," said Winter.

"There's not a lot to say. I looked up once and saw him but didn't really think about it. I mean, you often see people with video cameras nowadays, don't you? But then I looked again, and he was still there, filming—apparently filming us." She threw her hands up. "And when he seemed to notice that I'd seen him, that I was looking at his camera, he turned it away and pretended to be filming the buildings on the other side of the street, or whatever."

"Maybe he was," said Winter.

"Was what?"

"Filming the buildings. Maybe he wasn't pretending."

"It looked like he was."

"What happened next?" Winter asked. "Did you continue watching him?"

"Yes. I watched for a bit longer, but we had the children to think about. And he turned away after only a few seconds and walked off."

"In which direction?"

"Back toward Linnéplatsen."

"Did you see him from the side? Or from behind?"

"From behind, I think. I didn't watch very long. I mean, we had other things to think about. But then I remembered it again, later."

"Can you describe what he looked like?" Winter asked.

"Well . . . He was sort of normal looking. The camera was in the way so you couldn't see his face. His jacket was blue, I think, and trousers, I assume." She gave a laugh. "He wasn't wearing a skirt, I would've remembered that, and, well—that's about it." She was still thinking. Winter had sat thousands of times with witnesses trying to remember. Everything they said could be accurate, but it could also be totally misleading. Colors that were definitely green could be yellow, six-foot men could be dwarfs, women could be men, men women, trousers could be . . . skirts. Cars could be mopeds and 100 percent certainly dogs could turn out to be camels. No. No camels had cropped up in any of his cases, not yet.

Children could be children. Cease to be children, disappear. Cease to exist. Or never be children again, never be whole persons again.

"He had a cap!" she said suddenly.

"You said before he had a camera in front of his head."

"In front of his face. I said in front of his face. And not all the time I was watching him. I remember now that you could see the cap over the top of the camera. And I saw it as well when he turned to film the buildings on the other side, if that's what he was doing."

"What kind of a cap?"

"Well, it wasn't a Nike cap. Not one of those baseball things."

Winter thought about Fredrik Halders: He often wore a baseball cap over his shaven skull. Nike, or Kangol.

"More like an old man's cap," she said.

"An old man's cap?" said Winter.

"Yes. One of those gray or beige things old men always seem to wear."

Winter nodded.

"Yes, one of them," she said. "Gray, I think, but I'm not sure. A sort of gray pattern."

"Was he an elderly man?" Winter pointed to himself. "Like me?"

She smiled again, big teeth, perfectly shaped, white; Nordic, if you could call them that.

"I really couldn't say," she said. "But he could have been about your age.

Despite the cap. He walked normally, he wasn't fat or anything like that, he didn't seem old. He wasn't an old man."

"Would you recognize him if you saw him again?"

"I don't know. But if he was wearing the same clothes, and carrying a video camera—well, I might."

"Have you spoken to anybody else about this?" Winter asked. "Apart from Lena." He nodded in the direction of Lena Meyer.

"No."

"How many staff were out this afternoon with the children?"

"Er, three, including me."

"And none of the others noticed anything?"

"I don't know. As I said, I sort of forgot all about it. Until now."

Winter stood up. Thought. He could see the group in his mind's eye. Staff first, in the middle, and at the back. He'd seen a set up like that lots of times. What did they do? Pause, fuss around, carry on. It was December now. Not long to go before the holidays. Everybody was caught up in the spirit. Something to celebrate coming up. Everybody on vacation. In a way, the holiday had already started. What do you do when there's a holiday mood in the air? You sing. Dance. Have fun. Perhaps you might want to record these moments, or this mood. Record it. Watch it again later. Record it. Keep it.

He looked at Lisbeth Augustsson.

"Did any of you have a video camera with you when you went out?"

"Er . . . No."

"An ordinary camera, perhaps?"

"Er . . ."

He could see that she was thinking hard.

"Did any of you have a camera with you when you went out on this excursion?"

Lisbeth Augustsson looked at Winter with a curious expression.

"Good Lord! Anette had her camera with her! An ordinary film camera. She might have taken a few pictures when we were crossing the soccer field. She said she was going to take some, but I was looking in the other direction." Lisbeth Augustsson looked at her boss and at Winter again. "She might have a picture of him!"

"Could be," said Winter.

"Amazing that you thought of that," she said.

"We'd have found out anyway when we spoke to the others," Winter said. "Where can I get hold of Anette?"

Ringmar was waiting for Gustav Smedsberg. He could hear voices in the corridor, somebody trying to sing a Christmas carol. The echo was not to anybody's advantage. A peal of laughter, a woman's voice. Detectives winding down for the holiday.

But here we are not winding down, we're winding up, up, up.

He called home but there was no reply. Birgitta ought to be at home by now. He needed to ask her what she wanted him to buy from the market.

He tried Moa's mobile. "The number you have called cannot be reached at this time."

He would have liked to call Martin, if he'd known what to say.

The phone call came from the duty officer. Smedsberg was waiting downstairs in the cozy foyer, "the charm suite," as Halders called the reception rooms. The first stimulating contact the general public had with the police authorities, step one on the way to the ombudsman.

Gustav Smedsberg looked thin, standing on the other side of the security door. He seemed underdressed, wearing a cap that appeared to be more of an accessory than anything else. Denim jacket, a thin T-shirt underneath. Open neck. The boy's face was expressionless; he might have been bored stiff. Ringmar beckoned to him.

"This way," he said.

Smedsberg was shivering in the elevator up.

"It's cold out there," said Ringmar.

"Started yesterday," said Smedsberg. "A bastard of a wind."

"You haven't gotten around to digging out your winter clothes, I take it?"

"These are my winter clothes," said Smedsberg, scrutinizing the buttons in the elevator. He shivered again, and again, like sudden tics.

"I thought you were used to chilly winds where you come from out on the flats," said Ringmar. "And how to protect yourself from them."

Smedsberg didn't respond.

They exited the elevator. The brick walls were a big help to anybody who wanted to suppress the Christmas atmosphere. The thought had occurred to Ringmar that morning. Or perhaps in his case he had lost the Christmas spirit already. Birgitta had said nothing when he got up. He knew she was awake, she always was. Silent. He'd said a few words, but she'd just rolled over onto her other side.

"Please come in," he said, ushering Smedsberg into his office.

Smedsberg paused in the doorway. Ringmar could see his profile, a nose curved like that of his father. Perhaps there was something in his bearing reminiscent of the old man as well. And in his accent, although the boy's was less pronounced.

"Please sit down."

Smedsberg sat down, hesitantly, as if he were ready to leave at any moment.

"Will this take long?" he asked.

"No."

"What's it about, then?"

"The same thing we've talked about before," said Ringmar.

"I don't know any more about it than I did then," said Smedsberg. "He stirred things up about Josefin, and that's about it."

"What do you mean? Who's 'he'?"

"Aryan, of course. Isn't he the one we've been talking about all the time?"

"There are others involved as well," said Ringmar.

"I don't know them, like I said."

"Jakob Stillman lived in the same building as you."

"So did a hundred others. A thousand."

"You said before that you didn't know Aryan Kaite."

"Yes, yes." Smedsberg shook his head dismissively.

"What does that mean?"

"What does what mean?"

"Yes, yes. What do you mean by that?"

"I don't know."

"*Snap out of it,*" said Ringmar, sternly.

"What's the matter?" said Smedsberg, more alert now, but still with a remote, bored expression that wouldn't disappear that easily.

"We are investigating serious violent crimes, and we need help," said Ringmar. "People who lie to us are not being helpful."

"Have I committed a crime?" Smedsberg asked.

"Why did you tell us you didn't know Aryan Kaite?"

"I didn't think it was significant." He looked at Ringmar, who could see a sort of cold intelligence in his eyes.

"What do you think now, then?" asked Ringmar.

Smedsberg shrugged.

"Why didn't you want to tell us that you knew somebody who'd been assaulted the same way you almost were?"

"I didn't think it was all that important. And I still think it was just coincidence."

"Really?"

"The argument I had with Aryan had nothing to do with anything . . . anything like this."

"What *did* it have to do with?"

"Like I said before. He misunderstood something."

"What did he misunderstand?"

"Look, why should I answer that question?"

"What did he misunderstand?" said Ringmar again.

"Er, that he had something going with Josefin." Gustav Smedsberg seemed to smile, or at least give a little grin. "But he hadn't checked with her."

"Where do you fit in, then?"

"She wanted to be with me."

"And what did you want?"

"I wanted to be free."

"So why did you have an argument with Kaite, then?" Ringmar asked.

"No idea. You'd better ask him."

"We can't do that, can we? He disappeared."

"Oh yes, that's true."

"The girl vanished as well. Josefin Stenvång."

"Yes, that's odd."

"You don't seem to be particularly worried."

Smedsberg didn't answer. His face gave nothing away. Ringmar could hear a voice outside in the hall, a voice he didn't recognize.

"You and Kaite were such good friends that you both went to your home to help out with the potato picking," said Ringmar.

Smedsberg still didn't answer.

"Didn't you?" said Ringmar.

"So you've been to my dad's, have you?" said Smedsberg. All I need to do is to mention *die heimat,* Ringmar thought, and the boy's back home again on that godforsaken plain.

"Didn't you?" said Ringmar again.

"If you say so," said Smedsberg.

"Why didn't you tell us about your friendship with Aryan Kaite?" Ringmar asked.

Smedsberg didn't answer.

"What did your dad think of him?" Ringmar asked.

"Leave the old man out of this."

"Why?"

"Just leave him out."

"He's already in," said Ringmar. "And I have to ask you about another matter that is linked to this business."

Ringmar asked about Natanael Carlström's foster son.

"Yes, there was one, I guess," said Smedsberg.

"Do you know him?"

"No. He moved out before I—well, before I grew up."

"Have you seen him?"

"No. What are you getting at?"

Ringmar could see that the boy no longer looked bored stiff. His body language had changed. He was more tense.

"Do you know his name?"

"No. You'll have to ask old man Carlström."

Ringmar paused for a few moments.

"You were the one who mentioned that branding iron. Marking iron. We've looked into it but didn't get anywhere until we paid a visit to Carlström."

"Why did you go there?"

"It was your dad who thought that Carlström might have owned an iron like that."

"Oh."

"Which he had."

"Oh."

"Did you use to have one on your farm?"

"Not as far as I know."

"You said you did before."

"Did I?"

"Were you making it up?" Ringmar asked.

"No. What do you mean?"

"You said you used to have irons like that."

"I must have gotten it wrong," said Smedsberg.

"How could you have done that?"

"I must have phrased it wrong. I must have meant that I'd heard about irons like that."

We'll come back to that, Ringmar thought. I don't know what to think, and I don't think the boy does either. We'll have to come back to it.

"Carlström had one," said Ringmar. "Or maybe two."

"Really?"

"You seem to be interested."

"What am I supposed to say?"

Ringmar leaned forward.

"It's been stolen."

Smedsberg was about to come out with another "really" but controlled himself.

"It's vanished," said Ringmar. "Just like Aryan Kaite has vanished. And he has a wound that looks as if it might have been caused by a weapon like that. And that wound might be able to tell us something."

"Isn't it a bit far-fetched for you to meet an old man who's just had an iron like that stolen, and that it should turn out to be precisely the one that was used?" said Smedsberg.

"That's what we're wondering as well," said Ringmar. "And that's where you come in, Gustav." Ringmar stood up and Smedsberg remained seated. "If it hadn't been for you, we'd never have made that journey to the flats."

"I didn't need to say anything at all about a branding iron," said Smedsberg.

"But you did."

"Am I going to get fucked over for that, then?"

Ringmar didn't respond.

"I'll be happy to join in a search party for Aryan if that's what you need help with," said Smedsberg.

"Why a search party?"

"Eh?"

"Why should we send a search party out to look for Aryan?"

"I have no idea."

"But that's what you said."

"Come on, that's just something you say. I mean, a search party, for Christ's sake, call it what the hell you like when you're looking for somebody."

"Search parties don't work in big cities," said Ringmar.

"Oh."

"They work better in the countryside," said Ringmar.

"Really?"

"Is he somewhere out there in the flats, Gustav?"

"I have no idea."

"Where is he, Gustav?"

"For Christ's . . . I don't know."

"What's happened to him?"

Smedsberg stood up.

"I want to leave now. This is ridiculous."

Ringmar looked at the boy, who still seemed to be freezing cold in his thin clothes. Ringmar could lock him up for the night, but it was too soon for that. Or perhaps too late. But the evidence was too thin.

"I'll show you out, Gustav."

29

WINTER CALLED ANETTE RIGHT AWAY, FROM THE NURSERY-SCHOOL manager's office. She was at home and Winter could hear the humming of the exhaust fan in the background. Or perhaps it was a hair dryer. It stopped.

Camera? Yes, what about it? Yes, she had it on hand. The film wasn't finished. Yes, he could come and get it.

Winter sent a car to Anette's flat. The camera really was a very simple one. One of the technical division's labs had the film developed and copied after Winter had returned to his office.

He had the photographs on the desk in front of him now. They hadn't been taken by an expert photographer. Everything was overexposed and slightly blurred. All of them were of children, mostly in a location Winter recognized: the grounds of Elsa's nursery school. Some of the pictures featured members of staff he knew.

The park, the soccer field. A long line of children.

A man with a video camera could be seen in the background, perhaps thirty meters behind them. His face was hidden by the camera. That particular picture was sharper than the others, as if it had been taken by a different photographer. The man was wearing a cap. Winter couldn't make out the colors.

The man was wearing the kind of jacket you often see on elderly men who buy their clothes at charity shops. It was impossible to see what kind of trousers he was wearing. More careful copying was necessary, and a bigger enlargement.

Anette had taken two pictures in which the man was visible in the background, but not in succession.

In the second one he had turned his back on the camera and was evidently walking away. The jacket could be seen more clearly. It could easily have been made in the 1950s.

Perhaps the trousers as well. You couldn't see his shoes, the grass was up to the man's calves. Nor could Winter see the video camera.

"Is it still glued to his face?" asked Halders, who was poring over the photograph. "The video camera, I mean."

They were meeting in the smaller conference room: Winter, Ringmar, Halders, Djanali.

"It's not visible," said Winter.

"He dresses like an old man, but he's not an old man," said Djanali.

"What exactly does an old man look like?" Halders asked.

"You're not going to goad me into going on about that," said Djanali.

"But seriously, what is characteristic of an old man?" said Ringmar.

"He doesn't have the bearing of an old man," said Djanali. "He's just chosen to dress like one."

"Clothes make the man," said Halders.

"The question is what this particular man has done," said Ringmar, looking at the photograph that could possibly feature the abductor. He felt strangely excited.

"He was filming the children," said Winter.

"That's not a crime," said Ringmar, rubbing one eye. Winter could see tension in Ringmar's face, more noticeable than usual. "There are normal people who film anything in sight." Ringmar looked up. There was a red patch over one eye. "He doesn't have to be a pedophile or a kidnapper or a child molester."

"But he could be," said Djanali. "We have a crime on our hands. And he could be the one who did it."

"We'll have to work on the picture," said Winter. "Or pictures, rather. Maybe it's somebody we can recognize from the archives."

"The camera looks new. It doesn't fit in with the dress code," said Halders.

Nobody was sure if he was being serious or not.

It was so crowded that it was difficult to move your feet. A teeming mass of people, and he was sweating, and if it hadn't been for that woman with the stroller ten meters ahead of him, he wouldn't have been here at all, no, certainly not. He'd have been at home, on his own.

It had looked as if the child was sleeping when they were outside the Nordstan shopping center. Then they went inside, the black sea of people walking, walking, walking, shopping, shopping, shopping.

"The day before the day before the day before the day!" somebody yelled, or something of the sort. But what did he care about Christmas? Personally? Christmas was a time for children. He wasn't a child. But he had been one, and he knew.

It was a good idea. He'd had it before, but now it was stronger than ever. Christmas was a time for children. He was on his own and wasn't a child. But he knew what children liked at Christmastime. He was nice and he could do everything that would make Christmas really fun for a child. Really fun!

He wasn't at all sure that the woman in front of him could do that. He didn't think that the child lying asleep in an uncomfortable position thought she was fun. She didn't look very fun. He'd seen her before, when she had come to the nursery school and he'd been standing there, watching, or maybe just walking past. In fact he'd seen her several times.

He had seen the boy. And he'd seen a man who might have been the boy's father.

He'd filmed the boy.

He'd filmed all of them.

The woman had paused outside Nordstan to smoke a cigarette. He didn't like that. She had jerked her head back and looked as if she were drinking the smoke. He didn't think that she lived with this child. It might have been her boy, but he wasn't sure.

Somebody bumped into him, then somebody else. He couldn't see the stroller, but then it came into view again. He wasn't bothered about the woman at all, to be honest.

He'd followed them when they left the nursery school. He could come back for his car later.

The weather had turned colder, but he didn't feel cold. He thought the boy was cold: The woman hadn't tucked him in properly.

That didn't matter so much now; it was warm indoors. She was standing in front of one of the department stores that sold everything imaginable. The doors were open and as wide as sluice gates, and people were flooding in and out like torrents of black water, out and in, out and in.

He saw the sculpture, the one he admired. It looked so . . . so free, so liberated. Sculpted figures flying down from the sky. They were free. They were flying.

He looked around and noticed that she'd parked the stroller by a counter where they sold perfume and hair lotion and lipstick and all that kind of stuff, or maybe it was clothes, but he hadn't checked very carefully. Yes, it was clothes in fact, perfume was a bit farther on. He knew that really.

He could see the boy's feet sticking out, or one of them at least. She seemed to be standing there, looking at the boy or maybe something on the floor next to the stroller. Maybe it didn't make any difference to her. He moved to one side, out of the way of people flooding in and out. He was standing ten meters away from her. She didn't see him. She moved the stroller closer to one of the counters. She looked around. He didn't understand what she was doing.

She walked away. He saw her go to another counter, and then he lost sight of her. He waited. He could see the stroller, but nobody else was looking at it. He was standing guard while the woman was away, doing God only knows what.

He kept watch. People walking past no doubt thought the stroller belonged to somebody at one of the nearby counters. Maybe someone who worked there. He looked around but there was no sign of the woman. He checked his watch, but he didn't know what time it had been when she left and so he didn't know how long she'd been away.

He took a few paces toward the stroller, and then a few more.

When Ringmar got home he could feel that there was something seriously wrong. Even as he took his shoes off in the hall he could sense that the silence was heavier than usual. He hadn't heard a silence like that before in this house. Or had he?

"Birgitta?"

No answer, and there was nobody there when he went to the kitchen, up the stairs, through the rooms. He didn't turn on the lights upstairs as the neighbor's illuminations were quite enough to fill the rooms with a yellow day-before-the-day-before-the-day-before-the-day glow.

Back downstairs he called his daughter's mobile. She answered after the second ring.

"Hi Moa, it's your dad here."

She didn't answer. Perhaps she's nodding, he thought.

"Do you know where your mom is?"

"Yes."

"I tried to call her but there was no reply, and when I got home there was nobody there."

"Yes."

"Where is she then? Did she go shopping?"

Ringmar could hear her rapid breathing.

"She's gone away for a while."

"Eh? Gone away? Where to? Why? What's going on?"

That was a lot of questions, and she answered one of them: "I don't know."

"Don't know what?"

"Where she's gone."

"Didn't she say?"

"No."

"What the hell is this?!" said Ringmar. I'd better sit down, he thought. "I don't understand a goddamn thing," he said. "Do you, Moa?"

She didn't reply.

"Moa?" He could hear a noise in the background, as if something was moving fast. "Moa? Where are you?"

"I'm on the streetcar," she said. "On my way home."

Thank God for that, he thought.

"We can talk when I get there," she said.

───────

He waited on edge, opened a beer that he didn't drink. The thousand lights in the neighbor's garden suddenly started flashing. What the hell, he thought. They're winking like a thousand yellow compound eyes, like stars sending messages down to earth. Pretty soon I'll have to stop by and pass on an unambiguous message to that stupid bastard.

The front door opened. He went into the hall.

"It's probably not all that bad," was the first thing his daughter said. She took off her coat.

"What is going on?" asked Ringmar.

"Let's go into the living room," she said.

He trudged after her. They sat down on the sofa.

"Martin called," she said.

"I understand," he said.

"Do you?"

"Why didn't she talk to me first?"

"What do you understand, Dad?"

"It's obvious, isn't it? He wants to see her but under no circumstances does he want to see me." He shook his head. "And she had to promise not to say anything to me."

"I don't know anything about that," said Moa.

"When's she coming back?"

"Tomorrow, I think."

"So he's not that far away?" said Ringmar.

She didn't answer. He couldn't see her face, only her hair, which was speckled with the flashing light from the idiot's garden.

"So he's not that far away?" Ringmar said again.

"She's not going to meet him," Moa said eventually.

"I beg your pardon?"

"Mom isn't going to meet Martin," said Moa.

"What do you know that I don't know?"

"I don't know much more than you do," she said. "Mom called me and said that Martin had been in touch and she would have to go away for a short while."

"But what the hell did he say, then? He must have said something that made her take off?!"

"I don't know."

"This is the kind of thing that happens to other people," he said.

She said nothing.

"Aren't you worried?" he asked.

She stood up.

"Where are you going?" he asked.

"Up to my room. Why?"

"There's something else, isn't there?" he said. "I can see it in your face."

"No," she said. "I have to go to my room now. Vanna's going to call me."

He stood up, went to the kitchen and grabbed the bottle of beer, went back to the living room, and sat down on the sofa again. Birgitta didn't have a mobile: If she did he could have left her a message, said something, done something. This is a situation I've never been in before. Is it a dream? Or is it something I've said? Something I've done? What have I done?

Why had Martin called? What had he said? What had he said to make Birgitta pack a bag and take off? Without telling her husband.

He took a swig of beer, and the illuminations outside continued to flash and twinkle. He looked out of the window and saw that some kind of portal with lights had been created outside the neighbor's front door. That was new. He clutched the bottle in his hand and stood up. He saw his neighbor come out and turn around to admire his garden of light. Ringmar heard the phone ring and Moa's voice when she answered. He waited for her to shout down to him, but she continued talking. Vanna, no doubt, a fellow student who wore flowery shirts. Would do well as a lawyer.

He kept on staring at his idiotic neighbor. It looked as if the stupid bastard were fixing up some more floodlights in one of the maple trees. Ringmar slammed the bottle down onto the glass table with a loud bang and went out onto the veranda facing the lights. He didn't feel the frost through his socks.

"What the hell are you doing now?" he yelled straight across the flashing Dipper and the Great Bear and the Little Bear and everybody and their brother.

The neighbor's discolored and moronic face turned to look at him.

"*What the hell are you doing?!*" screeched Ringmar, and even as he did so he recognized that this was not the way to behave, that you didn't take out your own frustration or worries on other people, he knew that full well, but just then he didn't give a shit about that.

"What's the matter?" asked the neighbor, who Ringmar knew was some kind of administrator in the health service. A real butcher, in other words, as Winter's Angela would have said. I'll bet that bastard administrates fucking light therapy at the hospital, Ringmar thought.

"I can't take any more of your stupid lights in my face," said Ringmar.

The neighbor stared back with his stupid face. How can anybody like that be allowed to live? Where are you, God?

"My whole house is bathed in light all night long from your goddamn yard, and it only gets worse," said Ringmar in a louder voice than usual, to make sure the administrator heard. "Thank God Christmas will be over soon." He turned on his heel, went back inside, and slammed the door behind him. He was shaking. I managed that quite well. Nobody got hurt.

He was woken up at midnight, out of a dream that was brightly lit.

"Bertil, it's Erik. I need your help. I know it's late, but it can't be helped."

He could see the light was on in Winter's office as he crossed the parking lot. It was the only lit window in the north wall of police headquarters.

A man was sitting on the chair opposite Winter.

"This is Bengt Johansson," said Winter. "He's just arrived."

Ringmar introduced himself. The man didn't respond.

"Have you been there?" Ringmar asked, turning to Winter. "To Nordstan?"

"Yes," said Winter. "And I wasn't the only one searching. But the place is empty."

"Oh my God," said Bengt Johansson.

"Tell us your story one more time," said Winter, sitting down.

"This isn't the first time," said Johansson. "It's happened once before. They called from the kiosk. It was only a few minutes that time."

Ringmar looked at Winter.

"Tell us about what happened," said Winter.

"She was supposed to pick up Micke," said Johansson. "And she did. Eh! We'd agreed that they'd go out for an hour or so and buy some Christmas presents, and then she'd bring him back home to me." He looked at Ringmar. "But they never showed up." He looked at Winter. "I called her at home, but there was no answer. I waited and called again. I mean, I had no idea where they might go."

Winter nodded.

"Then I called various people I—we—know, and then I checked the hospital." He mimed a phone call. "And then, well, then I called here. Criminal emergency, or whatever they call it."

"They called me," said Winter, looking at Ringmar. "The mother—Carolin—had left the kid at H&M near the entrance, and vanished."

"And vanished?" said Ringmar.

"Shortly before six. Loads of people. They closed at eight."

Winter looked at Johansson. The man seemed as if he had come face-to-face with a horror that must have been worse than anything Ringmar had dreamed recently.

"Bengt here started calling when they didn't turn up. And eventually got through to us, as he said."

"Where's the boy?" Ringmar asked.

"We don't know," sighed Winter. Johansson sniffled.

"Where's the mother?" asked Ringmar. "Is the boy with her?"

"No," said Winter. "Bengt mentioned a few places he hadn't gotten around to phoning, and she was in one of them."

"What kind of places?"

Winter didn't answer.

"Pubs? Restaurants?"

"That kind of place, yes. We found her and identified her, but the boy wasn't with her."

"What did she have to say?"

"Nothing that's of any help to us at the moment," said Winter.

Johansson showed signs of life.

"What do I do now?" he asked.

"Is there someone who can keep you company for the time being?" Winter asked.

"Er, yes. My sister."

"One of our colleagues will give you a lift home," Winter said. "You shouldn't be on your own."

Johansson said nothing.

"I'd like you to go home and wait," said Winter. "We'll be in touch." Maybe somebody else will be in touch as well, he thought. "Could you call Helander and Birgersson, please, Bertil?"

"What the hell's going on?" asked Ringmar. They were still in Winter's office. Winter had tried to get in touch with Hanne Östergaard, the police vicar, but she was abroad on Christmas leave.

"A family drama of a more difficult kind," said Winter. "The mother left the boy all alone and hoped that some kind soul from the staff would look after him. Or some other generous passerby."

"Which might be what happened," said Ringmar.

"It looks like it."

"But now he's disappeared," said Ringmar. "Four years old."

Winter nodded, and drew a circle with his finger on the desk in front of him, and then another circle on top of that.

"Where's the mother now?"

"At home, with a couple of social workers. She might be on her way to Östra Hospital by now—I expect to be informed at any minute. She'd been drinking at the pub, but not all that much. She's desperate, and very remorseful, as you'd expect."

"As you'd expect," said Ringmar.

"She went back after a while, she couldn't say how long, but the boy was no longer there, and she assumed he'd been taken care of by the authorities."

"Did she check via the emergency police number?"

"No."

"And she never called her husband? Bengt Johansson?"

Winter shook his head.

"They are divorced," he said. "He has custody."

"Why did she do it?" Ringmar asked.

Winter raised both arms a bit.

"She can't explain it," he said. "Not at the moment, at any rate."

"Do you believe her?" asked Ringmar.

"That she abandoned the boy? Yes. What's the alternative?"

"Even worse," said Ringmar.

"We have to work with all possible alternatives," said Winter. "We need to check the father's alibi as well. The important thing is that the child is missing. That's what we need to concentrate on."

"Have you been to their home? The Johanssons'? The father?"

"Yes," said Winter. "And we're tracking down everyone who was working at the time on that floor of the shopping center. The first."

"So somebody might have abducted the kid?" said Ringmar.

"Yes."

"Is this a pattern we recognize from before?"

"Yes."

"Exactly," said Ringmar. "But it doesn't really fit in with the previous cases. The others."

"It might," said Winter. "This boy, Micke, went to a nursery school in the center of Gothenburg. Not all that far away from the others we are involved with, including mine—or Elsa's rather."

"And?"

"If there's somebody stalking the nursery schools from time to time, keeping them under observation, it's not impossible that the person concerned could follow somebody after they've picked up their child."

"Why?"

"To see where they live."

"Why?"

"Because he or she is interested in the child."

"Why?"

"For the same reason as in the earlier cases."

"Calm down now, Erik."

"I am calm."

"What's the reason?" Ringmar asked.

"We don't know yet."

Ringmar eased off. He recognized Winter's fervent involvement, and his own.

"Perhaps it's easier to abduct a child if you've been keeping it under observation for some time," said Ringmar.

"Perhaps."

"Instead of just marching up and wheeling the stroller away. I mean, the mother might have been within reach."

Winter nodded. He tried to picture the situation but wasn't very successful. There were too many people in the way.

"For Christ's sake, Erik, we could be dealing with an abducted child here." Ringmar rubbed away at his eye. "Or I suppose it's possible that the boy woke up and staggered off all by himself?" He peered out from underneath his rubbing. "It's a possibility."

"We have lots of officers searching," said Winter.

"Down by the canal?"

"There as well."

"Do you have a picture of the boy?"

Winter pointed at his desk, where a little photograph must have been lying all along.

"We're busy making copies," Winter said.

"You realize what will happen once the wanted notice becomes public?" Ringmar said.

"Goodbye secrecy," said Winter.

"And all the rest follows, like it or not."

"Just as well," said Winter.

"The media will give us hell," said Ringmar.

"Can't be helped."

"I get the impression, Erik, that . . . that you're looking forward to it."

Winter said nothing.

"This is going to be some Christmas," said Ringmar. "You're on your way to Spain, I gather?"

"I was. Angela and Elsa are flying tomorrow. I'll follow when I follow."

"I see."

"What would you have done, Bertil?"

"It depends what we suspect this is all about. If it's the worst-case scenario, then there's no question about it," said Ringmar.

"We'll have to interrogate the children soon," said Winter.

30

THE APARTMENT WAS BEING HAUNTED BY *THE GHOST OF TOM Joad* when Winter stood in the hall with his overcoat half off and heard the sound of Elsa's feet on the way to greet him. Angela dropped something hard on the bedroom floor and the volume was high and piercing: *The highway is alive tonight, but where it's headed everybody knows,* another bang from the bedroom, Elsa's face lit up, Winter was down on his knees.

It had started snowing outside. Flakes were still melting on his shoulders.

"Would you like to come outside with me and see the snow, Elsa?"

"Yes, yes, yes, yes!"

The pavement was white, and the park.

"We make snowman," said Elsa.

They tried, and managed to make a small one. The snow wasn't really wet enough.

"Have carrot for nose," said Elsa.

"It would have to be a little one."

"Can Daddy get?"

"Let's use this twig."

"Snowman breaking!" she said as she pressed the twig into the middle of the round face.

"We'll have to make another head," he said.

They were back home after half an hour. Elsa's cheeks were as red as apples. Angela came out into the hall. Springsteen was singing on repeat about the dark side of humanity, still loud: *It was a small town bank it was a mess, well I had a gun you know the rest.* Angela's songs had become his as well.

"Snow!" shouted Elsa, and ran into her room to draw a snowman like the real one she'd just made.

"And I'm going to take all this away from her," said Angela, looking at him with a faint smile. "Tomorrow we'll fly away from the first white Christmas of her life."

"It will disappear during the night," he said.

"I don't know if that was pessimistic or optimistic," she said.

"Everything depends on the context, doesn't it? Positive, negative."

He hung up his overcoat and wiped a few drops of water off his neck. He undid another shirt button.

"Where's your tie?" she asked.

"A guy out there borrowed it," he said, gesturing with his thumb at the park outside.

"A silk tie. Must be the best-dressed snowman in town."

"Clothes make the man," said Winter, going into the kitchen and pouring out a whiskey.

"Would you like one?"

She shook her head.

"You don't have to go," he said. "You could stay at home. I'm not forcing you to go."

"I thought that this afternoon as well," she said. "But then I thought about your mom. Among other things."

"There's nothing stopping her from coming here."

"Not this Christmas, Erik."

"Do you understand me?" he asked.

"What am I supposed to say to that?"

"Do you understand why I can't go with you now?"

"Yes," she said. "But you're not the only person in Gothenburg who can interrogate a suspect. Or lead an investigation."

"I've never claimed that I am."

"But you still have to stay here?"

"It's a question of finishing something off. And it's only just begun. I don't know what it is. But I have to follow it through to the end. Nobody else can do that."

"You're not the only one on the case."

"I don't mean it like that. I'm not talking about me as a lone wolf. But if I break off now, I won't be able to come back to it. I'll . . . lose it."

"And what does that mean? What will you lose?"

"I don't know."

She looked at the window that was being pelted with snowflakes hurled by strong gusts of wind. Springsteen was singing, again and again: *I threw my robe on in the morning.*

"Something terrible may have happened," said Winter.

"Have you appealed to the public for information?"

"Yes."

"Ah, that reminds me, your contact at the newspaper, Bülow, called."

"I'm not surprised. He'll call again."

"Can you hear the phone ringing? Of course you can't. That's because I've pulled the plug out."

"I can hear 'The Ghost of Tom Joad,'" he said.

"Good." She made a gesture. "Is this case going to take up the whole Christmas holiday?"

"That's why I'm staying behind, Angela." He took a drink of whiskey now; a cold heat passed down his throat. "I can't say any more than that. You know me. Don't you? I can do my job or I can pack it in. Either or. I can't do it by halves."

"Why bother to make plans for a vacation at all, then? It's pointless. It would be better to work all the time, eighteen hours a day, all year round, year after year. Always. Anything else would be half-assed, as you say."

"That's not what I'm saying."

"OK, OK. I understand that you have to keep going now. That things are happening all the time now. That what has happened to the little boy could be horrendous. Or is horrendous." She was still looking at the snow on the window. "But it never stops, Erik." She turned to look at him. "Horrible things happen all the time. And you are always there, in the thick of it. It never stops, never."

He said nothing.

I did take six months' paternity leave, he thought. That might have been the best time of my life. The only time of real value.

"I've been looking forward to this trip," she said.

What should he say? If we miss one Christmas together, there'll be a thousand more to come? How did he feel himself? What did it mean to him, not spending the special days with Angela? And Elsa?

How many days were they talking about?

"I might be down there with you the day after," he said.

"The day after the day?"

"Stay here, Angela. We'll go there together the moment all this is over."

"Sometimes when I think about you and your job it's like you're a sort of artist," she said. "No fixed working hours, you choose yourself when and how you work, you sort of direct the work yourself. Do you understand, Erik? You . . . create your work yourself."

He didn't respond. There was something in what she said. It wasn't possible to explain it, nobody could. But there was something in it. It was a frightening thought.

"I can't explain it," she said.

"I understand what you're saying."

"Yes."

"Of course, you should stay here over Christmas," he said again.

"Let me think about it," she said. "Maybe it's best for all concerned if we go to Spain, Elsa and I."

Five days, he thought out of the blue. It'll be all over in five days. It'll be over by Boxing Day.

He knew already that wasn't going to be something to look forward to. Regardless of what happened, he knew there was something dreadful in store after the Christmas holiday. Or during it. He knew that he would be surprised, find questions and answers that he hadn't formulated. He would be left with unanswered questions. See sudden openings that had previously been welded together. And new walls. But he would be on the way all the time, really on the way, and this moment at this table would be the last bit of peace he would have. When would he be able to return here, to this? To peace?

"Will you marry me, Angela?" he asked.

The telephone rang the moment he plugged it in again. It had just turned midnight. Nothing new on his mobile, and nobody had that number unless he'd given it to them personally. Hans Bülow wasn't among those.

"What's going on, Erik?" asked Bülow.

"What do you want to know?"

"You've sent out an appeal for information about a four-year-old boy called Micke Johansson?"

"That's correct."

"What happened?"

"We don't know. The boy is missing."

"In Nordstan? In the middle of the Christmas rush?"

"That's precisely where and when such things happen."

"Has it happened several times, then?" asked Bülow.

"I meant in general. Children get lost when there are lots of people around."

"But this one hasn't come back?"

"No."

"It's been almost a full day."

Winter said nothing. Bülow and his colleagues could follow the hands on a clock just as well as he could.

Angela moved in bed. He went quickly out into the kitchen and picked up the receiver of the wall telephone. The reporter was still there.

"So somebody kidnapped the boy?" said Bülow.

"I wouldn't use that term."

"What term would you use?"

"We don't know yet what happened," said Winter again.

"Are you looking for the boy?" asked Bülow.

"What do you think?"

"So he disappeared." Winter could hear voices in the background. Somebody laughed. They should be crying, he thought. "It sounds like a very serious business," said Bülow.

"I agree," said Winter.

"And then there was the abuse of that English boy." Winter could hear the rustling of paper near Bülow's telephone. "Waggoner. Simon Waggoner. He was evidently kidnapped as well and mistreated and abandoned."

"No comment," said Winter.

"Come on, Erik. I've helped you before. You ought to know by now, after all the contact you've had with the media, that facts are better than rumors."

Winter couldn't help laughing.

"Was that an ironic laugh?" asked Bülow.

"What makes you think that?"

"You know I'm right."

"The statement is true but the messenger is false," said Winter. "I deal in facts, you deal in rumors."

"That's what can happen when we don't get any facts to work with," said Bülow.

"Don't work, then."

"What do you mean?"

"Don't write anything until you know what you're writing about."

"Is that how you work?"

"I beg your pardon?"

"Do you sit around doing nothing until you get a little piece of the jigsaw?"

"I wouldn't find a little piece of the jigsaw if I sat around doing nothing," said Winter.

"Which brings us back to the point of this conversation," said Bülow, "because I'm also doing something to find a little piece of the jigsaw that I can write about."

"Ask me again tomorrow evening," said Winter.

"I have to write about this now," said Bülow, "tonight. Even you must understand that."

"Hmm."

"We've already got facts in connection with the Waggoner case."

"Why are you waiting to publish them, then?" asked Winter.

Winter could hear that Bülow was hesitating before answering. Was he going to say "no comment"?

"We've only just gotten hold of them," said the reporter. "In connection with the appeal for information about the other boy."

"Oh."

"Can you see a connection, Erik?"

"If I say yes, and you write that, it's hard to see what the consequences would be," said Winter.

"Nobody here is going to create panic," said Bülow.

Winter was about to burst out laughing again.

"What creates panic is the indiscriminate spreading of unconfirmed rumors, and I'm looking for facts," said Bülow.

"Haven't we had a conversation about that very topic before?" said Winter.

"Is there a connection?" asked Bülow again.

"I don't know, Hans. I'm being completely honest with you. I might know more tomorrow or the day after."

"That's Christmas Eve."

"And?"

"Will you be working on Christmas Eve?" asked Bülow.

"Will you?"

"That depends. On you, among other things." Winter heard voices in the background again. It sounded as if somebody was asking Bülow a question. He said something Winter couldn't hear and resumed the conversation. "So you don't want to say anything about a link?"

"I'd prefer you didn't raise that question just now, Hans. It could make a mess of a lot of things. Do you follow me?"

"I don't know. I'd be doing you yet another favor in that case. Besides, I'm not the one who makes all the decisions here," said Bülow.

"You're a good man. You understand."

The alarm clock woke him up from a dream in which he had rolled a snowball that grew to the size of a house, and kept on rolling. An airplane had passed overhead, and he'd been sitting on top of the snowball and waved to Elsa, who had waved back jerkily from her window seat. He hadn't seen Angela. He had heard music he'd never heard before. He'd looked down and seen children trying to make an enormous snowball, but nothing had moved, not even Elsa's hand as the airplane had passed by and vanished into a sky, where all the colors he'd seen earlier had been mixed together to form gray. He'd thought about the fact that when all those brilliant colors were mixed, the result was simply gray—and then he'd woken up.

Angela was already in the kitchen.

"The snow's gone," she said. "As you predicted."

"There'll be more."

"Not where we'll be."

"So you've made up your mind?"

"I want some sun." She looked at Winter, held up one of her bare arms. "I damn well want a bit of sun on this pale skin. And a bit of sun in my head."

"I'll join you on Boxing Day."

"How can you be so sure?"

"Or the day after."

"Should we stay there over New Year's?"

"At least."

"Have you spoken to Siv?"

"I'll call her now. I wanted to be certain what you were going to do."

She leaned over the table. There was a teacup in front of her, the radio was mumbling in a corner, words full of facts.

"Erik? Were you serious last night? Or were you just prepared to do anything at all in order to be allowed to stay at home and spend Christmas on your own, thinking to your heart's content?"

"I was as serious as it's possible to be."

"I'm not sure how to interpret that."

"Give me a date. I'm fed up with calling you my partner or my fiancée," he said.

"I haven't said yes yet," she said.

Winter's mobile rang as he was shaving. Angela handed it to him.

"That cap has popped up again," said Ringmar.

"Where?"

"We've heard from three witnesses during the night who think they saw a man pushing a stroller with a child in it from H&M or somewhere near there, and he was wearing a checked cap. No leading questions."

"What made them notice that?"

"A woman was working right by where the mother left the stroller, and she noticed that it was unattended for a while, and then a man came up after a while and went off with it."

"And she didn't react?"

"Well, it seemed natural enough at the time. She recalled the incident when we started rooting around."

"Good God, Bertil: If what she says is right, we're onto something here. What about the other witnesses?"

"Independently of each other, they both saw that cap in Nordstan."

"Nobody saw it outside?"

He could hear Bertil sigh. Bertil had had another sleepless night. Winter hadn't been able to stay with him, it wouldn't have been possible. It had been necessary to discuss the Christmas holiday with Angela. And to make a snow-man with Elsa.

"We've had the usual idiots who've seen everything you can imagine. There've been more than ever of them, but that probably has to do with Christmas," said Ringmar.

Winter didn't ask him what he meant by that.

"Have you made copies of the photo?" he asked.

"Hundreds."

"I'll be with you in half an hour."

"I haven't gotten around to talking to the parents yet," said Ringmar.

"I heard his father was taken into the hospital last night," said Winter.

"I've never seen anybody in such a state of shock," said Ringmar. "It hit him afterward, like an avalanche."

"Nothing new from the mother? Carolin?"

"She's told her side of the story," said Ringmar. "She didn't set up a kid-napping scenario, I don't think so. But we'll be talking to her again."

"I thought of trying again with Simon Waggoner later this morning," said Winter.

"At home? Or at the station?"

"At home. Do you have the video camera?"

"It's here on my desk."

"How are the checks on the nursery-school staff going?" Winter asked.

"It's progressing. It takes time, as you know."

"We have to check up on *everybody* who works, or has worked, at those places. I take it that Möllerström is aware of that? Even if we have to go back ten years, or even longer."

He embraced Elsa and whispered things into her ear that made her giggle. The bags were all packed.

"We should have had some sort of Christmas party last night," said Angela.

"We'll do it in a few days' time," he said.

"Don't fool yourself," she said.

He didn't respond.

"We've both hidden a Christmas present for you somewhere in the apartment," she said.

"You'll *never* find mine!" said Elsa.

"Animal, vegetable, or mineral, or somewhere in between?" he said.

"Fish!" Elsa shouted.

"It's a secret, Elsa!" said Angela.

"Is it easy to find the packages?" Winter asked.

"There's a letter in the kitchen with clues," said Angela.

———————

The taxi was waiting. The snow had gone, but the sun was there, located quite low in the blue expanse.

"Daddy is coming as well," said Elsa as she got into the car. She looked miserable.

What am I doing? Winter thought.

The driver crammed the bags into the trunk. He glanced at Winter. He'd heard.

Winter's mobile rang in his inside pocket—two, three rings.

"Aren't you going to answer?" asked Angela from the backseat, through the open door.

He saw "private number" on the display, and answered. It was Paul Waggoner, Simon's father: "I just wanted to check what time we could expect you," he said.

Winter exchanged a few words with him, then hung up.

"I'll take you to the airport," he said, starting to take the bags out of the trunk.

"Merry Christmas," said the taxi driver, as he prepared to drive his empty car away.

Winter and Elsa sang Christmas carols all the way to Landvetter airport.

The check-in line was shorter than he'd expected.

Angela smiled and waved from the escalator up to the terminal. He needed that. She was a good lady. She understood.

The question was how much she understood, he thought, as he drove back to Gothenburg from the airport. On the way he listened to the news reports about his own reality. Now that was his whole world.

31

WINTER CAME TO THE ROUNDABOUT AT LINNÉPLATSEN, CONTINUED
along the service road, and turned off toward Änggården.

The Waggoners lived in one of the English-type town houses. Of course.
There was a Christmas tree outside the front door. There was still snow on
the lawn, a thin rectangular drift that could have been a snowman once upon
a time. Winter thought he could make out an orange carrot as he rang the
doorbell. He rang again. He was carrying his equipment himself.

Simon Waggoner had not spoken, not drawn anything, not said anything
about what had happened. It hadn't worked in the room they'd set up at po-
lice headquarters. Maybe it would work now.

When a child is about one, it communicates in single words; at about
eighteen months it starts using two-word sentences, and later it uses three-
word sentences. He knew that from the interrogations he'd conducted with
children, and from the literature. Christianson, Engelberg, Holmberg: *Ad-
vanced Interview and Interrogation Methodology*.

And he knew from his conversations with Elsa.

He knew that a child's language exploded between the ages of two and
four.

After the age of two a child is aware that it is an individual in its own
right.

The child can start to link its experiences to a concept of itself, and ex-
plain to others what it has experienced. It has a memory. It is possible to find
that memory, find paths leading to it. Forgetfulness disappears as language de-
velops.

Four-year-olds can talk about experiences they have been through.

Simon Waggoner was four. He was nowhere to be seen as Winter stood
in the hall, greeting the parents, Paul and Barbara. There was a smell of
Christmas spices in the house, but not quite the same as in a typical Swedish

home. Perhaps there was a Christmas pudding on the stove, slowly cooking for another few hours.

"Simon is very tense," said Paul Waggoner.

"I understand that," said Winter.

"As far as we can gather he's been telling his teddy bear what happened," said Barbara Waggoner. "He confides in his teddy bear." She looked at her husband. "I don't know what we should make of that."

"The teddy bear can be present at the interview," said Winter. "What's his name?"

"Billy."

Billy can do the talking, Winter thought. Billy can talk via Simon.

"We've prepared the guest room," said Barbara Waggoner. "We moved some of the furniture."

"Is Simon used to being in the room?"

"Oh yes. He's in there every day. He likes to sit there drawing."

"Good."

"Follow me, I'll take you to it."

The room was on the ground floor. They passed through the kitchen, which was big and light and had a window facing east. Sure enough something was cooking in a large saucepan, and it wasn't a Christmas ham. There were newspapers and drawing paper and colored pencils on the kitchen table, various small molds, wrapping paper, and a stick of sealing wax. Two candles were burning in low candlesticks. There were Advent candles in the window, with three of them burning. The fourth one would be lit tomorrow, on Christmas Eve. But being an English family, their main celebration would be the day after, on Christmas Day. With full stockings in the morning.

The radio was murmuring away on the kitchen counter, just as in Winter's flat, and he recognized the BBC voice, dry, reliable, clear. Facts, no rumors.

He hoped the Waggoners would avoid reading the newspapers, miss all the rumors and speculation.

The guest room was good, out of the way, no voices audible from elsewhere. No distracting toys on the floor or table, no Christmas decorations.

"Good," said Winter again.

"Where shall I put the tripod?" asked Paul Waggoner.

"We need the camera to be as far away from Simon as possible," said Winter. "But he must be able to see it."

They placed it against the north wall, in the middle, clearly visible. Winter would work it himself, using the remote control.

The picture would have to contain both himself and Simon all the time, it was the interplay between them that had to be documented; he would need to keep coming back to the recording to see if something he did, some movement or other, affected the boy.

And he needed to capture Simon's face, his body movements. The technology would assist him; he had the latest camera, which enabled him to focus on Simon's face in a separate picture.

"It's ready," said Winter. "I'm ready."

He went out of the room and waited in the little hallway that led to the staircase. There was a window in the wall behind, so he couldn't really see Simon's face properly as he came down the stairs against the light, holding his mother's hand.

This wasn't the first time Winter had met Simon. It might have been the third time, possibly the fourth.

He squatted down so that he could greet Simon at eye level.

"Hi, Simon."

The boy didn't answer. He clung to his mother's hand and took a step to one side, diagonally backward.

Winter sat down on the floor, which was polished and varnished wood, possibly pine. It was soft.

Simon sat down on Barbara Waggoner's knee. After a short while he slid down onto the floor.

He was holding Billy tucked under his arm. The teddy bear's eyes were aimed straight at Winter.

"My name's Erik," Winter said, "and we've met before, haven't we?"

Simon didn't answer. Clung to his teddy bear.

"What's your teddy called?" Winter asked.

The boy looked at his mother, who nodded and smiled.

"I used to have a teddy called Willy," said Winter. It was absolutely true. It suddenly occurred to him that there was a photograph of Willy in the family album, with Winter wearing overalls, sitting and looking up at something outside the picture, holding the teddy bear with his left hand. When had he last looked at it? Why hadn't he shown it to Elsa yet?

Simon looked at Winter.

"Mine was called Willy," said Winter again, looking at Simon's friend.

"Billy," said Simon.

That was the first word Winter had heard Simon utter.

"Hello, Billy," said Winter.

Simon held Billy out with his uninjured arm.

"I'm a policeman," said Winter to both his interviewees, and then he looked at Simon: "My job is to find out about things. Things that have happened." He slowly adjusted his position on the floor. "I want to ask you about that."

Winter knew how important it was to start by placing the interview in a frame. He needed to de-dramatize the whole thing while still being clear and natural, and to make the boy feel secure. He must use simple words, short sentences, try to speak like Simon did. He must approach the center in ever-decreasing circles. Perhaps he would never get to the very center. Or perhaps he would get there amazingly quickly.

"I want to have a little talk with you," Winter said.

Simon looked at his mom.

"You don't have to answer, Simon."

He moved again. He was getting stiff from sitting on the floor.

"Erik's going to talk to you in the guest room," said Barbara Waggoner.

Winter nodded.

"Why?" asked Simon.

"I have a camera there. It will film us," said Winter.

"A camera?"

"It will film us," said Winter. "When I press a button."

"We have a video camera too," said Simon, looking at his mother.

"We lent it to Grandma," said Barbara Waggoner. "You remember when we were there with it, Simon, don't you?"

The boy nodded.

"Do you want to see my camera?" Winter asked.

The boy seemed to hesitate, then he nodded.

Winter stood up and led the way into the guest room. That was important. Simon came in with his mother. Normally relatives were not allowed to sit in on interviews, but this wasn't normal. Winter knew that Simon wouldn't say a word if he couldn't see his mother.

"It's not very big," said Simon.

"I'll show you," said Winter, and nodded to Mrs. Waggoner, who lifted Simon up while Winter sat on the chair Simon would be sitting on. Simon looked into the camera.

"Can you see me?" Winter asked.

Simon didn't answer.

"Can you see when I move my hand?" asked Winter.

"Yes," said Simon.

They sat down where they were supposed to sit. The camera was rolling. Winter started his journey toward the center in ever-decreasing circles. He had to start with neutral subjects: That would give him an indication of how well Simon spoke, what he could talk about, his linguistic ability, imagination, behavior patterns. His ability to pin down time in relation to events.

"Have you made a snowman, Simon?"

Simon nodded.

"When did you make it?"

The boy didn't answer.

"Where's the snowman now?"

"Out there," said Simon, pointing at the window.

"On the lawn out there?"

"It's broken," said Simon, gesturing with his uninjured hand.

Winter nodded.

"It's melted," said Simon.

"I saw the nose when I arrived," said Winter.

"I fixed the nose," said Simon.

Winter nodded again.

"Have you made a snowman at the nursery school, Simon?" he asked.

The boy nodded.

"Have you made lots?"

"There hasn't been snow."

"Do you play indoors then?"

Simon didn't answer. He was still holding Billy, the teddy bear, but not so tightly now. He didn't look as often at the camera, nor at his mother.

For the first few minutes Winter had wondered if it was a mistake to allow her to be in the room, but he didn't think so now.

"Do you play indoors when it isn't snowing, Simon?"

"No. Play outside."

"What games do you play?"

The boy seemed to be thinking about what to say. Winter was trying to make him start saying more. Perhaps it was too soon.

"Do you play hide-and-seek?"

"Yes."

"Do you play tag?"

Simon didn't answer. Perhaps he didn't know what tag was.

"Do you chase each other?"

"Yes."

"Do you play on the swings?"

"Yes. And the slide."

"Do you like the slide?"

"Yes. And the train."

"Do you have a train at the nursery school?"

Simon didn't answer. Winter thought. Suddenly they were at the playground where Simon had disappeared, next to the big park. A regular outing for the nursery school. There was a wooden train, as close to life-size as it could be for children. Engine and coaches, on the edge of the big playground that was always full of children.

Suddenly they were there, he and Simon. Should he take them back to the secure place where they had been before, back home, and to the nursery school, continue the circular movement? Or should they stay where they were and get closer to the boy's trauma, continue the inward journey into the darkness? Winter knew that if he moved forward too quickly he might not be able to go back to a position where the boy would say what actually happened. They would revert to silence, and they wouldn't find anything out.

"Did you drive the train?"

"Yes."

"Where did you drive the train, Simon?"

"At the playground."

"Was that an outing from the nursery school?"

Simon nodded.

"Driven lots of times," said Simon, shuffling on the chair.

Soon we'll stop for juice and a bun and a coffee and a cig . . . no, not a cigarillo. But he felt the desire; it increased as he became more tense himself.

"Do you often drive the train?"

"Yes!"

"Are there lots of people traveling with you, Simon?"

"Arvid and Valle and Oskar and Valter and Manfred and . . . and . . ." he said, and Winter had time to think about how times change, old-fashioned names become fashionable again, old people revert to their childhood. Twenty years ago Simon could only have been describing a group of old-age pensioners clambering into a toy train.

"Did Billy travel with you as well?"

"No."

"Where was Billy?"

Simon looked baffled. It was a difficult question.

"Was Billy at home?" Winter asked.

Simon still looked confused. What was wrong? What am I doing wrong? Winter thought.

"Was Billy at the nursery school?" he asked.

Simon looked at Billy and leaned down closer to the bear's little face, which was turned toward the boy now, as if he no longer had the strength to listen to this conversation. Simon whispered something to Billy, but very quietly. He looked up again.

"Can Billy say where he was?" asked Winter.

"On the train," said Simon. "Billy rode the train."

"Billy rode while you were driving?"

Simon nodded again.

"Billy rode on the train all the time?"

Simon nodded.

"Not the car," he said out of the blue, and leaned over Billy again, as if he wanted to hide his own face in the teddy bear's. Winter could see that the boy had become more tense, from comfortable calm to sudden unrest.

My God, Winter thought. This is quick. I've gotten us to this point, but has it been too quick? But it was Simon who had said that, of his own accord.

"Didn't ride in the car," said Simon.

He's starting to tell us what happened, Winter thought. But what does he mean? We know he was abducted. Wasn't it in a car?

"Tell me about the car, Simon."

What Winter needed to do now was let Simon tell his story at his own pace, in his own way. He hoped Simon felt sufficiently secure to *start* telling the tale. That was all he could ask for.

He remembered what he had read, and passed on to his colleagues:

Hand control over to the child and let the child decide who is going to be described. Let the child decide on the scenario. It's important that the interviewer makes it clear that he or she doesn't know what happened.

He would try to break down Simon's reluctance to tell.

He must give the boy time.

He suddenly felt the need to make a note, but resisted it. He hadn't said anything about making notes before the interview started. It would only distract Simon now, perhaps spoil something.

"Tell me about the car, Simon."

Simon turned to Billy again. He whispered something that Winter couldn't hear.

Now it's time for Billy. Winter said Billy's name and then Simon's. Simon looked up.

"Have you told Billy about the car?" Winter asked.

Simon nodded.

"Do you think he could tell me about it?"

Simon leaned down over Billy again, and Winter waited while the pair of them discussed the matter.

"Billy wants to hear the question," said Simon.

"I want Billy to tell me what you told him about the car," said Winter.

"You have to ask," said Simon.

"Was the car next to the train?"

"Simon says it was in the woods," said Simon. His tone of voice was darker. The shift was barely noticeable, as if he had left his own body and moved into Billy's little brown one, which he had now lifted up to face level and was holding out like an overdemonstrative ventriloquist. Winter felt a shudder, and another. I've used cuddly toys before, but this is different, he thought. He looked at Barbara Waggoner. She looked scared stiff.

"Tell me about the car, Billy," said Winter.

Simon held Billy in front of his face, then lowered the teddy a little bit.

"It was a big car in some big, big woods," chanted Simon in his changed voice, as if he were about to tell a fairy story, or a ghost story. "The boy went into the big woods and the car drove through the woods."

Simon was looking at Winter now, not at his mother, not at the camera, and not at Billy. Winter stayed motionless. Barbara Waggoner tried not to move.

"The mister had some candies and there were candies in the car," said Billy. "Brrrrrrmmm, brrrrrrrm, the car drove off with candies!"

Billy paused. Simon looked up.

"Billy rode in the car," said Simon.

Winter nodded.

"Yes, so he said."

"No, no, Billy didn't ride in the car!" said Simon. He looked at Winter, then at his mom.

"No, no, *Billy* rode in the train. Billy rode in the car!"

"Did Billy ride in the train and the car as well?" asked Winter.

"No, no."

Simon shuffled restlessly on the chair. They were getting close to the incident.

"There was a Billy that rode in the car?" said Winter.

"Yes, yes!"

"But it wasn't your Billy? The Billy who's sitting here?"

"No, no!"

"Was it a teddy who rode in the car?" Winter asked.

"No!"

"What was it?"

"Billy, Billy. Billy Boy!" Simon was almost shouting now, in yet another voice, almost croaking. "Billy Billy Boy!"

"Did the mister have a Billy?" asked Winter.

Simon picked up his teddy again, returned to the teddy bear's voice: "The mister had Rotty on the mirror."

"Rotty?" asked Winter.

Simon lowered the teddy, and croaked: "Rotty, Rotty! Billy Boy, Billy Boy!"

Pretty Rotty, Winter thought. Pretty Polly.

"Did the mister have a parrot?"

Simon put the teddy bear in front of his face again and said:

"Yes, yes. Billy Rotty!"

Rotty on the mirror. The man had a parrot hanging from his mirror. A bird hanging from his rearview mirror.

Jesus, we're on our way.

32

ANETA DJANALI HAD GOTTEN THOSE RESPONSIBLE TO FURNISH the interrogation room with armchairs children could creep onto, in warm colors. Everything that Ellen Sköld might regard as a toy had been taken away. The girl's interest had to be concentrated on Djanali.

Aneta entered the room first. Now she was holding the remote control—Ellen had already familiarized herself with the camera.

Lena Sköld was waiting outside. Djanali wanted to try that first. We'll see how long the girl can sit still.

Ellen was cheerful and inquisitive. Djanali watched her trying out various sitting and lying positions on the armchair.

This is not a traumatized child. I must try to bear that in mind when the questions are asked and the answers given. If they are.

They chatted for a while. Ellen played with her fingers as she answered Djanali's questions. Or rather, commented on them, it seemed to the detective inspector.

"Your mom told me that it was your birthday a month ago, Ellen."

The girl nodded, up and down, up and down, but said nothing.

"How old are you now?"

"Four," said Ellen, holding up a bunch of fingers.

"Wow," said Djanali.

Ellen nodded again, forcefully.

"Did you have a fun birthday party?" asked Djanali.

"Yes!"

"Tell me about it!"

Ellen looked as if she wanted to talk about it but couldn't choose between all the fun things that had happened on her birthday.

"Dad came," she said, when Djanali was on the point of asking a follow-up question. "Dad came and brought some presents."

Djanali thought about the single mother on the chair in the corridor. Lena Sköld had sole custody, she knew that. Even so there was an absent father who came to his four-year-old daughter's birthday party with presents. Not all children with a single parent were so lucky. The children are just as single as their parents, she thought.

"What presents did you get?"

"From Dad?" asked the girl.

"Yes," said Djanali. This girl is bright, she thought.

"I got a doll called Victoria. And I got a car that the doll can ride in." She gave Djanali a meaningful look. "Victoria has a driver's license. Really." She looked at the door, next to the camera. "Mom doesn't have a driver's license." She looked at Djanali. "Do you have a driver's license?"

"Yes."

"I don't have a driver's license."

"It's mostly grown-ups who have a driver's license," said Djanali.

The girl nodded. Djanali could picture her in a front seat with a grown-up who had a driver's license. Did the girl have Victoria with her in the car? Did they have any information about that? Victoria wasn't with her now. But if Victoria had in fact been in the car as well, she might have seen something Ellen hadn't seen. Victoria had a driver's license, after all.

"Do you like riding in cars, Ellen?"

Ellen shook her head and her expression seemed to tense—barely noticeable, but even so. I must check the recording afterward, Djanali thought.

"Do you and your mom have a car, Ellen?"

"No. My mom doesn't have a driver's license. I said that."

"Yes, you did say that. I forgot. So in your house it's only Victoria who has a car and a driver's license, is that right?"

The girl nodded, up and down, up and down.

"Where's Victoria now?"

"She's sick," said Ellen.

"Oh, dear."

"Mom and me are going to buy some medicine for her."

"What's the matter with her?"

"I think she has a cold," said Ellen, looking worried for a moment.

"Has the doctor taken a look at her?"

She nodded.

"Was it a nice doctor?" asked Djanali.

"It was me!" shouted Ellen, and giggled.

Djanali looked at her and nodded. She looked at the eye of the camera that might be seeing everything. She wondered how long Lena Sköld would be able to wait outside. Victoria had to have her medicine. Christmas would be here soon. It was the day before the day now. She hadn't bought all her presents, nothing yet for Hannes and Magda, although she had bought two CDs for Fredrik, Richard Buckner and Kasey Chambers, because that's what Fredrik had wanted, among other things. She had written a wish list herself. She would have a Christmas meal on Christmas Eve, Swedish style, with the Halders family, or what was left of it; she might even try the super-Nordic tradition of "dipping in the pot" (she'd never tried dipping bread into the stock from the Christmas ham before) and hoped to avoid having to listen to jokes from Fredrik apologizing for not having camel meat and tapioca pudding, today of all days. She would open presents piled under the Christmas tree.

She looked at the girl, who had left the armchair now. It was almost a miracle that she had sat on it for so long.

Would Dad come back to the Sköld family, or what was left of it?

"You told Mom that you went for a ride with a mister," said Djanali.

"Not ride," said Ellen.

"You didn't ride in the mister's car?"

"Didn't ride," said Ellen. "Stood still."

"The car stood still?"

She nodded.

"Where was the car?" asked Djanali.

"In the woods."

"Was it a big forest?"

"No! At the playground!"

"So the woods were at the playground?"

"Yes."

"Was Victoria with you when you sat in the car?"

Ellen nodded again.

"Did Victoria want to drive the car?"

"No, no." Ellen burst out laughing. "The car was big!"

"Was the mister big as well?"

The girl nodded.

"Tell me how you met this mister!" said Djanali. Ellen was now standing next to the brightly colored armchair. A split had developed in the cloud cover that lay like paper over Gothenburg as it waited for Christmas to arrive, and the split let through a beam of sunshine that shone in through the window and onto the back of the armchair. Ellen shouted in delight and pointed at the sunlight that suddenly disappeared again as the clouds closed.

"Tell me about when you met the mister with the car," said Djanali.

"He had candy," said Ellen.

"Did he give you some candy?"

She nodded.

"Was it good?"

She nodded.

"What kind of candy was it?"

"Candy," she said dismissively. Candy was candy.

"Did you eat all the candy?"

She nodded again. They had searched the place looking for candy wrappings, but had naturally realized before long that it was like looking for a needle in a haystack. This was a playground, a park, children, parents, candy . . .

"What did the mister say?"

Ellen had started to dance around the room, like a ballerina. She didn't answer. It was a difficult question.

"What did the mister say when he gave you the candy?"

She looked up.

" 'You want a candy?' "

Djanali nodded, waited. Ellen performed a little pirouette.

"Did he ask you anything else?"

Ellen looked up again.

"Ca-ca-ca-ca," she said.

Djanali waited.

"Swee-swee-swee-swee," said Ellen.

Time for a break, Djanali thought. Past time, in fact. The girl is tired of all this. But Djanali had intended for Ellen to look at a few different men from around police headquarters—a twenty-year-old, a thirty-year-old, a forty-year-old, a fifty-year-old, and a sixty-year-old, and ask her to point out the one that looked most like the man in the car. If that was possible. This collection of Swedish manhood was so vain that the fifty-year-old wanted to be forty, and the forty-year-old would have looked devastated if she'd guessed his age correctly. Only the twenty-year-old and sixty-year-old were unconcerned. That must mean something. Perhaps for men most of all. Men were people too. She must try to remember that.

She'd also hoped that Ellen would be persuaded to draw something, including a car in some trees.

"Pa-pa-pa-pa-pa," said Ellen now, and she danced around the room again.

"Do you mean your papa, your dad?"

The girl shook her head and said, "Pa-*pa-pa-pa*!"

"Did the mister say that he was your dad?"

She shook her head again.

"We-we-we-we," she said.

Djanali looked at the camera, as if seeking help.

"Why did you say that?" she asked.

The girl didn't understand the question; or perhaps it was Djanali who didn't understand if she'd understood.

"Co-co-co-co," said Ellen.

Djanali said nothing. She tried to think.

"Had a radio," said the girl now. She'd moved closer to Djanali.

"This man had a radio?"

Ellen nodded.

"Did he have a radio in the car?"

Ellen nodded again.

"Was the radio on?"

Ellen nodded again.

"Was the radio playing a song?"

Ellen didn't answer.

"Was there somebody singing on the radio?" Djanali asked.

"The mister said bad words," said Ellen. By now she was standing next to Djanali, who was sitting on the floor that was colder than it looked.

"Did the man in the car say bad words to you?"

Ellen shook her head. But her expression was serious.

"Who said bad words?" Djanali asked.

"The radio," said Ellen.

"The radio said bad words?"

Ellen nodded, solemnly.

"Did a mister on the radio say bad words?"

Ellen nodded again. That's not *allowed*.

A man on the radio says bad words, Djanali thought. It's afternoon. Somebody is sitting in the studio and swearing. Does that happen every day? Can we trace the program? And what do children think is a bad word? Often the same ones as we do. But children are so much better at picking up on them. But I won't ask her now what the words were.

"I held my hands over Victoria's ears," said Ellen.

"So Victoria didn't hear anything?" asked Djanali.

Ellen shook her head.

"Has she said anything about it to you?"

She shook her head again, more firmly this time.

Djanali nodded.

"*Bad* words," said Ellen.

"What did the mister in the car say about these bad words?" asked Djanali.

Ellen didn't answer.

"Did he think they were bad words too?"

Ellen didn't answer. There must be something in the question that's too subtle, Djanali thought. Or in her failure to answer. She's not answering because the man didn't make any comment about the bad words. He didn't hear them.

"Bi-bi-bi-bi-bi-bi," said Ellen.

He made a cup of hot chocolate for the boy the old-fashioned way: First he mixed the cocoa with milk and sugar, then he added the hot milk and stirred it with a spoon. In fact, he had made an extra effort, and had mixed the cocoa and sugar with cream!

But the boy didn't want it. Would you believe it? He must be both hungry and thirsty, but he drank nothing, ate nothing, he cried, and he shouted, and it had been necessary to tell him that he had to be quiet because the neighbors needed to sleep.

"Sl-sl-sl-sl," he said. He tried again: "Sl-sl-sleep. You must sleep."

He pointed at the chocolate, which was still quite hot.

"Cho-cho-cho-chocolate."

He could hear his voice. It had to do with the excitement. He could feel a hot force gushing through his body.

The boy had been asleep when he carried him into the building, and then into the apartment. He had driven him around the main circular roads and through the tunnels until he was so fast asleep that nothing would wake him up.

The stroller was in the trunk. It was safe there, just as the boy is safe here, he thought, nodding at the chocolate once again. Now he felt calmer, as if he had found peace and knew what was going to happen, maybe not right now, but shortly.

He knew that the boy was called Micke.

"Micke Johansson," the boy had said. His pronunciation was good.

"Drink now, Mick," he said.

"My name's Micke," the boy said.

He nodded.

"Want to go home to Daddy."

"Don't you like it here?"

"Want to go home to *Daddy*."

"Your dad's not at home."

"I want to go home to *Daddy*," the boy said again.

"It's not good, being at home with your daddy," he said now. He wondered if the boy understood. "It's not good at all."

"Where's Mommy?" asked Micke.

"Not good."

"Mommy and Daddy," said Micke.

"Not good," he said again, because he knew what he was talking about.

The boy was asleep. He'd made up a bed for him on the sofa. He had a Christmas tree that he was decorating. It was made of plastic, which was good because it didn't shed any needles. He was longing for the boy to wake up so that he could show him the pretty Christmas tree.

He had phoned work and told them he was ill. He couldn't remember what he'd claimed was wrong with him, but the person who received his call simply said, "Get well soon," as if it didn't matter if he was at work or not.

He had shown the boy how you drive a streetcar, and drawn the tracks and the route he was most familiar with.

That was where he always went back to when he wanted to talk to children and look after them. He had seen the places from his driver's window, and thought, this is where I want to come back to.

Just as he liked to go back to the Nordstan shopping center when there were a lot of people around, the brightly lit windows looking festive, the families, the moms and dads with children in strollers that *they didn't look after properly* but just left in any old place, *in any old place,* as if the stroller and its contents were a sack of trash that didn't matter. What would happen if he were not there? Like on this occasion? What would have happened to Micke?

It was hardly worth thinking about.

When most of the Christmas holiday was over he and Micke would go back there, like everybody else would be doing, Micke in his stroller and him pushing it.

He'd shown Micke his Billy Boy.

The press conference was as chaotic as usual, but worse than ever on this occasion: Winter could smell the stench of fear that would spread once the idio . . . the journalists assembled here had published their articles.

There were honest people here. But what could they do? The moment they had left this room their influence would be over. Come to that, it was over even before they entered it.

He saw Hans Bülow two rows back. So far Bülow had behaved honorably.

It could be that his colleagues would consider him to be a traitor, but his willingness to compromise had made his articles better than the others, and more truthful, if such an expression still existed.

Winter was dazzled by three flashbulbs going off simultaneously.

He was on the stage once again. The show must go on.

Birgersson had backed out at the last moment. An important meeting with the chief of police. At the same time as the press conference. I wonder what that means.

"What traces have you found of the boy?" asked the woman who always asked the first questions at shows like this, and always wrote articles without an ounce, without a single gram of fact or credibility.

"At the moment we are working on information we have received from the general public," said Winter. "A lot of people contacted us as a result of our appeal."

Far too many, he thought. Thousands of Gothenburgers had seen men with small boys in strollers, in cars, on the way into and out of buildings, into and out of shops, department stores, cars, streetcars, buses, even more than usual because so many people were out doing last-minute Christmas shopping.

"Do you have a suspect?" asked the same woman, and somebody in the pack of journalists smirked in the same cynical way that Halders sometimes did.

"No," said Winter.

"You must have a long list of pedophiles and others who go after children," said the woman. "Who abduct children."

"We don't know if Micke has been abducted," said Winter.

"Where is he, then?"

"We don't know."

"So are you saying he got out of the stroller and wandered off on his own?"

"We don't know."

"What *do* you know?"

"We know we are doing all we can to make sure this boy returns home," said Winter.

"So that his mother can abandon him again?" asked a male journalist sitting next to Hans Bülow.

Winter said nothing.

"If she hadn't left the boy, this would never have happened, would it?"

"No comment," said Winter.

"Where is she now?"

"Any other questions?" said Winter without looking at the man.

"How are you ever going to be able to find this boy?" asked a woman who was young and wore her hair in pigtails. It's a long time since I last saw an adult in pigtails, Winter thought. They make everybody look younger.

"Like I said, we are doing everything we can," he said.

A man in the fourth row raised his hand. Here it comes, Winter thought. Until now this has been kept away from the public, but not anymore. I can see it in his face. He knows.

"What connection does this disappearance have with the other children who have had contact with a strange man this last month?" asked the man, and several heads turned to look at him.

"I don't understand what you mean," said Winter.

"Isn't it a fact that several children have been approached by a man at playgrounds in various parts of Gothenburg?"

"There have be—"

"In one case a little girl was actually kidnapped and was eventually found with injuries," said the man.

Boy, Winter thought. Not girl.

Winter said nothing.

"Why don't you answer my question?"

"It sounded more like a statement to me," said Winter.

"Then I'll ask it again: Have children been picked up by a man at playgrounds? Or simply approached? Are the police aware of any such cases?"

"I can't answer that question at this moment for reasons connected with the case," said Winter.

"Well, that's a pretty clear answer, isn't it?" The male reporter looked at Winter. He was wearing a leather jacket and had long black hair and a black mustache, and his whole body language expressed an attitude that Winter often came across in journalists, a sort of rueful arrogance that suggested that the truth wouldn't make anybody happier, just as lies wouldn't make people all that much unhappier. Perhaps in fact it was better to take lies with you on a journey that wasn't anything special, and life wasn't anything special.

"So there is a link?" the reporter persisted.

"No comment," said Winter.

"Have children been kidnapped from nursery schools here in Gothenburg?" asked another reporter, a woman Winter didn't recognize as an individual but was familiar with as a type.

Winter shook his head.

"What kind of cover-up is this?!" shouted a young man who seemed to have wandered into the room from a film, and with exaggerated gestures he started making his way toward the stage where Winter had hitherto been the only entertainer: "What are you trying to conceal from the public?"

"We are not concealing anything," said Winter.

"If you'd laid your cards on the table from the start, Micke Johansson might not have been kidnapped," said the young reporter who was now only a meter away from Winter, and looked up at him. Winter could see that the man's eyes were bloodshot, and it might not have been only from excitement.

"Cards on the table? This is not a game of cards," said Winter.

He also thought about the man in the checked cap who had been filming the children as they crossed the soccer field. They had good enlargements now, but he had waited before making the pictures public. Had that been a mistake? He hadn't thought so thus far. The flood of tips would be even more overwhelming and difficult to oversee, running off in all directions. Who would be able to absorb all this, sort it, filter it? He didn't have the resources, the staff. Perhaps he could borrow this big group of people in front of him, a onetime thing. No, he didn't have the time to coach them.

"I declare this press conference closed," he said, and turned his back on the big flood of questions that always comes when the event is over.

33

WINTER TRIED TO TALK TO BENGT JOHANSSON. THERE WAS A framed photograph of Micke on the desk, and also a PC.

Micke was climbing up a jungle gym with an expression on his face suggesting that he wanted to climb up, up, up. There was wind in his hair and in the trees behind him. He was wearing overalls, blue or possibly black. His tongue was visible between his narrow lips.

Johansson sat on his swivel chair swaying back and forth, back and forth as if he were merely a part of an intricate balancing system. Which is what he is, in a way, Winter thought. He's swaying on that chair in order to keep his balance, whatever good that might do him.

Johansson had just come home from the hospital. It wasn't easy to talk to him, but it was necessary. Now more was expected of him.

Johansson looked up.

"Is it true that this has happened before?" he asked.

"What do you mean?"

"That Micke isn't the first."

He's forgotten, Winter thought. Repressed it.

"I told you at the hospital about another boy. Simon Waggoner. And about our suspicions regarding a man who makes contact with children."

"Hmm."

"I asked you if you'd seen or heard anything that you maybe didn't think twice about at the time but which stayed in your mind. Anything suspicious."

"Yes, yes." He sounded very weary.

Now he has seen the newspapers. Winter saw a newspaper on the floor, folded up, or rather *crunched* up behind Johansson. The words of the press weigh more heavily than mine. It becomes clearer when it's written down.

"And now I want to ask you again," said Winter. "Has anything occurred to you?"

Open questions. He felt that to some extent he was in the same interview position as with a child. Bengt Johansson was traumatized, his own private hell had fallen in on him.

"What might that be?" asked Johansson.

"Well, for example, have you ever noticed a stranger talking to Micke? Or trying to talk to him?"

"You'll have to ask the nursery-school staff about that."

"We have."

"And?"

"No. Nobody noticed anything."

"I'm with Micke for nearly all the rest of the time," said Johansson. "It's him and me." He looked up. "The one you should talk to is Car . . . Carolin. My ex-wife." He looked again at the photograph. "Jesus Christ . . ." He buried his face in his hands. "If only I'd known, if only I'd realized. Oh, God!"

"If only you'd known what?" Winter asked.

"What she . . . what she intended to do." He looked up again at Winter with his bloodshot eyes. "That she'd intended . . . that she wanted . . ." And he burst out crying. His shoulders started to shake, slightly at first, then more and more violently.

Winter stood up and walked over to him, kneeled down and embraced the man as best he could, and it was sufficient. He could feel the man's movements echoing in his own body, his spasms, his noises close to his own face. He could feel the man's tears on his own cheek. It's part of the job. This is the work I've chosen to do. This is one of the better moments. It's not much of a consolation, but it's an emotion shared with a fellow human being.

Bengt Johansson gradually calmed down. Winter continued to embrace him, waist hold, half nelson, whatever—he didn't need any macho excuse. The man snorted loudly.

Neither of them spoke. Winter could hear the sound of passing cars. There was an overhead streetlight outside, flashing at intervals through the open venetian blinds.

Johansson disentangled himself.

"I'm . . . I'm sorry," he said.

"For what?" Winter asked, rising to his feet. "Would you like something to drink?"

Johansson nodded.

Winter went to the kitchen that was next to the bedroom they had been sitting in: Johansson's king-size bed, the desk, the photograph of Micke.

Winter took a glass from the drain board, waited until the tap water turned cold, filled the glass, and took it in to Johansson, who drank deeply and said: "I don't think I can cope with this."

"I understand that you are going through hell," said Winter.

"How can you understand? Nobody can understand." Johansson shook his head. "How can you understand?"

Winter stroked the right side of his head with his right hand. His hair felt cool, like something that was a secure part of himself. He could see Angela's face seconds after they had *hacked* their way into that horrific apartment where she'd been held captive. His thoughts when she had disappeared, his thoughts about her thoughts when she was held there. Not knowing what she had been feeling, what she had been thinking. That had been the worst part of all.

"I've been there," he said.

It was Halders who took the call, via Möllerström.

"I take it you are looking for me." It was Aryan Kaite's voice at the other end of the line.

"That was a hell of a long piss break you took, kid," said Halders. "Three days."

Kaite mumbled something.

"Can you tell me where you are?" asked Halders. "Or are you still straining away somewhere?"

"I'm at Josefin's place." Halders heard a voice in the background. "Josefin Steinv—"

"Stay where you are," said Halders. "I'm coming."

"There's some . . . something else as well," said Kaite.

"Well?"

"I have a mark. A mark on my head. I thought it was just a scar but Josefin says it looks like something."

"Stay where you are, or there'll be hell to pay," said Halders.

Aneta was trying to interrogate a child, Bergenhem was trying to interrogate a child, Winter was trying to interrogate a missing child's father. Halders and Ringmar were in a police car. The heavens had closed again, or opened up if you preferred: Rain was pelting down, whipped up by a northerly wind.

"This is also what I'd call a hell of a long piss break," said Halders, indicating the rain being swept off the windshield by the wipers.

"Break?" said Ringmar.

"Ha ha."

Ringmar took a piece of paper out of his inside pocket. Halders saw something that looked like a crude drawing, which is what it was: Natanael Carlström's sketch of his farm's symbol.

"Do you think it will be possible to detect a similarity?"

Ringmar shrugged. Halders looked at him, at the streets flashing past them, then at Ringmar again.

"How are you, Bertil?"

"Eh?"

"How are you feeling?"

Ringmar didn't answer. He seemed to be perusing his notes, but when Halders looked more closely at the piece of paper he couldn't see any notes.

"You give the impression of being extremely worried about something," said Halders.

"Drive straight through the roundabout, don't turn right," said Ringmar. "It's quicker that way."

Halders concentrated on driving. He continued south after the roundabout. They could see the apartment buildings on top of the hill. Josefin Stenvång lived in one of them.

"Perhaps he's been there the whole time," said Ringmar.

"No," said Halders. "The girl has also been uncontactable. You know that."

"That's only because we haven't felt up to looking for her," said Ringmar.

"'Felt up to looking for her'?" said Halders. "I have."

"I haven't," said Ringmar.

"For Christ's sake, Bertil. What's the matter?"

Ringmar put the piece of paper back in his inside pocket.

"Birgitta's taken off," he said.

"Taken off? What do you mean, 'taken off'?"

"I don't know," said Ringmar. Did Fredrik know about Martin? he wondered. What did it matter? "I'll have to prepare the Christmas ham myself."

Halders gave a laugh.

"Sorry, Bertil."

"No, it's OK. I think it's funny too. And I haven't even bought it yet."

"So you can relax," said Halders. "All the good ones have gone. You have to order six months in advance."

They drove into the rectangular-shaped parking lot. Ringmar unfastened his seat belt.

"Good, that means I can relax," he said.

Aryan Kaite's face was shadowed with fear, if that is possible in a face like his, Halders thought. There were scars on the back of his head from his wound. But why not? There were always scars after wounds. This one could be a brand or an owner's mark, but it could also be part of the natural healing process, as far as Halders could see. Pia Fröberg had better take a look at it. The weapon might have come from Carlström's farm, but it might not. Still, Kaite has been out there in godforsaken land. Maybe the old coot didn't like darkies, and so he flew to Gothenburg on a broomstick and dived down from the sky and branded those bastards with his seal. That sounded logical enough, didn't it? Even if we drop the broomstick part.

There is a connection between these frisky students, Halders had thought in the car on the way there. And the same thought occurred to him again.

Josefin Stenvång was sitting next to Kaite and looked guilty, even more guilty.

"It's a *crime* to fail to appear for questioning," said Halders without bothering to sugar his words.

Kaite said nothing.

"Why?" asked Ringmar. He was standing beside Halders, who was sitting down.

"I'm here now," said Kaite. He looked up. "I called you, didn't I?"

"Why?" asked Halders.

"Why what?"

"Why did you call? Why did you get in touch with us?"

"It was these marks, Josefin said that they—"

"Don't give me that *crap* about it being because of some marks on the back of your head or on *your ass*," said Halders. "Maybe you're aware that we are busy right now with a case concerning a missing child and *we don't have the time* to sit here listening to you feed us *a load of shit*." He stood up. Josefin flinched, so did Kaite. "I want to know *here* and *now* why you took off."

Kaite said nothing.

"OK," said Halders. "You're coming home with us."

"Ho . . . home with you?"

"To jail," said Halders. "So put on your gloves and your wool hat." He headed for the door. "You'd better take a piss first, to be on the safe side." He turned around and looked at the girl, who looked at Kaite. "You too, Miss. You're coming too."

She was the one who replied to the big question *why*. "He was scared," she said.

"Josefin!"

Kaite started to stand up. Ringmar took a step forward. Stenvång looked at Halders. Halders saw that she had made up her mind. She looked at Kaite again.

"Are you going to tell them, or should I?" she said.

"I don't want to finger anybody," he said.

"You're just being stupid," she said. "You're only making things worse for yourself."

"It's private," said Kaite. "It's got nothing to do with *that*."

"Will one of you kindly tell us what this is all about?" said Halders. "If not, we're going to the station."

Kaite looked up, at something halfway between Halders and Ringmar.

"I was out there," he said. "At . . . at Gustav's place."

"We know," said Ringmar.

"W . . . what? You know?"

He looked genuinely surprised.

"We've been there," said Ringmar. "We've spoken to Gustav's father."

Kaite still looked just as surprised. Why does he look like that? Ringmar thought. What's so surprising about our going to see old man Smedsberg? Or could it be that we have been talking to Smedsberg and still don't *know*? What don't we know?

"He said that you and Gustav had been on the farm. And helped with the potato picking."

Kaite nodded. His face was different now.

"Is that where you were when you disappeared?" asked Ringmar.

Kaite looked up. Yet another expression: How the hell could you think that?

"What does this have to do with Gustav?" asked Ringmar.

Kaite didn't answer.

"Is he the one who threatened you?"

Kaite nodded.

"Have you felt threatened by Gustav Smedsberg?"

Kaite nodded again.

"I want to hear an answer," said Ringmar.

"Yes," said Kaite.

Ringmar could see relief in the boy's face now. It was a reaction he'd often seen before. But his face revealed not only relief. There was something else as well. He couldn't quite make out what it was. He recognized it, but he would have to think more about what it stood for.

"Is that why you've been hiding?"

"What?"

"Why have you been in hiding?"

"He was *scared*," said Stenvång. "He already told you."

"I'm asking Aryan," said Ringmar calmly. Halders glared the girl into silence. "Why did you disappear for three days even though you knew we were looking for you, Aryan?"

"I was scared," he said.

"Were you scared of Gustav?"

"Yes."

"Why?" asked Ringmar.

"Something . . . Something happened out there," said Kaite.

"Out there? Do you mean at Gustav's place? At the farm?" Talk about leading questions, Ringmar thought.

Kaite nodded.

"What happened out there?" asked Ringmar. Here it comes, he thought. Now we'll solve this business, or parts of it.

"He hit him," said Kaite. "He hit him."

"What do you mean? Who hit who?"

"Gustav's dad. He hit Gustav," said Kaite. "I saw it."

"You saw Gustav being beaten by his father?"

"Yes."

"How?"

"What do you mean?"

"What happened?"

"He just hit him. On the head. I saw it." He looked up, at Halders and Ringmar, and then at the girl. "He saw that I'd seen."

"Who saw?"

"Gustav."

"Gustav?"

Kaite mumbled something they couldn't hear.

"What did you say?" asked Ringmar.

"I don't know if his father saw," said Kaite.

"Why do you feel threatened by Gustav then, Aryan?"

"He didn't want it to get out."

"To get out? That he'd been beaten by his father?"

Kaite nodded.

"Why didn't he want it to get out?"

"I don't know," said Kaite.

"And you expect us to believe this? That you feel so threatened by him that you disappear?"

"It's the truth," said Kaite.

"It's not that Gustav has hit you, is it?" Ringmar asked.

"Eh?"

"You heard the question."

"No," said Kaite.

"No what?"

"Gustav hasn't hit me."

"He wasn't the one who clubbed you down in Kapellplatsen?"

"No." Kaite looked up. "I don't know who it was."

"You weren't with Gustav at the time?"

"No, no."

"Or with his father?"

"Eh?" That look of surprise again. And something else. What is it? Ringmar wondered.

"Has Gustav's father hit you as well, Aryan?"

"I don't know what you mean," said Kaite.

"Let's take it one step at a time," said Ringmar. "When you saw Gustav being beaten at home on the farm—were *you* attacked as well?"

"No."

"Have you ever been attacked by Gustav's father?"

"No."

"But Gustav doesn't want you to tell anybody what happened?"

"No."

"Why?"

"You'd better ask him that."

"We will," said Ringmar. "We definitely will." He looked at Halders. "Should we call?" He looked at Kaite again. "You don't need to come to the station with us, but we'll wait here until a car comes to pick you up and take you to our doctor so that she can take a look at that wound."

———

Ringmar and Halders drove back to the city center. It had stopped raining, but it was still just as dark.

"He's holding something back," said Halders.

"Of course," said Ringmar.

"You could have leaned on him a bit more."

"I thought I did a pretty good job," said Ringmar.

"Of course."

"We'll pick him up tomorrow," said Ringmar. "He can think over what he's said. What he's set in motion."

"You met old man Smedsberg in his element, up to his knees in dirt," said Halders. "What do you think?"

"Nothing," said Ringmar. "I don't think anything."

"There's nothing to think," said Halders.

"Was that a philosophical statement?" asked Ringmar.

"No," said Halders. "I was referring to this case. Nobody knows what to think."

Ringmar produced a piece of paper again, read something, then put it away.

"There was one thing you didn't ask about," said Halders.

"So you noticed?"

"Don't insult me."

"I was only joking, Fredrik."

"Why did you hold back on that?"

"As I said, I think he should have a bit of time to think over what he's already said."

Halders thought about the other boys. If there was a connection, it would have been appropriate to ask Kaite about it now, when he seemed vulnerable. But Bertil had waited. He hadn't asked about them. He hadn't leaned on the girl, Josefin. He had chosen not to press ahead. There was one reason above all others:

"Our black friend tells lies like a cow shits," said Halders.

Ringmar nodded. He was miles away, deep in thought.

"Do you think he feels relieved now?" Halders asked.

"Relieved!" shouted Ringmar, wide awake again.

Halders drove along Per Dubbsgatan. The hospital was glittering faintly, ten thousand windows with Advent candles in a blackish red wall.

"What?" said Halders. "What do you mean?"

"When I asked him if Gustav Smedsberg had threatened him and he eventually got around to saying that he had, he looked relieved!" said Ringmar.

"Maybe he had it inside him and needed to let it out," said Halders. "Maybe it's actually true. Or partly true. Or only partly a lie."

"Maybe he wasn't threatened by Gustav," said Ringmar.

"You mean it was the old man who threatened the Aryan?"

"The kid seemed to be relieved, but there was something else there, too," said Ringmar. "There was something else."

"Maybe he had to take a piss," said Halders, and Ringmar laughed out loud.

"Was it that funny?"

"I needed to laugh," said Ringmar. He laughed again.

"You'd better make another trip to the flats," said Halders.

"If one more is enough," said Ringmar.

"We're going to crack this one now," said Halders. "We'll sort it out rapido, and then we have other things to think about."

"We always have other things to think about," said Ringmar.

"I'm going to grab young Mr. Smedsberg right away," said Halders. "Young Mr. Cowshit."

They were approaching the intersection.

"Can you drive me home, please, Fredrik? I need to check something."

"Er . . . Yes, of course."

"Left here."

They drove past Slottsskogsvallen. Dusk fell during the six minutes it took Halders to get to Ringmar's house. The symphony of light in the neighbor's garden was magnificent.

"Now I've seen everything," said Halders.

"He's mentally defective," said Ringmar, getting out of the car.

"You don't need to turn any lights on in your place, Bertil." Halders looked sympathetic. "Look at it like that."

But Ringmar had to switch the hall light on as it was shielded by the living room. But that didn't help. No message on the answering machine on the hall table. No message in the mail he'd picked up from the box on the way in. He dropped the crap on the floor. Silence everywhere. No kitchen fan buzzing away at full speed. No voices. No Christmas ham boiling on the stove.

34

PIA FRÖBERG HAD A FURROW BETWEEN HER EYEBROWS THAT
seemed to grow deeper the longer she examined the injury on Kaite's head.
There was something there she was scrutinizing between her splayed hands.

Kaite appeared to be lost in thought, gazing out of the window, head to
one side.

"Hmm," said Fröberg.

"What?" asked Ringmar.

"Well, you can see something, but you can also see nothing."

"Great. Thank you for that."

"But Bertil, I can't say here and now if this is a special mark, or just . . .
just a mark. A scar. A wound in the process of healing."

"OK, OK, I'm with you, Pia."

"But it could be an imprint."

"Which in that case would represent something?" said Ringmar.

"In that case, yes."

"Could it be this?" said Ringmar, holding up a copy of Carlström's
drawing.

"It could be. It's not possible to say here and now."

"Let's go," said Halders.

They headed for the door.

"What am I supposed to do?" said Kaite, raising his head.

"I have no idea," said Halders without turning around.

"Shouldn't I go with you?"

"Do you want to?" asked Halders, turning around.

"N . . . No, no."

"Go home and take it easy," said Ringmar, who had also turned around.
"We'll be in touch."

"What will happen to this thing, then?" said Kaite to Pia Fröberg, moving his head slightly. "Will it leave a permanent mark?"

"It could."

"Oh my God."

"It's too early to tell," said Fröberg, feeling sorry for the boy.

<hr>

They drove toward the city center. There were more and more lights and lamps and glittering garlands hanging over the streets.

"Call young Smedsberg and see if he's at home," said Ringmar.

There was an answer after the third ring.

"This is Detective Inspector Fredrik Halders."

<hr>

Smedsberg was in Ringmar's office in an hour. He won't run away, Halders had said.

"Please sit down," said Ringmar.

Smedsberg sat down on the modest visitor's chair.

"Shouldn't we go to another room?" said Halders.

"Oh yes, of course," said Ringmar. "Please come this way, Gustav."

"What's this all about?" asked Gustav Smedsberg.

"What was that?" said Halders.

"I don't underst—"

"Are you still sitting down?" said Halders.

"It's only two floors down," said Ringmar.

Neither of the police officers spoke in the elevator. Smedsberg looked as if he were on the way to the electric chair. Either that or he's the type who always looks worried, Halders thought.

It was not a cozy room. It was the opposite of the interview rooms set up to make a child feel secure. There was a nasty lamp on the desk and an even worse one hanging from the ceiling. There was a window, but the view of the ventilation duct was unlikely to raise anybody's spirits. The room seemed to be fitted out for its purpose, but everything was accidental—a window in the wrong place, a ventilation duct in the wrong place.

"Please sit down," said Ringmar.

Smedsberg sat down, but cautiously, as if he expected a different instruction from Halders, who he was looking at now. Halders gave him a friendly smile.

Ringmar switched on the tape recorder that was standing on the table.

Halders was fiddling with the tripod for the video camera, which was making a humming noise, the coziest thing about the room.

"Will you be celebrating Christmas at home this year, Gustav?" asked Ringmar.

"Er . . . What?"

"Will you be celebrating Christmas at home on the farm, with your dad?"

"Er . . . No."

"Really?"

"What difference does it make to you?" asked Smedsberg.

"It's just standard interview technique," said Halders, who was still next to the camera but leaning over the desk. "You start with something general and then come around to the heavy stuff."

"Er . . . Hmm."

"Why have you been threatening Aryan Kaite?" asked Ringmar.

"The heavy stuff," said Halders, gesturing toward Ringmar.

"Er . . ."

"You seem to have a limited vocabulary for a student," said Halders.

"We have been informed that you threatened Aryan Kaite," said Ringmar.

"W . . . What?"

"What do you have to say to the accusation that you threatened him?"

"I haven't threatened anybody," said Smedsberg.

"We have been informed that you did."

"By whom?"

"Who do you think?"

"He would never da—"

Ringmar looked at him.

"What were you going to say, Gustav?"

"Nothing."

"What happened between you and Aryan, Gustav?"

"I don't understand."

"Something happened between the two of you. We want to know what. We might be able to help you."

Smedsberg looked as if he might be smiling. Ringmar saw the smile come and go within a fraction of a second. The camera saw it. What did it mean?

"What really happened between you and Aryan, Gustav?"

"I already told you, a hundred years ago. It was a girl."

"Josefin Stenvång," said Halders.

"Er . . . Yes."

"But that's not all, is it?" Ringmar eyed Smedsberg. "There are other reasons as well, aren't there?"

"I don't know what he told you, but whatever he said, it's wrong," said Smedsberg.

"But you can't know what he's said, can you?"

"It's wrong in any case," said Smedsberg.

"What's the truth, then?"

Smedsberg didn't reply. Ringmar could see something in his face that he thought he recognized. It wasn't relief. It was at the other end of the emotional register, the dark side.

"It will be better for you if you tell us."

That same smile again, like a flash of cynicism, combined with the darkness in the boy's eyes. What has he been through? Ringmar didn't know, couldn't begin to guess.

"Gustav," said Ringmar, "that story you told us about how you were attacked on Mossen—it's not true, is it?"

Smedsberg said nothing. He wasn't smiling anymore.

"You were never attacked, were you?"

"Of course I was."

"It doesn't matter if you change your story."

"Of course I was," Smedsberg said again.

And again: "Of course I was."

Are we talking about the same thing? Ringmar thought.

"Were you attacked by your father, Gustav?" Ringmar asked.

Smedsberg didn't answer. That was an answer in itself.

"Was it your father who attacked you at Mossen, Gustav?" Ringmar asked.

"No."

"Did he attack you at home, Gustav?"

"It doesn't matter what he said."

"Who, Gustav? Who said what?"

Smedsberg didn't answer. Ringmar could see that the kid wasn't feeling well now, not well at all. What the hell was he concealing? Is it something that has nothing to do with this business? Something worse?

Ringmar looked at Halders, and winked.

"That story about the branding iron you told us the first time we met—you made it up, didn't you?"

"Did I?" said Smedsberg.

"Nobody uses those things, do they?"

"Not nowadays, maybe."

"And they've never used them at your farm," said Halders.

A special look in Smedsberg's eyes again, something different this time. Is he playing games with us? Ringmar wondered. No, it's something different. Or it might be a game, but not his.

"What made you think of that branding iron, Gustav?"

"Because it *looked like it.*"

Oops, Ringmar thought.

Halders seemed to be waiting for more.

"Haven't you been able to check it out?" asked Smedsberg.

"Check what out?" asked Halders.

"The iron, for Christ's sake!"

"Where would we be able to do that?"

Smedsberg looked at Halders, and now there was something different in his eyes. Perhaps it was desperation now, and insecurity.

"Do I have to spell everything out for you?" he said.

"He hasn't told us a single thing," said Halders, as they drove past Pellerin's Margarine Factory.

"Or everything," said Ringmar.

"We should have grilled those other two student brats right away," said Halders.

"You're talking about people who have been badly assaulted," said Ringmar. "One of them so badly that he was on the point of being a permanent invalid."

"He'll recover," said Halders. "He'll be OK."

"Still," said Ringmar.

"He'll be able to play for the Blue and Whites six months from now," said Halders. "Even if he's still lame. Nobody would notice the difference on that team."

"You must be getting them mixed up with Örgryte soccer club," said Ringmar.

"I think the most important thing now is to go out there again," said Winter from the backseat.

He watched the townscape change and eventually disappear. Forests and an endless network of lakes now. Commuter trains.

He had been poring over the transcripts of the interviews with the children and trying to conjure up a picture of the man who had talked to them, done other things. He'd searched and searched. There was something he could make use of. The man had a parrot who might be called Billy. Winter had gone back to Simon Waggoner with ten toy parrots in ten different colors, and Simon had picked out the green one.

Simon had also pointed at the red one.

The man might well have been in his forties, possibly a worn-out thirty-year-old, possibly a fit and active fifty-year-old. Winter had been talking to Aneta Djanali when Halders and Ringmar returned from interviewing Smedsberg.

"We sent him home," Ringmar had said.

"Hmm," said Winter.

"I think it's the best thing for now."

They had made up their minds to make the journey out to the flats.

"I'll come with you," Winter had said. "I've been there before and I can think about this other stuff in the car."

He was sitting in the backseat hunched over his laptop. Lakes and forests and hills turned into plains.

"That's it," said Ringmar at the crossroads.

"Drive straight to old man Carlström's," said Winter.

Ringmar nodded, and they passed a hundred meters away from Smedsberg's house. They couldn't see a tractor; there was no sign of life.

"It's like being at sea," said Halders.

Ringmar nodded again and drummed on the steering wheel.

"A different world," said Halders. "When you see this you begin to understand a thing or two."

"What do you mean?" asked Winter, leaning forward.

"Smedsberg is an odd character, isn't he? When you see this it becomes easier to understand why." They passed a man on a tractor who raised a hand in greeting. The tractor had emerged from a side road a hundred meters ahead of them, from a little copse. Like a tank coming out of a patch of camouflaging bushes. "A different world," said Halders again. They could see two figures on horseback in what appeared to be the far distance.

They were being followed by birds. A minor twister whistled across a little field, whipping up a swirl of dead leaves. Ringmar drove past the same house as before. They suddenly found themselves in a forest, shadows. Then they were back among the open fields again. They passed Smedsberg's wife's family home. Gerd.

They were there.

They got out of the car and walked toward the house. Nobody came out to greet them.

"How do we explain our visit this time?" said Ringmar.

"We don't need to explain ourselves this time either," said Winter.

The winds circled around the house. Everything was just the same as the last time. In the distance Winter could see the tower he'd noticed before, like a lighthouse. Darkness was closing in quickly. It felt colder here than any-where else. On their last visit he'd thought that if they returned soon every-thing would be white, and it really would look like a wintry sea.

When he raised his hand to knock, he thought about the feeling he'd had when he'd last stood there: the certainty that he would return, and he hadn't been able to explain that feeling. But it had to do with darkness. It was a pre-monition that forebode something terrible. Now that I've experienced the feeling, it won't go away, he'd thought. He could feel it again now. That's why he'd chosen to accompany the others, to see if he would experience it again. Yes. There was a secret buried here. And something had made him come here again, and it had nothing to do with the assaults on the young men, with this case. What was it? It must have some connection with it, surely. But simulta-neously he thought that he would have to bear it in mind again, remember that not everything was what he saw and thought it was, that there was some-thing else about this place.

Why am I thinking like this?

After the third salvo of hammering they could hear somebody moving inside, and a voice said: "What do you want?"

"It's us again," said Winter. "From the police. May we come in and ask you a few more questions?"

"About what?"

The voice was as gruff as before and still seemed to be in several layers, an old man's voice. Life is a series of repeats, Ringmar thought. At best.

"Can we come in?" Winter said again.

They heard the same mumbling and a clanking of bolts. The door opened and the man inside again appeared as a silhouette, illuminated by a low light from the hall and perhaps also the kitchen. Winter held out his ID. The man ignored it but nodded at Halders.

"Who's he?"

Halders introduced himself and showed the man his ID.

"What's it about this time, then?" said Carlström, who appeared to be even more hunched than before. His head was still shaved, and he was wear-ing what might have been the same whitish shirt, suspenders, trousers of no particular style, and thick woolen socks. He hadn't abandoned his classic rural attire.

Talk about contrasts, Halders thought, looking at the two men facing each other. Winter's white shirt made the old man's look black.

Halders could smell a wood-burning oven and recently cooked food. Pork. It was damp and chilly in the hall, and this was not entirely due to the air coming from the outside.

"We just have a few things we'd like to clarify," said Winter.

The old man made a sort of sighing noise and opened the door wider.

"Well, come in, then."

He showed them into the kitchen, which seemed to have shrunk since the last time, just as he seemed to be more hunched.

This is one of the solitaries, Winter thought. One of the most solitary men on earth.

The wood-burning stove was alight. The air in the kitchen was dry and distinctly warm, in contrast to the raw damp in the hall.

Carlström gestured for them to sit down. He didn't offer coffee. The kitchen seemed to be overfilled by the four men, as if a new record was about to be set for a country kitchen in the *Guinness Book of World Records,* Halders thought.

"Do you remember us talking about marks made by a branding iron the last time we were here?" Winter asked.

"I'm not senile," said Carlström.

"We've found one," said Winter. "One that looks like a brand. On one of the boys."

"Really?"

"It looks like your mark, Carlström."

"Really."

"What if it is your mark?"

"What am I supposed to do about it?"

"How could your mark have ended up on the skin of a young man in Gothenburg?" asked Ringmar.

"I don't know," said Carlström.

"We don't know either," said Winter. "It's a mystery to us."

"I can't help you," said Carlström. "You could have saved yourselves the journey."

"Have any of the stolen goods come back?" asked Winter.

"Before any stolen goods come back pigs will have learned to fly from here to Skara," said Carlström.

Winter thought of his own drawing, the flying pig. That felt like a long time ago.

"You understand why I'm asking, don't you?"

"I'm not stupid," said Carlström.

"Somebody might have stolen that iron from here, and used it."

"That's possible," said Carlström.

Halders knocked against a little iron poker lying on the stove, and it fell on the floor with a hollow clang. Natanael Carlström gave a start and whipped around. Rather nimbly, Winter thought. His back had straightened out for a second. Winter looked at Halders, who was bending down and caught his eye. Halders was not stupid.

"I must ask you again if there's anybody you suspect," said Winter.

"Not a soul," said Carlström.

"You didn't see anything suspicious?"

"When are you talking about?"

"About the time of the theft," said Winter. "You said last time that you discovered the theft more or less right away."

"Did I say that?"

"Yes."

"I don't remember that."

Winter said nothing. Carlström looked at Ringmar, who remained silent.

"You had equipment out there that was stolen."

"Yes, that's probably what happened."

"I don't suppose you've found any other, er, tool or equipment with your owner's mark on it since we were here last?" Winter asked.

"Yes, I have," said Carlström.

"You've found something?"

"Yes, I just said so."

Winter looked at Ringmar.

"What is it?" asked Winter.

"It's a little iron," said Carlström. "It was in the old barn."

The old barn, Halders thought. Which is the new one?

35

NATANAEL CARLSTRÖM FETCHED HIS . . . CONTRAPTION. SOMETHING
for very small creatures, Winter thought.

"So this is your owner's mark, is it?" said Ringmar, holding up the disk
that was attached to the short handle. Everything was small, but solidly
made, as if it had been cast in a single piece.

Crazy-looking thing, Halders thought.

Carlström nodded in response to Ringmar's question.

"Have you ever used this?"

"A long time ago."

"How long ago?"

Carlström made a gesture that could encompass the last two thousand
years.

"And it wasn't stolen?"

"I don't know. Somebody could have stolen it and brought it back again."

"Wouldn't you have noticed if they had?"

"Yes, I suppose so."

"We would like to borrow this iron from you," said Winter.

"Please do," said Carlström.

I wonder what he's thinking, Halders thought. About us here in his tum-
bledown house that looks as if it will be blown away any minute over the
plain, like pigs heading for Skara.

"So that we can make comparisons," said Winter. We don't really need to
explain anything, he thought. But sometimes it makes things easier.

"I'd also like a bit of information about your foster son," said Winter.

He could see that the old man gave a start.

"Say that again?"

"Your foster son," Winter repeated.

Carlström turned around, like a very old man, lifted the lid of the stove, bent down awkwardly, and peered at the fire that was showing no signs of dying.

"Did you hear what I said?" asked Winter.

"I heard you," said Carlström, slowly straightening his back. Either what I said has made him more ancient, or he's trying to think. Winter watched the old man close the lid and look at him. "I'm not deaf." He glanced at the other two intruders then looked at Winter. "Who said anything about a foster son?"

Does *everybody* have to keep secrets to themselves in this world? Halders thought. He had sat down on one of the wooden kitchen chairs. They looked fragile, but this one felt stable under his weight.

"Do you have a foster son, Mr. Carlström?"

"What's he done?"

"Do you have a foster son?"

"Yes, yes, yes. What's he done now?"

"What's his name?" Winter asked.

"What's he done now?" asked Carlström again.

Now, Winter thought. What had happened earlier?

"Nothing as far as we know," said Winter. "But since we've been here before and discussed those things that were stolen from your farm, we ca—"

"Mats hasn't taken nothing," said Carlström.

"No?"

"Why should he? He's not interested."

"Mats?" said Winter.

"Yes, Mats. That was the name he had when he came here and it was the name he had when he left."

"The last time we asked you, you said you didn't have any children," said Winter.

"Well?"

"That wasn't quite true, was it?"

"This has nothing to do with them thefts," said Carlström, "nor with them assaults or whatever they were." He turned around again, bent down, and picked up a piece of firewood, which he pushed into the stove. Winter could see the flames and sparks from where he stood. "And besides, he's not my son."

"But he lived with you, didn't he?"

"For a while."

"How long?"

"What difference does it make?"

Yes. What difference did it make? I don't know why I'm asking that. All I know is that I have to ask. It's like that feeling before I knocked on the front door.

"How long?"

Carlström seemed to sigh, as if he felt obliged to answer all these stupid questions so that the townies would drive away over the fields again and leave him in peace.

"A few years. Probably about four years."

"When was that?"

"It was a long time ago. Many years ago."

"What decade?"

"It must have been the sixties."

"How old is Mats?"

"He was eight when he came," said Carlström. "Or maybe it was ten, or eleven."

"When was it?"

"The sixties, like I said."

"What year?"

"For Christ's . . . I don't remember. The middle, I suppose. Sixty-five or so."

"Has he been back here often since he moved out?" Winter asked.

"No."

"How often?"

"He didn't want to come back here." Carlström looked down, then up again. There was a new expression in his eyes. Perhaps it denoted pain. It could also mean: He didn't want to come back here and I don't blame him.

"What's his surname?"

"Jerner."

"So his name is Mats Jerner?"

"Mats is his first name, I've already told you that."

Winter thought: Did this Mats Jerner come here and steal a weapon so that this man would take the blame? Is the foster son so self-confident that he knows he can get away with it?

Is any of this probable?

Did something happen out here on the flats that involves the Smedsberg family and old man Carlström?

Smedsberg's wife grew up not far from here. What was her name? Gerd. She knew Natanael Carlström.

How could he be a foster parent? Was he different then? Maybe he was a nice man once upon a time. Maybe such considerations didn't matter. Very strange things happened in those days between adults and children, just like now, Winter thought.

"When was Mats here last?" Winter asked.

"It's odd," said Carlström. He seemed to be studying the wall behind Winter.

"I beg your pardon?" said Winter.

"He was here a month ago," said Carlström.

Winter waited. Ringmar was bent over the stove, about to open the lid. Halders looked as if he were studying Carlström's profile.

"He came to say hello."

"A month ago?" Winter asked.

"Or maybe it was two. It was this autumn in any case."

"What did he want?" Halders asked.

Carlström turned to look at him.

"What did you say?"

"What did Mats want?"

"He didn't want anything," said Carlström.

"Could he have taken your branding irons?" asked Winter.

"No," said Carlström.

"Why not?"

Carlström didn't answer.

"Why not?" asked Winter again.

Carlström still didn't answer.

"So can we assume that he took them?" asked Halders. "It's looking very much like it."

"He would never go near them," said Carlström.

"Never go near them?" said Winter.

"There was an accident once," said Carlström.

"What happened?"

"He burned himself."

"How?"

"He got in the way of the iron." Carlström looked up again. His head had become increasingly bowed as the interview proceeded, and in the end he was forced to straighten himself up, but soon his head began to droop again. "It was an accident. But he got scared of the iron. It got a grip on him."

"Got a grip on him?"

"Fear got a grip on him," said Carlström.

"He's a grown man now," said Halders. "He knows that these tools can't burn him."

Winter saw something definite in Carlström's face: doubt about what Halders had said, or certainty.

"What did Mats say when he was here?" Winter asked.

"He said nothing."

"Why did he come, then?"

"No idea."

"Where does he live?" Winter asked.

"In town."

"What town?"

"The big town. Gothenburg."

That surprised Winter: Gothenburg referred to as "town." He'd thought the old man was referring to one of the smaller towns situated to the north, like spiky little growths on the enormous featureless plain. Perhaps Gothenburg was the only town of real significance when the young ones left this desolation for the city. There weren't many alternatives.

"Where does he live in Gothenburg?" Winter asked.

"I don't know."

"What does he do?"

"I don't know that either."

Winter couldn't make up his mind if Carlström was lying or telling a sort of truth. Maybe it didn't matter. But once again Winter could sense the pain the old man was enduring. What was causing it? Was it longing, or regret, or . . . shame? What had happened between the man and the boy? Smedsberg had said the boy was badly treated. How did he end up here in the first place? Where did he come from? Suddenly, Winter wanted to know.

"Tell me about Mats," he said.

Open questions.

"What do you want me to say?"

That soon closed.

"How did you get custody of him?"

"Don't ask me!"

"You offered to take care of him?"

We'll go on to leading questions instead.

"It just happened, I guess."

Which work well, and hence are just as worthless as ever.

"Where did he come from?"

Carlström didn't answer. Winter noticed the moment of pain in his eyes again.

"Did he have any parents?" Winter asked.

"No," said Carlström.

"What had happened?"

"They were not worthy to be his parents," said Carlström.

That was a very odd expression to come from this man.

"Not if you can believe the woman from the Child Support Agency," said Carlström.

Who entrusted a young boy to the care of a lone man, Winter thought. Possibly a psychologically damaged and scared little boy.

"Have you always lived alone, Carlström?"

"Eh?"

"Were you living without a woman when Mats was here?"

Carlström looked at him.

"I've never been married," he said.

"That's not what I asked," said Winter.

"A woman was living with me," said Carlström.

"When? When Mats was here?"

Carlström nodded.

"The entire time?"

"In the beginning," he said.

Winter waited with his follow-up question. Carlström waited. Winter asked a different question: "What had happened to Mats?"

"I don't know details like that."

"What did the woman from the Child Support Agency say?"

"Somebody had . . . raped him."

"Who? His father?"

"I don't want to talk about it," said Carlström.

"It co—"

"*I don't want to talk about it.*"

There was a loud crackle in the wood-burning stove, a birch log had protested, the sound underlined Carlström's words.

Winter glanced at Ringmar, who shook his head almost imperceptibly.

"Was Mats, er, exposed to anything while he was here?" asked Winter, and noticed that Carlström gave another start. "What I mean is, did anybody in the village hurt him in any way? Interfere with him in some way or other?"

"I don't know," said Carlström.

"Anything. Anything at all."

"So that now he's getting his own back, is that what you mean? Attacking people in Gothenburg? Is that what you're saying?"

"No," said Winter.

"But is it what you're thinking?"

"The boys who were clubbed down weren't even born when Mats was a little boy," said Winter.

"No, precisely," said Carlström.

But you were, Winter thought. And Georg Smedsberg.

Nobody answered the door at Smedsberg's house. It was empty, black. It stood like a crumbling fortress on the plain north of Carlström's farm.

"Maybe he's playing bridge," said Halders.

"Where?" said Ringmar.

There was nothing around them but darkness, a sky with pale stars that seemed to be covered by dark veils that only allowed thin wisps of light through. They could hear a humming noise that could be traffic from a long way away or Smedsberg's ventilation system or just the wind itself that hadn't come up against any resistance out there.

They went back to Halders's car and headed south. Their headlights clove through the fields, shone up heavenward when Halders drove up a little hill, the only one for miles around. Nobody in the car spoke; all were deep in thought. Winter felt cold, especially after the conversation with Natanael Carlström, who had watched them drive away without waving.

Winter could see flakes from heaven through the window.

"It's snowing," he said.

"The day before the day," said Halders.

"It'll be Christmas Eve in two hours," said Ringmar.

"Merry Christmas, gentlemen," said Halders.

He parked outside police headquarters, which had Advent candles in every other window.

"Now that really is a neat way to illustrate the shortfall in the police budget," Halders had said when they set off and it was already dark. "Pretty and neat and symmetrical, but half baked."

Now he was driving home, to Lunden. They watched his rear lights disappear into the snow.

Winter looked at Ringmar.

"Leave your car here, Bertil. I'll drive you home."

Home, Ringmar thought.

They drove in silence. Winter waited while Ringmar walked to his front door. Bertil seemed to be dressed in gold thanks to the ridiculous glare from the neighbor's lights. Winter watched Ringmar close the door behind him, and immediately got out of his car and walked up the yellow brick road to the door.

Ringmar opened it immediately.

"Are you alone in the house, Bertil?"

Ringmar burst out laughing, as if Winter had said something funny.

"Come back home with me instead. We can talk and have a beer. And celebrate Christmas. I have a guest room."

They walked back along Ringmar's path. The neighbor's Christmas decorations swayed in the wind.

"He's opened the pearly gates," said Ringmar, gesturing toward the neighbor's garden.

36

THE WALL CLOCK IN THE KITCHEN SHOWED IT WAS PAST MIDNIGHT; it was Christmas Eve now. The shepherds would be watching their flocks.

"Merry Christmas, Erik."

"Merry Christmas, Bertil."

Ringmar raised his glass to the skies. Winter had put Paul Simon on the CD player in the kitchen: *She's so light, she's so free, I'm tight, well that's me.* Ringmar's head swayed from side to side in time with the palliative music.

"Do you really want to hear about it?" he asked.

"With you celebrating Christmas on your own, without your family? Don't insult me, Bertil."

"You're alone, too."

"That was by choice, or necessity. I'm off as soon as we've cracked the case."

"When will that be?"

"Soon," said Winter.

"Martin got it into his head that I, well, did something," said Ringmar.

Paul sang: *It's cold, sometimes you can't catch your breath, it's cold.*

Winter finished off his beer and waited.

"Did you hear what I said?" Ringmar asked.

"What do you mean, Bertil? Did something?"

"The reason why he's gone into hiding."

"What does he say you did?"

"I can't tell you," said Ringmar. "I can't bring myself to say it."

"When did you discover whatever it is that you can't bring yourself to say?"

Was he being brutal? No. Bertil was too close a friend.

"Yesterday. Birgitta called. Finally."

"And what did she say?"

Bertil was asleep, or at least he was in bed in the spare room. An hour earlier he had been crying his eyes out over Winter's kitchen table. Winter was standing in the balcony doorway, smoking. There was snow down below. Tomorrow morning he wouldn't be trying to build a snowman with Elsa.

Silence reigned. It was as if everybody was sleeping the sleep of the pious before being nice to everybody on Christmas Eve morning, as tradition demanded.

Winter closed the balcony door and returned to his desk and the laptop. Paul Simon had accompanied him into the living room. *We think it's easy, sometimes it's easy, but it's not easy.* He stared at his notes that flowed in straight lines, like heartbeats that had ceased to beat: They were straight, devoid of life.

They had spoken. Then Bertil had immersed himself in the case again. The cases. Do you really want to? He'd seen from Bertil's intensity that it was necessary.

"It could be the foster son," Ringmar had said. "He's been the victim of something that has to do with one of these students. Smedsberg. Or it could be the old man. Georg, is that his name?"

"Yes," said Winter.

"Yes to what?" Ringmar wondered.

"His name is Georg."

"The foster son, Mats. He might have stolen the branding iron from Carlström and used it. We know that he was there."

"Carlström might have done it himself," Winter had said. "He's not a cripple."

"But why?"

"The big question."

"We always come up against the Big Question," said Ringmar. "We'll have to have a word with him tomorrow."

"Carlström?"

"Jerner. The foster son."

"Assuming he's at home," Winter said.

He'd looked up the name and address in the telephone directory and called the moment they'd gotten back home, but there was no reply. As they'd driven home from the flats they'd talked about calling HQ and asking them to send out a car to take a look, but it was too soon. And what was the point? If they really were onto something, doing that could cause problems for the investigation. Better to pace themselves.

"The woman," Ringmar said. "Gerd. Smedsberg's wife. What happened to her?"

"How deep should we dig out there in the flats, Bertil?"

"We might have to dig as deep down as it goes," said Ringmar.

"It might be a bottomless pit," said Winter. "Should we call it a day, Bertil? It will be a long day tomorrow."

"We haven't talked about the most important thing," said Ringmar. "We haven't gone through it again."

"I'll talk to Maja Bergort tomorrow morning," Winter said. "And the Waggoner boy."

"I'll listen to the tapes as soon as possible."

"I want to go through them again too."

"They are still around," Ringmar said.

"Aneta will try again with the Skarin boy. And the Sköld girl. Ellen."

"The absent father," said Ringmar.

"There are lots of them to choose from," said Winter.

"What do you mean by that?"

"There are lots of them we can interview, suspect, investigate."

"That wasn't the only thing you were thinking about, Erik."

"No. I was thinking of myself as well."

"You were thinking about me."

"I was thinking about me, and about you too."

———

He was staring at the screen, which was the only source of light in the room, apart from the standing lamp by the leather armchair next to the balcony door. He checked his watch. Two o'clock.

Paul Simon was singing something that he didn't catch, but it was beautiful.

He reached for the telephone and dialed the number.

His mother sounded like a jazz singer after two in the morning when she eventually answered.

"Hel . . . hello?"

"Hello, Mother. It's Erik."

"Er . . . Erik. Did something happen?"

"No. But I'd like to speak to Angela."

"She's asleep. Upstairs. And Els—" He heard a voice in the background, then his mother's voice again. "Well, you've woken her up, so here she is."

"What's the matter, Erik?" Angela asked.

"Nothing. I just wanted to call."

"Where are you?"

"At home, of course."

"What's that noise I can hear?"

"It could be the computer, or it could be the Paul Simon CD you bought me."

"I can hear it now. Hmmm."

She sounded half asleep, a little hoarse, delightful. Her voice was on low frequency, as if partly in a dream.

"How's it going down there?"

"Splendid. The sun's shining, the stars are glittering."

"What's Elsa doing?"

"She tried to go swimming in the sea but thought it was too cold."

"What else?"

"Playing on the lawn. And pointing at the snow on top of the mountain."

"The White Mountain," said Winter.

"She can say that in Spanish. If we stayed here for six months, she'd be bilingual."

"That might not be a bad idea," said Winter.

"And what would you be doing meanwhile?"

"I'd be there," he said.

Six months in Spain. Or a full year. He could afford it.

Once this case was over. Who knows?

"It's Christmas Eve tomorrow. Elsa doesn't talk about anything else. *Feliz Navidad.*"

"Today."

"Hmm. Did you call to remind me of that?"

"No."

"Do you still plan on coming on Boxing Day?"

"Yes."

"Siv couldn't believe it. That you didn't come with us, I mean."

"She'll have to make up for that."

"She? She doesn't need to make up for anything."

"No."

"You sound absolutely worn out, Erik."

"Yes."

"Will you be able to make progress tomorrow?"

"Yes."

"Steer clear of the whiskey tonight."

"We hid the bottle the moment we came through the door."

"Ha ha." Then he heard her take a deep breath. "We?"

"Bertil. He's spending the night here."

"Why?"

"He needs to."

"What does Birgitta have to say about that?"

"She doesn't know about it," said Winter.

"What's going on, Erik?"

He tried to explain what was going on. That was why he'd called, one of the two main reasons. He felt he simply had to talk to someone else about the situation.

"Good God," she said. "Bertil?"

"You don't have to believe it," said Winter.

"Is that what Bertil says?"

"Of course he says he's innocent."

"Good God," she said again.

"Birgitta rang from—from wherever she is. She didn't want to say where. And Martin was there too. And Moa. She's the daught—"

"I know who she is," said Angela. "What are they up to? Figuring out how to trample all over Bertil?"

"I think they're trying to work out what Bertil's son's problem is."

"Is this the first time he's said anything? Martin, I mean."

"Evidently."

"So what did he say?"

"Well, Birgitta was a bit, er, vague about that. Something about . . . abuse. I don't know what. When he was a little boy."

"For God's sake. Bertil. It doesn't make sense."

"No," said Winter.

"So why did he say that? Martin?"

"I'm not a psychologist," said Winter. "But my guess is that it has something to do with the company the kid keeps. All that brooding. He's evidently gotten mixed up with some damn sect or other since he ran off."

"But there must be some reason he ran away in the first place?" said Angela.

"Presumably. But it might only exist in his own head."

"How's Bertil taking this?"

"Hmm. What can I say? He's trying to fulfill his work commitment. As best he can."

"Will it come to . . . an official complaint to the police?"

"I don't know," said Winter. "But if it does I want to be a thousand miles away from here."

"Five hundred will do," she said. "On the Costa del Sol."

"I don't want to be there for a reason like that."

"Do you want to be there at all?"

"Come on, Angela. You know why I'm still here in Gothenburg. I'll come down there as soon as I can, obviously. If not sooner."

"OK. Sorry, Erik. What are you going to do now?"

"Try to get an hour or two's sleep. I've stopped thinking. Switched off."

"Have you found your Christmas presents yet?"

"I'll start looking tomorrow morning."

He was flying over the plain on the back of a bird that kept repeating his name, and then a four-word sentence: Klara want a cookie, Klara want a cookie, Klara want a c—Hush, I can't hear what the children are thinking, what the children are thinking down below. Four young men were wandering over the plain, one of them smiled. His face was black. A tractor was crossing the field, Winter could see the dust rising up into the sky. Ringmar was chasing one of the boys. Lies! Ringmar yelled. Lies! Lies! Winter was in town. Christmas everywhere, packages, shops, a square. It was indoors. A man passed by with a stroller. The man was wearing a checked cap. He turned around toward Winter. You are not listening! You are not looking! You have stopped but you don't see. Don't see. Now he was playing the guitar. Winter followed him. The stroller had gone, flown up into the air. There was a sun in the sky, and stars. He was standing up there on the earth, looking down at heaven. It was night and day. Up was down. The cap came past again with the stroller. There were feet in the stroller that didn't move. Small feet, motionless. The cap rang a bell, shook it upward, downward, riiiiiiiiiiiiiiing, riiiiiing.

He woke up in darkness. The alarm clock was screeching seven.

Ringmar was sitting in the kitchen with a cup of coffee in front of him. The darkness outside was lighter because of the thin covering of snow everywhere. Ringmar was reading the newspaper.

"You're already up," said Winter.

"I never went to sleep."

There was coffee in the pot. Winter prepared a cheese sandwich. He was shivering in his bathrobe.

"Professor Christianson, a research genius in the psychology department here in Gothenburg has concluded that the police should rethink the way they conduct interrogations," said Ringmar, staring hard at the newspaper.

"Sounds interesting," said Winter, and took a bite of his sandwich.

"He maintains that we've always thought that somebody who's telling lies is shifty-eyed, seems nervous, and gesticulates a lot." Ringmar gave a laugh, loud, brief, and sarcastic. "This white knight who has come to rescue us in our distress has concluded that liars don't act like that!" Ringmar looked up at Winter and quoted: "'Liars often look you straight in the eye and tell their lies calmly.'"

"Just think, if we'd only known that," said Winter. "Now our interviewing methodology will be revolutionized."

"All those mistakes we've made," said Ringmar.

"Thank God for academic research," said Winter.

Ringmar continued reading the article, then gave another laugh:

"I'll quote you some more: 'Research also shows that it is easier to expose a lie when the interrogation is recorded on video than when using the standard method.'"

Winter laughed, just as briefly and sarcastically. "And we've only been using the video technique for five years now."

"Without knowing why," said Ringmar.

"Get this on our intranet, pronto," said Winter.

"To be on the safe side he states that the judicial authorities are badly informed about modern forensic psychology but have promised to read up on it," said Ringmar. "Hallelujah."

"But first he will have to write the books for them," said Winter.

"I wonder what Professor Christianson thinks about this," said Ringmar.

"I don't think he needs any sympathy," said Winter.

"Gesticulates a lot," said Ringmar, "shifty-eyed."

"Sounds like a film by Fritz Lang. *Doctor Mabuse, M.*"

"Maybe Göteborgs Posten found this research report in an old archive?" Ringmar suggested.

"Researcher," said Winter. "They found the researcher there."

Ringmar looked for further wisdom in the article.

"This might be interesting despite everything. Our researcher has noticed that parents are better than others at detecting lies. They can also detect when other people's children are not telling the truth. Adults without children are significantly worse at it." Ringmar looked up. "We're OK on that score, Erik." Then his face fell, and despite his purported lack of knowledge about human behavior, Winter knew immediately what Ringmar was thinking.

Winter's mobile rang on the countertop, where it was recharging. He could reach it without standing up.

"Hello?"

"Hi, Lars here."

Bergenhem's voice sounded small, as if it were coming from a tunnel.

"What's up?"

"Carolin Johansson overdosed," said Bergenhem. "Micke's mother. Some kind of pills, they don't know yet."

"Is she alive?"

"Barely."

"Is she alive or isn't she?"

"She's alive," said Bergenhem.

"There were no drugs at her place," said Winter. "We should have a record."

"Sleeping pills, they think. She had visitors at the time," said Bergenhem.

"I want to know exactly who was there," said Winter.

"That's not so—"

"I want to know, Lars. See to it."

"OK."

"Is she in Östra Hospital?"

"Yes."

"Do we have somebody there?"

"Sara."

"OK. How's the father taking it? Where is he?"

"He's there as well."

"Who's keeping an eye on his telephone?"

"Two new officers. I don't know their names. Möllerström can ask—"

"Forget it for the time being. Have you spoken to Bengt Johansson this morning?"

"No."

Just as well, Winter thought. I'll stop in on him this afternoon at his home. Assuming he's back there by then.

Bertil had gathered what had happened, and stood up.

"Time for a day's work," he said. "Another day's work. Christmas Eve or no Christmas Eve." He looked at Winter. "They work on Christmas Eve in the USA."

"How are you feeling, Bertil?"

"Excellent after a good night's wake."

"Won't Birgitta be looking for you?"

"How the hell should I know?"

"You know where you stand with me, Bertil," said Winter.

"I beg your pardon?"

"I believe you," said Winter.

"How can you be so sure, Erik? Just because I'm swaying around like a

Christmas tree in a storm and blinking like a lighthouse it doesn't necessarily mean that I'm telling the truth."

Winter couldn't help smiling.

"You're not swaying and you're not blinking."

"Oh shit, then I'm really screwed."

"Never read newspapers," said Winter.

"I didn't even show you the front page," said Ringmar.

"I can imagine," said Winter.

"And it's not even a tabloid," said Ringmar.

He went into the hall.

"I'll be going now. Merry Christmas again."

"See you shortly," shouted Winter, but the door had already closed.

He went to his desk and checked the telephone number he had added to his computer notes. He dialed it.

"Hello?"

The voice could belong to anybody, could be young, could be old. There was a noise in the background that he couldn't identify.

"I'm looking for Mats Jerner."

"Wh-wh-who's asking?"

"Are you Mats Jerner?"

"Yes . . ."

"My name's Erik Winter, I'm a detective chief inspector. I'd like to meet you. Preferably today. This afternoon."

"It's Ch-Ch-Christmas Eve," said Jerner.

It's Christmas Eve for me too, Winter thought.

"It will only take a couple of minutes," said Winter.

"What's it about?"

"We're investigating a series of vicious attacks and, well, one of the victims comes from your home district, and we're trying to get in touch with everybody who's had cont—"

"How do you know where I come from?" asked Jerner.

Winter noticed that he sounded calmer. That was often the case. If you mentioned that you were a police officer, and especially a DCI, most people's voices sounded a bit unsteady at first.

"We've spoken to your foster father," said Winter.

Jerner said nothing.

"Mr. Jerner?"

"Yes?"

"I'd like to meet you today."

Silence again. That noise again.

"Hello? Jerner?"

"I can come to see you this afternoon," said Jerner.

"Do you mean come to police headquarters?"

"Isn't that where you work?"

"Yes . . ." said Winter, looking around his apartment.

"When do you want me to come?"

Winter looked at his watch.

"Four," he said.

"That's fine," said Jerner. "I finish up at twenty to."

"Finish up?"

"Finish my shift."

"What's your work?"

"I'm a streetcar driver."

"I see. It sounded a minute ago as if you wanted to keep Christmas Eve . . . free."

"It was just because of the ph-ph-phone call," said Jerner. "Realizing that you're at work on Christmas Eve. Calling people up and asking questions and telling them to come in for more questioning and all that. Ordering them, or whatever the right word is. That was what surprised me."

It's not an order, Winter thought.

"What do I do, then?" asked Jerner.

"I beg your pardon?"

"I need to know where in police headquarters I should report to, don't I? Or do you expect me to find my own way around the building?"

37

THE CITY WAS STILL WHITE WHEN HE DROVE SOUTH. METHENY and Haden oozed calm from the CD, *The Moon Is a Harsh Mistress*.

He was blinded for a second as he drove into the tunnel. There was no light. On the way to the darkness at the end of the tunnel, he thought. A horrific thought.

It occurred to him that he'd forgotten to look for the Christmas presents from Angela and Elsa.

Snow lay like cold powder on the fields. Beyond them the sea formed a concave mirror. It wasn't moving at all.

The Bergorts' truck was bathing in one of the day's first sunbeams as he got out of the car. There were Advent candles in two of the windows.

He could smell fresh-brewed coffee as he stepped into the hall.

Kristina Bergort offered him a coat hanger.

"I apologize for disturbing your Christmas Eve," said Winter.

"But this is important," she said. "God, it's awful."

He could see the open newspaper on the kitchen table: What happened to Micke? The police have no leads.

He could smell the pungent scent of Christmas hyacinths through the living room door. That was the dominant Christmas smell as far as he was concerned, full of memories.

"I just made coffee."

"Thank you."

Winter sat down. He could see the illuminated Christmas tree through the door to the living room. Did Elsa have a Christmas tree in Nueva Andalucía? Surely his mother would have dreamed up something. Lights in the palm trees in the garden? That made him think of Bertil. Where was Bertil supposed to be going this morning?

Smedsberg. The other students.

"What's Maja doing?" he asked.

"She's watching TV. Kids' shows."

"Where can we go?"

"Well, you didn't want to be in her room, so I thought maybe we could use Magnus's room. It's a sort of little office. And sometimes I sit there and do some sewing."

"OK."

"Shall I tell Maja?"

"Yes, please."

The routine, if that was the right word for it, was the same as usual, and the same as at Simon Waggoner's home: Winter squatting down on the floor and displaying a genuine interest in the child. Being a nice man. Merry Christmas, Maja. I have a little girl just one year younger than you. Her name is Elsa.

She looked down. She'd said her name very quietly when they were introduced.

He led the way into the room.

"So, here we are," he said.

She didn't want to follow him.

"Erik just wants to have a few words with you in there," said Kristina Bergort to her daughter.

The girl shook her head. She was bouncing a little ball that went off course and disappeared into the room. Winter was in there already.

"Aren't you going to fetch the ball, Maja?"

She shook her head again.

"That's Daddy's study," said Kristina Bergort.

"Where's Daddy?" asked the girl.

"He has to work, darling. I told you that this morning."

On Christmas Eve, Winter thought. Is there anybody else in Sweden who needs to work on Christmas Eve?

"Don't want to," said Maja.

"We can move to the kitchen," he said. "Why don't you bring along some paper and crayons, Maja?" He wanted her undivided attention, but he wanted something else as well.

He set up the camera next to the door.

She was perched on her chair like a bird. The smell of coffee had dispersed, but the hyacinths were still there.

His questions had started to zoom in on her meeting with the stranger.

Winter had started by asking Maja about her favorite colors. They'd drawn something using them, and then something with colors she didn't like as much. She knew her colors, all of them.

"Did you lose your ball, Maja?"

She looked at the ball on the table between them.

"The other ball," said Winter. "The green ball."

"That's gone," she said. "I lost the green ball."

"Where did you lose it?"

"In the car," she said.

"In what car?"

"The mister's car."

Winter nodded.

"Were you sitting in the mister's car?" he asked.

"Yes."

"What color was that car, Maja?"

"It was black," she said, but she didn't look sure.

"Like this?" said Winter, and he drew a black line.

"No, not that black."

He drew a blue line.

"No."

A different blue.

"Yes!"

"So the mister's car was this color?"

"Yes! Blue!"

Maybe they'd hit the jackpot. But then again, a witness claiming to recognize a color was among the most unreliable pieces of evidence in existence, with the possible exception of car makes. Somebody could swear to God that it was a white Volvo V70 that had driven away from the scene of the crime, but shortly afterward it could be established that it was a red Chrysler Jeep. That sort of thing. It had become more difficult to distinguish between makes of cars since their cloning procedures had become more sophisticated. They all had the same slick design, the same nuances. He'd thought a lot about that. He'd had to.

They tried showing the child various makes of car, but it wasn't possible to narrow it down.

He took a piece of paper, and drew a car using a blue pencil. It could have been a Volvo, or a Chrysler. In any case, it had a basic outline, and four wheels.

Maja laughed out loud.

"Was this the car?" he asked.

"No, don't be silly," she said, but coquettishly.

"Why don't you draw it, then?"

"I can't," she said.

Winter slid his drawing over to her.

"Let's help each other," he said. "Why don't you draw yourself?! Where were you sitting in the mister's car?"

"It wasn't that car," said Maja.

"Let's pretend that this was the mister's car," said Winter.

He took a yellow pencil and drew a head in the front seat. She took a black one, and drew an eye, a nose, and part of a mouth. A profile of a face.

"Where was the mister sitting?" Winter asked.

"We can't see him," said Maja.

"What would he have looked like if we could see him?" Winter asked.

She drew a head in black, and on top of it something that could possibly be a cap.

"What's that?" asked Winter.

"That's the mister's hat."

Before Winter had time to ask his next question, she drew a green dot in front of her portrait of herself sitting in the car.

Her ball, Winter thought. Perhaps it was on top of the dashboard until he took it. Assuming that's really where it vanished. If any of this really took place.

But he asked even so, pointing at the green dot.

"What's that, Maja?"

"That's the mister's birdie," she said.

Aneta Djanali met Kalle Skarin for the second time. The first meeting had suggested that something might have been taken from Kalle.

"The car," Kalle had said.

They had gone through all the things he had at home, and what was missing.

"He usually took it with him," Berit Skarin had said. "I couldn't find it, so maybe . . ."

Now Kalle was playing with a new car on the carpet. Aneta Djanali was sitting beside him. Kalle had proved to be a bit of an expert on cars, and might have identified the abductor's car as a Japanese make, possibly a Mitsubishi. He had pointed at the Lancer as if he had recognized the car model, but he had been less sure of the colors.

He hadn't heard any bad words on the radio.

"Did the mister have any toys, Kalle?" asked Djanali.

"Kalle got candies," said the boy, interrupting his brrrruuumming with the car, which was a Chrysler Jeep.

"Did the mister have candy?" Djanali asked.

"Lots of candy," said Kalle.

She asked about what kind of candies, what they looked like, what they tasted like. She should've conducted this part of the interview in Gothenburg's best candy shop so that they could compare different ones, but that might have been too distracting.

"Candy!" said Kalle, who wasn't too concerned about details. Unfortunately.

"Was there a toy in the mister's car, Kalle?"

"Brrrrruuuuuum."

He drove the car in circles, in a figure eight. She saw his little head and thought of the injured Simon Waggoner, and Micke Johansson who had disappeared. Was there a connection? They didn't know yet, so what could they do? They were doing their best at the moment.

Kalle Skarin might have met the same person as Micke Johansson. She thought about that again now. His head bowed over the car and the gray carpet that was thin but soft.

It had been a very short meeting. Why? What did he want from Kalle? Was Kalle a part of a pattern? The other children: Ellen, Maja, and then Simon. Was there a pattern in the different meetings? Were they building up toward something? Did *the man* change? Why did he assault Simon? Was that a step on the way? Was he preparing himself? For what? For Micke Johansson? She didn't want to think about that, not now, not ever in fact.

Erik had spoken to the forensic psychologist. There were various possible scenarios, all of them frightening.

We have a goal, and that is to find Micke Johansson. Please help me, Kalle.

"Brrrruuuuuuumm," said Kalle, and looked up. "Birdie."

"What did you say, Kalle?"

"Birdie."

"Did the mister have a birdie?"

"Birdie?" said Kalle, parking by the edge of the carpet.

"Was the birdie called Billy?"

"Birdie."

"Birdie," she repeated.

"Said Kalle. 'Birdie,' said Kalle!"

"I heard you say Birdie," said Djanali.

Berit Skarin had been sitting in an armchair during the interview. Kalle had forgotten about her, as had Djanali. But she heard the mother's voice now: "I think he means that the birdie said his name. Said Kalle to him."

Winter had asked Maja Bergort about the mister's birdie. She couldn't remember a name. Was it a parrot? Winter had asked. The reply he got was not 100 percent certain. We'll have to get pictures of all kinds of birds, he thought. Starting with parrots. Where in Gothenburg do they sell that kind of thing?

The parrot Maja Bergort spoke about was hanging from the rearview mirror, or so he gathered from his follow-up questions. If it really was a parrot. What she called a parrot might have been one of those tree-shaped things supposed to remove nasty smells from your car. No, not this time, not this one.

Maja's arm gave a sudden twitch.

"Does your arm hurt, Maja?"

She shook her head.

Winter could hear Kristina Bergort moving around the house. He had asked her not to stay in the kitchen while he spoke to Maja. He heard her again, close by. Perhaps she was listening. Maja didn't see her.

"Have you had a pain in your arm, Maja?"

The girl nodded solemnly.

"Was the mister nasty to you?" Winter asked.

She didn't answer.

"Did the mister hit you?" Winter asked.

She was drawing circles now with the black pencil, circles, more and more circles.

"Did the mister hit you, Maja? The mister you sat in the car with? The mister with the birdie?"

She nodded now, up and down, without looking at Winter.

"Was that when you got those marks?" Winter asked.

He held his own arm, tapping at the inside of it.

She nodded without looking at him.

There was something wrong. She was drawing more circles now, one on top of the other, like a black hole on which the center grew smaller and smaller every time. The darkness at the end of the tunnel, Winter thought again. The same terrible thought.

There was something wrong here.

"What did the mister say when he hit you?" Winter asked.

"He said I was bad," said Maja.

"That was a silly thing to say," said Winter.

She nodded solemnly.

He thought of the difference between the truth and a lie. There was something evasive about Maja now. A lie, even if he had led her into telling it. Had the man hit her? Which man? There could be several reasons why children don't say who did it. And there could be several reasons for why they tell lies. But in most cases they feel threatened, he thought, as Maja filled in her tunnel and started on a new one. Children are scared, they want to avoid being punished. They sometimes want to protect somebody they are dependent on. Children want to avoid feeling guilt, embarrassment, or shame. It can sometimes happen that the traumatization makes it impossible for them to distinguish between reality, fantasy, and dream.

"Did the mister hit you many times?" asked Winter. The man had become several now, or two.

She didn't answer. The pencil had stopped moving, halfway through building a tunnel. Winter repeated his question.

She held up her hand, slowly. Winter could see three fingers pointing up at the ceiling.

"He hit you three times?" Winter asked.

She nodded, extremely solemnly now, and looked at him. He heard a deep intake of breath behind him, turned around, and saw Kristina Bergort, who could no longer hide behind the half-open kitchen door.

In the car on the way back he spoke to Bertil, who was in police headquarters going over all the interviews, which were spreading in all directions now—or maybe some of them were heading in the same direction.

"It's very quiet here," said Ringmar. "You can hear your own feet on the stairs."

"Has Aneta come back yet?"

"No."

"Is she aware that she has to wait until I get back?"

"Aneta is no doubt just as eager to speak to you as you are to her, Erik."

He drove around the Näset roundabout. A car ahead of him had a Christmas tree strapped to its roof. It looked a bit desperate, a last-minute transaction.

"I think Bergort beats his daughter," said Winter.

"Should we bring him in?" asked Ringmar without hesitation.

"Damned if I know, Bertil."

"How sure are you?"

"I'm fairly certain. The girl made it very obvious, between the lines. With her body lànguage."

"What does her mother say?"

"She knows. Or suspects it, in any case."

"But she hasn't said anything?"

"You know how it is, Bertil."

Silence.

Oh my God, what have I said? thought Winter.

"That's not what I meant, Bertil."

"OK, OK."

"I tried to talk to her, but she seems to be scared as well. Or wants to protect him. Or both."

"He seems to have a solid alibi," said Ringmar.

They had checked up on all the parents involved, as far as possible. The problem with Bergort was that he didn't work regular hours and had a lot of freedom. Was Magnus Himmler Bergort, as Halders called him (among other things), something more than just a child beater?

"Bring him in," said Winter.

"Will he be in his office?"

"Yes."

"OK."

"I'm going to the Waggoners' now," said Winter.

They hung up. Winter drove along the main road leading to the other end of Änggården. Here comes Santa Claus. Have you all been good little boys and girls?

The traffic was denser than he'd expected. Normally he would be sitting with a cup of excellent coffee and a large sandwich of freshly roasted ham at this time—at least, that had been normal for the last three years. We'll never get through it all, Angela always said. This is the best part, he would say. The first slice after roasting.

No Christmas ham this year, not here in Gothenburg. No Christmas tree, not at the moment at least. He saw several desperate men with Christmas trees on their car roofs, an odd sight for somebody on their first visit from, say, Andalucía. This is Sweden: Take up thy fir tree and drive. Where to? Why? Porqué? He suddenly felt an intense longing for some peace and quiet, some food, a strong drink, a cigarillo, music, his woman, his child, his . . . life, the other one. He could see Maja's face, the photograph of Micke on Bengt Johansson's desk. Simon Waggoner. And just as suddenly the longing had vanished, he was back at work. He was on his way, on the move. You can never let yourself stop, as Birgersson used to say, but less often now. Never stand still. Never lack faith, never doubt, never let it get to you, never run away, never cry, always put up with everything. *Bullshit,* Winter thought. Birgersson had also gotten the message, but later.

He turned off at the Margretebergs junction. The attractive wooden houses were at their best. Torches were burning in the cautious daylight. It was a clear day. The sun could be glimpsed here and there in the gaps between the houses. There was still a thin layer of snow on paths and lawns. God was smiling.

Winter saw some children in a playground in the center of town. There were a lot of grown-ups with them. Two men turned to look as he drove slowly past in his black Mercedes: Who was he, what was he doing here?

He parked outside the Waggoners' house.

A wreath was hanging on the front door.

There was a smell of exotic spices in the hall.

"For us tomorrow is the big day," said Paul Waggoner with his English accent, as he took Winter's overcoat and hung it on a coat hanger. "Tomorrow's Christmas Day."

"Is that pudding I smell?" asked Winter.

"Which one?" asked Waggoner. "We're making several." He gestured toward the living room. "My parents have come over from England."

I'll call Steve Macdonald when I get home, Winter thought. Or maybe from the office. Merry Christmas and all that, but maybe he can do some thinking for me, before all that pudding gets to work on him.

"How's Simon?"

"He's doing pretty well," said Waggoner. "He's speaking only English at the moment, has been for a few days now. It just happened. Perhaps he wanted to prepare himself for his grandparents."

"I'd better speak English to him, then," said Winter.

"Maybe," said Waggoner. "Will that be a problem?"

"I don't know. It might be an advantage."

It was the same room as before. Simon seemed more relaxed, recognized Winter.

"Will you get any Christmas gifts this evening?" Winter asked.

"Today *and* tomorrow," said Simon.

"Wow."

"Grandpa doesn't really like it."

"And this is from me," said Winter, handing over a package he had in his shoulder bag.

The boy took it, obviously pleased. There was a gleam in his eyes.

"Oh, thank you very much."

"You're welcome."

"Thank you," said Simon again.

He opened the little package. Winter had thought about giving the boy a watch to replace the one that had disappeared. Should he or shouldn't he? In the end he'd decided not to. It could have been regarded as a bribe in return for information. By Simon. Perhaps it was.

Simon held up the squad car, which was one of the latest models. It was an expensive toy, with a lot of details. The word POLICE was painted on the side. He couldn't very well give the boy a remote-controlled Mercedes. CID model.

The police car could be driven wherever there was no speed bump in the way.

"Want to try it?" Winter asked, handing over the control panel that was hardly any bigger than a matchbox.

Simon put the car down on the floor, and Winter showed him the controls without actually touching anything himself. The car took off, and crashed into the nearest piece of furniture. Winter bent down and turned it in the right direction. Simon reversed, then drove forward. He switched on the siren, which was very loud for such a little car.

I wonder if he heard the siren when he was lying on the ground? Winter thought. When they had found him?

"Great," said Simon, looking up with a smile.

"Let me try it," said Winter.

It was fun.

38

WINTER SAT ON THE FLOOR AND STEERED THE POLICE CAR THROUGH
tunnels made of chairs and tables and a sofa. There was a blue light rotating
on the roof. He switched on the siren as the car went past the door. He
switched it off.

Simon had agreed to accompany Winter to the place where he had been
found. That was how Winter had preferred to see it: agreed to accompany
him. It felt important for Winter.

He knew that it was usually difficult for a child under seven to re-create
an outdoor setting.

He had driven along various roads, back and forth. Where had the mister
been taking Simon? To his home? Was he interrupted? Did anything happen?
Did he see anything? Anybody? Did anybody see him? Did the mister throw
Simon out of the car close to his home?

The police had made door-to-door inquiries everywhere, it seemed.
Gone back to places where there had been no answer the first time around.

They had made inquiries along possible routes the car might have taken,
makes of car, times, what the driver looked like. In-car decorations. Rearview
mirrors. Items hanging from rearview mirrors. Green, perhaps. A bird, per-
haps. A parrot, perhaps.

They had been in touch with the Swedish Motor Vehicle Inspection Com-
pany. Repair workshops. Salesrooms. Real-estate companies. Staffed multi-
story parking garages.

They had checked all the cars owned by staff at the nursery school. Cars
that had been parked nearby, were parked nearby.

Simon had tried to explain something. They were sitting on the floor.

Winter tried to interpret it. He knew that several studies suggested that a
child's memory was very consistent and reliable when referring to situations
that had affected its emotions and had been stressful. He knew this, regardless

of what university researchers might say about the ignorance of him and his colleagues.

Between the ages of three and four, children have a particularly good memory for things that are emotionally charged and central to a situation, while they can forget details that are less important in the context.

Several years after being kidnapped, children could still supply accurate details of things central to the abduction, but often got peripheral details wrong.

That meant that the details the children spoke about were significant.

Nevertheless, everything had to be regarded with skepticism, of course, and carefully considered. He had heard of a case where a five-year-old boy had been asked to describe what he had seen and experienced while with his abductor. The boy made some gestures and said he had seen "one of those things that have lots of telegraph wires hanging from it." The interviewer took him out in a car, in the hope that the boy would be able to point out what he meant. In the end he indicated a high-voltage electricity pylon, broad at the base and getting narrower toward the top.

But in fact he'd been trying to describe something else. In the abductor's house the police found a souvenir, a model of the Eiffel Tower. That's what the boy had meant.

Simon hadn't pointed anything out, hadn't spoken about anything. But was there something? That was what Winter was trying to find out now.

He had tried to transport the boy back to that horrendous journey again. So far Simon hadn't said anything about it.

"Did you see anything from the window in the car?" Winter asked.

Simon hadn't answered. Winter suggested they should park the police car in the garage under one of the chairs.

"You're a good driver," said Winter.

"Can I drive again?" asked Simon.

"Yes, soon," said Winter.

Simon was sitting on the carpet, moving his feet as if practicing swimming strokes.

"When you went with that man," said Winter. He could see that Simon was listening. "Did you go for a long ride?"

Simon nodded now. Nodded!

"Where did you go?"

"Everywhere," said Simon.

"Did you go out into the countryside?"

Simon shook his head.

"Did you go close to home?"

Simon shook his head again.

"Do you think you could show me? If we went together in my car?"

Simon didn't shake his head, nor did he nod.

"Your mom and dad could go with us, Simon."

"Followed," Simon said suddenly, as if he hadn't heard Winter.

"What did you say, Simon?"

"He said follow," said Simon.

"Did he say follow?"

"Yes."

"I don't understand," said Winter.

Simon looked at the car again, then at Winter.

"We followed," said Simon now.

Winter waited for the rest of the sentence that never came.

"What did you follow, Simon?"

"Follow the tracks," said Simon.

"The tracks?" asked Winter. "What tracks do you mean?"

He was sitting in front of a boy who was translating into English what somebody had said to him in Swedish. Assuming they had been speaking Swedish. Or had they spoken English? He couldn't ask that right now.

"What tracks do you mean, Simon?" Winter asked.

"Follow the *tracks*," said Simon again, and Winter could see that the boy was growing more agitated, the trauma was coming back.

Simon burst into tears.

Winter knew full well that he shouldn't sit a weeping child on his knee, shouldn't hold him, or touch him during the interview. That would be unprofessional. But he ignored that and lifted Simon onto his knee. Just as he'd tried to console Bengt Johansson the previous day, and now he did the same to Simon Waggoner.

He knew he wouldn't be able to keep going, not for too much longer. He would need consoling himself. He saw himself on the flight to Málaga, a picture of the future for a fraction of a second. What state would he be in by then?

Simon's parents made no complaint when he left, but he felt very guilty. What had he done to the boy?

"We're just as anxious as you," said Barbara Waggoner. "It'll be all right."

Simon raised one hand when Winter left, holding the car in the other one. An elderly man, Paul Waggoner's father, eyed Winter up and down from beneath bushy eyebrows, and mumbled his name in a thick accent as he held out his hand. Tweed, port wine nose, slippers, unlit smelly pipe. The works.

Winter folded his Zegna overcoat over his arm, fastened a button in his suit jacket, collected his belongings, and went out to the car. He had taken his video equipment into the house with him but hadn't used it.

His mobile rang before he'd got as far as Linnéplatsen.

"Any news?" asked Hans Bülow. "You said we were going to help each other. In a meaningful way."

"Will there be any newspapers published tomorrow?" Winter asked.

"GT runs every day," said Bülow. "Every day all year round."

"Shouldn't there be a law to prevent that?"

"How's it going, Erik? You sound a bit tired."

"I need to think about it," Winter said. "About what to publish. I'll call you this afternoon."

"Will you really?"

"I said I would, didn't I? You have my top-secret professional mobile number, don't you? You can get through to me at any time, can't you?"

"Yes, yes, calm down. Bye for now."

Shortly afterward the phone rang again. Winter thought he recognized the breathing even before the caller spoke.

"Any more news?" asked Bengt Johansson.

"Where are you calling from, Bengt?"

"Ho . . . From home. I've just gotten back." He could hear the breathing again. "Nobody's called me." More breathing. "Has anything happened? Anything new?"

"We're getting tips all the time," said Winter.

"Are there no witnesses?" asked Johansson. "The place was flooded with people. Has nobody contacted you?"

"Lots of people have been in touch," said Winter.

"And?"

"We're going through all the tips."

"There might be something there," said Johansson. "You can't just put them to the side."

"We're not putting anything to the side," said Winter.

"There might be something there," said Johansson again.

"How's Carolin?" Winter asked.

"She's alive," said Johansson. "She'll live."

"Have you spoken to her?"

"She doesn't want to talk. I don't know if she can."

Winter could hear the pause. It sounded as if Johansson was smoking.

Winter hadn't smoked at all so far today. I haven't had a smoke today. The craving had vanished without a trace.

"Could she ha . . . have done something?" asked Johansson. "Could it have been her?"

"I don't think so, Bengt."

No. Carolin wasn't involved, he thought. They had started off by including that as a possibility. Everything horrendous was a possibility. But they hadn't found anything to suggest that there was any substance to the thought, not as far as she was concerned, not under the circumstances. She was overcome by guilt, but of a different kind.

He drove along the Allé. There were remains of snow in the trees. Traffic was heavy, the shops were still open. Service was good. There were more pedestrians in the Allé than on a normal weekday, carrying more packages. Of course. We are slowly becoming a population of consumers rather than citizens, but you don't need to moan about that today, Erik.

He stopped at a red light. A child wearing a Santa Claus hat passed by accompanied by a woman, and the child waved at him. Winter looked at his watch. Two hours to go before the traditional Christmas Donald Duck program on TV. Would this boy make it home in time? Was it as important now as it used to be? Winter wouldn't be home in time. Elsa would be able to watch last year's Donald on her grandma's VCR. He'd made sure the cassette was in their luggage.

Still red. A streetcar rattled past, festive flags flying. Lots of passengers. He watched it forging ahead. Another streetcar approached from the opposite direction, a number 4. A bit of snow between the lines. The tracks for streetcars heading in both directions were side by side here. In the middle of the road. It was possible for a car driver to follow them.

The tracks.

Was it the streetcar lines Simon Waggoner had been talking about? That might have been a question Winter would have asked if they had continued their conversation, but the boy had started crying and Winter had brought the interview to a close and not continued with his line of thought.

He'd be able to call shortly: "Please ask Simon if . . ."

Had they been following the streetcar lines, Simon and his abductor? A specific route, perhaps? Was it a game? Was it of significance? Or were "the tracks" something completely different? Tracks on a CD? Railway tracks? Some other kind of tracks? Fantasy tracks in a mad abductor's imagination? Simon's own tracks. He cou—

Angry honks from the car behind. He looked up, saw the green light, and took off.

A group of young men were playing soccer on Heden. They seemed to be having fun.

He parked in his allocated spot. As usual, the Advent candles were burning in every other window of police headquarters—the money-saving symmetry that Halders had griped about.

Reception had been deserted by its usual line of the good and the bad: the owners of stolen bicycles, police officers, legal aid lawyers on their way to and from the usual discussions about will-he-won't-he be released, car owners, car thieves, other criminals at various stages of professional achievement, various categories of victim.

The corridors echoed with Christmas—the lonely version of Christmas. The lights on the tree at the entrance to CID had gone out. Winter poked at the switch, and they came on again.

He bumped into Ringmar, who was on the way out of his office.

"What's the latest, Bertil?"

"Nothing new from my nearest and dearest, if that's what you mean."

"That's not what I meant."

"I tried to get hold of Smedsberg junior but failed," said Ringmar.

"Are you coming home with me this evening?" asked Winter.

"Are you expecting to be able to go home?"

"If going home is in the cards."

"I hope not," said Ringmar.

"Would you prefer to sleep here?"

"Who needs sleep?"

"You, by the looks of it."

"It's only young guys like you who need to be dropping off to sleep all the time," said Ringmar. "But we can rent a video and while away the gloom of Christmas Eve in your living room."

"Your choice," said Winter.

"*Festen,*" said Ringmar. "A hot film. It's about a fath—"

"I know what it's about, Bertil. Come off it, for Christ's sake! Otherwise we'll—"

"Maybe I'd better go into hiding right away," said Ringmar. "Are you going to report me to the police?"

"Should I?" asked Winter.

"No."

"Then I won't."

"Thank you."

"Do we have Bergort?"

"No. I didn't get around to—"

"Where is he?"

"Nobody knows."

"Is there anybody in his office?"

"Yes, there are a few. But he never showed up."

"At home?"

"He hasn't come back yet, according to his wife."

"Damn it! I should never have let him slip through our fingers. But I told him not to be at home. I thought the girl wou—"

"You did the right thing, Erik. He would've taken off either way."

"We'd better slam an APB on him right away."

"But he's not our kidnapper," said Ringmar.

"He's been abusing his daughter," said Winter. "That's enough to set the police on him as far as I'm concerned. We'll have to see about the other business."

The coffee room was quiet; they were the only ones there. Winter could see the day turning outside. A big spruce fir on a hill toward Lunden had been decorated and was glittering in the distance. He thought of Halders and his children. What were they doing now? Was Halders capable of boiling a ham, coating it with egg and bread crumbs, and roasting it for the right length of time?

"Something else has come up," said Ringmar, putting two steaming mugs of coffee down on the table.

"Oh yes?" Winter blew at his machine-made coffee, which smelled awful but would do him some good nevertheless.

"Beier's forensic boys got the results of the analyses of the boys' wounds, and established a few other things."

They had taped the injured students' clothes and vacuumed their shoes, which was standard practice after violent crimes.

The children's clothes had been carefully scrutinized in the same way, and the technicians had found dust and hair that could have come from anywhere until they had something to compare them with.

"They found some kind of clay," said Ringmar.

"Clay?"

"There are traces of the same kind of mud on the students' shoes," said Ringmar. "And one of them—Stillman, I think—had it on his pants as well."

"When did you hear about this?"

"An hour ago. Beier isn't there, but a new officer came down to tell us. Strömkvist or something. I have—"

"And they've been working on this today?"

"They're working overtime on the kiddies' clothes, but the other stuff was sitting around doing nothing, as he put it. They had to put it on hold when the Waggoner thing happened, and the manslaughter out at Kortedala, and they just came back to it."

"Anything else?"

"No. The rest is up to us. For the time being."

"Mud. There's mud everywhere. Gothenburg is full of mud. The town is built on clay, for Christ's sake!"

"I know," said Ringmar.

"It could be the mud outside the student dorms at Olofshöjd."

"I know."

"Have they started comparing?"

"Yes, but they can only do one thing at a time. The other—"

"There's a quicker way," said Winter.

"Oh yeah?"

"The mud out at Georg Smedsberg's place."

"You mean . . ."

"Bertil, Bertil. They were all there! There's the connection! Gustav Smedsberg and Aryan Kaite were there, we know that. Why couldn't the others have been there too?"

"Why haven't they mentioned it, then?"

"For the same reason that Kaite didn't mention it. Or lied about it. Or tried to keep quiet."

"What is there to lie about?" said Ringmar. "What happened out there?"

"Precisely."

"Why did they all go there together?"

"Precisely."

"Did they witness something?"

"Precisely."

"Are they being threatened?"

"Precisely."

"Is that why they're keeping quiet?"

"Precisely."

"Were the assaults a warning?"

"Precisely."

"Somebody will have to drive out there and do some digging," said Ringmar.

"Precisely," said Winter.

"What is this?" said Aneta Djanali, who was standing in the doorway of the coffee room.

39

"NOW LISTEN, MICKE. I HAVE TO GO OUT FOR A BIT. CAN YOU BE a good boy and behave yourself till I get back?"

The boy's eyes opened then closed again, but he didn't know if the boy had heard, or understood.

"I want you to nod if you understand what I say."

The boy seemed to be asleep, didn't nod. He could hear him breathing. He'd checked carefully to make sure that the scarf wasn't covering the boy's nose. If it was, he wouldn't have been able to breathe!

The boy had said "hurt" when he untied the scarf some time ago, and he tried to find out where it was hurting but that was hard. He wasn't a doctor. The boy must have been hurt even before he'd decided to look after him. Seeing as nobody else was. His mother, or whoever she was, hadn't been taking care of him.

"It's the best I can do."

"Hurts," the boy had said.

"It'll pass."

"Want to go *home*."

What should he say to that?

"Want to go *home*," the boy had said again.

"And I want you not to shout."

The boy mumbled something he couldn't hear.

He'd told the boy about himself. Things he'd never told anybody else before.

He'd adjusted the boy's arms, which seemed to be lying awkwardly behind him. There were no marks from the string he'd used to tie him with, of course not. He'd only done that because he thought the boy needed to rest, he'd been running around too much. He needed some rest, as simple as that.

Micke was being well taken care of here.

He'd shown him the ceiling, the stars on one side and the blue sky and the sun on the other.

"I painted that myself," he said. "Can you see? No clouds!"

It was his sky, and now it was the boy's as well. They had lain side by side, looking up at the heavens. Sometimes it was night and sometimes it was day.

"When I come back you'll get your Christmas present," he told the boy, who was lying nicely now after the adjustments. "I haven't forgotten. Did you think I'd forget?"

Winter, Ringmar, and Aneta Djanali were watching the video recordings, over and over again. The children looked so small, smaller than any of them had remembered, and the police officers looked like giants. It sometimes seems almost threatening, Winter thought. It's not easy.

Ellen Sköld's face was in the picture:

"Pa-pa-pa-pa-pa," she said, and pirouetted like a ballerina.

"Do you mean your papa? Your daddy?" asked Djanali.

The girl shook her head and said: "Pa-*pa-pa-pa*!"

"Did the mister say that he was your dad?"

She shook her head again.

"We-we-we-we," she said.

Djanali looked at the camera, as if hoping for help.

"This is the part I was thinking of," she said, nodding toward the picture of herself. She turned to Winter. "She says that over and over again."

"Co-co-co-co," Ellen's voice came through the speakers.

Winter said nothing, continued watching and listening. Ellen told how some mister had said bad words on the radio. It was obvious she objected to that.

Winter came to the same conclusion as Djanali: The man hadn't heard the bad words. But he'd had the radio on.

Maja Bergort had also heard bad words.

Simon Waggoner had nodded. Perhaps he had heard them as well.

"He has a special time," said Winter. "He goes on his excursions at the same time."

Djanali suddenly went cold at the thought.

Ringmar nodded.

"Is that because of his job?" wondered Djanali. "His work?"

"That's possible," said Winter. "It's during the day. He has to adapt. He does shift work. Or he doesn't work at all and so has all the time in the world."

"But even so, it always happens at the same time?" said Djanali.

"We don't know that for certain," said Winter. "I'm just thinking out loud."

"Who is the man swearing on the radio?" asked Djanali.

"Fred Gustavsson," said Ringmar. "He swears all the time." He looked at Djanali. "Radio Gothenburg. He's been on ever since it started."

"Is he still on now?" asked Winter.

"I don't know," said Ringmar. "But if there's somebody saying bad words on the radio it's bound to be him."

"Find out if he's still working for Radio Gothenburg, and if so when that program is broadcast," said Winter.

Ringmar nodded.

Djanali wound back to the beginning and pressed "play" again.

"Pa-pa-pa-pa-pa," said Ellen Sköld.

Winter didn't listen this time, he simply tried to study her face, her facial expressions. That was the main reason they used the video recorder. Her face was in a separate picture now.

There was something there. In her face. In her mouth. Her eyes.

"She's aping somebody!" said Winter. "She's imitating somebody!"

"Yes," said Djanali. "It's not her face anymore."

"It's not her own face when she says her pa-pa-pa-pa-pa," said Winter.

"She's imitating *him*," said Ringmar.

"Bi-bi-bi-bi-bi," said Winter.

"Co-co-co-co-co," said Ringmar.

"Pa-pa-pa-pa-pa," said Winter.

"What is she trying to say?" asked Ringmar.

"It's not what *she's* trying to say," said Winter. "It's what he's trying to say to her."

"Pa-pa-pa-pa-parrot," said Djanali.

Winter nodded.

"He stutters," said Djanali, looking at Winter, who nodded again. "He stutters when he talks to the children."

———

They were sitting in Winter's office. Ringmar had called for Thai delivery in attractive cardboard cartons. Winter could taste coriander and coconut with prawns in red chili paste. It was spicy, and he could feel the beads of sweat on his forehead.

"Anyway, Merry Christmas," said Aneta Djanali, waving her chopstick in the air.

"It's not head cheese and red cabbage, I'm afraid," said Ringmar.

"Thank God for that," said Djanali.

"Do you eat any of the traditional Swedish Christmas meals?" asked Ringmar.

"I was born here in Gothenburg," said Djanali.

"I know that. But the question stands."

"Do you think it's genetic, or something?" she said, fishing up a prawn with her chopsticks.

"God only knows," said Ringmar. "I'm just curious."

"Jansson's Temptation," she said. "I just love the herring baked in cream with onions and potatoes."

"Did your African parents make Jansson's Temptation at Christmastime?" asked Ringmar, dropping a lump of chicken, which fell back into the carton.

"Thai food shouldn't be eaten with chopsticks," said Winter. "We can blame Chinese restaurants for drumming the wrong idea into our heads. The Thais use a fork and spoon."

"Thank you for that, Mr. Know-it-all," said Ringmar, "but couldn't you have mentioned that sooner?"

"It was just a thought," said Winter. An attempt to distract you, he thought.

"Do you have any forks in your office?" Ringmar asked.

"In Thailand they never stick the fork in their mouths," said Winter in an exaggeratedly pompous tone of voice. "It's just as bad as when we put a knife into our mouths."

"No wonder they're all so small and thin," said Ringmar.

"You've got it all wrong, Bertil," said Djanali. "You can shovel more food down if you use a spoon."

"Do you have any spoons in your office, Erik?" Ringmar asked.

It was dusk. Winter had turned on the lights in his office. He was smoking by the window, the day's first Corps. It was a must after the food, even though the chili and coriander didn't really go with the spices in the cigarillo.

He could see the stars, very faintly. It might just be a clear Christmas Eve evening. A sky full of stars. The silent beauty in the sky. He thought of Simon Waggoner. He had decided not to do any telephone interviews. That might only confuse the boy, spoil the possibilities.

He took a drag at his cigarillo. He had a taste of roasted onion in his mouth that disappeared, thanks to the smoke. Many thanks. Peeling an onion, he thought. This job is like peeling an onion, layer after layer. What will be in the center? That's our problem, isn't it, Erik? An onion is made up of its layers. When the last one has gone, there's nothing left. But we keep on peeling.

He heard a streetcar approaching before he saw it. A distant and muffled clattering on the tracks.

They'd talked about it.

"Chasing after a streetcar?" Ringmar had said.

"Follow the tracks," Djanali had repeated. "Why streetcar lines, or streetcar tracks, Erik?"

"It was the first thing I thought of," he'd said. "I was standing in the Allé and I could see the streetcars and the streetcar lines and I just associated them with what Simon had said."

That was where they had gotten to now. He turned around.

"Be careful," said Ringmar.

"I know," said Winter. "But we don't have much time. If an idea pops up, you go with it."

"But what if we think of other tracks?" said Djanali.

"We should," said Ringmar.

"His own tracks," said Djanali. "He was driving around with Simon and following his own tracks."

"A criminal returns to the scene of the crime," said Ringmar. "Or retraces his tracks."

"What were his tracks?" wondered Winter.

"Where he'd been before with the children," said Djanali.

"But then the question is: *Why there?*" said Winter. "If we assume that the places weren't chosen at random, that there was a reason why he picked those particular ones."

"Maybe he lives nearby?" said Djanali.

"Near what?" said Ringmar. "The locations of those playgrounds and nursery schools cover an area several kilometers in diameter."

"Near one or more of them," said Djanali.

"We've already followed up that possibility," said Ringmar. "We're checking up on all the various housing estates."

"But he might not live there at all," said Winter. "The point could be that he lives for away from all the places."

"Which are *quite* close to one another nevertheless," said Djanali, glancing at Ringmar. "Central. Apart from Marconigatan."

"Which is only ten minutes by streetcar from Linnéplatsen," said Ringmar.

Winter took another drag at his cigarillo. He could feel the chill from the open window.

"Say that again, Bertil."

"Er, what?"

"What you just said."

"Er, well . . . Marconigatan, which is only a ten-minute streetcar ride away from Linnéplatsen. But the same from lots of other places as well, I assume."

"The streetcar," Winter said.

"Wasn't the idea that we should forget the streetcar link for a moment or two?" asked Djanali.

"Where were we, then?" said Winter.

"A criminal returns to the scene of the crime," said Ringmar.

"I want to drive around with Simon again," said Winter. "It's necessary. It might work better this time."

"Does he remember what route they took?"

"I don't know," said Winter. "Probably not. But we know where he was picked up, and we know where he was dropped off. Obviously, we know the area in between—but there are lots of possible routes. Then again, there can't be *that* many different ways of getting from A to B."

"Assuming that he took the direct route from A to B," said Djanali.

"I didn't say he did," said Winter,

"He could have circled around again and again," said Djanali. "Tunnels, roundabouts."

"He didn't have unlimited time," said Ringmar.

"We know approximately when Simon went missing," said Winter, "and approximately when he was found."

"Which isn't the same as when he was dropped off there," said Djanali.

"The radio program," said Ringmar.

"I'll try to take him for a spin tomorrow morning," said Winter.

"Were they on the way to the kidnapper's home?" wondered Djanali, mainly to herself. "But something got in the way?"

"The question is: Who got in the way?" said Ringmar.

"Good," said Winter.

"Was it something Simon said or did?"

Winter nodded.

"Something that disappointed our kidnapper?"

Winter nodded again.

"Or was that the intention from the start?" said Djanali. "Part of a plan. A plan that didn't work out?"

"What sort of a plan?" asked Winter, looking at Djanali.

"The same plan that did work the next time," she said. "Micke Johansson."

"He got scared when he was with Simon," said Ringmar. "He didn't dare . . . Didn't dare to go through with it."

Go through with what? thought Aneta Djanali, and she knew that the others were asking themselves the same question.

"But the way of going about it is very different," she said instead. "It might not be the same person at all."

"It isn't different," said Winter. "Or doesn't need to be. He might have followed Carolin and Micke from the nursery school. He might have been standing outside there day after day, waiting for an opportunity. There and at the other places as well."

"And filming," said Ringmar.

"Or he might have been roaming around Nordstan," said Djanali. "It's no accident that everything happened there, OK? Not just a coincidence. Just as likely that he stood day after day outside a playground or a nursery school is the possibility that he wandered around Nordstan. For instance. Maybe the same days, the morning here, the afternoon there."

"Good, Aneta," said Winter.

"He might live out in the countryside," said Ringmar, looking at Winter. "As far away as possible from Nordstan, which is the image mentally deficient people have of a big city."

"The countryside's a big place," said Winter.

"How many people do we have on the case?" said Djanali.

"Not nearly enough," said Ringmar. "The Christmas holiday presents problems with overtime, not to mention law and order and neighborhood policing."

"But for Christ's sake, this is more important than Christmas dinner!" said Djanali. "A boy is missing, kidnapped, but no kidnapper has announced himself. We could be looking at a matter of hours."

Kidnapping, Winter thought. A kid napping. A little snooze. Fast asleep when Santa Claus arrived with his presents. If only.

40

RINGMAR RECEIVED A TELEPHONE CALL THAT HE WANTED TO take in his own office. Winter could see how nervous he was when he left, and the shadows under his eyes. What was he going to hear now? What would he say?

"I'll pay a visit to Ellen Sköld again," said Aneta Djanali. "I know what I'm going to say, and how to say it."

Winter looked at the clock. The traditional Donald Duck cartoon on TV would be over. The long night had fallen outside the window. It was too late to drive through the streets with Simon Waggoner to follow streetcar lines.

"Ellen has probably already told us what we need to know," said Winter.

"I want to be certain."

"Go home to your family," said Winter. "Celebrate Christmas."

"That will be at Fredrik's," she said.

Winter nodded and started gathering together some papers.

"Are you surprised?" asked Djanali.

"Why should I be surprised?"

"Well . . . Fredrik and I."

"The odd couple?" he said with a smile. "Oh, come on, Aneta."

She hesitated in the doorway.

"You're welcome as well," she said.

"I beg your pardon?"

"You can come by for a while if you like. We'll be eating later on, so the Christmas buffet is still waiting." She smiled and looked up at the heavens. "Fredrik made something based on polenta. He said it was the closest he could get to yam porridge."

"Fredrik Halders, always looking to build bridges between cultures," said Winter.

Aneta Djanali burst out laughing.

"Unfortunately, I'll have to work," said Winter.

"Where?"

"Here. And at home."

"Erik, it's Christmas Eve and you're all alone. Some company won't hurt you."

"I'll see," he said.

"You can call us late this evening, in any case."

"I'll call," he said. "Say hello to Fredrik. In any case."

She smiled again, and left. He went over to the CD player and turned it on. He stood by the window, lit a Corps, and opened the window slightly. The smoke was whisked away by a wind he hadn't noticed until now.

The room behind him was filled with Trane's *Slo Blues,* Earl May's bass and Arthur Taylor's drums, doom doom doom doom doom doom, then Coltrane's tenor saxophone creating calm and restlessness at the same time, that difficult simplicity he still hadn't found anywhere else in jazz, even if he had discovered different music that he liked and that he could make use of in his life.

Lush Life now, the beautiful introduction, like a soundtrack to the smoke wafting in a shiny silver cloud from his cigarillo and out into the evening glowing in gold from all the Christmas lights. It was music to dream to, but he wasn't dreaming.

His mobile rang on the desk. He turned down the volume of the music and picked up the mobile with his free hand.

"Merry Christmas, Daddy!"

"Merry Christmas, sweetie!"

"What are you doing, Daddy?"

"I was standing here thinking it was time to call Elsa," he said, letting a little column of ash fall into the tray.

"I was first!"

"You are always first, sweetie," he said, and was glad that Angela couldn't hear him saying that. What was he doing here when they were there? "Did you open your presents yet?"

"Santa Claus hasn't come yet," she said.

"He'll show up any minute, I'm sure."

"Did you find the Christmas present?!"

My God, he thought. The Christmas present.

"I'll open it later tonight," he said.

"When are you coming, Daddy?"

"Soon, sweetie."

"You must come *now,*" she said, and he could hear other voices on the line. Perhaps they all had the same message tonight.

"I'll be there before Christmas is over," he said.

"I want Christmas to go on forever," she said.

"Oh, I'll be there long before that. We'll be able to go swimming."

"It's cold," she said. "It's *freezing cold.*"

"What have you been doing?"

Open questions, he thought.

"Played with a pussy cat," she said. "She's called Miaow."

"That's a good name for a cat."

"She's black."

Winter heard an echo and her voice disappeared, then came a different voice: "Hello?"

"Hello," he said.

"It's Angela. Where are you?"

"In my office," he said.

"Lucky you," she said.

"Merry Christmas," he said.

"How's it going?"

"Progressing, I think."

"How are you?"

"It's . . . a bit difficult. It's a difficult case."

"No news about the boy?"

"I don't know. We might be getting closer. But we haven't found him."

"Be careful, Erik."

"We're close. I can feel it."

"Be careful," she said again. "I know you have to be careful with this case."

"Hmm."

"You must think about it all the time, Erik. Being careful."

"I promise. I heard from Elsa that—"

His office phone rang on the desk.

"Excuse me a moment, Angela."

He picked up the other phone.

"Hello Winter, it's Björck in the front office. You have a visitor. A Mr. Jerner, Mats Jerner."

Winter looked at his watch. Jerner was an hour late. He'd forgotten about him, forgotten about him altogether. Had anything like this ever happened before? Not as far as he could remember. All that flashed through his mind before he said: "I'll be right down."

He spoke into his mobile again: "I'll call you back a little later, Angela. Say hello to Mother in the meantime."

"I can hear that you're working."

"It's not in vain," he said. "I love you."

———

The visitor was still standing in the waiting room. He could be around Winter's age, possibly a bit older. I know roughly how old he is. Carlström told us.

Winter opened the glass door.

"Mats Jerner? Erik Winter."

Jerner nodded and they shook hands in the doorway. His hair was blond and his eyes blue. He was wearing a brown Tenson jacket and blue jeans, and heavy shoes suitable for the current weather. He was carrying a briefcase under his left arm. His hand was cold. Winter saw that he was carrying his gloves in his left hand. Jerner's eyes had a transparent intensity that almost made Winter want to turn around in order to see what the man was looking at straight through his head.

"We'll take the elevator up," said Winter.

Jerner stood beside him without speaking. He avoided looking in the mirror.

"Are there any passengers at all at this time on Christmas Eve?" Winter asked as they stepped out of the elevator.

Jerner nodded again, straight ahead.

"No problems with snow on the lines?" Winter asked.

"No."

They entered Winter's office.

"Would you like coffee or something?" asked Winter.

Jerner shook his head.

Winter walked to his desk chair and gestured toward the visitor's chair opposite. He had recently had a sofa and armchairs installed in one corner, but this was better for the moment.

"Well," said Winter, "we're trying to solve a series of attacks on young men here in Gothenburg. As I explained on the telephone."

Jerner nodded.

How can I put this? Winter thought. You haven't by any chance stolen a branding iron from your foster father's farm, have you? Or two?

"The fact is, weapons that could have been used in these assaults have been stolen from your foster father's farm. Natanael Carlström." Winter looked at Jerner. "He is your foster father, is that right?"

Jerner nodded, and said: "One of them."

"Did you have several?" Winter asked.

Jerner nodded.

"Living in that area?"

Jerner shook his head.

He's the silent type, Winter thought. But you've met your match.

He hasn't said a word about arriving over an hour late for an interview at police headquarters. Doesn't even seem to be aware of the fact. Some people are like that. Lucky them.

"Have you heard your foster father say anything about a robbery?"

"No."

Jerner crossed his legs, then recrossed them in the other direction. He had put his gloves on the table in front of him. Something was bulging in the left-hand pocket of his jacket. Maybe a hat of some kind.

Maybe he gets a discount on Tenson jackets, Winter thought. The Tenson League has threatened its way to a deal.

The Tenson League was the popular name for the inspectors working on Gothenburg's streetcars, sullen men and women who had a lot to put up with as they rode the streetcars looking for fare dodgers. Halders had once been caught, and spent the whole afternoon on the telephone trying to convince the man in charge of his innocence, pleading absentmindedness, police business—no, not that—taking the kids to nursery school, taking his car to Mölndal for repairs, or whatever. But he had failed. Halders had never set foot on a Gothenburg streetcar after that.

"Did you ever see one of those branding irons?" Winter asked.

Jerner shook his head.

"But you knew about them?"

Jerner nodded.

We'll have to put a stop to this, Winter thought. He doesn't *want* to speak.

"When were you last at home?"

Jerner looked confused.

"I mean at Carlström's."

"I d-don't know," said Jerner.

"What month?"

"No-november, I think."

"What did he say about the theft?"

Jerner shrugged.

"He told me he mentioned it to you."

"Possibly," said Jerner. Nothing else.

Winter stood up and went to the ugly filing cabinet he tried to hide behind the door. He retrieved a folder, returned to his desk, and took out the photographs.

"Do you recognize this person?" he asked, holding out a photograph of Aryan Kaite.

Jerner shook his head.

"He's one of the young men who was attacked."

Jerner seemed uninterested, as if he were looking at a stranger.

"He's also visited your home village," said Winter. "He knows Gustav Smedsberg." Winter looked at Jerner. "Do you know anybody called Smedsberg?"

The man seemed to be thinking that over. He brushed his thin blond hair to the side. It was long.

He looks as if I'd asked him a perfectly normal follow-up question, Winter thought. No "Who's Gustav Smedsberg?" He recognizes the name, or he's trying to look uninterested. It's been a long day. For him, for me. This conversation is getting nowhere. He can go home, I can go home. He has nothing to do with this. Or maybe he did steal the irons, maybe even used them. No. Not him. The only odd thing is that he seems to be able to keep on sitting here without getting annoyed. He was annoyed before, irritated, on the telephone. But now. Now he's shaking his head.

"Georg Smedsberg?" said Winter.

"No."

"A neighbor."

Jerner's calm face moved slightly to one side, perhaps as a protest: Smedsberg isn't a neighbor. Too far away.

"Gerd," said Winter.

The man gave a start. He looked at Winter, raised his head slightly. His eyes still had that same transparency.

"When did you meet Gerd?" Winter asked.

"Wh-what Gerd?"

"The Gerd who was one of your neighbors."

What does she have to do with this business? He doesn't ask that. He doesn't say: Who's Gerd? His face is exactly like it was before. I'll put a stop to this now. I have to devote my energies to Micke Johansson.

"I won't take up any more of your time on Christmas Eve," said Winter. "But I might be in touch again if I need some more details."

Jerner stood up and nodded.

"When do you have to work again?" Winter asked.

Jerner opened his mouth and looked as if he were swallowing air, then he closed it again.

"When's your next shift?" Winter asked.

"Tomo-mo-mo-morrow," said Jerner.

He *is* nervous. Nervous about something.

"You're working the whole holiday?"

Jerner nodded.

"Tough luck," said Winter.

They went out into the corridor and took the elevator down. Jerner had his left hand in his jacket pocket. He was carrying his gloves in his right hand, and his briefcase was tucked under his left arm. He was staring straight at his own reflection in the elevator mirror. Winter could see himself standing beside Jerner, but Jerner didn't seem to see him. As if I were a vampire that doesn't have a reflection. But I'm not a vampire. I am there. I look tired. Jerner looks more alert.

"What route do you drive?" Winter asked at they walked toward the exit.

Jerner held up three fingers.

This is almost comical, Winter thought.

"Number three?" he said, interpreting the sign language, and Jerner nodded.

Ringmar came out of his office just as Winter was getting out of the elevator. He didn't look quite the same as before.

"I'm off now," said Ringmar.

"Where to?"

"Home."

"Is there anybody there?"

"No. But I have to check that everything's OK."

"You can come to my place later if you want," said Winter.

"Last night was enough. But thanks for the offer."

"Just come if you change your mind."

Ringmar nodded. He started walking off.

"Did you find out anything new?" Winter asked.

"It was Birgitta," he said.

"And?"

"She wanted to talk to me, at least."

"What about?"

"Don't push your luck, Erik."

"What about?" said Winter again.

"About Martin, what the hell do you think?"

Winter said nothing. They could hear footsteps in the distance, in the stairwell. The elevator clattered into action.

"There's light at the end of the tunnel," said Ringmar.

"Come home with me," said Winter.

"I'll be in touch," said Ringmar, pulling on his overcoat as he walked away.

"Your car's outside," said Björck as he passed the front office.

Ringmar drove out to the highway in his official car, heading north. He drove in silence, no radio. He didn't know if Smedsberg would be at home.

Winter turned off the lights and left. His footsteps echoed in the brick corridor. His mobile rang.

"I can't accept that you'll be alone tonight, Erik."

His sister. She hadn't accepted that he was alone. She'd called yesterday, and the day before that. And the day before that.

"I have to work, Lotta."

"You mean that you have to be alone in order to think, is that it?"

"You understand how it is."

"You should have food."

"That's true."

"You should have company."

"I might come by a bit later," he said.

"I don't believe you."

"Come on, Lotta, I haven't chosen this of my own free will."

"You're welcome to come whenever you want," she said, and hung up.

There was a layer of ice on the car windows. He scraped and smoked. The smoke was like breath.

He was alone in the streets, the only person out and about at this hour. No buses, no streetcars, no taxis, no private cars, no police cars, no motorbikes, no pedestrians, nothing at all.

Vasaplatsen was white and silent. He stood in the entrance and breathed in the air that felt cold without being raw.

He poured himself a Springbank in the kitchen and took it into the living room, where he lay down on the sofa with the glass on his chest. He closed his eyes. The only sound to be heard was the faint hum from the freezer. He leaned his head forward and took a sip of the whiskey.

He sat up and ran his hand through his hair. He thought about playgrounds and nursery schools, parks, cars, squares such as Doktor Fries, Linnéplatsen, Kapellplatsen, Mossen, about Plikta, about—tracks. Tracks heading in all di-di-di-directions.

He thought about all that simultaneously. He couldn't keep things apart, everything came at the same time, as if they were linked. But they weren't linked.

He rubbed his face. A shower and something to eat, then I can think again. And I have Christmas presents to look for as well.

He took off his clothes as he walked to the bathroom. I'll take a bath. The whiskey can keep me awake.

Nevertheless, he reached for the telephone in the hall and called England. It was one of several such calls that late autumn and winter.

Steve answered.

"Merry Christmas, Steve," said Winter.

"Same to you, Erik. How are things?"

Winter told him how things stood.

"Have you checked all the parents thoroughly?" asked Macdonald. "All of the parents?"

Winter would remember that question when it was all over.

41

HE PUT ON HIS BATHROBE AND LEFT THE STEAMING BATHROOM.
His drowsiness fell away as he walked around the apartment. He glanced at
the whiskey bottle in the kitchen, but left it untouched. The centimeter he
had drunk already would have to suffice for the time being. He might need to
drive later tonight.

He read the instructions in the kitchen, and started his search. Elsa's present was indeed like a fish under a rock—in a flat box taped underneath the
double bed. Drawings: the sea, the sky, beaches. Snowmen. Angela's present
was hidden in among the drawings: another volume for the bookcase. Some
newly discovered texts by Raymond Carver, *Call If You Need Me.*

He sat in the bedroom and phoned Spain.

"Siv Winter."

"Hello, Mom. Erik here."

"Erik. We wondered when you would call."

"That moment has come," he said.

"It's after nine. Elsa's almost asleep."

"Can I speak to her? Merry Christmas, by the way."

"Are you at Lotta's?"

"Not tonight," said Winter.

"Are you spending Christmas Eve all alone, Erik?"

"That's why I stayed behind here."

"I don't understand you," said Siv Winter.

"Can I speak to Elsa now?"

He heard her voice, she was halfway into a dream. He recognized Angela
in her. It was the same voice.

"Thank you for the doll," she said. "It was lovely."

"Thank you for the wonderful drawings."

"You found them!"

"The snowman seemed to be having a good time on the beach."

"He's on vacation," she said.

"Good for him."

"When are you coming, Daddy?"

"Soon. When I get there we'll have another Christmas Eve!" he said.

She giggled, but as if in slow motion.

"Are you tired, Elsa?"

"Nooo," she said. "Grandma said I could stay up as long as I want."

"Is that what she said?"

"As looong as I want," said Elsa, sounding as if she might drop the receiver at any moment and lie down to sleep on the marble floor.

"Have a nice evening, sweetie," said Winter. "Daddy loves you."

"Love and kisses, Daddy."

"Can you ask your mommy to come to the telephone, sweetie?"

He heard Mooommy in the half distance, and then Angela's voice.

"Are you still at work?"

"No. I'm still working, but not at work."

"You sound tired."

"Drowsy, more like it, but I'm waking up again. I took a bath."

"Good thinking."

"I wasn't thinking much at all at the time."

"Any news since we last spoke?"

"I found the book and called right away."

He heard a giggle, just like Elsa's.

"I've got a question for you," he said. "Do you know anybody at the nursery school who stutters? An adult. Staff or parents."

"Stutters? As in st-st-stutters?"

"Yes."

"No. I can't say I do. Why do you ask?"

"Or Lena Sköld. When you spoke to her. Did she say anything about somebody stuttering then?"

"No, not as far as I recall. What are you getting at, Erik?"

"We think the person Ellen met stuttered. I think she is trying to tell us that. Or, has told us already."

"What's that got to do with the nursery school?"

"You know that we are checking up on everybody connected with the place."

"I was thinking about all this earlier today," said Angela. "What if the things the children have been saying were just figments of their imagination after all?"

"It wasn't a figment of the imagination for Simon Waggoner."

"No. But the others."

"Three parents have reported the same thing," said Winter.

"Have you spoken to them?" she asked. "About the stuttering?"

"No. We didn't get this lead until late this afternoon. I'll speak to them."

"Tonight?"

"Yes."

"It's starting to get late," she said.

"Everybody understands how serious this is," he said. "Christmas Eve or no Christmas Eve."

"Any new tips on the boy? Micke Johansson?"

"All the time. We have extra staff on the switchboard throughout the holiday period."

"Are you sending out a search party?"

Winter thought of Natanael Carlström when she said "search party." That had been one of the first things he'd said.

"There are a lot of people out looking," he said. "As many as we can possibly muster. But Gothenburg is a big city."

"What do your local stations have to say?"

"What do you mean?"

"The officers who took the phone calls in the first place. Do they have anything to say about a stutter, or any other details?"

"Am I talking to DCI Angela Winter?"

"What do they have to say?" she repeated. "And it's DCI Angela Hoffman."

"I don't know yet. I've tried to contact the ones at Härlanda and Linné-staden, but they're off duty and not at home."

He called the Bergorts, who were still a man short. When Magnus Bergort vanished Winter had called Larissa Serimov and asked her point-blank if she could go be with the mother and daughter. He had no right to do that, and she was under no obligation. She was off duty.

"I'm not doing anything special tonight anyway," she'd said, and he thought he could hear her smiling.

"It's a lonely family," Winter had said. "Kristina Bergort has nobody who can be with her and the girl tonight."

"What if he comes home?" she'd asked. "He might be violent."

What could he say? Use your SigSauer?

"I could always shoot him," she'd said.

"He won't come home," Winter had said. "Be careful, but he won't come home."

"Do you think he's offed himself?"

"Yes."

He'd been waiting for news that somebody had driven into a cliff or a tree on one of the roads heading east. Nothing yet. But he thought that Magnus Bergort was no longer of this world, or soon wouldn't be.

Serimov answered:

"Bergort residence, Serimov speaking."

"Erik Winter here."

"Hello, and Merry Christmas," said Serimov.

"Is Maja in bed?"

"She's just gone to sleep."

"Can I speak to her mother?"

Kristina Bergort sounded tired but calm. Maybe it's a relief for her. Regardless of what happens next.

"Has anything happened to Magnus?" she asked.

"We still don't know where he is," said Winter.

"Maja is asking for him," said Kristina Bergort.

Winter could see the girl in front of him, when she didn't want to enter her father's study.

"Has she said anything about the man she sat with in the car stuttering?" Winter asked.

"No, she's never said anything about that."

"OK."

"Do you want to ask her about that?"

"I think so, yes."

"When? Now?"

"Maybe tomorrow. If that's all right?"

"Yes, that should be OK. Everything is so . . ." and he could hear that she was losing her grip on her voice, not much, but enough for him to be clear that the call must come to an end now.

His mobile rang. For a moment he wasn't sure where it was. He found it in the inside pocket of his jacket, hanging in the hall.

"You didn't call."

"I haven't had time, Bülow."

"You never do."

"I'm up to my neck in it at the moment," said Winter.

"So am I. I'm staring at an empty computer screen."

Winter had gone to his study. His laptop was gleaming vacantly on his desk.

"The situation is very sensitive at the moment," said Winter.

"The night editor has sent reporters out to Önnered," said Bülow.

"What the hell did you say?"

"To the Bergorts'. Since you put an APB on—"

Winter pressed as hard as he could on the red key. The problem with mobile phones was that there was no receiver to slam down. You would need to hurl the whole thing.

It rang again. Winter recognized the number.

"We ha—"

"It's not my fault," said Bülow. "I don't like it either." Winter could hear voices in the background, a snatch of music that could have been a Christmas carol or some such stuff being played for the lowlifes in the newsroom. "Are *you* always happy with your job, Winter?"

"If I'm allowed to do it," he said.

"Carolin Johansson is interviewed in tomorrow's edition," said Bülow.

"Words fail me," said Winter.

"You see? It only gets worse."

"Who's next? Simon?"

"Who's that?" asked Bülow. "What's happened to him?"

"That was only an example."

"I don't believe you."

"Are you sending out the reporters now?" asked Winter.

"I'm not the night editor," said Bülow.

"How long are you working tonight?"

"I'm on until four in the morning. So much for my Christmas."

"I'll call."

"I've heard that before."

"I'll call," said Winter again and pressed the red key for the second time, put his mobile down on the desk, and picked up the receiver of the main telephone.

A patrol car drove past in the street below, its siren wailing. That was the first sound he'd heard from outside. He could see the top of the Christmas tree in Vasaplatsen, a lone star.

The Bergorts' phone was busy. He considered calling the Frölunda station, but what would they be able to do? He called Larissa Serimov's mobile number, but didn't get through.

He called Ringmar at home, but there was no answer. He tried Ringmar's mobile. No contact.

He was beginning to feel manic, standing in the middle of the quiet, dark room with his fingers hovering nervously over the keys. He tried a number he'd looked up in his address book.

He waited. Three rings, four. The world was unavailable tonight. A fifth ring, a crackling, an intake of breath.

"Car-Carlström."

Winter said who he was. Carlström sounded worn out when he mumbled something.

"Did I wake you up?" Winter asked.

"Yes."

"I'm sorry. But I have a couple of questions about Mats."

Winter heard a sound coming from somewhere close to Carlström. It could have been a stick of firewood crackling in the stove. Did Carlström have a telephone in the kitchen? Winter hadn't thought about that when he was there.

"What about Mats?" asked Carlström.

"I met him today," said Winter, checking the time. It wasn't midnight yet.

"And?"

"Does he know Georg Smedsberg?" Winter asked.

"Smedsberg?"

"You know who he is."

"I don't think he knows him."

"Could they have had any contact at all?"

"What difference does it make?"

"Smedsberg's son is one of the young men who've been attacked," said Winter.

"Who said that?" asked Carlström.

"Excuse me?"

"He said that himself, didn't he?" said Carlström.

"I've been thinking about that," said Winter.

"Maybe not enough," said Carlström.

"What do you mean by that?"

"I'm not saying any more," said Carlström.

"Did Mats have any contact with Georg Smedsberg?" Winter asked again.

"I know nothing about that."

"Any contact at all?" said Winter.

"What if he did?"

That depends on what happened, Winter thought.

"What kind of a life did Mats have with you?" Winter asked. I've asked that before. "How did he get along with other people?"

Carlström didn't answer.

"Did he have a lot of friends?"

It sounded as though Carlström gave a laugh.

"I beg your pardon?"

"He didn't have any friends," said Carlström.

"None at all?"

"Them round here couldn't stand th' boy," said Carlström, his accent getting broader. "Couldn't stand the boy."

"Was he mistreated at all?"

That same laugh again, cold and hollow.

"They made a mockery of him," said Carlström. "He might have been able to stay, but—"

"He ran away?"

"He hated 'em and they hated 'im."

"Why was he hated?"

"I don't know the answer to that. Who knows the answer to a question like that?"

"Was Georg Smedsberg one of those who abused him?"

"He might have been," said Carlström. "Who can keep track of that?"

"What did his wife think about it?"

"Who?"

"Gerd. His wife."

"I don't know."

"What does that mean?" asked Winter.

"What I said."

"How did you know Gerd?" Winter asked.

Carlström didn't answer. Winter repeated the question. Carlström coughed. Winter could see that he wasn't going to say anything else about Gerd, not at the moment.

"Would Mats have been up to attacking those boys?" he asked. "As some sort of revenge? An indirect revenge? In return for what the others had done to him?"

"That sounds crazy," said Carlström,

"Has he ever said anything along those lines? That he wanted to get someone back?"

"He never said much at all," said Carlström, and Winter detected a touch of tenderness in his voice. Unless it was tiredness. "He didn't want to say much. Avoided anything hard. That's the way he was when he first came here."

"Have you spoken to him this Christmas?" Winter asked.

"No."

Winter said good night. He checked his watch again. Almost midnight now. He could still hear Carlström's voice echoing in his ears.

Carlström could have done it, Winter thought. He could have taken revenge on old man Smedsberg, for instance, and everything associated with him. For something Smedsberg had done to Mats. Or to himself.

There was something else Carlström had just said. Winter hadn't thought about it at the time, but now, a minute later, he was going over the conversation again, in his head.

He didn't want to say much, Carlström had said about his foster son. That's the way he was when he first came here. There was something else. *Avoided anything hard.* What did he mean by anything hard?

Winter dialed Carlström's number again and listened to the ringing. This time nobody answered in the house in the flats.

Winter hung up and thought. He lifted it again and dialed Mats Jerner's number. He listened to the ringing just as he'd listened to the ringing at Jerner's foster father's house.

He hung up, went to the kitchen, and made a cup of double espresso. He drank the drug while standing by the kitchen window. The courtyard down below was glistening from a thin layer of snow and frost. The outside thermometer showed minus four degrees. The light from the Christmas tree in the courtyard shone all the way up to Winter's apartment. He was reminded of Bertil's neighbor, the mad illuminator, and of Bertil. He took his cup back into the study and called Bertil again, but there was no answer from any of the numbers. He left a message on Bertil's mobile. He called Police Operations Center but they had no information about Ringmar. Nor any other kind of information. No car accident, no boy, no abductor.

He could hear his stomach. Some Thai curry the day before, or whenever it was, and since then nothing but whiskey and coffee. He went back to the kitchen and made an omelette with chopped tomatoes, onion, and quick-roasted paprika. The telephone rang as he was eating. He could reach the kitchen telephone from the table, and answered with his mouth full.

"Is that Winter? Erik Winter?"

"Chllm . . . mmm . . . yes."

Winter could hear the sound of an engine—the call seemed to be coming from a car.

"Ah. Good evening, er, good morning, er, Janne Alinder here. Linné—"

"Hello, Janne."

"Er, we've just come back from the country. No mobile in the world gets through to our cottage. I saw you'd been trying to contact me."

"Good that you called."

"No problem. We had some trouble with the electricity in the cottage, so we had to pack up and go home in the end. I'm not a hundred percent sober, but luckily the wife is."

"Can you remember if Lena Sköld mentioned anything about her girl saying that the man whose car she sat in stuttered?" Winter asked.

"Stuttered? No, I can't remember anything about that off the top of my head."

"Or if she spoke about a parrot?"

"A what?"

"A parrot. We've just sent out a message to all the Gothenburg police stations about that. We think the abductor had an ornament or something hanging from his rearview mirror. A parrot. A bird in any case. Green, or green and red."

"A parrot? No. Have the witnesses seen a parrot or something?"

"The children have," said Winter.

"Hmm."

"It feels reliable," said Winter.

"You're certainly doing overtime on this case," said Alinder.

"You will be too," said Winter. "Right now, and maybe more later. If you're prepared to."

"Overtime? Of course, for Christ's sake—I know what's involved." Winter could hear a slight slurring, but Alinder wasn't so drunk that he wasn't thinking straight. "What do you want me to do?"

"Check your notes one more time."

"Have you checked with any of the others?"

"I've tried to contact Josefsson at Härlanda, but I haven't gotten ahold of him yet."

"When do you want this done?"

"As soon as possible."

"I can instruct my chauffeur to drive me to Tredje Långgatan. Even if I can't find the station, she will."

⸺

The silence after the phone call almost took him by surprise. He stood up and shoveled the remains of the Basque omelette that had been his Christmas dinner into the trash. It was past midnight now. He turned on one of Angela's CDs that had now become his too. He opened the balcony door, breathed in the night air, and contemplated the Christmas tree and its star that seemed to be reflecting images of the city all around. The stars in the bright sky. Away in a manger, no crib for a bed. He thought about Carlström, his barn, and lit a cigarillo, the music from U2 behind him, delicate synthesizers, the words, *Heaven on Earth, we need it now.*

The telephone rang.

42

WINTER RECOGNIZED NATANAEL CARLSTRÖM'S BREATHING, HEARD
the rush of air in the wood-burning stove, the wind howling around the god-
forsaken house, all that solitary silence.

"Sorry to disturb you so late," said Carlström.

"I'm up," said Winter. "I tried to call you not long ago. Nobody an-
swered."

Carlström didn't answer now either. Winter waited.

"It's Mats," said Carlström eventually.

"And?"

"He called here, not long ago."

"Mats called you?" Winter asked. He could hear Carlström nod. "What
did he want?"

"It was nothing special," said Carlström. "But he was upset."

"Upset? Did he say why?"

"What he said didn't . . . didn't make sense," said Carlström. "He talked
about the sky and heaven and other things that I couldn't understand. I was
very upset."

It sounded as if he'd been surprised to hear himself saying that, Winter
thought.

Things I couldn't understand, Carlström said.

"When I tried to call you again it was regarding something you'd said
about Mats earlier on. You said he avoided anything hard. What did you mean
by that? What exactly was it that he avoided?"

"Well, er, it was sort of everything that he found hard to say. And it was
harder for him when he was upset. Like he was when he called just now."

Winter could picture Mats Jerner in his office in police headquarters. The
calm, the few seconds of uncertainty, which was normal. The impression that
he had all the time in the world in a very unusual place on Christmas Eve.

"Are you saying that he found it hard to pronounce words?"

"Yes."

"That he stuttered?"

"He stuttered then, and he stuttered now, just now, when he called."

"Where did he call from?" Winter asked.

"Where? He must have called from home, surely?"

"Can you remember what he said? Tell me as exactly as possible."

"I couldn't make heads or tails of it."

"The words," said Winter. "Just tell me the words. Don't bother about the order."

Ringmar parked behind a copse on one of the narrow dirt roads that skirted the fields. Dark shapes were flying across the sky, like bats. He seemed to be walking over a frozen sea. The plain was white and black in the moonlight. He could feel the wind blowing through his body. The wind was the only sound.

There was a light and it came from Smedsberg's farm. It was flickering, moving back and forth in the wind. It grew as he approached, acquired an outline, and became a window. He went closer, but not before picking up a handful of mud and dropping it into a plastic bag inside another one, which he then put in the pocket of his overcoat.

He stood next to a bush five meters from the window, which was at eye level. He heard his mobile vibrating in his inside pocket, but he didn't touch it.

He recognized the kitchen, a late-medieval version of old man Carl-ström's iron-age room. Georg Smedsberg was leaning over his son, who sat with his head bowed, as if expecting a blow. His father's mouth was moving as if he was shouting. His whole body was a threat. Gustav Smedsberg raised an arm, as if to protect himself. For Ringmar it was a scene that said every-thing, that confirmed what had brought him here, Georg Smedsberg's words that first visit: They mebbe got what they deserved.

He remembered what Gustav had said the first time they interviewed him: "Maybe he didn't want to kill us. The victims. Maybe he just wanted to show that he owned us."

Ringmar suddenly felt colder than he had ever been in his fifty-four years. He stood there as if frozen fast in the sea.

Then he found the strength to walk toward the house.

Winter rang Mats Jerner's number again.

No, no, that couldn't be it.

But everything was getting mixed up. Nevertheless, Jerner's name had come into his head. Jerner had attacked the boys. His foster father had attacked them. They'd both done it. Neither had done it. Yes they had. There had been a lot of hatred or despair, and a lust for revenge. There were several people taking part in this dance: Georg Smedsberg, his son Gustav, Gustav's mother Gerd (was she the mother?), Natanael Carlström, his foster son Mats Jerner (that was definitely true, Winter had read parts of Jerner's grim curriculum vitae), the other students: Book, Stillman, Kaite.

Jerner didn't answer. Winter looked at the clock. Had he gone back to work? Another overtime shift for the solitary man? Surely there weren't any streetcars running now?

No sound of traffic from Vasaplatsen down below. He hung up, walked through the hall to the living room, and looked down at the street. There was no traffic, and nobody waiting at the streetcar stops. A taxi cruised by slowly from Aschebergsgatan, hunting for fares. The star on top of the Christmas tree smiled at him.

He called Police Operations Center and asked them to find somebody who would know. He didn't have any timetables.

"I want to speak to somebody from their personnel department as well," he said.

"Now?"

"Why not now?"

"There's nobody there."

"I realize that. But some of the staff will be at home, won't they?"

"OK, OK, Winter. We'll get back to you."

He loosened the cord around the boy's wrists, even though the little boy hadn't asked him to.

It had been so quiet in there for so long.

He felt calmer now.

He'd called the old man when he got back from the interview with that superior policeman who had everything this world had to offer. He'd been so angry! Look at the clothes he's wearing! As if he's on his way to a ball at the Royal Palace! But the policeman hadn't shaved! They'd never let him in!

That policeman had everything, but even so he'd been sitting *there*, on Christmas Eve, in his ugly office, with a visitor's chair that was worse than anything they had in the coffee room at the streetcar sheds.

Did that policeman live there, in his office? Why wasn't he at home, with his . . . with his family? The policeman had a family, he could tell that. Superior.

I have and you don't have. That was what the superior person had meant, and demonstrated.

There was something familiar about the policeman. He'd thought about that as he'd hurried home. He'd been in a hurry when he left the policeman's house.

The boy wasn't moving, but he didn't remove the cord. The boy hadn't touched the food he'd left for him, but it struck him that maybe it wasn't so easy to reach the dish. Perhaps it had been impossible.

Micke. When he'd removed the scarf placed so delicately and gently over the boy's mouth, Micke had tried to scream again, and it was just like when that little boy had started screaming in English at him. As if the boy thought he wouldn't understand! As if he was stupid!

It was the little boy who was stupid. Everybody was stupid. That little boy who spoke English had been nasty to him, just like all the others.

And now Micke was starting to be nasty to him as well.

When he tried to say something to the boy, he refused to answer. He either screamed or didn't say anything. That was no way to behave.

He'd driven the car on the carpet next to where Micke was lying. Br-rrrmmm! That was only one of the things he'd done. He had all the other toys that children liked, their favorite things. He'd borrowed them for Micke's sake. Well, not exactly borrowed . . . He could give them to Micke and they'd become his best things as well. He'd done all that for him. He'd bounced the ball, but it hadn't bounced very well on the carpet, and so he'd stood up and bounced it on the bare floorboards and that had been much better. Hiiigh! Micke had been given the little bird that gleamed like silver. Maybe it was silver. It was hanging from Micke's shirt. He'd noticed that the shirt smelled unpleasant when he'd pinned the bird to it, so he'd done it quickly. The watch was on the table next to the bed. The English watch, as he'd said when he gave it to Micke. It might be an hour slow!

He carried the boy out into the living room now.

They watched films. Look, Micke: That's you!

He told the boy how he knew he was called Micke. Easy. It was in your jacket! A little tag sewn in.

But he'd known that before. He'd heard both the boy's father and mother say "Micke" to him. You could see that they were saying Micke on the video, and they were doing that just now. They were too far away for it to be heard, but you could read their lips. He'd zoomed in, and you could see.

"Look, Micke! You're sitting in the stroller now!"

It was in the hall, the same stroller. He'd show it to the boy later if he doubted it.

He showed a few more recordings from a different nursery school. A little girl, then another. They were in several of the sequences. The first girl, and the other one. And a boy he'd filmed later.

Would you like a brother and sister, Micke? We've got room for them here.

He looked at the first girl in the film. He watched somebody come to collect her, a man, a back, an overcoat. They went into the building then came out again. It was a long way away and he'd used the zoom.

He recognized the man in the overcoat. Recognized him.

Now he didn't feel calm anymore; he wanted to feel calm. He also wished that Micke wasn't being so nasty to him.

———

Winter was standing with yet another cup of espresso, in the middle of the biggest room. He felt stiff, but his eyes were still open.

It was tonight. A magic night.

He turned up the volume on the CD that had been on repeat all evening, U2's *All That You Can't Leave Behind,* louder, a pencil on a piece of paper on the coffee table started to tremble. He was standing in the midst of a deafeningly loud blast when he saw the red light on his mobile on the desk and switched off the music and heard the phone.

He went over to the mobile, his ears ringing, like an overpowering silence.

"Hello?"

"Str . . . klrk . . . prr . . ."

A buzzing, even louder than the one in his ears.

"Hello?" he said.

". . . nt thing . . ."

It sounded like Bertil.

"Where the hell are you, Bertil? Where have you been?"

Ringmar's voice came and went.

"I can't hear you," Winter yelled.

"Sme . . . hrrrlg . . . bo . . . bllrra . . . cal . . ."

"I can't hear you, Bertil. Reception is bad."

"I . . . ca . . . ho . . . the . . ."

"Can you hear me? Eh? Come to my place as soon as you can. I repeat, as soon as you can."

He hung up, and immediately called Ringmar's mobile number on both his own mobile and the desk phone, but couldn't get through. He repeated what he had just said for the answering machine.

His mobile rang again, for the thousandth time. As long as the phone keeps ringing, there is still hope.

"I'll put you through to an angry man from personnel," said Peder, a colleague from Police Operations Center. "That's what you wanted, isn't it?"

"Hello? Hello? Hello, for fuck's—" Winter heard.

"DCI Erik Winter here."

"Hello? Who?"

"I'm the one who's been trying to contact you," said Winter. "We're busy with a case and I need some information."

"Now?!"

"You have a streetcar driver by the name of Mats Jerner. I want to know what route he drives, and what his working hours are."

"What!?"

Winter repeated his question, calmly.

"What the hell . . . What is this?"

"We are busy with an extremely serious case, and I *want your help*," said Winter, still calm but louder. "Can you be of assistance?"

"What was the name again?"

"Jerner. Mats Jerner."

"I'm one of . . . I can't keep track of all the names. Jerner? Wasn't he the one in that accident?"

"Accident?"

"There was a crash. I think he was suspended. I can't remember. Or maybe he's on sick leave? He reported sick later, I think. I'm not sure." Winter heard a scraping noise, then something fell and broke. "Shit!"

"How can I find out more about this?" asked Winter.

"Why don't you ask him?"

"He's not home."

"He isn't, eh."

"He's been working this afternoon and is due to work tomorrow," said Winter.

"I know nothing about that," said the official, whose name Winter still didn't know.

"Who will know?"

Winter was given a telephone number, evidently a new one as the receiver at the other end was put down for quite a while and he could hear muffled curses in the background.

Before he had chance to call the number he'd been given, his desk phone rang.

"Janne Alinder here."

"Hello."

"I'm still at the station. Sorry about the delay. I had a—"

"Forget it. Have you found anything?"

"I saw your message on the intranet and a few memos. I've been away for a few days."

"Did you find anything in your notes on the report from Lena Sköld?"

"No. But I found something else."

"And?"

"I don't know what it means. But I've found something."

"Well? Out with it."

"We had a crash at Järntorget on November 27. A streetcar and several cars. No fatalities or anything like that, but a drunk standing next to the driver's cabin had fallen into the windshield and smashed his skull. It was a mess. And the driver was . . . odd."

"What do you mean?"

"He'd run a red light, but it wasn't really his fault. But, well, he was odd. He was sober and all that. But with regard to what you asked about: He stuttered." Alinder had the conversation on tape, and had just listened to it:

"We can help you."

"H-h-h-h-h-h."

"I beg your pardon?"

"Ho-ho-ho-ho-how?"

"He was really stressed," said Alinder. "Maybe not all that surprising, but he was extremely nervous. I don't know. He was odd, as I said."

Winter could hear paper being turned over at the other end of the line.

"That's about all I can come up with on the stuttering front," said Alinder.

"What was the driver's name?" Winter asked.

More rustling of paper.

"His name is Mats Jerner," said Alinder.

Winter felt his hair stand on end, a draft of wind blew through the room he was standing in.

"Could you say that again?"

"His name? Mats Jerner. With a J."

"He crops up in another case," said Winter. "I interrogated him yesterday. Today."

"You don't say."

"What route was it he drives?" Winter asked.

"Hang on a minute." Alinder looked it up and reported: "Number three."

"What direction was he coming from when the accident happened?"

"Er, from the west. Masthugget."

"OK."

"There's another thing," said Alinder.

"What?"

"It makes the whole thing even odder."

"Well?"

"I don't have any notes about it or anything like that. I didn't remember it tonight in the car when I called you, or as we were driving to the station. It came to me when I was reading the reports from the accident and the interviews."

He remembered it like this:

He had been the first one to enter the streetcar after he'd managed to get the driver to open the doors. He'd looked around: The man at the front with the blood pouring out of him, a woman weeping and making high-pitched wailing noises, some children huddled together on a seat with a man who was still holding his arm around them as protection against the crash that had already taken place. And two young men, one white and one black.

The driver had just sat there, staring straight ahead. Then he'd slowly turned his head to look at Alinder. He'd seemed uninjured and calm. He'd lifted up his briefcase and placed it on his knee. Alinder hadn't noticed anything special in the driver's cab, but then again, he didn't know what they normally look like.

There had been something hanging from a peg behind the driver. Alinder had registered that it was a toy animal, a small one, *a little bird perhaps, green in color* that didn't stand out from the wall it was hanging against. It had a beak. Maybe there was a bit of red there as well. It had looked like a sort of ornament.

The driver had swiveled around in his seat, raised his left hand, unhooked whatever it was, and put it into his briefcase. Aha, Alinder had thought. A mascot. We all need some kind of company. Or protection, perhaps. To ward off bad luck. But that bundle of feathers hadn't done much to help this poor bastard, he'd thought.

A little bird, green in color.

43

JERNER HAD BROUGHT A BROWN BRIEFCASE WITH HIM THAT
looked to be about as old as he was. Winter had seen it. Jerner had it tucked
under his arm, Winter had seen it leaning against the visitor's chair when they
stood up to leave.

Oh my God.

Winter felt he couldn't really control the hand still holding the damn re-
ceiver, which had almost become a part of him over the last few hours.

Was that a car he could hear outside? Had traffic started moving? Was it
that early, or late?

Stay *calm* now, Winter.

There was one thing he had to do, without delay. He dialed the number
for Police Operations Center.

"Hello Peder, it's Winter again. Send a car immediately to this address."

He listened to what his colleague had to say.

"It's to the home of somebody called Mats Jerner," he said. "No, I don't
know exactly which apartment, I've never been there. But send the nearest team
there as quickly as possible. What? No, wait outside. Outside the door to the
apartment, on the landing, yes. They are to wait for me. I'm on my way." He
needed to clear his throat. "Send a locksmith there as well. Tell him to step on it."

What was the number three route? Westward from the city center? East-
ward, southward? Maybe Jerner didn't drive that route exclusively. Did he re-
member correctly that they had changed the number three route recently? It
had stopped passing by Winter's flat, didn't stop at Vasaplatsen anymore.
Then it had come back again. I seem to remember noticing that.

He put on a sweater, stepped into his boots, wriggled into his leather
jacket, and grabbed the door handle just as the bell rang from the other side.

He opened it and found Ringmar standing there.

"Are you on your way out, Erik?"

"Where's your car?"

"Just outside your front door."

"Good. I can drive," said Winter. "Come on, I'll explain on the way."

They took the elevator. Ringmar had left the sliding doors open so that it didn't automatically return to the ground floor.

"It's Smedsberg," said Ringmar as they rattled down.

"What?"

"Old man Smedsberg. Georg Smedsberg. He was the one who attacked the students."

"Where have you been, Bertil?"

Ringmar's face was blue in the red light of the elevator, which tended to highlight his features. There was fire in his eyes. Winter detected a smell coming from Ringmar that he'd never noticed before.

"His son knew the whole time, of course," said Ringmar. "Or almost the whole time."

"Have you been *out there,* Bertil?" Winter looked askance at Ringmar, who was staring straight ahead. "Did you go there *on your own?*" Ringmar continued to stare straight ahead. "For Christ's sake, Bertil. I've been trying to reach you."

Ringmar nodded and continued to tell his story as if he hadn't heard Winter's question.

"They've all been out there. All the guys. I have half a kilo of dirt that will prove it, though we don't even need technical evidence in this case."

"Did he confess?" Winter asked.

Ringmar didn't answer the question, but continued telling his story.

"I went into the house just as he was about to do God only knows what to the boy. His son. Then it was just a matter of listening. He wanted to talk. He'd been waiting for us, he said."

They were down. Winter opened the door and Ringmar accompanied him, almost tentatively, still absorbed in his story. Their footsteps echoed in the stairwell. Ringmar's voice echoed: "Gustav knew his father wanted to punish the others—or warn them, rather, give them a serious warning that they were not to say anything, that he'd already done it, and would do it again, so Gustav came to us with his story about branding irons."

They were standing on the pavement. Ringmar's unmarked police car felt warm when Winter touched the hood.

"I'll drive," he said. "Give me the keys."

"But it wasn't really a story, was it?" said Ringmar, as they sat down in the car. "Branding irons like that *did* exist, and we checked up. And came to Carlström. And from him to old man Smedsberg. Or was it vice versa?" Ringmar stroked his nose and took a deep breath. "The boy wanted us to get to his father." Ringmar looked at Winter. "He didn't dare say anything himself. He was too scared. He knew he'd never be able to get away from the old man."

"Did he tell you that?" asked Winter, running a red light in the deserted Allé. The traffic lights weren't working.

"He came home with me in the car," said Ringmar.

"Good Lord. Where is he now?"

"In his room."

"Are you sure?"

Ringmar nodded.

"Do you believe it all?"

"Yes." Ringmar turned to look at Winter. "You weren't there, Erik. If you had been, you'd have understood."

"Where's old man Smedsberg?"

"With our colleagues in Skövde by now," said Ringmar, checking his watch. "Christ, is that the time?" He looked at Winter again. "They were out there, Kaite and the other guys, and saw the old man attack his son. I'm not clear about all the details, but they surprised the bastard. The boy, Gustav, must have been unable to move. Paralyzed. His father laid into him." Ringmar rubbed his face. "It must have been going on for ages." He rubbed his face again, making a scraping noise against the stubble on this chin. "Destroyed, of course. Ruined." He rubbed, and rubbed again. "There's nothing to see on the surface, of course, but it's there inside. Ruined by his father. It came—"

"Bertil."

Ringmar gave a start, as if waking up out of something else, from a different dimension. The word came into Winter's head, "dimension." We're moving in different dimensions here, one, two, three. The heavens, the ocean, the earth, out and in, down and up. Dreams, lies.

He ran another red light—the system seemed to be stuck on the merry color of Christmas. He drove in a semicircle, past old Ullevi Stadium, the Göteborgs Posten offices, Central Station. It was early morning, but still black night. Dark taxicabs were parked alongside the railway lines. Follow the tracks, Winter thought.

"He set off for the city and paid them a visit," Ringmar continued. "And, well . . . we know the rest."

"So he was the one who stole the iron from Carlström's barn?" said Winter.

"Yes."

"That's not the only connection we have out there," said Winter.

"What do you mean?"

"Smedsberg was married to Gerd, who had previously been a neighbor of Carlström's. Do you remember that?"

"Of course. We checked up on the marriage."

"I think that Carlström and Gerd Smedsberg had an affair."

"What makes you think that?"

"Go back and read the case notes, Bertil. Think about how people have reacted. You'll realize then."

"Is it relevant?" Ringmar asked.

"Carlström's foster son, Mats Jerner, wasn't unknown to Smedsberg," said Winter. "I could see that from the start. It was obvious."

"And?"

"Smedsberg is just as guilty for what's happened. He probably abused Mats Jerner. I'm almost convinced that he ruined Jerner as well, when he was a boy. Or was one of the people who did. Abused him sexually. Smedsberg is just as guilty for what's happened."

"Just as guilty of what, Erik?" asked Ringmar, who seemed to have only just become aware of the fact that they were heading somewhere. He looked around as they drove up onto the bridge. "Where are we going?"

"To Mats Jerner's place," said Winter.

They were on the bridge. Lights were burning everywhere, as if on a dome rising out of the sea and the land around them on all sides. It's as if the city were alive, Winter thought. But it isn't.

They were alone on the apex of the bridge, then started descending again. Winter could see the water glittering from the reflection of the illuminated oil storage tanks that were the most attractive objects in sight. They passed a streetcar and a bus. Neither had any passengers.

"I've also got some news," said Winter, and summed up his Christmas Eve night in one minute flat. They were approaching Backaplan. He turned right, then left. He could feel the adrenaline pumping through his body, creating a heat that cooled him down.

"It could be coincidence," said Ringmar. "He just happens to stutter like others do, and has a bird like others do."

"No, no, no, no."

"Yes, yes, yes."

"We need to take a look at where he lives no matter what," said Winter and parked. He could see the discreet blue light on his colleagues' car illuminating the sky over the residential area where Jerner lived in one of the three-story apartment blocks. It looked almost like a new day.

The Hisingen police were waiting outside the building. They had switched off the blue light now. Their squad car was covered in dirt, as if they'd had to cross a muddy field in order to get there.

"We weren't sure if the flat was in A or B," said one of the inspectors, gesturing toward the entrance doors.

"Has anybody entered or left?" asked Winter.

"Not since we arrived, ten minutes ago."

Another car arrived and parked in the parking lot opposite the buildings. A man got out, carrying a small case.

"The locksmith," said Winter, gesturing in his direction. "That was quick."

The smith opened the front door for them. Jerner lived on the second floor, the door on the right. Winter rang the bell and heard the ringing inside the apartment. He drummed with his fingers on the yellow tiled wall that resembled the corridors at police headquarters. The echo died down and he rang again. There was a scraping noise behind the door opposite. The neighbor was evidently watching them through the peephole.

"Open the door," he said to the locksmith.

"Is there anybody in there?" asked the locksmith.

"I don't know," said Winter.

The locksmith looked scared, but he had the door open within twenty seconds. After the click he practically leaped to one side. Winter opened the door with his gloved hand. He crossed the threshold with Ringmar close behind him. The two uniformed officers waited on the landing. Winter had asked the locksmith to wait as well.

The hall was lit up by streetlights shining into a room at the far end. Street lighting was slowly beginning to mix with the faint light of dawn. Winter saw an open door and the corner of a sofa.

"I'm going to switch on the light," he said.

He could see Bertil blinking. The light seemed very bright.

There were shoes scattered all over the floor, items of clothing. There was something at his feet and he bent down and saw that it was a length of cord, frayed at one end.

He stepped over a man's boot. Ringmar went into the room at the end of the hall, and switched on a light. Winter joined him and stopped dead to stare up at the ceiling that Ringmar was also staring at. There was no other possible reaction.

"What the hell . . ." said Ringmar.

The ceiling was split into two. On the left it was black with bright yellow stars some fifteen centimeters in diameter. On the right was a blue sky.

The sofa was red and there were several video cassettes on the table, which was low and wide. There was a television set to the left and a VCR on top of it.

Things were scattered over the wrinkled carpet. Winter squatted down again. He could see a toy car, a green ball, a watch.

He was prepared for this. Ringmar wasn't.

"Jesus," said Ringmar. "It's *him*. It *is* him."

Winter stood up straight again. He was aching all over; it felt as if he'd broken every bone in his body during the last twenty-four hours.

They moved quickly through the apartment. The bed was a mess. There were newspapers on the floor. There were remains of food on the table, butter, bread. On the floor next to the sofa was a plastic cup with a spoon in it. Inside the cup were remains of food, something yellow.

There was a little sock half a meter from the cup.

Winter bent down over a cushion on the sofa and thought he could see small, fine strands of hair.

An unpleasant smell pervaded the flat, a most unpleasant smell.

"He's not here," said Ringmar, emerging from the bathroom. "The boy's not here."

Good for you, thinking first and foremost about the boy, Winter thought.

They examined all the closets, every nook and cranny, looked underneath everything, looked up as well.

In the bedroom Winter found a thin cord tied to one of the bedposts. There were red stains on the cord. He leaned over the bed and saw a green parrot hanging with its beak pointing toward the wall. It was no bigger than the stars in the sky.

"Did he leave without taking that with him?" asked Ringmar, peering from behind Winter.

"He doesn't need it anymore," said Winter.

"What does that mean?"

"You'd rather not know, Bertil." Winter took his mobile from the inside pocket of his leather jacket. "And I'd rather not tell you." He almost dropped it. Suddenly, he was no longer in full control of his movements. "Jerner has a car. We'd better see if it's parked outside."

He rang for all the reinforcements available.

They were still alone in the apartment some minutes later. Winter had phoned Bengt Johansson and then Hans Bülow. They were now faced with a hunt.

There was water on the bathroom floor, and on the drain board in the kitchen. Jerner wasn't on the other side of the world. Micke wasn't far away.

Winter had gone out and checked the parking lot, but there was no point. Within the next half hour everybody in this building would be telling the police everything they knew and had seen.

"Didn't anybody react to the fact that he had a little boy in his apartment?" Ringmar wondered.

"Did anybody see?" asked Winter. "He might have waited until it got dark and then carried the boy up."

"But later?"

"They never went out."

Ringmar turned away. Winter stood in the middle of the room. He contemplated the video cassettes in their black cases. He went to the table and lifted them up, one after another. There were no markings, no text.

He looked around. There was a shelf of cassettes on the right, most of them marked. Videos he'd bought. He knew that pedophiles copied their films onto innocent thrillers or comedies. Winter had sat watching films containing everything possible under the sun—at any moment an entirely different sequence could appear, a child who . . . who . . .

But he didn't need to do that now.

Pedophile. If Jerner wasn't a pedophile, what was he? Winter wasn't sure.

"I don't suppose you've seen a camera in here, Bertil?" he said, waving a cassette at Ringmar.

"No."

There was no cassette in the VCR. Winter picked an unmarked cassette at random, put it into the player, found the video channel, and started the tape. Ringmar came to stand beside him. They waited while the initial blurred images and buzzing passed.

The picture suddenly *jumped* onto the screen, unexpectedly sharp.

Trees, bushes, grass, a soccer field. Children in a long line. Adults at both ends and in the middle. A woman's face that Winter recognized. Another of the women was pointing a camera in various directions. The sound was vague, streaky.

The woman suddenly started to grow as the zoom came into play. Her camera was directed at Winter as he stood beside Ringmar in this disgusting room.

We had him, Winter thought. *I had him,* I talked to him. Micke was here while he was with me. It was only half a day ago. One night. But I didn't see.

Jerner had stood exactly where Winter was standing now and seen the camera pointing at him. What had he thought? Did he care? Did he think the video camera and the cap would protect him?

There was a checked cap hanging out there in the hall. They didn't need it anymore. Jerner didn't need it anymore.

The buildings on the other side of the road now appeared on the television screen. It was like seeing images of a story you'd been told, Winter thought. Or watching the movie of a book you'd read.

A blackout, then Micke Johansson was in the picture, in a stroller with Bengt Johansson. Winter recognized the location, and so did Bertil.

"Can you call and ask them to send a car there right now?" he said, without taking his eyes off the screen.

Ringmar dialed, and they continued watching the video. Micke Johansson with his dad, with his mom, on his own on a swing, leaving the nursery in his stroller, half asleep, his legs sticking out. On the way through Brunnsparken heading for the entrance to Nordstan's shopping mall.

"My God," said Ringmar, "it's just before it happened."

"He must have taken the camera in there with him," said Winter.

Another cut, a brief sequence of disturbance, then a steady picture taken on a day that was grayer, wetter, perhaps starker.

"November," said Ringmar.

"The chronology on the cassette is mixed up," said Winter.

The picture showed a different playground with children playing. Winter suddenly felt sick: He recognized the building. It was Elsa's nursery school.

It was Elsa on the swing.

It was her face that the camera zoomed in on, as close as the *goddamn* lens could get, her mouth smiling out into the wonderful world she'd only recently been born into.

The camera followed her as she jumped down from the swing and scampered toward the playhouse.

Winter could feel Bertil's supportive hand around his arm.

"She's in Spain, Erik. Spain."

Winter tried to breathe, to break the spell. He was here, Elsa was there, Angela, his mother. He felt an overwhelming urge to reach for his mobile and call Nueva Andalucía.

He saw himself appear on the screen. The camera followed him from the gate to the door. He vanished. The camera waited, still aimed steadily at the door. Winter turned around in the room where he was standing now. He was in that film! Both here and there at this very moment!

There is a mound on the other side of the road, in front of the cemetery. That's where he's standing, Jerner.

The camera waited. Winter and Elsa emerged. He said something and she laughed. They walked back to the gate, hand in hand. He lifted her up and she tried to open it. They went out, and he closed the gate behind them. He lifted Elsa into the front seat of the Mercedes and strapped her into her child seat. I'm a detective chief inspector, but I'm a father as well.

The camera followed the car as it drove off, signaled right, disappeared around the corner.

Black screen. Winter looked at the next cassette on the table. We didn't take them in order, he thought. That one will feature Kalle Skarin, Ellen Sköld, Maja Bergort, and Simon Waggoner. Before and during. Maybe after. These were future victims. Ringmar had called again. Sent another car to another place.

"There's more to come," said Ringmar.

Another place, swings in the background, a slide, a wooden train showing its age that the children could play around in.

"The playground at Plikta," said Ringmar.

Winter nodded, still thinking about Elsa.

"The conductor," said Ringmar.

A little boy of about four was busy checking the tickets. The children sat down. The camera concentrated on the conductor, and followed him when he grew tired and wandered off. Followed him back to the swings, watched him swinging back and forth, back and forth. The cameraman moved the camera in sync with the swing, and Winter had the feeling that this was the worst he'd been through, one of the worst things he'd ever experienced during yet another day at work. There were more pictures of the same boy, in different places. The sun shone, it was raining, the wind thrashed its way through the trees.

"Who the hell is that?" said Ringmar, and Winter could hear the desperation in his voice. "Who's the boy?"

They watched the little boy slip and fall, and burst out crying after the usual intake of breath before the pain and the surprise. They watched a woman come to bend down over him and console him. Winter recognized her. He even remembered her name. Yes. Ingemarsson. Margareta Ingemarsson.

"That's the nursery school in Marconigatan," he said. "She works there."

"Eh," said Ringmar. "Well done. We have to get ahold of her as soon as possible and show her this. She'll know who the boy is."

"Ring Peder at the Police Operations Center. He'll still be there, and he's good."

Winter raised his head and saw morning on the other side of the window, a heavy mist. He suddenly heard a million noises in the hall. Everybody had arrived.

44

THE NURSERY-SCHOOL MANAGER FROM MARCONIGATAN WAS AT home; she was switched through from the operations center to Winter, who was still in Jerner's living room. He couldn't describe the boy over the telephone. She wasn't going anywhere, to tell the truth she was barely awake.

Winter drove to her house in Grimmered, following her directions.

"Can I have my car back one of these days?" Ringmar had asked as Winter was on his way out.

"I hope so," Winter had replied. "Will you call Skövde station?"

"Already done," Ringmar had said. "They're on their way to the old man's house."

It was a possibility, Winter thought as he drove through the morning. Jerner going back to his old home in the sticks. He could be there already. Natanael Carlström would let him in.

But Carlström couldn't know.

Winter remembered Carlström's telephone number. He called from the car. After six rings he hung up, then called again, but there was no reply this time either.

He met three taxis on the highway, but no other traffic at all. A solitary bus stood in Kungsten in a cloud of steam and exhaust fumes, waiting for nonexistent passengers. Nobody crossed the streets. Snow was still lying as a thin layer of powder that would be blown away by the slightest breeze, but at the moment there was no sign of any wind in the city.

He saw three squad cars emerging from the tunnel. He heard a snatch of siren and saw another squad car approaching from Högsbo höjd.

The police radio was rapping out instructions regarding the hunt for Jerner and the boy.

He turned off Grimmeredsvägen and found the house. The Christmas tree in the garden was tastefully lit up. Winter thought of Ringmar's neighbor. Did Ringmar murder him yesterday?

The sky behind the timber-built house was alternating between bright yellow and wintry blue. It was going to be a beautiful Christmas Day. It was cold. The time was just past nine.

She was dressed when she opened the door. The man beside her had tousled hair, bloodshot eyes, a hangover.

"Come in," she said. "The tape player is in here."

He found the sequence with her and the boy. The man smelled of alcohol and looked as if he were going to throw up when he saw the scene.

"It's Mårten Wallner," she said without hesitation.

"Where does he live?"

"They live at—just a moment, I have the address list on the fridge. It's not far from here."

Winter phoned from the kitchen.

"Mårten's at the playground," said his mother. "He's an early bird."

"On his own?"

"Yes." He heard her intake of breath. "What's going on?" she asked, a new sharpness audible in her voice.

"Go and get him immediately," said Winter, replacing the receiver and hurrying into the hall.

"I heard," said Margareta Ingemarsson. "The playground—assuming it's the one near here—is on the other side of the hill. That's the quickest way."

She pointed, and he ran through the undergrowth. You could never be certain. *Never.* He could see Elsa's face in Jerner's recording.

There were some fir trees on the top of the hill, and there was a little playground a bit farther on, and a little boy in a wool hat walking away from it hand-in-hand with a man in a thick jacket and a cap. Winter could see only the man's back, and he started sliding down the slope and scraped his thigh on the frozen ground under the thin layer of snow, and he shouted and the boy turned around and the man turned around, and they stopped:

"It's only us," said the man. The boy looked at Winter, then up at his father.

Ringmar was making a Basque omelette in the kitchen, Winter had explained how to do it before sitting down in the living room and calling Angela.

He wouldn't say anything about the video. Not now.

"My God," she said. "How will you find him?"

She meant the boy.

It was a difficult question. They knew who the abductor was, but not *where* he was. Winter was very familiar with the opposite situation: the body of a victim but no identity for the killer. Sometimes they didn't know the identity of either.

Children disappeared and never came home again. Nobody knew, would never know.

"We're trying to think of every possibility," said Winter.

"When did you last get some sleep?"

"I don't know."

"Forty-eight hours ago?"

"Something like that."

"Then you're not functioning now, Erik."

"Thank you, doctor."

"I'm being serious. You can't keep going for another day on nothing but cigars and coffee."

"Cigarillos."

"You have to eat. For God's sake. I sound like a mother."

"Bertil's making a Basque omelette at this very moment. I can smell paprika burned black."

"It's supposed to be burned black," she said. "But Erik. You have to get some rest. An hour at least. You have colleagues."

"Yes. But right now I have all the details in my head, everything, that's how it feels. So does Bertil."

"How is he?"

"He's spoken to his wife. He doesn't want to tell me what they said. But he's, shall we say, calmer now."

"Where's Martin?"

"I don't know. I don't know if Bertil knows. I haven't asked yet. He'll talk when he wants to talk."

"Say hello for me."

"I will."

Winter heard Ringmar shout from the kitchen, which was a long way away.

"Lie down for a few hours," she said.

"Yes."

"What are you going to do then?"

"I don't have a clue, Angela. I have to think about it over the food. We're looking everywhere."

"Have you canceled the ticket?"

"What ticket? Tomorrow's flight?"

His ticket for the late afternoon flight to Málaga, return two weeks later. It was lying on the hall table, as a sort of reminder.

"Of course that's what I mean," she said.

"No," he said. "I'm not going to cancel it."

"Where the hell are they?" asked Ringmar over the kitchen table, but mostly muttering to himself.

They were trying to contact any friends of Jerner's, colleagues, nonexistent relatives. He didn't seem to know anybody.

Jerner had been off sick for the last few days. When he came to see Winter it wasn't after work. He drove straight back *there*, Winter thought when he heard.

And then possibly left immediately for somewhere else. Where?

Winter looked up from his plate. He'd felt slightly dizzy when he sat down, but that was gone now.

"Let's drive out to the old man," he said.

"Carlström? Why? The Skövde boys have already been there."

"It's not that. There's something . . . there's something to do with Carlström that's linked with this business."

Ringmar said nothing.

"Something else," said Winter. "Something different." He pushed his plate to one side. "Are you with me? Something that can help us."

"I'm not sure I understand," said Ringmar.

"It's something he said. Or didn't say. But there's also something in that house of his. It was something I saw. I think."

"OK," said Ringmar. "There's nothing more we can do in town at the moment. Why not?"

"I'll drive," said Winter.

"Are you up to it?"

"After this restorative meal? Are you kidding?"

"We can always get someone to drive us," said Ringmar.

"No. We need every single officer for the door-to-door."

The telephone rang.

"Press conference in an hour," said Birgersson.

"You'll have to take it yourself, Sture," said Winter.

Winter smoked before they set off. The nicotine bucked him up. He didn't look at the headlines outside the newsstand.

The city streets seemed to be deserted. Normal for Christmas Day, perhaps. Now that was drawing to a close as well. Where was it going? Dusk was lying in wait over Pellerin's Margarine Factory.

"I checked with Skövde again," said Ringmar. "No sign of anything at Carlström's place, no tire tracks, and they'd have seen those in the newly fallen snow if there's been any." Ringmar adjusted the two-way radio. "And old man Smedsberg is saying nothing in his cell."

"Hmm."

"And now it's starting to snow," said Ringmar, looking skyward through the windshield.

"It's been looking dull for ages," said Winter.

"The tracks will disappear again," said Ringmar.

They'd discovered a new, faster way of getting to Carlström's farm. It meant that they didn't need to pass Smedsberg's house.

It seemed to have been snowing quite heavily on the plain.

Winter hadn't announced their visit in advance, but Carlström seemed to take it for granted.

"Sorry to disturb you again," said Winter.

"Save it," growled Carlström. "Would you like a cup of coffee?"

"Yes, please."

Carlström went to the wood-burning stove, which seemed to be on all day long. It was warmer in the little kitchen than anywhere else Winter could imagine. Hell perhaps, but Winter thought that was a cold place.

The heat in this kitchen could induce him to fall asleep in midsentence.

"It's a terrible situation," said Carlström.

"Where could Mats be now?" Winter asked.

"I don't know. He's not here."

"No, I've gathered that. But where could he have gone?"

Carlström tipped coffee into the saucepan straight out of the tin, which was covered in rust.

"He liked the sea," he said eventually.

"The sea?"

"He didn't like the flats," said Carlström. "It looks like a sea, but it isn't a sea." Carlström turned around to face them. Winter noticed a warmth in his eyes that could have been there all the time, but he hadn't detected it. "He could go and fantasize about the sky up there, the stars and all that, and the sealike plain."

"The sea," said Winter, and looked at Ringmar. "Do you know any of the places he used to go?"

"No, no."

Carlström came with the coffee. There were small cups on the table that looked out of place, elegant. Winter looked at them. They told him something.

It was linked to what had inspired him to come here.

Ringmar told Carlström about Georg Smedsberg.

Carlström muttered something they couldn't hear.

"What did you say?" asked Winter.

"It's him," said Carlström.

"Yes," said Ringmar.

"Just a minute," said Winter. "What do you mean by 'it's him'?"

"It's his fault," said Carlström, staring down at the little cup hidden inside his big hand. His hand was twitching. "It's him. It wouldn't have happened but for him . . ."

Winter saw. It was coming to him now, he knew why they'd had to come out here again. He remembered. He stood up. Jesus *Christ*.

He'd seen it the second time, or was it the first? But he hadn't *thought*, hadn't *realized*.

"Excuse me," he said, and went back into the hall; the ceiling light with no shade cast faint light onto the upper part of the cupboard in the far corner where there was a little collection of photographs in old-fashioned frames gleaming vaguely gold or silver. That's what Winter had seen, only a passing glimpse of something you find in every home, and he'd seen the face, the second from the left, and it was a young woman with blond hair and blue eyes and the reason why he *remembered*, why he had re-created this photo in his mind's eye, was her features that he had recognized later, yesterday, or whenever the hell it was, on Christmas Eve, in his office. Her face had stuck in his memory, her eyes, they were transfixing him now, that remarkable piercing quality that almost made him want to turn around to see what she was looking at straight through his head.

He went closer. The woman's face had a cautious smile that ought to have vanished by the time the photograph was taken. The similarity to Mats Jerner was astonishing, frightening.

He had seen that face previously as a framed portrait on a desk on the other side of the table in Georg Smedsberg's kitchen. He could see that in his mind's eye as well. The woman in that portrait was middle-aged, and smiling a cautious black-and-white smile. It's my wife, Smedsberg had said. Gustav's mom. She left us.

He heard a shuffling sound, Carlström's slippers.

"Yes," said Carlström.

Winter turned around. Bertil was standing behind Carlström.

"It was many years ago," said Carlström.

"What happened?" was all Winter could say. Open questions.

"She was very young," said Carlström. He sank down onto the nearest chair, the only one in the hall. He looked at Winter's face, which was a question mark.

"No, no, I'm not Mats's father. She was very young, like I said. Nobody knows who he was. She never said."

Carlström made a sort of gesture.

"Her parents were old, and they couldn't cope. I don't know if it killed them, but it all happened quickly. First one then the other."

"Did you look after her?" Winter asked.

"Yes. But that was after."

"After what?"

"After the boy. After she'd had him."

Winter nodded and waited.

"She came back without him. It was best, she said." Carlström squirmed on the chair, as if in pain. Winter felt wide awake, as if he'd been resurrected. "I guess they had some kind of contact, but . . ."

"What happened next?"

"Then, well, you know what happened. Then she met h . . . She met him."

"Georg Smedsberg?"

Carlström didn't answer, as if he didn't want to utter the man's name.

"He did it," said Carlström, and now he looked up. Winter could see tears in his eyes. "It was him. It is him. He ruined the boy." He looked at Winter, then at Ringmar. "The boy was damaged before, but he ruined him altogether."

"What . . . How much did Gerd know?" asked Winter.

Carlström didn't answer.

"What did she know?" said Winter again.

"They'd already had the other boy by then," said Carlström, as if he hadn't heard the question.

"The other boy? Do you mean Gustav?"

"She was already getting on in years by then," said Carlström. "One came early, the other one late." He squirmed on the chair again, and it creaked. "And then . . . and then . . . she vanished."

"What happened?"

"There's a lake in the next parish," said Carlström. "She knew. She *knew*. She wasn't . . . wasn't healthy. Not before either."

Carlström bowed his head, as if in prayer, Our father . . . thy kingdom come, on earth as it is in heaven; Carlström's head dipped farther. "I had to look after him, Mats. When she couldn't cope. He came here." Carlström stood up slowly. "You know about that."

How much did the social services know? Winter thought. It was unusual for a single man to be allowed to take charge of a child. He'd wondered about that before. But Carlström had been regarded as safe. Had he been safe?

"I'd tell you where Mats was if only I knew," said Carlström.

"There's one other place," said Ringmar.

They didn't speak as they drove through the fields. The distance seemed shorter this time. Smedsberg's house was hidden by the barn as they approached from this direction. The mixture of dusk and snowfall made it difficult to see. The road was a part of the field that stretched as far as the horizon that couldn't be seen. There were no tracks on the road in front of them. There were no tracks outside the house when Winter turned in and parked some twenty meters away. If there had been any tracks, they'd been covered up by the snow.

There was a light in one of the upstairs windows.

Ringmar opened one of the barn doors and examined the floor that was covered in bark and sawdust.

"A car was parked here not long ago," he said, and he wasn't referring to Smedsberg's Toyota that was standing to the right.

Winter picked the lock on the front door of the farmhouse. The light from the floor above lit up the stairs at the far end of the hall.

"Did the Skövde boys forget to turn a light off?" wondered Ringmar.

"I don't think so," said Winter.

There was a packet of butter on the drain board, and a glass that seemed to have contained milk.

"Only one glass," said Ringmar.

"Let's hope it was the boy who used it," said Winter.

"They've been here today," said Ringmar.

Winter said nothing.

"He managed to get out of Gothenburg," said Ringmar. "We didn't have time to seal the place off. How could we have?"

"There was nothing for him here," said Winter. "This was just a temporary refuge."

"Why not Carlström's place?"

"He knew we'd go there." Winter looked around the kitchen that smelled cold and damp. "He assumed this house would be boarded up and forgotten about."

"How could he be sure of that?" said Ringmar, and stiffened, just as Winter had stiffened as he spoke.

"Fucking hell!" exclaimed Winter, whipping out his mobile and barking Gustav Smedsberg's address to a colleague at Police Operations Center: Chalmers student dorm, room number, "but stay outside, unmarked cars only, he might be there already or he could turn up at any time, he might be on his way there right now. Don't scare him off. OK? *Don't scare him off.* We're on our way."

"I was blind, *blind*," said Ringmar as Winter drove quickly south. Darkness was falling fast. "I was distracted by my own problems. When I was out here last night."

"Old man Smedsberg attacked those boys," said Winter.

"My God, Erik. I gave Gustav a lift back home! I presented Jerner with somewhere to hide. Two places, in fact! Gustav must have told him that the old man was in jail and the house was empty." Ringmar shook his head. "I gave him time. That's time he has taken from us."

"We don't know if he's been at Gustav's place," said Winter.

"He's been there alright," said Ringmar. "He's his brother."

The information had hit home like a punch to the solar plexus when Natanael Carlström told them. The truth. Winter was convinced that he'd been told the truth. Gustav Smedsberg and Mats Jerner were brothers, or half brothers. They hadn't grown up together, but they had the same mother and the same man had destroyed their lives. One of their lives, at least.

Why hadn't Carlström reported Georg Smedsberg to the police long ago? How long had he known? Had Mats told him recently? As recently as Christmas Eve night? Was that why Carlström had telephoned Winter? Was he incapable of saying that over the telephone? He was that sort of man, an odd man.

"I wonder when they discovered that they were brothers," said Ringmar.

"We'll ask Gustav," said Winter.

They drove past Pellerin's Margarine Factory. There was more traffic now than when they'd left Gothenburg.

People were roaming the streets in the city center as if it were a normal Saturday night, more than on a normal Saturday night.

"Christmas Day is when everybody goes out nowadays," said Ringmar in a monotonous tone of voice.

Taxis were lining up outside the Panorama. The glass wall of the hotel was decorated with a star pattern.

Winter parked outside the student dorm, where most of the windows were just as dark as the facade.

Bergenhem slipped into the backseat.

"Nobody has come out or gone in through this door," said Bergenhem.

"Nobody at all?"

"No."

"OK, let's go in," said Winter.

WINTER KNOCKED ON GUSTAV SMEDSBERG'S DOOR. THE BOY opened it after the second knock. He let go of the handle and went back in without greeting them or saying anything at all.

Why had he been left alone? Ringmar wondered. It wasn't the intention that he should be on his own.

They followed Gustav into his room that looked out over Mossen. The high-rise buildings on the hill opposite towered up toward the heavens. The field in between was deserted and flecked here and there with black snow.

Gustav Smedsberg remained standing without speaking.

"Where's Mats?" Winter asked.

Smedsberg gave a start.

"It's urgent," said Winter. "A little boy's life is at stake."

"How do you know about Mats?" asked Smedsberg.

"We'll tell you," said Winter. "But just now this is *urgent*."

"What's all this about—a boy?"

"Has Mats been here?" asked Ringmar.

Smedsberg nodded.

"When?"

"I don't kn . . . This morning some time. Early."

"Was he alone?"

"Yes. What's all this about a boy?"

"Haven't you read the newspapers or watched television or listened to the radio?"

"No."

Winter could see that his ignorance was genuine.

"Didn't Mats say anything?"

"About *what*?"

Winter explained, briefly.

"Are you absolutely sure?"

"Yes. We've been in his apartment."

"Oh, shit."

"What did he say?"

"That he was going away. Far away."

"On his own?"

"He didn't mention anybody else. No boy, nobody at all."

"Far away? Did you tell him about me?" Ringmar asked. "About what happened at your father's place? And about Georg? Last night?"

"Yes."

"He cried. He said he was pleased."

"Where might he be, Gustav? Where could he have gone?"

"He could have gone there, I suppose."

"He was there, but he isn't now," said Ringmar. "We just came from there."

Smedsberg looked weary, or worse.

"I don't know," he said. "I don't know where he is. You have to believe me. I don't want anything to happen either."

"Could something happen?" Winter asked. "What could happen? You've seen him recently. You know him."

"I don't know him," said Smedsberg, "I don't kn—" Then he looked at Winter and said: "He . . . He said something about flying."

"Flying? Flying to where?"

"I don't know."

"Where from?"

"He didn't say."

"Where might it be? You know him."

"No, no."

"You've met him more often than I have," said Winter.

"He's never said anything about this to me," said Smedsberg, looking up. "Nothing at all. But . . ."

"Yes?"

"He has seemed, I don't know, creepy. I don't know how to put it. As if everything was coming back to him. I can't explain it."

You don't need to explain, Winter thought.

"We have to leave now, but one of our officers will stay here and then somebody else will help you," he said. "We can keep talking later."

Gustav didn't seem to hear. He was still standing there in his room when they left. The lights on the staircase went out as they were walking down it. From the outside Winter could see Gustav's silhouette through the window.

"This is the country we have built, the New Jerusalem," said Ringmar. Winter made no comment.

"He told me about something in the car," said Ringmar. "Gustav."

"What?"

"That fake newspaper boy was Aryan Kaite. Aryan was following him."

"Why?"

"He suspected it was Gustav who had attacked him."

"He was wrong."

"And he had confirmation of that," said Ringmar. "He saw the old man trying to club down his own son."

"Have you had time to check this with Kaite?"

"Yes."

"Good God. Did Gustav know?"

"He didn't see who it was. But Kaite did."

"And Gustav saw Kaite?"

"Yes, but he didn't recognize him."

"So it was Kaite who told Gustav?"

"Yes."

"And Gustav didn't want to believe him," said Winter.

"It's complicated," said Ringmar.

"This is the country we have built, the New Jerusalem," said Winter. They walked to the car.

"Let's go to my place and have something to eat," said Winter, thinking about Angela.

"Am I hungry?" said Ringmar.

"You can do the cooking."

"Basque omelette?" Ringmar asked.

"Why not?"

Winter spoke to Bengt Johansson on the phone again. He could hear the busy traffic in the street below, a stark contrast with the previous day.

"I can check in on you for a while later this evening, if you like," said Winter.

"I spoke to Carolin earlier," said Johansson. "It felt good."

Aneta Djanali had continued to interrogate Carolin Johansson, but she was unable to add any further details. They might have seen the video film by now. Aneta hadn't called Winter yet.

They ate. Ringmar had cut the tomatoes for the omelette the opposite way this time.

"We need meat," said Winter.

"We need a housekeeper," said Ringmar. "We need women."

Cooking isn't our first priority right now, Winter thought.

"Are you tired, Bertil?"

"No. Are you?"

"No."

"He might have driven to the seaside," said Ringmar. "Could be on a beach somewhere."

Winter had sent all the officers available to scour the coastline.

They tried to set up checks at Landvetter and other smaller airports. But Winter didn't believe Jerner would be taking a flight to anywhere. He thought his own flight would be more likely.

"How many people do we have at Nordstan?" he asked.

"Now? Not many. It's empty. None of the shops are open today. But they are supposed to have scoured the place pretty thoroughly."

"That was where he grabbed Micke," said Winter. "Is he intending to take him back there?"

"He's not there, Erik. The place is empty."

"He used to go there a lot. You've seen a few of the other films. He seemed to like going there."

"He's not there," said Ringmar again.

"Maybe there's something special that draws him there?" said Winter.

Ringmar made no comment.

"Something we don't see," said Winter. "Something he sees but we don't?"

"I think I know what you mean," said Ringmar.

"When do they open again?" Winter asked.

"Tomorrow at ten o'clock. The Boxing Day sales."

"Is it Boxing Day tomorrow? The second day of Christmas?"

"Christmas will soon be over," said Ringmar.

"And I haven't bought you a Christmas present, Bertil."

"I'm afraid I haven't bought one for you either."

Winter stood up.

"I didn't call Moa either. I promised I would."

"Don't even think about it," said Ringmar. "No doubt you would have only made things worse."

"I agree," said Winter. "Are you coming with me?"

"Where to?"

"To Nordstan."

"It's *empty*, Erik."

"I know, I know. But it's better than sitting here. Bengt Johansson lives on the other side of the station as well."

There was snow in the air again, a light snow shower. Some people out in the streets had their umbrellas open. Winter drove slowly.

"People shouldn't use umbrellas when it's snowing," said Ringmar. "It doesn't seem appropriate."

"It was old man Smedsberg who told us that Carlström had a foster son," said Winter.

"Do you think that I haven't thought of that?" said Ringmar.

"If he hadn't said anything, we probably would have never spoken to Carlström."

'No."

"And still wouldn't have gotten Jerner's identity."

"No."

"So the question is why?" said Winter, turning to look at Ringmar. "Why?"

"Yes."

"Come on, give me an answer. You've spoken to old man Smedsberg."

"Not about that."

"But you must have an idea?"

"Everything will be revealed by forensic psychology," said Ringmar.

"I think we've uncovered quite a lot already," said Winter.

"That's true."

"The father did exactly the same thing as the son did," said Winter. "He gave us clues."

"Yes."

"It all has to do with guilt," said Winter.

"Gustav's guilt? What guilt?"

"Don't you think the son feels guilty?" Winter looked at Ringmar again. "Don't you think he's been feeling guilty for ages?"

"Yes."

"Just like the other boys. Their silence is due to the fact that they were afraid their friend would be beaten again by his father, or even worse. Fear makes you keep quiet." Winter changed gear. "And shame also makes you keep quiet. The boys were ashamed of having been attacked. Ashamed, and shocked. That's the way it is with rape victims."

"Yes," said Ringmar again.

"Gustav led us to his father," said Winter.

"And maybe the father intentionally put us onto Carlström and hoped we would change direction and understand who it was really all about. Who the guilty one really was."

Winter nodded.

"Guilty of everything," said Ringmar, thinking of Mats Jerner and Micke Johansson.

"Do you think Gustav knew?" Winter asked. "Did he know about Mats? Mats and the children?"

"No," said Ringmar. "We'll find out eventually, but I don't think so. As far as Gustav was concerned, it was all about his father. The old man."

"And for old man Smedsberg it was all about himself," said Winter. "He turned himself in indirectly the moment he told us about Natanael Carlström and the foster son."

His mobile rang.

"We've found Magnus Heydrich," said Halders.

"Eh? Come again?"

"Bergort. We've got him."

"Where is he?"

"Safe and sound, locked up in a cell."

"Has he said anything?"

"No. But who cares? He's guilty. There's no doubt about that, is there?"

"No," said Winter.

"Chicken shit," said Halders.

"What did you say, Fredrik?"

"The bastard didn't even have the guts to drive into a tree."

The square in the center of the Nordstan shopping mall was illuminated by every kind of light you could think of. The area around the square was silent and glittering. The display windows of the shops and department stores cast shadows onto the stone floor.

Nordstan was a training area for all rookies joining the Gothenburg police force. Winter had patrolled there. A fair number of those he'd kept an eye on in those days were still around, sometimes inside the mall, sometimes outside in Brunnsparken; they had also been rookies in their own way, alcoholics and junkies who had once been young just like him.

He stood in the middle of the square, with his back to the travel agency. From there the lights from KappAhl and Åhléns and H&M and the Academy Book Shop looked warm and inviting. He couldn't see any security guards or police officers just now. He could have been the only person in the world. Ulf Silén's sculptures from 1992 were hanging down above his head—the work of art known as *Two Dimensions* comprised figures diving and jumping into the water, flying through the air, changing under the surface of the water from white to sea green, and turning into other shapes that became a part of the water. He had never really looked at the hanging sculptures in this way before, never given them a thought, just as none of the other passersby ever did, no doubt, thousands of them every day, going to and from the shops, to and from Central Station via the pedestrian subway. The work of art became a part of the square, and that was doubtless the intention.

He heard Ringmar's voice behind him:

"Twenty officers have been through all the basement areas."

"OK."

"Have you finished here?" Ringmar asked.

"What time is it?"

"Past eleven."

"I'll stop in on Bengt Johansson," said Winter.

"I'm going home," said Ringmar.

Winter nodded. It was time for Ringmar to go home.

"But I might come by later tonight," said Ringmar. "If I can't sleep."

"You mean you've thought of sleeping?"

Bengt Johansson was calmer than before.

"It helped to talk to Carolin," he said. "I think it helped her too." He was pacing up and down. "You're not going to get me to watch those films." He held up his hands in Winter's direction. "Carolin said she had to because it was her fault, as she put it. But I'm not going to watch that shit. Never."

"You don't need to see Micke," said Winter. "But the man doing the filming. You might see something that strikes a chord."

But what would that be? The only help they could get from Bengt Johansson would be if he recognized Jerner from some particular place.

"I don't want to," said Johansson.

Winter noticed the photographs of Micke on the wall and on the desk. There were more now than there had been when he was here last.

"I'd like to tell you about Micke," said Johansson. "About all the new words he's learned recently. Would you like to hear?"

Winter was poring over a map of Gothenburg and maps showing the streetcar routes. It was past two when he got home from Bengt Johansson's. His car was parked in the street outside, in a space reserved for the disabled because that's how he felt.

In the morning they would cast the net farther afield, concentrating in the first place on the number 3 streetcar route. It was an enormous task. He fell asleep halfway through a stroke of the pen. He dreamed about a child's voice shouting "Daddy," and then again, "Daddy," but farther away now, faint, and toneless. He woke up in the armchair, staggered into the bedroom, and collapsed into bed.

He was woken up by a noise. He sat up with a force that startled even himself. He checked the clock on the bedside table: nine-thirty. He'd slept for five hours.

Nobody had woken him up, nobody had called. He knew they were aware at headquarters that he was working around the clock, and maybe they were simply trying to prevent him from burning himself out. He almost smiled. But his mobile? Where was it? He looked for it in the bedroom. It felt as if he were still asleep. He looked for it in the other rooms, in the kitchen. He called the number from his landline telephone in the kitchen. No ringing. He eventually found the mobile on the washbasin in the bathroom, turned off. He had no recollection of taking it there, or of switching it off. Why had he turned it off? But if there had been any developments, he would have been called by Halders, who was back on duty now. So nothing had happened. He checked the answering machine. Then took a cold shower.

As he was drinking coffee he thought again about Nordstan. Jerner had kept visiting Nordstan. There were usually so many people there that they merged into one another. He looked at the clock. The shopping mall would be open now.

On the way there Aneta Djanali called.

"Ellen Sköld said a name."

"Have you spoken to her again?"

"Yes, just now, this morning. She keeps saying the name Gerd. It must be Gerd she keeps saying."

"Jerner's mother," said Winter.

"He's told Ellen about her," said Djanali.

There were plainclothesed police officers in all the arcades, Postgatan, Göt-gatan, in the department stores. All the entrances and exits were under obser-vation.

People were thronging in there now. The Boxing Day sales had exploded in everybody's face. Winter could barely move as he tried to make his way over the square. Yesterday he'd been the only person on earth, today there were thousands there.

The headlines outside the newsstand were screeching at top volume.

Ringmar was waiting outside H&M, as agreed.

"Did you get any sleep, Erik?"

"Yes, but it was not intentional."

"I've spoken to Martin," said Ringmar.

"About time."

"He wants to meet me."

"What does he have to say?"

"That he's never gotten over the fact that I hit him once. Once. That was it. That was all it was. But it just grew and grew on him."

"Did you?"

"Hit him? Not in that way."

"What other way is there?"

"I *didn't* hit him," said Ringmar, and Winter could see that the relief in Bertil's face was that of an innocent man. I haven't even done *that,* was what he wanted to say.

"Where is he?" asked Winter, as he observed people moving slowly around in clumps.

"In New York."

"In *New York*?"

"Yes. He left that damned sect he was a member of."

"Deprogrammed?"

"He sorted it out himself." Ringmar looked at Winter. "This might only be the beginning, of course. Such things take time."

"What's he doing?"

"Working in a restaurant."

"Is he coming home?"

"Next week."

"When's Birgitta coming home?" Winter asked, watching a man sitting on the ground with people stepping around him.

"She's already home. So's Moa."

"Who's checked out that guitar player?" said Winter, pointing in the direction of the plinth in the middle of the square.

"Eh? What guitar player?"

"Who's the *guitarist*?!" said Winter. He stepped quickly forward, collided with a woman, apologized, and continued barging his way forward like a rugby player forcing his way through tackling backs, and he reached the guitar player who was sitting underneath the hanging and whirling bodies of *Two Dimensions,* strumming away at some tune or other, and Winter came up behind him, saw the checked cap and knew that it was possible, and that anybody could hide himself away like this for as long as they liked, it was a devilishly clever disguise, a disguise that would work in any public place, and Winter's hand was shaking as he reached out for the man, who strummed a chord, and Winter pulled off his cap and found himself looking at a mop of black hair and an unknown, terrified face looking up at him.

"Oh, I'm sorry," said Winter.

Nobody seemed to have noticed. Nobody had been listening to the busker. He stood up, grabbed his empty guitar case and his guitar, and hurried away.

The sculptures were hovering over Winter's head. He took a step backward and looked up at the roof that extended from the north arcade to the square. Four enormous ventilation shafts were fixed under the roof, like pedestrian tunnels. He followed them with his gaze. They opened out just in front of the work of art. You could see the sky through a circular window. The highest of the figures were surrounded by mirrors that formed a circular prism reflecting the display windows of the shops around about. He could see the reflections of people moving. The white sculptures were of naked bodies, on the way down from heaven to earth. He'd looked closely at them for the first time the previous day. He was the only person looking up. Before long, several more people would wonder what was happening, and look up as well.

The bodies were attached to transparent lines that seemed to freeze their movements.

Some were jumping.

Some were diving.

Then he saw him.

There was a new body hanging up there.

He hadn't seen that one yesterday,

White like the rest of them, as white as snow.

Jerner's features had stiffened just like the rest of them. He was on his way down from heaven in a frozen movement.

His arms and legs were attached to wires that he must have carried with him through the ventilation shafts.

He'd tied the last of the wires around his neck.

Then he'd jumped.

Winter was able to work all that out in a flash.

Winter closed his eyes and looked again. Jerner was hanging there, frozen in his death leap. He was flying, just like he'd told his brother he would, flying

ÅKE EDWARDSON

in his own way. Winter looked around, and he could see that he was the only one who had *seen*. Bertil had disappeared in the sea of humanity.

Winter looked up again, he couldn't help it. Next to Jerner's left shoulder he could see the reflection of H&M's display window. The mirror was curved in a strange way that made it possible for him to see the bottom part of some clothes racks inside the shop. He saw a small, shiny wheel and something that could be a stay, or a stand of some sort. Winter turned around and forced his way through the crowd and ripped the clothes off the racks, and there was the stroller and Micke's head was leaning to one side, and a little arm hung down and he could feel a faint pulse.

On the plane he kept his leather jacket on, and his sunglasses. Somebody started singing as they rose up through the black, friendly skies. Somebody laughed. He put on the earphones and turned on his portable CD player and closed his eyes. A cart arrived eventually and he asked for four of the ridiculously small bottles of whiskey. He put the earphones back on and drank and tried to think of nothing, but failed. The woman next to him looked away. He turned up the sound, and the trumpet of Miles Davis blew everything else out of his mind.